The Complex Tapestry of Free Will

The Complex Tapestry of Free Will

A Philosophical Odyssey

ROBERT KANE

OXFORD
UNIVERSITY PRESS

Oxford University Press is a department of the University of Oxford. It furthers
the University's objective of excellence in research, scholarship, and education
by publishing worldwide. Oxford is a registered trade mark of Oxford University
Press in the UK and certain other countries.

Published in the United States of America by Oxford University Press
198 Madison Avenue, New York, NY 10016, United States of America.

© Oxford University Press 2024

All rights reserved. No part of this publication may be reproduced, stored in
a retrieval system, or transmitted, in any form or by any means, without the
prior permission in writing of Oxford University Press, or as expressly permitted
by law, by license, or under terms agreed with the appropriate reproduction
rights organization. Inquiries concerning reproduction outside the scope of the
above should be sent to the Rights Department, Oxford University Press, at the
address above.

You must not circulate this work in any other form
and you must impose this same condition on any acquirer.

CIP data is on file at the Library of Congress

ISBN 978-0-19-775140-4

DOI: 10.1093/oso/9780197751404.001.0001

Printed by Integrated Books International, United States of America

To
My son, Nathan Robert Kane, his wife Caitlin O'Brien, and their children,
Liam O'Brien Kane and Michaela Quinn Kane

In Memoriam
Our son, Russell Hilary Kane, and my wife Claudette Drennan Kane,
whose wisdom is reflected on every page.

Contents

1. Introduction — 1
2. Compatibility and Significance Questions (Part I): The Freedom Path — 9
3. Compatibility and Significance Questions (Part II): The Responsibility Path — 29
4. The Intelligibility Question (Part I) — 58
5. The Intelligibility Question (Part II) — 80
6. The Libertarian Spectrum (Part I): Deliberative or Non-centered Views — 113
7. The Libertarian Spectrum (Part II): Event-Causal Views, Centered and Non-centered — 135
8. The Libertarian Spectrum (Part III): Agent-Causal and Noncausal Views — 182
9. The Compatibilist Spectrum — 208
10. Skepticism and Illusionism about Free Will and Moral Responsibility — 247
11. Ultimate Desert, the Dialectic of Selfhood, Kant's Three Questions, Aspiration, Eastern Views, Theism, and Predestination — 274

Notes — 303
References — 329
Index — 359

1
Introduction

1.1. A Bit of History and the Aims of This Book

It is now more than fifty years since I first began thinking about issues of free will. In this long period there has been something of a renaissance of writing by philosophers and other scholars and researchers in the sciences and humanities on this ancient and venerable problem, new avenues pursued and theories proposed, novel thought experiments introduced, and many new ideas debated. My own writings have contributed to these debates. The views about free will I developed over this long period in books and many articles, as well as edited volumes, including two editions of *The Oxford Handbook of Free Will* (2002, 2011a), have been much debated and have been refined and further developed in numerous ways over the years in response to the critical literature.

The goal of this book is to provide an overview of the more recent developments of my views along with responses to some of the latest critical literature on them over the past twenty-five years since the publication of my book *The Significance of Free Will* (Oxford University Press, 1996). During this period, I have attempted to respond to many objections and to the critical literature, refining my views in the process. But these responses are scattered in journal articles, symposia, anthologies, and other venues. I thought it was time to bring them together; and that is what this book aims to do. It should not be read as a replacement for *The Significance of Free Will*, but as a sequel to that book, adding to and refining the view presented there and developed in earlier and subsequent writings.

As such, this book continues an ongoing dialogue with many other thinkers to whom I am much indebted, philosophy being the collective enterprise it is. As Plato intimated centuries ago, the Truth (with a capital T, one of his ideal forms along with Justice and the Good) is not something any one person or group can wholly own, hoarding it from others like a pot of gold. The Truth in this ideal sense is something we can only (to use his words) "participate in" with other persons to some degree from our own necessarily limited and finite perspectives. Hence its pursuit is said to be a kind of love (*philia*) of wisdom (*sophia*).

In prior writings, I've often quoted the thirteenth-century Sufi Muslim poet and philosopher Jalal ad-Din ar-Rumi, who said, "there is a disputation that will continue till mankind is raised from the dead, between the necessitarians and the partisans of free will."[1] The problem of free will and necessity or determinism of which he speaks has arisen in history whenever humans have reached a higher stage of self-consciousness about how profoundly the world may influence their behavior in ways unknown to them and not controlled by them. The rise of doctrines of determinism or necessity in the history of ideas is an indication that this higher stage of self-consciousness has been reached. People have wondered at various times whether their actions might be determined by Fate or by God, by the laws of physics or the laws of logic, by evolution, genes, or environment, by unconscious motives, by psychological or social conditioning, or, with the latest scientific threats from the neurosciences, by the activity of their brains of which they are not conscious.

Despite differences, there is a core idea running through all these historical doctrines of determinism, whether they are religious, secular, or scientific, that shows why many people have felt they are a threat to free will. They all imply that, given the past at any time and the laws governing the universe, there is only one possible future. Whatever happens is therefore inevitable, it cannot but occur, given the actual past and laws. Free will by contrast seems to imply that (i) the future is open, with multiple possible paths into the future, and (ii) it is sometimes "up to us," and no one and nothing else, which of these possible paths will be taken.

Like Rumi and many other thinkers of the past, I had always believed there was some kind of conflict lurking here that was very deep and could not be easily dismissed by facile arguments. Yet I was also aware that many philosophers and scientists, especially in the modern era, have argued that doctrines of determinism pose no real threat to free will, or at least to any free will "worth wanting." Even in a determined world, these compatibilists argue, we would want to distinguish persons who are free from such things as physical restraint, addiction or neurosis, coercion, compulsion, covert control, or political oppression from persons who are not free from these things; and we could affirm that these freedoms could exist and would be preferable to their opposites *even in a determined world*. In addition, it is commonly argued that requiring that free actions must be *undetermined* would not enhance our freedom but would rather reduce it either to chance or luck or mystery.

This dialectic in its modern forms was firmly in place when I first began thinking about free will in the 1960s. But the contours of philosophical debates about it were simpler then than today. The common assumption was that if you had scientific leanings, you would naturally be a *compatibilist* about free will (believing it to be compatible with determinism), unless you were a *free will skeptic* or *hard determinist*, denying free will altogether. And if, by contrast, you were a *libertarian* about free will, believing in a free will that was *incompatible* with determinism, it was assumed that you must inevitably appeal to some kind of mysterious forms of agency or causation to make sense of it—to uncaused causes, immaterial minds, noumenal selves outside space and time, prime movers unmoved, or other examples of what P. F. Strawson called in his seminal 1962 essay "Freedom and Resentment" the "panicky metaphysics of libertarianism."

I began thinking about free will shortly after Strawson's essay appeared, when my philosophical mentor at the time, Wilfred Sellars, challenged me to reconcile a traditional incompatibilist or libertarian free will with modern science. Sellars was a compatibilist about free will, like Strawson, who believed that a libertarian or indeterminist free will could not be accounted for without reducing it to mere chance or appealing to what Strawson had dubbed panicky metaphysics. While Sellars granted that free will in some sense was an integral part of what he notably called the *manifest image* of the world, the world of our ordinary experience, he did not believe a traditional libertarian or incompatibilist free will could be reconciled with what he called the *scientific image* of the world; and he challenged me to show otherwise.

Meeting that challenge turned out to be a longer task than I expected, sixty years and still ongoing. The reason, as I learned, was that it would require rethinking nearly every facet of the traditional problem of free will. Strawson and Sellars, as it turned out, were part of a long modern tradition of skepticism about the possibility of a free will that must somehow be incompatible with determinism. Such a traditional idea of free will has been under sustained attack in the modern era as outdated, obscure, and unintelligible and has been dismissed by many modern philosophers and scientists since the seventeenth century for its supposed lack of fit with modern images of humans and the cosmos in the natural and human sciences.

Friedrich Nietzsche summed up this prevailing skepticism in his inimitable prose when he said that such a traditional notion of freedom of the will "in the superlative metaphysical sense," as he called it, that would underwrite an "ultimate responsibility for one's actions" and require that one somehow be an undetermined "cause of oneself" was "the best self-contradiction that has been conceived so far" by the human mind (1889, sec. 17.8).

1.2. Questions to Be Addressed and the Plan of the Book

I agree that a traditional idea of free will that would require its being incompatible with determinism is likely to appear utterly mysterious and unintelligible in a modern context unless we learn to think about it in new ways. Hence my long struggle. Yet the struggle seemed worth the effort. For, like many another issue of modernity, the question was whether *something* of this traditional idea of free will in what Nietzsche called "the superlative metaphysical sense" can be retrieved from the dissolving acids of modern science and secular learning. Or would it become, along with other aspects of our self-image, yet another victim of what Max Weber notably called the "disenchantments" (*entzauberungen*) of modernity?

But any retrieval, as I came to realize, would be no simple matter, if possible at all. It would require piecing together a complex tapestry of ideas that would involve rethinking the relations of many different and related notions: agency, choice, action, selfhood, will, control, responsibility, power, and many others. It would also require making a host of distinctions, many of which are still often not made, or fully appreciated, in contemporary discussions of free will, despite the sophistication of these discussions. You cannot get to the heart of historical debates about free will, I argue, without distinguishing different kinds of *freedom*, different senses of *will*, different dimensions of *responsibility*, and different notions of *control*, among many other distinctions.

The purpose of this book is to spell out this complex tapestry of ideas as I currently envisage it and address some of the latest critical literature related to it. Hence the book's title. The rethinking required involves addressing two related strands of the modern attack on libertarian free will. The first strand, just mentioned, comes from compatibilists who argue that, despite any appearances to the contrary, determinism does not really conflict with free will. We can have all the freedoms "worth wanting," even if determinism should turn out to be true. Addressing this first challenge requires addressing two related questions. First is the so-called Compatibility Question: Is free will compatible or incompatible with determinism? Second is what I call the Significance Question: What kinds of freedoms are "worth wanting" and why?

The second strand of the modern attack goes further. The claim in this case is that a libertarian or incompatibilist free will of this traditional kind is impossible or unintelligible and has no place in the modern scientific picture of the world. It is not a kind of freedom we *could* have anyway. Addressing this second challenge requires addressing, among other things, what I have called the "Intelligibility Question" about free will: Can one make sense of a libertarian or indeterminist free will without reducing it to mere chance or luck, on the one hand, or to mystery, on the other, and can such a free will be reconciled with modern scientific views of the cosmos and of human beings?

Chapters 1 through 5 of this book begin to spell out my updated views concerning the Compatibility and Significance Questions (in Chapters 2 and 3) and the Intelligibility Question (in Chapters 4 and 5), which also has implications for the Significance Question as well as various Existence Questions about free will. Numerous objections to the view of free will developed are also addressed in these chapters. Subsequent chapters compare, and contrast, the view presented with other competing views of free will that have been a part of current debates, especially over the past fifty years. These later chapters also involve addressing more recent objections and topics and, in the process, further developing and adding additional pieces to the account of free will in the first five chapters. Throughout all the chapters, I will be adding significant refinements to my view as it was developed in earlier writings.

1.3. Teleological Intelligibility:
My View Is Both Agent-Causal and Event-Causal

Before turning to these tasks, however, I want to mention at the outset one particular refinement of my view that will also be discussed in more detail later,[2] but is especially important and relevant to how that view is discussed and labeled in the current literature.

It has become customary in the past several decades to distinguish libertarian views of free will into three kinds: *noncausal* (NC), *agent-causal* (AC), and *event-causal* (EC). Noncausal libertarian views hold that free choices or volitions are intrinsically active doings that are uncaused events. Agent-causal libertarian views hold that free choices and actions are caused by agents in a special manner that for various reasons (which differ, depending on the particular version of the view) cannot themselves be caused by events, either deterministically or indeterministically. Event-causal views hold that free choices or actions are caused by events, but indeterministically.

In the 1960s, when I began thinking about these issues, most libertarian views were either noncausalist (NC) or agent-causalist (AC), or some combination of the two. Those who held dualist views of mind and body usually had elements of both views: free choices or actions were uncaused by physical events, yet were caused in some manner by agents, qua immaterial minds. All such views and historical versions of them are what prompted Strawson's complaint in 1962 about the "panicky metaphysics of libertarianism."

What have since come to be called event-causal (EC) views were not yet on the horizon in those days when I began. Some philosophers, such as David Wiggins (1973), Richard Sorabji (1983), and Robert Nozick (1981), later suggested the possibility of libertarian theories that did not appeal to panicky metaphysics and might somehow be reconciled with contemporary scientific views.[3] But my own view, developed in the 1970s and subsequent decades, was the first to attempt to develop such a view in considerable detail. Other libertarian views with similar goals have been subsequently developed in the past several decades, and they will also be discussed in later chapters.

All libertarian views with such goals thereafter came to be designated "event-causal" (EC) libertarian views to distinguish them from traditional NC and AC views. And since my view was one of the first of this new kind, it was often identified and discussed as a prime example of such an EC view. Yet I was never happy with this designation and did not use it myself in earlier writings, including *The Significance of Free Will*. In that work and elsewhere I preferred to call my view a "teleological intelligibility" view, an expression suggested by Gary Watson. But I now think it necessary to go one step further and repudiate the simple designation "event-causal" altogether for my view because of its misleading implications.

For one thing, the designation "event-causal (EC)" misleadingly suggests (and has suggested to many) that one must choose between saying that event causation, on the one hand, or agent (or substance) causation, on the other, is fundamental to making sense of libertarian free will; and I have never believed that. What I believe and have consistently argued is that both agent and event causation are necessary to account for libertarian free will and neither is reducible to the other, in a manner to be further explained in this book.

As a consequence, I have come to believe and will argue in these chapters that to avoid numerous potential misunderstandings in current debates about free will, we should distinguish at least four different kinds of libertarian theories, not merely the three common ones, NC, AC, EC, but also a fourth kind, which might be called agent-causal/event-causal (AC/EC). In writings over the past decade, I refer to this as "a fourth way forward" in making sense of a free will that is not compatible with determinism.[4]

My view has always been of this fourth kind, though I have not always made this clear in earlier works. It differs from noncausal (NC) views in not requiring that basic libertarian free actions be uncaused. It differs from EC views in rejecting claims that libertarian free actions can be adequately explained merely by claiming they are indeterministically caused in appropriate ways by beliefs, desires, intentions, and other mental states of agents. I argue that to explain what these "appropriate ways" amount to, one must bring in references to agents, as *complex dynamical systems*, exercising a certain kind of *teleological guidance control*, to be discussed, over some of their own processes; and such references I will further argue are not reducible to mere causation by mental states and events of agents alone. As I explain in the following chapters, such complex dynamical systems and the teleological guidance control they may involve play significant roles in current natural sciences of complex systems and in recent developments in the neurosciences.[5]

Finally, this fourth kind of view (AC/EC) I shall defend differs from traditional AC views in not having any of the following features, one or more of which has been claimed for AC views by their historical and recent defenders: (1) The view to be defended here does not involve a "sui generis" or "metaphysically primitive" notion of causation by an agent or substance. (2) Nor does it involve a notion of agent or substance causation that is *not also* required by compatibilist accounts of free agency. (3) The view defended here also does not appeal to a notion of agent causation whose *exercise* does not essentially involve causation by states, processes, and events (hence AC/EC). (4) Nor does it require a special kind of causation by an agent or substance that is in principle, or by its very nature, incapable of being itself caused by prior events, either deterministically or indeterministically. (5) Nor does the view developed here require a special kind of causation by an agent or substance that is not subject to or governed by laws of nature of the natural sciences, (6) nor one that involves appeals to immaterial substances (Descartes and other substance dualists), noumenal selves outside space and time (Kant), prime movers unmoved, or other examples of what Strawson called the panicky metaphysics of libertarianism.

In sum, the irreducible agent causation involved in this fourth kind of view (AC/EC) (7) is not of a kind that is only needed for libertarian free will. It is needed as well for any kind of voluntary agency, whether compatibilist or incompatibilist. And (8) it is consistent with determinism *or* indeterminism. Its irreducibility to event causation is thus not a sufficient reason for saying (i) that it is not compatible with determinism or (ii) that its *exercise* does not *involve* event causation.

I will therefore refer to the view developed in this book throughout as this fourth kind, as an AC/EC view ("if that doesn't sound too much like a modern rock group," as I added in a recent work [2014] where this label AC/EC was used). And let me reiterate that my view has always been of this AC/EC kind, though this label was first introduced in my writings in Kane 2011b. I will occasionally also refer to the view defended here by my previously favored title, "teleological intelligibility," a title that also remains appropriate for reasons that will become clear as we proceed.

2
Compatibility and Significance Questions (Part I)

The Freedom Path

Is free will compatible or incompatible with determinism? And what kind of freedoms are "worth wanting"? These are respectively the Compatibility and Significance Questions about free will. I believe there are two paths to adequately addressing these questions from both historical and contemporary perspectives—two paths that ultimately converge. The first path, undertaken in this chapter, begins by reflecting on different *kinds of freedom*. The second path, pursued in the next chapter, begins by reflecting on practices and grounds for holding persons responsible for their choices and actions, and it leads to a distinction between different *dimensions of responsibility*.

By following each path and exploring their convergence, one can begin to piece together the complex tapestry of ideas that I believe is necessary for understanding these and other important questions about free will. From this point onward, I designate the pieces of this tapestry by P1, P2, etc. We begin with the first of the two paths, the freedom path.

2.1. Multiple Meanings of Freedom and Freedom of Will

(P1) The first significant step on this freedom path involves recognizing that as the Compatibility Question is formulated in many modern discussions of free will—"Is freedom compatible or incompatible with determinism?"—the question is too simple. For *there are many meanings of "freedom"* (as one would expect from such a much-disputed and much-debated term) *and many of these meanings are compatible with determinism.*

Even in a determined world, as suggested in the opening chapter, we would want to distinguish persons who are free from such things as physical restraint, coercion, compulsion, covert control, or political oppression from persons who are not free from these things; and we can and should acknowledge that these freedoms are significant (i.e., "worth wanting") and would be preferable to their opposites even in a determined world.

(P2) Libertarians about free will (those who believe in a free will that is incompatible with determinism) should, I argue, concede this point to compatibilists and others. What libertarians should insist upon instead is that *there is at least one significant kind of freedom worth wanting that is not compatible with determinism.* This further freedom is freedom *of will*, which I define as "the power to be the ultimate source and sustainer to some degree of one's own ends or purposes." What this amounts to will be made clear as further pieces of this tapestry are added.

2.2. Alternative Possibilities and Ultimate Responsibility

The first of these further pieces involves recognizing that

(P3) There are two features of free will that have led persons to believe historically that it is threatened by determinism. We believe we have free will when we view ourselves as agents capable of influencing the world in various ways. Open alternatives or alternative possibilities seem to lie before us (a "garden of forking paths," to use the much-cited image of Jorge Luis Borges's well-known short story).[1] We reason and deliberate among these alternatives and choose. We feel (i) it is "up to us" what we choose and how we act: and this means we "could have chosen or acted otherwise." As Aristotle noted: when acting is "up to us," so is not acting. This "up-to-us-ness" also suggests that (ii) the ultimate sources of our actions lie to some degree in us and not entirely outside us in factors beyond our control (Kane 1985, p. 78). As the ancient philosopher Plotinus put it in response to the deterministic Stoics of his day, if the ultimate sources or causes (*archai*) of our actions were not in us, but in conditions that we did not control, we would not be responsible for the actions (1950, p. 87).[2]

(P4) Most modern debates about the Compatibility and Significance Questions have tended to focus on the first of these two requirements, that free agents must have alternative possibilities or open alternatives for action. But arguments about whether determinism is or is not compatible with this *condition of alternative possibilities* (or AP as we may call it) have led to contentious debates in modern philosophy that have tended to stalemate over differing interpretations of what it means to say that agents have the "power" or "ability" to act and to act otherwise and about the meaning of related expressions such as "can do otherwise" and "could have done otherwise."

(P5) These contentious debates about the meaning of such expressions, and the resulting disagreements about the role of this AP condition in modern debates about free will, I contend, are symptoms of a deeper problem. The problem is that focusing on alternative possibilities alone is too thin a basis on which to rest the case for the incompatibility of free will and determinism. It is not that alternative possibilities and the power to do otherwise are unimportant for free will. Far from it. They are very important, and we will return shortly to consider why. It is rather that other considerations must also be brought into the picture in arguing for the incompatibility of free will and determinism. *The Compatibility Question cannot be resolved by focusing on alternative possibilities or the power to do otherwise alone.*[3]

(P6) Realizing this, I have argued in past writings that one must revisit the long history of debates about free will to see where else to look. When doing so, one finds there is another historical condition fueling incompatibilist intuitions that to my mind is even more important than the alternative possibilities condition (AP). This other condition is related to the second requirement for the "up-to-us-ness" of freedom of will mentioned in P3—namely, (ii) that "the ultimate sources of our actions must lie to some degree in us and not entirely outside us in factors beyond our control."

(P7) I call this further condition ultimate responsibility, or UR. The basic idea is this: *to be ultimately responsible for an action, an agent must be responsible to some degree for anything that is a sufficient reason (a sufficient condition, cause, or motive) for the action's occurring.* If, for example, a choice issues from, and can be sufficiently explained by an agent's character and motives (together with background conditions), then to be ultimately responsible for the choice, the agent must be at least in part responsible by virtue of choices or actions voluntarily performed in the past for *having* certain features of the character and motives he or she now has. Compare Aristotle's claim that if a man is responsible for wicked acts that flow from his character, he must at some time in the past have been responsible for forming the wicked character from which these acts flow (1985, p. 63).

This UR condition accounts for the "ultimate" in the original definition of free will in P2: "the power of agents to be the ultimate sources and sustainers to some degree of their own ends or purposes." This ultimacy condition also helps to explain why historical debates about free will have so often been intertwined with metaphysical debates about the so-called principle of sufficient reason.

2.3. Self-Forming Actions, Self-Formation, and the Will

(P8) Importantly, this condition of UR does not require that we could have done otherwise (AP) for *every* act done "of our own free will." It thus partially vindicates compatibilists and others who insist that we can be held morally responsible for many acts even when we could not have done otherwise than perform them.

This condition UR shows, for example, that what Harry Frankfurt calls the Principle of Alternative Possibilities (PAP) is false, as Frankfurt argues. It is not true, as his principal PAP says, that "agents can be held morally responsible for their actions *only if* they could have done otherwise at the time than perform those actions" (1969, p. 12).

(P9) But this vindication is only partial. For this condition of UR *does* require that we could have done otherwise with respect to *some* acts in our past life histories by which we *formed* our present characters and wills. I call these *self-forming actions*, or SFAs, and they represent a ninth piece of this tapestry involved in rethinking the Compatibility Question.

To bring out the importance of these SFAs, consider a familiar compatibilist line of argument purporting to show that moral responsibility does not require the power to do otherwise *at all*. It is a line of argument illustrated, for example, by compatibilist Daniel Dennett's much-discussed example of Martin Luther (1984, pp. 131–33). When finally breaking with the Church of

Rome, Luther said, "Here I stand, I can do no other." Suppose, says Dennett, Luther was literally right about himself at that moment. Given his character and motives, he literally could not then have done otherwise. Does this mean he was not morally responsible for this act? Not at all, Dennett says. In saying, "I can do no other," Luther was not disowning responsibility for his act, but taking full responsibility for it. Thus, Dennett concludes, "could have done otherwise," or the power to do otherwise, is *not* required for free will in a sense demanded by moral responsibility.

(P10) In response, I have argued that incompatibilists may, and indeed should, grant that Luther could have been responsible for this act, *even ultimately responsible in the sense of UR*, though he could not have done otherwise *then and there*, and even if his act was determined by his existing will at that moment. But this would be so, incompatibilists about free will should argue, to the extent that Luther was responsible for his present motives and character by virtue of some earlier struggles and self-forming choices (SFAs) that brought him to this point where he could do no other. Luther's biography provides ample evidence of many such prior struggles.

(P11) Often we act from a will already formed, but it is "our *own* free will" by virtue of the fact that we formed it by other choices or actions in the past, self-forming actions (SFAs), for which we could have done otherwise. If this were not so, *there is nothing we could have ever done differently in our entire lifetimes to make ourselves different than we are*—a consequence, I believe, that is incompatible with our being (at least to some degree) ultimately responsible for being the way we are and having the wills we do have.

2.4. Freedom of Action and Freedom of Will

(P12) Focusing on this condition of ultimate responsibility or UR tells us something else of importance about the traditional problem of free will. It tells us why it is a problem about the freedom *of the will* and not just about the freedom *of action* and why these freedoms must be distinguished if the Compatibility and Significance Questions and other questions about free will are to be adequately addressed.

There has been a tendency in the modern era, beginning with Thomas Hobbes ([1654] 1999) and John Locke ([1690] 1975) in the seventeenth century, and coming to fruition in the twentieth century, to reduce the problem of free will to a problem of free action.

> (P13) I believe such a reduction oversimplifies the problem. *Free will is not just about free action*, though it involves free action. It is about *self-formation*, about *the formation of our "wills," or how we got to be the kinds of persons we are*, with the characters, motives, and purposes we now have. Were we ultimately responsible to some degree for having the wills (characters, motives, and purposes) we do have, or can the sources of our wills be completely traced back to something over which we had no control, such as Fate or the decrees of God, heredity and environment, social conditioning, hidden controllers, and so on? Therein, I believe, lies the core of the traditional problem of "free *will*."

John Locke ([1690] 1975) famously said in the seventeenth century that the so-called problem of free will, which had so exercised medieval and earlier philosophers, was really a problem about *free agency*, or the freedom *of the agent*, and not about the freedom *of the will*. Like other thinkers of the modern era, Locke was skeptical of medieval references to the "will" in general, which often made it out to be a mysterious inner power capable of influencing actions and events in ways not countenanced, Locke believed, by the emerging sciences of his day.

Many moderns down to the present time have followed Locke in this skepticism. They argue, as did Ludwig Wittgenstein (1948) and Gilbert Ryle (1949) in the mid-twentieth century, that references to the *will* and *acts of will* were outdated remnants of premodern modes of thought and should go the way of witches and phlogiston. Even some modern libertarians and incompatibilists about free will have joined compatibilists in arguing that the historical "problem of free will" is really about the freedom of agency and hence about the freedom of action, and *not* about the freedom of the will.[4]

> (P14) I believe this is a mistake. It is *not* wrong, to be sure, to say as Locke does, that the traditional problem of free will is really a problem about *free agency*. But it *is* wrong to say it is not therefore *also* about the freedom of the will. For, as described in these pieces, *freedom of will is an important aspect of free agency*; and moreover, freedom of will *is that particular aspect*

of free agency which has been the subject of historical debates about whether free will is or is not compatible with determinism.

2.5. The Compatibility Question Revisited

(P15) For if the case for the incompatibility of free will and determinism cannot be made by appeal to alternatives possibilities or AP alone, the case can be made if this condition of UR is added. I have thus argued that this condition of UR should be moved to center stage in free will debates.

(P16) To be ultimately responsible for an action in the sense of UR, an agent must be responsible to some degree for anything that is a sufficient reason (cause or motive) for the action's occurring. This entails, as noted in P7, that if a choice can be sufficiently explained by an agent's character and motives (together with background conditions), then to be ultimately responsible for the choice, the agent must be at least in part responsible by virtue of choices or actions voluntarily performed in the past for having relevant aspects of the character and motives he or she now has.[5] But this being the case, an impossible infinite regress of past actions would be required unless *some* actions in the agent's life history (SFAs) did not *have* either sufficient causes or sufficient motives (and hence were undetermined).[6]

Yet if one can arrive at the incompatibility of free will and determinism from UR alone in this manner, one might wonder whether appeals to alternative possibilities or AP are needed at all for free will. Some recent philosophers who are sympathetic to incompatibilism, and are impressed by arguments of the above kind, have in fact suggested that appeals to alternative possibilities or the power to do otherwise are not needed at all for free will. These *source incompatibilists*, as they are sometimes called, insist that, while free will is incompatible with determinism (by virtue of a source or ultimacy condition, such as UR), alternative possibilities or AP are not needed at all for free will or moral responsibility.[7]

(P17) I believe this is also a mistake. While I am usually regarded as one of the first of these so-called source incompatibilists in recent modern discussions of free will because of my emphasis on UR, I have never been a source incompatibilist of this kind. *Both conditions, I believe—UR and AP—are needed for free will.* Kevin Timpe (2008) has made a useful distinction between what he calls "narrow" and "wide" source incompatibilism.[8] Narrow source incompatibilists believe that alternative possibilities or AP are not needed at all for free will or moral responsibility. Wide source incompatibilists, like myself (and Timpe), believe that both ultimate responsibility and alternative possibilities are needed for free will and moral responsibility, at least for some choices and actions in the course of our lives.

But the reasons why both conditions, UR and alternative possibilities, are needed for free will are more subtle than is generally realized; and understanding them requires further pieces in rethinking the Compatibility and Significance Questions about free will.

2.6. Plurality Conditions and Free Will

(P18) The first of these further pieces concerns what I call *plurality conditions* for free will. When we wonder about whether the wills of agents are free, it is not merely whether they could have done otherwise that concerns us, even if the doing otherwise is undetermined. What interests us is whether they could have done otherwise *voluntarily* (or *willingly*), *intentionally*, and *rationally*. Or to put it more generally, we are interested in whether agents could have acted voluntarily, intentionally, and rationally *in more than one way*, rather than in only one way, and in other ways merely by accident or mistake, unintentionally, inadvertently, or irrationally.[9]

(P19) I call such conditions—of more-than-one-way voluntariness, intentionality, and rationality—"plurality conditions" for free will (Kane 1996, pp. 107–11). They seem to be deeply embedded in our intuitions about free choice and action. Most of us naturally assume that freedom and responsibility would be deficient if it were *always* the case that we could *only* do otherwise by *accident* or *mistake, unintentionally, involuntarily, or irrationally*.

But *why*, one might ask, are these plurality conditions so deeply embedded in our intuitions about free choice and action? Answering this question takes us to several further pieces of this tapestry.

2.7. Austin-Style Examples

(P20) It is normally assumed that what incompatibilists and libertarians need for free will are (i) alternative possibilities (AP) *plus* (ii) indeterminism. But these two conditions alone are not sufficient for incompatibilist free will, even if each should be necessary. One can see this by paying greater attention to a significant class of actions for which the agents could have done otherwise (had AP) *and* the actions are undetermined—and yet the agents lack free *will* in performing them.

(P21) The actions I have in mind go back to examples put forward more than fifty years ago by J. L. Austin (1961), Philippa Foot (1966), Michael Ayers (1968), Elizabeth Anscombe (1971), and others. These "Austin-style examples," as I call them, were originally conceived for purposes having to do with analyses of what it means to say that agents "can" do and do otherwise and "could" have done otherwise. But it is not always noticed that examples of this kind have a significance beyond what was originally envisaged for them.

Here are three such examples, the first from Austin's influential "Ifs and Cans" (1961). Austin imagined that he must sink a three-foot putt to win a golf match, but owing to a nervous twitch in his arm, he misses. The other two examples are ones I have used on other occasions. An assassin is trying to kill a prime minister from a distance with a high-powered rifle when, owing to a nervous twitch, he misses and kills the minister's aide instead. I am standing in front of a coffee machine intending to press the button for black coffee when, owing to a brain cross, I mistakenly press the button for coffee with cream.

In each of these cases, we can further suppose, as Austin suggests, that an element of genuine chance or indeterminism is involved. Perhaps the nervous twitches or brain crosses are brought about by amplified undetermined quantum events in our brains or nerve pathways. We can thus imagine that examples of this sort, such as Austin's sinking his putt or the assassin's hitting his target, would be genuinely undetermined events. They might miss by chance, and, in the examples, they do miss by chance.

Now the important question Austin asked about his example was this: Can we say in such circumstances where he missed the putt that "he could have done otherwise" than miss it? Austin's answer is that we can indeed say this. For he had made many similar putts of this short length in the past. He thus had the *ability* to hole putts of this length and the *opportunity, since the outcome of this attempt was also undetermined*, and so he might well have succeeded in holing the putt, as he was trying to do.

(P22) But this means we have an action (missing the putt) that is both (i) undetermined and (ii) such that the agent could have done otherwise. Yet *missing* the putt is not something that would be regarded as *freely* done in any normal sense of the term because it is not under the agent's *voluntary* and *intentional* control. Missing the putt was not something he wanted to do or was trying to do. The same is true of the assassin's missing his intended target and my accidentally pressing the wrong button on the coffee machine. These are things done by accident, unwillingly and unintentionally.

One might be tempted to think these occurrences are not *actions* at all because they are undetermined and happen by accident. But Austin rightly warns against such a conclusion as well. Missing the putt, he says, was clearly something he *did*, even though it was not what he wanted or intended to do. Similarly, missing the prime minister and killing the aide was something the assassin did, though unintentionally; and pressing the wrong button was something I did, even if only by mistake or inadvertently.

(P23) Austin's point is that many of the things we do *unintentionally* or *inadvertently, by accident* or *mistake*, are things we *do*. We may sometimes be absolved of responsibility for doing them (though not always, as in the case of the assassin). But it is for *doing* them that we are absolved of responsibility when we are absolved; and this can be true even if the accidents or mistakes are genuinely undetermined.

2.8. A Scenario: Plurality Conditions and Plural Voluntary Control

To see what this implies about free will, consider the following scenario. Imagine a world in which there is a considerable amount of genuine indeterminism or chance in human affairs as well as in nature. In this world, people set out to do things—kill prime ministers, sink putts, press buttons, punch computer keys, hit targets, etc.—usually succeeding, but sometimes failing by mistake or accident in the Austinian manner.

Now further imagine that *all* actions in this world in the lifetimes of agents, whether the agents succeed in their purposes or not, are such that their *reasons, motives, and purposes* for trying to act as they do, are always settled, or preset by prior formative circumstances. Whether the assassin misses the prime minister or not, his *intention* to kill the prime minister is already settled, we may imagine, by his past circumstances prior to his attempt. Whether Austin misses his putt or not, his *wanting* and *trying* to make it were already settled by his circumstances. Whether I press the button for coffee without cream, my wanting to do so because of my dislike of cream is already settled by features of my circumstances. And so it is, for all persons and all their actions in this imagined world.

(P24) I would argue that persons in such a world lack free *will*, even though it may often be the case that they have (i) *alternative possibilities* and that their actions are (ii) *undetermined*. For agents in such a world can sometimes do otherwise than they do, but only in the Austinian manner—by mistake or accident, unintentionally or inadvertently—and this is a limited kind of freedom at best. What they cannot do is *will* otherwise than they do. *All their reasons, motives and purposes have been already "set one way" before and when they act, so that if they do otherwise, it will not be "in accordance with their wills."*

(P25) What this shows is that when we wonder about whether the *wills* of agents are free, *it is not merely whether they could have done otherwise that concerns us, even if the doing otherwise is undetermined*. What interests us is whether they could have done otherwise *voluntarily* (in accordance with their wills), *intentionally* (knowingly rather than inadvertently and on purpose rather than accidentally), and *rationally* (having reasons for so acting and acting for those reasons). Or to put it more generally, when we wonder about whether the *wills* of agents are free, we are interested in whether there are situations in which they have the power to act voluntarily, intentionally, and rationally in more than one way, rather than in only one way, and in other ways merely by accident or mistake, unintentionally, involuntarily, or irrationally.[10]

20   THE COMPLEX TAPESTRY OF FREE WILL

(P26) We thus arrive at an answer to the question of why these "plurality conditions" are so deeply embedded in our intuitions about free choice and action. We naturally assume that freedom and responsibility would be deficient if it were *always* the case that we could *only* do otherwise by accident or mistake, unintentionally, involuntarily, or irrationally. If free will involves more than alternative possibilities plus indeterminism, these plurality conditions appear to be among the significant additional requirements.

(P27) Moreover, as (P24)–(P25) make clear, satisfying these plurality conditions implies that agents must be able to exercise a certain kind of *control* over some of their choices or actions that may be called *plural voluntary control* (PVC): agents have such PCV during a time period over a set of options (such as competing choices) when they have the power to bring about whichever of the options they will to bring about rather than any alternative option, when they will to bring it about, and they have the power to do this *voluntarily* (without being coerced or compelled), *intentionally* (knowingly and on purpose), and *rationally* (for *reasons* that they then and there wish to act upon), *whichever* choice may be brought about.

These conditions can be summed up by saying, as we sometimes do, that the agents can choose or act either way *at will*, or, alternatively, that it is *up to them* what they will to choose and do when they act.

2.9. Will-Settled vs. Will-Setting Actions

Focusing in this way on plurality conditions and plural voluntary control leads to a further important and often neglected topic in free will debates that I call "*will-setting*" (1996, pp. 113–15).

(P28) In the imagined scenario of the previous section, all of the motives and purposes of agents in every situation are already "set one way" *before* they act. The assassin's desires and purposes are set on killing the prime minister, not on missing or killing the aide. My desires and purposes are set on pressing the button for black coffee and not any other button, Austin's on making, not missing, his crucial putt. In such cases, where the motives and purposes of agents are already "set one way" at the time they act, we may say their actions are *will-settled*.

(P29) By contrast, actions are *will-setting* when the wills of agents (including their motives and purposes) are *not* already set one way *before* they act. Rather they set their wills one way or the other *in the performance of the actions themselves*. Choices or decisions that are SFAs in the sense understood here are will-setting in this sense. The agents' wills are not already set one way before they choose, but they set their wills one way or the other, voluntarily, intentionally, and rationally, in the act of choosing itself. Such self-forming or will-setting actions would thus also satisfy the plurality conditions.

(P30) The imagined world in which all the motives and purposes of agents are already set one way whenever they act thus provides a clue to the deep connection between will-setting, UR, free will, alternative possibilities, and the plurality conditions. If we are to be to some degree ultimate determiners of our own wills, as UR requires, some actions in our lifetimes, SFAs, must be will-setting in the above sense and hence must satisfy the plurality conditions. But these actions will then also satisfy the condition of alternative possibilities. For if one can do or do otherwise, either way voluntarily, intentionally, and rationally, it follows a fortiori that one can do or do otherwise. Alternative possibilities or AP would therefore be necessary for free will after all, at least sometimes in our lives *when we engage in self-formation*.

Yet we saw earlier that one could argue for incompatibilism from UR alone without appealing to AP. How are we to make sense of this?

2.10. The Dual Regress of Free Will

(P31) The answer, I argue, lies in UR. *Both* alternative possibilities (AP) *and* indeterminism follow from the condition of ultimate responsibility, but by different argumentative routes. I have called this "the dual regress of free will" (Kane 2000a). Two separate regresses are associated with UR. The first begins with the requirement that agents be responsible by virtue of past voluntary actions for anything that is a *sufficient reason* or ground for their actions in the sense of a *sufficient cause*; and it leads to the conclusion that some actions in the life histories of agents possessing free will must be *undetermined* (i.e., they must lack sufficient causes).

(P32) The second regress begins with the requirement that agents be responsible for anything that is a *sufficient reason* or ground for their actions in the sense of a *sufficient motive*; and it leads (by way of *will-setting* and *plurality*) to the conclusion that some actions in the life histories of agents must be such that the agents could have (willingly) done otherwise—that is, to a strong (plural voluntary) version of AP.[11]

(P33) Agents, it is important to note, can have a sufficient *motive* for an action even when the action does not have a sufficient *cause*, and hence is not determined. Such is the case, for example, with Austin-style examples. The assassin has a sufficient motive for killing the prime minister even though his killing of the prime minister is undetermined and therefore lacks a sufficient cause. The assassin's will is nonetheless set on doing it. So, if we want to know whether he is ultimately responsible for the act, we have to ask whether he is responsible for his will's being settled in this vicious way by past voluntary actions that were not also will-settled when they occurred, but some of which were will-setting or self-forming actions (SFAs). In other words, *if an agent has a sufficient motive for an action, so that the agent's will is settled on performing it, we need to ask whether the agent is ultimately responsible for the fact that his or her will is settled in this way.*

(P34) The first of these regresses results from the requirement that we be ultimate sources of our *actions*, the second from the requirement that we be ultimate sources of our *wills* to perform those actions. In this manner, the requirements of indeterminism and alternative possibilities have a common origin in the idea that we must be to some degree ultimate sources of our *willed actions*.

(P35) To stop both regresses, it is not sufficient that some actions in the lifetimes of agents be undetermined or lack sufficient *causes*. Such actions also cannot have sufficient *motives*. The regress-stopping actions must therefore not only be undetermined, but also be *will-setting* and *not will-settled* and hence must satisfy *plurality conditions* if agents are to be to some degree ultimate creators or shapers of their own wills. The resulting actions—which must be undetermined, will-setting, and satisfy plurality conditions—are the "self-forming" actions (SFAs) needed to satisfy UR.

With this in mind, we can return to P11, putting a further gloss on it:

(P36) Often we act from a will already formed, but it is "our *own* free will" by virtue of the fact that we formed it by other choices or actions in the past (SFAs) for which we had the power to have *willingly* (voluntarily and intentionally) done otherwise. *If this were not so, there is nothing we could have ever willingly done differently in our entire lifetimes to make ourselves different than we are.*

2.11. Three Notions of Freedom

Putting these pieces together, we may add that

(P37) To understand the full meaning of free will, one must distinguish at least three different *kinds* of *freedom*, or free acts, each of which is essential to making sense of free will. Free acts may be
(1) Acts done voluntarily, on purpose and for reasons that are not coerced, compelled, or otherwise constrained and not subject to control by other agents.
(2) Acts (free in sense 1 that are also) done "of our own free will" in the sense of a will that we are ultimately responsible (UR) to some degree for forming.
(3) "Self-forming" or "will-setting" acts (SFAs) by which we form and reform the will from which we act in sense 2.

Acts free in sense 1 are compatible with determinism. Freedom of kind 1 is thus a compatibilist kind of freedom. Free acts of kinds 2 and 3, by contrast, are incompatibilist or libertarian free acts. They could not exist in a determined world. But importantly, only acts of kind 3 (SFAs) have to be themselves undetermined. Acts done "of one's own free will," or kind 2, may be determined by our existing will plus background circumstances (though they need not be). Such free acts of kind 2 done "of our own free will" are nonetheless incompatibilist or libertarian free, because they could not exist *in a determined world*, since they presuppose other will-forming or self-forming acts (of kind 3) that are not determined. Hence, they are incompatible with determin*ism*,

> (P38) Freedom of kind 1 is *freedom of action* simpliciter, while freedoms of kind 2 (acts done "of our own free will" in the sense of a will we are ultimately responsible for forming) and of kind 3 (self-forming acts by which we form and reform the will from which we act) represent *freedom of will*. If we were always free only in sense 1, we would have a measure of freedom of action (to act *as* we will), but we would not possess a deeper freedom *of the will itself*.

> (P39) Yet the three freedoms are related. Free acts of kind 3 (SFAs) are also free acts of kind 2 (they are also ultimately responsible acts of free will, albeit of a special kind). And acts of both kinds 2 *and* 3 (acts of free will) are also free acts of kind 1 (they must also be voluntary, uncoerced, non-compelled, etc.). So, *freedom of will* (of kinds 2 and 3) *is a kind of freedom of action* (of kind 1), albeit a special kind.

> (P40) An important consequence of this nesting is that incompatibilist freedom (of will) presupposes compatibilist freedom (of action): acts of free will (of kinds 2 and 3) must also be compatibilist free acts (of kind 1).

2.12. Three Senses of Will

Another takeaway from this discussion is the following:

> (P41) If we are to fully understand issues about free will, we must not only distinguish different kinds of freedom as in the previous section. It's also necessary to distinguish *different notions of will*. Three notions of will, in particular, play significant roles in historical discussions of agency, choice, and action; and, importantly, *all three of these senses of will play essential roles in the account of free will and self-forming action developed here*. The three notions may be called respectively *Motivational Will*, *Rational Will*, and *Striving Will*.

(P42) The first sense of will, *Motivational Will*, designates *a complex set of psychological attitudes* or *dispositions* that incline an agent toward or against performing or omitting certain actions. These psychological attitudes or dispositions include wants, desires, preferences, likes and dislikes, beliefs, or judgments (factual, evaluative, or normative), emotions (including fears and hopes, anger, love, hate, resentment, and other "reactive attitudes"), among other psychological attitudes that may motivate agents to act in various ways.

(P43) By contrast, the second sense of will, *Rational Will*, is a *complex set of conceptually interrelated powers*, whose focal point is *practical reasoning*, including the powers to deliberate or reason practically, to decide or choose, to form intentions or preferences, to make evaluative or normative judgments, to critically evaluate reasons for action, and so on.

In the medieval period, it was customary to single out *Will* in this sense of Rational Will, as a set of conceptually interrelated powers whose focal point was practical reasoning, and to distinguish Will in this sense from *Intellect*, a set of conceptually interrelated powers whose focal point was *theoretical* reasoning (powers to infer, conclude, surmise, and critically evaluate theories about the world).

Among medieval, and some later, thinkers, Intellect and Will, understood in these senses, were often called *faculties* of mind. The term "faculty" has been out of fashion for some time and was often dismissed by early modern philosophers, along with the Will itself, as an outdated remnant of medieval modes of thought. But the notion of a faculty has a clear and useful meaning in this context.[12] A faculty of mind is nothing more nor less than a *set of conceptually interrelated powers*, related in this case of Rational Will, to the exercise of reason in its practical mode.

(P44) The third sense of "Will" is what Brian O'Shaughnessy (1980) has aptly called "Striving Will." It is "willing" as *trying* or *making efforts* or *exerting willpower* or *endeavoring* or *striving* to attain certain goals where some sort of resistance (mental or physical) must be overcome if the goals are to be achieved.

One can now see that

(P45) All three of these senses of will play essential roles in the accounts of free will and self-forming actions developed here. Wants, desires, preferences, and other expressions of Motivational Will are among the *inputs* to practical reasoning. They function as reasons or motives for action or choice, whereas decisions and intentions, which are outcomes of Rational Will, are the *outputs* of practical reasoning.

(P46) What is distinctive about SFAs is that the inputs in practical deliberation in the case of SFAs, that is, the reasons, motives, and other psychological attitudes of Motivational Will, may offer conflicting signals about what the outputs of Rational Will in practical reasoning should be. As a result, in self-forming choices, Striving Will must also be involved. Efforts of will or exercises of willpower must be involved to overcome resistance in the will to making either choice or decision to which the agent may be inclined at the time by practical reasoning and Motivational Will.

(P47) Note finally that the idea of will in all three of these senses is essentially *teleological* in nature. The different senses of will represent different ways in which agents may be directed toward or tend toward various goals, purposes or ends: (i) being attracted to them in various ways (Motivational Will), (ii) reasoning and deciding which purposes or ends are to be pursued (Rational Will) and (iii) making efforts or striving to attain purposes or ends in the presence of obstacles or resistance of various kinds to their attainment (Striving Will). Involving all three of these senses of will, as it does, free will itself is an essentially teleological notion.

2.13. *Walden Two* Revisited

I conclude this chapter with a bit of personal history about how I came to be interested in the issues considered in it. When quite young, I don't remember exactly when, I read B. F. Skinner's utopian novel *Walden Two* (1962). I recall Frazier, one of the designers of the community, boasting to the visitors he was showing around the place that *Walden Two* was the freest place on earth, the freest place imaginable. There were no jails, no need for them, no restraints. People could have and do whatever they wanted or chose, he said, because they were behaviorally conditioned from childhood to want and choose only what they could have and do. And my reaction was: "What? This is the freest place imaginable? Something seems to be missing here." And this was a common reaction among my schoolmates. For in one sense there was a great deal of freedom in *Walden Two*, but in another sense, it was a *controlled* society.

My special interest in *Walden Two* was inspired by the fact that I grew up not too far from the original Walden, which was of course a pond and not a utopian community. It was a place where friends and I might occasionally jump the fences and swim after high school dances or on warm summer evenings. So we naturally took an interest when asked in school to read Henry David Thoreau's reminiscences about the place and about life in general. I asked myself back then whether Thoreau himself would have thought *Walden Two* was the freest place imaginable. And the answer seemed obvious: lover of freedom that he was, Thoreau would not have thought it was the freest place imaginable.

(P48) I lacked the resources back then to say in detail what was missing in *Walden Two*—to say, as I eventually would, that there are different dimensions of freedom (a complex notion, to be sure). And what Frazier and his colleagues were doing in *Walden Two* was maximizing freedom in one dimension—surface *freedom of action*—by minimizing it in another dimension, the freedom of agents to form their own wills and what sorts of persons they would become—a deeper *freedom of the will*.

(P49) If freedom is not a one-dimensional concept, but something with multiple dimensions, one can maximize it in some dimensions while minimizing it in others. And freedom *is* a complex notion. You can have it to varying degrees in some dimensions, but not in others; and there necessarily are trade-offs. Political theorists know this all too well.

Now, let's be clear: Skinner was writing in the heyday of behaviorism in psychology, which soon after became passé. There are plenty of legitimate doubts that one could exercise such control over human behavior by behavioral conditioning alone. If such control were possible at all, many would now believe it would have to involve genetic and neurological conditioning of humans from earliest ages. But the same dialectic would hold, whatever the means, if it were possible at all. That is, the same dialectic would hold *if* people were completely conditioned from childhood so that they would *always* want and choose only what they could have and do.

(P50) Note here that worries about such conditioning are greater *to the extent* that the conditioning *by whatever means* implies that the agents could *never* in the course of their lives voluntarily and intentionally choose or do otherwise than they were conditioned to do, that they could *never resist this conditioning*. In other words, the worry grows to the extent that the conditioning may be completely *determining*, whatever form the conditioning may take.

In fact, it was intimated in the novel that some young people might chafe under the restrictions on what they could have or do in Walden Two to the degree that the founders' conditioning might not be completely successful. These young people would not necessarily think the Walden Two way of life was bad. But they would want to chart their own course, make their own decisions about what they might want or choose to become, even if that meant taking chances of choosing wrongly and being disappointed, or worse. In other words, they might want the experience of *self*-formation, and would be willing to *take responsibility* for what the consequences of their life-forming actions should be. Anyone who has raised teenagers knows what I mean. They may respect you and what you are, but they do not want to be you. They want to be and become themselves.

Yet we know that many modern compatibilists want to make a distinction between being determined by the actions of manipulators or controllers, like the founders of Walden Two, on the one hand, and being determined merely by natural processes of heredity and environment, on the other. If we are determined by other persons, these compatibilists argue, we are controlled by those other persons and to that extent are not free in some important senses of freedom worth wanting. But if we are determined by natural processes alone and not by the actions of other persons, then, these compatibilists argue, we would not lack freedom in any important sense worth wanting. I believe this familiar compatibilist line of reasoning does not relieve legitimate concerns about determinism for reasons that will be discussed along with other topics in the next chapter and subsequent chapters.

3
Compatibility and Significance Questions (Part II)

The Responsibility Path

There were two paths, I suggested, to adequately addressing the Compatibility and Significance Questions about free will. The first of these paths, pursued in the previous chapter, focuses on different *dimensions of freedom*. The second path, to be pursued in this chapter, begins by reflecting on ordinary practices of holding persons morally and legally responsible; and it leads to a distinction between different *dimensions of responsibility*. The two paths ultimately converge, as this chapter will also show.

3.1. The Insulation Thesis: P. F. Strawson's "Freedom and Resentment"

In his influential 1962 article "Freedom and Resentment," which was cited earlier, P. F. Strawson famously argued that the application and justification of our ordinary practices of holding persons morally responsible and related "reactive attitudes" (such as blame, praise, resentment, indignation, and moral approval) were wholly "internal" to the ordinary practices themselves and could be "insulated" from traditional philosophical and metaphysical worries, including worries about free will and determinism. Strawson argued that to believe these ordinary practices of holding persons responsible would have to be modified in some ways—mitigated or even possibly abandoned— if we found that the persons' actions were determined by prior causes was to "overintellectualize" the issues.

This "insulation thesis" (as it has sometimes been called) is a controversial feature of Strawson's article; and it has had numerous proponents and critics.[1] Interestingly, one of the most prominent of these critics was

Strawson's son, Galen Strawson, who in his 1986 book, *Freedom and Belief*, took issue with his father's contention in "Freedom and Resentment" that ordinary practices of blaming and other reactive attitudes could be entirely insulated from metaphysical concerns about determinism. Against this contention, Galen Strawson argued that "the roots of the incompatibilist intuition [that free will is incompatible with determinism] lie deep in the very reactive attitudes that are invoked in order to undercut it. The reactive attitudes, he argued, "enshrine the incompatibilist intuition" rather than being insulated from it (p. 89).

I agree with Galen Strawson on this issue, though my reasons (to be considered in this chapter) are not all the same as his. Like him, I believe our ordinary practices of holding persons morally responsible and related questions about blameworthiness and other reactive attitudes cannot be *entirely* insulated from philosophical worries about free will and determinism that have engaged philosophers for centuries. This genie cannot be kept in the bottle, annoying as he may be.

I stated this agreement with Galen Strawson against his father's view in a review of Galen's *Freedom and Belief* (1986) that appeared in the *International Philosophical Quarterly* in 1988. In the review, I suggested that the disagreement on these issues in the Strawson family seemed to track the development of British analytic philosophy from the 1950s and early 1960s to the 1980s. When P. F. Strawson's "Freedom and Resentment" appeared in 1962, ordinary language was all the rage, under the influence of Wittgenstein's later writings, among other influences. But by the 1980s, when Galen's book appeared, metaphysics had made a comeback in British analytic philosophy and issues about free will, moral responsibility, and determinism could not be dismissed merely by appeals to ordinary language. There were metaphysical concerns to be addressed as well.

I sent a copy of this review to Galen, who was then at Oxford. In his reply, which arrived sometime later, he said, "I showed your review to P. F. He said that he agreed with your observation that our differences and the disagreement between us tracked the development of British analytic philosophy from the 1950s and early 60s when ordinary language was in vogue, to the 1980s when metaphysics had made a comeback in British analytic philosophy." But then Galen added at the end of his reply, "Of course he [P. F.] still believes he is right, and I am wrong."

I have noted my agreement with Galen that our ordinary practices of holding persons morally responsible cannot be entirely insulated from philosophical worries about free will and determinism that have engaged philosophers for centuries, as his father contends in "Freedom and Resentment." There are a number of ways to show this. Some important ones will be pursued here.

3.2. Fair Opportunity to Avoid Wrongdoing: Hart and Others

The first way focuses on ordinary practices of ascribing responsibility, culpability, and blame in courts of law and other legal contexts. A widely cited condition among legal theorists for such ascriptions was stated by the influential legal theorist H. L. A. Hart. Hart (1970) argued that a necessary condition for ascribing responsibility and culpability to agents in legal contexts was that the agents must have had a "fair opportunity to avoid wrongdoing," or more generally, a "fair opportunity to have done otherwise" than they have done.

In an important recent article (2014), David Brink and Dana Nelkin argue persuasively that this "fair opportunity" criterion of Hart's is crucial for understanding legal and criminal responsibility and crucial as well for understanding moral responsibility in general, in what is often called an *accountability* sense that would justify blame, sanction, and punishment. Hart's fair opportunity condition, they argue, is thus a crucial part of the "architecture" of ordinary practices of ascribing moral as well as legal responsibility (p. 284).

> (P51) If this is the case, as I would agree it is, it has implications for the insulation thesis. For appeals to Hart's "fair opportunity" criterion for assigning responsibility in ordinary legal and moral practices lands one squarely in the center of traditional philosophical debates that have concerned incompatibilists about whether causal determinism rules out the freedom to do otherwise and whether and to what degree the freedom to do otherwise is required for moral responsibility.

> (P52) To show this, it is instructive to consider the following: if causal determinism was true, anything you might have done differently in the course of your life to make yourself different than you are, would have been *causally impossible*. Your character, your motives, your dispositions, your intentions, the quality of your will at any time—anything you might

have done to make these things different about yourself at any time—would have been causally impossible if causal determinism was true. For causal determinism implies that given the past and the laws governing the universe at any time, there is only one causally possible future.²

(P53) To put the meaning of causal impossibility assumed here more formally, we can say that an event E's occurring at a time t is causally impossible just in case

in every logically possible world in which the past prior to t is as it is in the actual world and the laws of nature are as they are in the actual world, E cannot possibly occur at t.

If an event E's occurring at a time t is *causally determined*, then E's *not* occurring at t is *causally impossible* in this sense. And *if an agent's avoiding wrongdoing was always causally impossible in this sense, it would appear that the agent lacked a "fair opportunity" to avoid the wrongdoing.*

(P54) An important qualification must immediately be added here, however, that is crucial for understanding Hart's fair opportunity criterion and is crucial as well for understanding ascriptions of responsibility generally in ordinary moral and legal contexts. This qualification is that the causal impossibility of avoiding wrongdoing *in certain particular circumstances* will not always imply that agents are excused from moral responsibility *in those circumstances*. It implies this only conditionally.³

For example, if it could be shown that it was causally impossible for a drunk driver to have avoided hitting a pedestrian on a dark and rainy night, given all the circumstances at the moment of the accident, that fact alone will not excuse the driver of responsibility. For one must also ask whether the driver was responsible by virtue of earlier actions or omissions for the existence of some of those crucial circumstances that made it now causally impossible for him to have avoided the accident, such as his prior decisions to drink and then to drive. In other words,

(P55) The causal impossibility of doing otherwise *now* will not excuse, if some of the crucial circumstances that made it now causally impossible to do otherwise were the results of actions or omissions by the agent in the past, *which the agent had a "fair opportunity to avoid" when they occurred.* And this last phrase is crucial. For the problem is that if determinism is true, there would be no actions or omissions in an agent's past that were not causally impossible for the agent to have avoided when *they* occurred.

Yet it might also be objected that the causal impossibility of doing otherwise is not among the *usual* excusing or exempting conditions commonly cited in ordinary moral and legal practices of holding persons responsible, such as incapacity, ignorance, coercion, duress, insanity, mental impairment, etc. In fact, a line of argument of this kind is floated by Strawson himself in "Freedom and Resentment" in an attempt to show that the causal impossibility of doing otherwise does not function as an excusing or exempting condition in ordinary practices of holding persons responsible. It is a line of argument that other compatibilists have also pursued before and after Strawson. Yet it is a more problematic line of argument than is usually realized, for several reasons.

(P56) First, one may grant that the causal impossibility of doing otherwise is not among the commonly *cited* conditions excusing or exempting agents from responsibility, such as those mentioned. But it does not follow that the causal impossibility of doing otherwise cannot itself be an excusing condition in many ordinary circumstances or that it does not often imply one or another of these commonly cited excusing conditions, such as *a lack of opportunity to exercise a capacity to do otherwise in particular circumstances.* There are numerous examples showing that it can and does so function.

Consider an accident at an airport in which an incoming aircraft has run off the runway, injuring many passengers and seriously damaging the aircraft. The initial assumption of investigators is that pilot error was involved. But further inspection shows that there was a subtle defect in the design of the aircraft that made it *causally impossible* for the pilot to have avoided the disaster, given the conditions of the runway and the weather at the time. The pilot, it is concluded, consequently lacked a "fair opportunity to avoid the outcome" and therefore could not be held responsible or blameworthy for the accident.

Similarly, imagine that an explosion occurs in an empty factory one evening. The security guard in the control room monitoring conditions throughout the factory may be legitimately excused of responsibility for not preventing the explosion, if an investigation shows it was causally impossible in the circumstances for him to have acted to prevent the explosion because of a defect in the monitoring systems which gave him no warning.

It is a mistake therefore to assume that the causal impossibility of doing otherwise cannot function as an excusing condition in ordinary practices of holding persons responsible. It can and often does so function.[4]

> (P57) In response to such examples, it might be argued that if the causal impossibility of now doing otherwise is due to the *quality of will* of the agents when they act, whether they act from a bad will or goodwill, that is different than if the causal impossibility is due to external factors over which the agents have no control (such as faulty aircraft design or faulty monitoring systems). But, by the same reasoning, if it is causally impossible for agents to do otherwise now, given the present quality of their wills, that alone will not excuse, *if* the agents themselves were responsible for the present quality of their wills by virtue of some acts in their prior histories by which the present quality of their wills was formed, earlier acts *that were not causally impossible for the agents to have avoided when they occurred*. And if determinism was true, there would have been no such formative acts that it was causally possible for the agents to have avoided now or at any time in the past.[5]

3.3. Reactive Attitudes, Criminal Trials, and Transference of Responsibility

Another significant way of highlighting problems with the thesis that issues about responsibility and the reactive attitudes can be entirely insulated from philosophical concerns about determinism is discussed by a number of writers, most recently by Shaun Nichols in his book *Bound: Essays on Free Will and Responsibility* (2015). Nichols's book focuses on the implications of new research in empirical psychology and experimental philosophy for traditional philosophical debates about free will and moral responsibility. The passages of interest here are where Nichols discusses Galen Strawson's claim, mentioned earlier, that our ordinary practices of holding persons responsible, and the reactive attitudes related to them, "enshrine" incompatibilist intuitions about freedom and responsibility rather than being entirely "insulated" from these intuitions.

In discussing what he takes to be important arguments supporting this claim of Galen Strawson, Nichols introduces two examples that play a pivotal role in his subsequent discussion. One of these examples is from Gary Watson's (1987) well-known and much-discussed account of the ruthless murderer Robert Harris, on death row in California for multiple murders. The other example Nichols considers is taken from my own writing about the trial of a young man who assaulted and raped a teenage girl. The examples have similar import. But I will focus on my example because it brings out some key points that Watson does not emphasize. As Nichols points out, my example is roughly based on experience, triggered by the trial of the young man accused of the assault and rape.

My initial reactions attending the trial of this young man were filled with anger and resentment against him, since we knew the family of the teenage girl who was his victim and who lived in our neighborhood. But as I listened daily to the testimony of how the young man came to have the mean character and perverse motives he did have—a sordid story of parental rejection, sexual abuse, bad role models and other factors (not entirely unlike Watson's case of Robert Harris)—some of my resentment toward the young man decreased and was directed toward other persons who abused and influenced him.

But—and here is a key point—I wasn't yet ready to shift all the blame away from the young man himself. I resisted this "transference of responsibility" and "blame" entirely to other persons and wondered whether some residual responsibility might not belong to the young man himself. My question became: Was his behavior *all* a matter of bad parenting, neglect and abuse, social conditioning, and like factors, or did he have any crucial role to play in choosing it?

(P58) We know that parenting and society, genetic makeup, and upbringing have a profound influence on what we become and what we are. But were these influences entirely *determining*, or did they "leave anything over" for the young man to be ultimately responsible for? Note that the question of whether he was merely a victim of bad circumstances or had some residual responsibility for being the way he is—the question, that is, of whether he became the person he is to any degree *of his own free will*— seems to depend on whether these other factors were or were not *entirely* determining. It seems to depend, in other words, on whether or not it was *ever causally possible for the young man to have resisted the influences of his background and upbringing* and to have acted differently at some points in his life *to make himself different than he now is*. And if determinism was true, acting differently than he actually did at *any* time in his lifetime would have been *causally impossible*.

One might argue here that my particular reactions at this trial to the young man—the fact that my reactive attitudes of resentment and blame toward him were mitigated to some degree and transferred to others when I learned about his sad history—were the reactions of a philosopher ("overintellectualizing" the issues?") and not the reactions of ordinary folk. But this was far from being the case. My wife and I sat in this courtroom with friends and other neighbors of the young girl's family, none of whom were philosophers. They were firemen, businesswomen, store owners, high school football coaches, teachers, and many others; and all had similar reactions to ours. Keep in mind that, like us, they all resisted mightily transferring responsibility entirely away from the young man. But their reactive attitudes, including retributive ones, were nonetheless mitigated to some degree and influenced by hearing the sordid stories of his history.

Moreover, if there *were* any persons in that courtroom whose reactive attitudes were not in any way influenced by listening to the history of the young man (as I am sure there were), then I would not want to see those persons anywhere near a jury deciding the fate of persons I cared about, or any other persons whatever. For they would not be capable of responding in ways I believe would be *fair* to those they judge. They would not be capable of responding fairly, if they were not capable of appreciating that, to the extent that the young man's sad history made it *causally impossible* for him to have turned out differently, to that extent he would not have had a *fair opportunity to avoid wrongdoing*.

3.4. Transference of Responsibility and Compatibility Questions

(P59) It is worth reflecting further on this interesting notion of "transference of responsibility." We are inclined to do this transference to some degree to other persons who may have influenced agents to be the way they are and act as they do *to the extent we believe that the influences of these other persons were difficult for the agents to have resisted when they occurred*. In such cases, we are inclined to "transfer" some of the responsibility and blame to those others who so strongly influenced the agents (parents, caregivers, role models, abusers, etc.) and mitigate the responsibility to some degree of the agents themselves accordingly.

(P60) In some extreme cases, such as Watson's Robert Harris or possibly the young man of my example, we might conclude that the influences were so strong that resisting them to any substantial degree was not causally possible. We could be wrong about this. Such judgments are fallible and should be made with great caution. But the crucial point is that *such judgments are relevant to our ordinary practices of holding agents responsible and blameworthy*, including who should be held responsible and to what degree. Moreover, as noted in P56, such judgments seem to depend on whether or not it was ever causally possible for the agents to have resisted the influences of their environment and upbringing and to have acted differently at some points in their lives to make themselves different than they are. And if determinism was true, this would never have been causally possible.[6]

There are other interesting and relevant implications of this notion of transference of responsibility for free will debates. For example, many compatibilists—Daniel Dennett (1984) being a prominent example—are willing to concede that transference of responsibility and related reactive attitudes, such as blame and resentment, to other persons who may have abused or otherwise exerted powerful influences over agents, is indeed a normal feature of our ordinary practices of holding persons responsible.

But compatibilists who concede this point usually go on to argue, as does Dennett, that such transference is only reasonable if the responsibility, blame, resentment, etc. is transferred to some other *persons*. If the influences on the agent's behavior and quality of will are due to natural causes alone and no other persons can be blamed, then, these compatibilists argue, it is not reasonable to transfer responsibility and other reactive attitudes, such as blame and resentment, to nature. For, as Dennett succinctly puts it, "nature is not a person."[7]

(P61) This is true enough and should be admitted by incompatibilists as well. It *is* an important fact about this transference of responsibility phenomenon that transference of moral and legal responsibility must be to other *persons* and cannot be to natural causes alone. Moreover, this fact is related to something important about the reactive attitudes, such as blame and resentment, in general. Namely, they are appropriately directed only at beings capable of *responsible agency*. But rather than providing a decisive argument for compatibilism, further reflection on this significant fact can take us in an opposing direction.

To see this, return for a moment to the young man at trial. Since he seems to have acted voluntarily and intentionally from a perverse and vicious will, our reactive attitudes of blame and resentment are initially focused entirely on him. But when we hear more about his past, we wonder whether some of the blame at least should be transferred to the sexually abusive father and others who may have enabled the father.[8] But now suppose we learn the abusive father was as he was because *he* was sexually abused by his father and so on back indefinitely. Perhaps it was all in some bad genes. Or suppose the young's man having the perverse will from which he acted was all a matter of determining genetic mutations in his fetal development for which we cannot blame the father *or* any other persons.

(P62) Suppose further that, as evidence unveiled in the courtroom made clear, the young man's acting from his perverse will in this incident satisfied familiar compatibilist conditions for free and responsible agency: he acted voluntarily, without being coerced or forced by others; he acted intentionally, knowing exactly what he was doing and doing it on purpose; he was reasons-responsive in the sense that he was calculating and would have altered his behavior appropriately, if his beliefs, desires, or circumstances had been different in various ways. Nor was he acting compulsively, like Frankfurt's unwilling addict, who wanted to resist the desire to take a drug but could not resist taking it anyway. To the contrary, this young man had, in Frankfurt's terms, "the will he wanted to have," and he was "wholehearted" and not ambivalent in his commitment to act in accordance with the will he had, perverse though it might be.[9]

(P63) It was indeed the evidence of all this, coming to light in the proceedings, that led most of those present in the courtroom to our initial attitudes of resentment and moral anger toward the young man. We transferred these reactive attitudes, at least to some degree, to others when we learned more about the sordid details of his upbringing. But we are now imagining a different situation. We are now supposing that the young man's having the perverse will from which he acted was a matter of determining genetic mutations in his fetal development for which we cannot blame the father or any other persons.

Yet we can't blame *nature* either in a moral sense, since it is not a person. Which prompts the following question: If the young man's acting from the perverse will, as he did, satisfies familiar compatibilist conditions for free and responsible agency, as spelled out in P58, and we can't find any other persons to blame, then do compatibilists want us to conclude that we can fully blame the young man?

(P64) Imagine two young men, possessing exactly the same wills and motives as this young man, and satisfying all the same compatibilist criteria for responsibility spelled out in P58 (uncoerced, reasons-responsive, etc.). Yet one of these young men was strongly influenced to be the way he is by the actions of other persons, the other by natural, impersonal causes alone. The first young man is not fully responsible, it might be said, to the extent that other persons made him this way. Some responsibility transfers to those others. But then should we say the second young man *is* fully responsible because no other persons, but only natural causes, made him the way he is—in other words, because we cannot find anyone *else* to shift some of the blame to?

(P65) Such reasoning seems not only perverse, but completely unfair to the second young man. For the question that begs to be answered *in both cases* is whether it was ever *causally possible* for either young man to have resisted the circumstances that influenced him, and to have made himself different than he turned out to be, *whether* those influencing circumstances were the result of the actions of other agents or of natural causes alone. For if these circumstances were determining either way, *it would not have been causally possible for either young man to have resisted them*. Neither of the young men would have had a "fair opportunity" to have done otherwise.

3.5. Two Dimensions of Responsibility

(P66) Reflections such as those in P53–P65 suggest that if full justice is to be done to our understanding of moral and legal responsibility and to our practices of holding persons responsible, two dimensions of responsibility must be distinguished. Both dimensions, I would argue, are necessary for a fully adequate account of that understanding of moral and legal responsibility and the associated practices; and neither dimension alone is sufficient. The first dimension is responsibility for *expressing the will* (the character, motives, and purposes) *one has in action*, and doing so voluntarily (without being constrained or hindered or forced) and doing so intentionally (knowingly and purposefully).

(P67) The second dimension of responsibility is another matter. It is not responsibility for expressing in action the true quality of will one has or the real self one is, but rather responsibility for *having* the quality of will one *expresses* in action and for *being* the kind of self one *is*. The distinction put succinctly is between

(1) Responsibility for *expressing* the (quality of) will one *has* in action (first dimension), and
(2) Responsibility for *having* the (quality of) will one *expresses* in action (second dimension).

(P68) To be responsible in this second dimension it must be that at least some time in one's life, when one acts responsibly and hence voluntarily and intentionally in the first dimension, it was also possible for one to have voluntarily and intentionally *done otherwise*, not by being forced or by accident, but in a manner that would also have expressed the true quality of one's will and the self that one was at the time. To be responsible in this second dimension, in other words, it cannot be at all times in one's life that only one possible action is expressive of one's *already existing will*. Some choices or actions in one's life must be, as explained in P24–P25 (section 2.8), *will-setting*, and not already *will-settled*.

This distinction between two dimensions of responsibility is not the same as Gary Watson's well-known distinction between two "faces" of responsibility in his important article "Responsibility and the Limits of Evil."[10] But the distinctions are related. Watson distinguishes between responsibility as *attributability* and as *accountability*. Agents are responsible for their actions in the attributability sense when the actions are attributable to them as actions they have willingly performed. Agents are responsible in the accountability sense when they can be justly held to be blameworthy or praiseworthy for their actions.

(P69) Each of the two dimensions of responsibility defined here in P66 involves both "faces" of responsibility, attributability and accountability, defined by Watson in his article. For agents to be responsible for expressing the wills they have in action as well as for having the wills they express in action, their actions and wills must be attributable to them, and they must be accountable to some degree for them.

(P70) Each of the two dimensions of responsibility defined here also involves a third notion that plays a significant role in contemporary discussions of responsibility, namely *answerability*.[11] Persons can be answerable to others for expressing the wills they have in action. But they can also be answerable for *having* the wills they express in action, and hence for *being* the sorts of persons they are with the ill will or goodwill their actions toward others express. *It is very much a part of our ordinary practices of holding others responsible and the reactive attitudes, that these attitudes can be applied to others for being the sorts of persons they are, whether kind and generous or nasty and selfish, etc., as well as for doing what they do.*[12]

Whether agents are answerable and accountable for the quality of the wills they express in action (whether for ill or for good) as well as for the actions themselves that are the products of their wills, has therefore always seemed to me a significant matter if one is looking for a complete account of moral responsibility. Hence the emphasis on both of these two dimensions of responsibility.

3.6. Convergence of the Two Paths: Freedom of Action and Freedom of Will Revisited

(P71) It should now be clear what was meant by saying that the two paths to addressing the Compatibility and Significance Questions—the freedom path of the previous chapter and the responsibility path of this chapter—ultimately converge. For the first of these dimensions of responsibility is historically associated with *freedom of action*—the ability to freely express the will one already has in action, voluntarily and without constraints. By contrast, the second dimension of responsibility is related to *freedom of will*—the freedom to *form* or *shape* the will that one expresses in action and to act of "one's own free will" in the sense of a will that one has to some degree freely formed or shaped.

So understood, freedom of will, as noted earlier, is about *self-formation*, about the formation of our "wills" or how we got to be the kinds of persons we are with the characters, motives, and purposes we now have; and this is distinctly related to the second dimension of responsibility, which was called in the previous chapter *ultimate responsibility*.

It is also instructive to view this convergence of the freedom and responsibility paths to addressing questions of free will in the light of the three notions of freedom distinguished in P30–P31 of the previous chapter. Free acts, it was said, may be (1) acts done voluntarily, on purpose and for reasons that are not coerced, compelled, or otherwise constrained or controlled by others. Or free acts may be (2) acts (free in sense 1 that are also) done "of our own free will" in the sense of a will that we are ultimately responsible to some degree for forming. Finally, free acts may be (3) "self-forming" or "will-setting" acts (SFAs) by which we form and reform the will from which we act in sense 2.

Freedom of kind 1 is *freedom of action*, the ability to freely express the will one has in action without constraints. By contrast, freedoms of kinds 2 and 3 represent *freedom of will*, the freedom to form or shape the will one expresses in action and to act of "one's own free will" in the sense of a will that one has to some degree freely formed or shaped.

(P72) Freedom of kind 1 is thus related to the first dimension of responsibility—responsibility for expressing the quality of will one has in action without constraints. By contrast, freedoms of kinds 2 and 3 (acts of free will of a libertarian kind)) are related to the second dimension of responsibility, responsibility for forming and having formed or shaped the quality of will one expresses in action.

What is noteworthy here is that free acts of kinds 2 and 3 (acts of free will) also presuppose the first dimension of responsibility as well as the second dimension. This is a consequence of the "nesting" of the three freedoms noted in P32. Free acts of kind 3 (self-forming actions) are also free in sense 2 (they are ultimately responsible acts of free will, albeit of a special kind). And free acts of both kinds 2 and 3 (acts of free will) are also free acts of kind 1. They must be done voluntarily, on purpose and for reasons and are not coerced, compelled, or otherwise controlled. Hence agents who perform libertarian free acts of kinds 2 and 3 must also be responsible for expressing the wills they have in action, voluntarily and without constraints; that is, they must be responsible in the first dimension of responsibility as well as in the second dimension.

These features of the three freedoms are a further consequence of an important theme I have emphasized in many writings and expressed earlier in P32, namely, that libertarian or incompatibilist freedom of will (of kinds 2 and 3) presupposes compatibilist freedom of action (of kind 1). Libertarians about free will thus can and should concede that adequate compatibilist requirements for both freedom and responsibility are necessary (though not sufficient) requirements for any adequate libertarian account of freedom and responsibility as well.[13]

3.7. Freedom to Do Otherwise: Further Compatibilist Responses

The preceding steps explain why I agree with critics of Strawson's insulation thesis that ordinary practices of holding responsible, and the reactive attitudes associated with them, cannot be entirely insulated from traditional philosophical concerns about freedom of will and determinism. But rejecting this insulation thesis alone does not settle the Compatibility Question. For many compatibilists are also critics of Strawson's insulation thesis, while continuing to defend compatibilism on other grounds.[14]

These compatibilists agree with P. F. Strawson that ordinary practices of holding responsible and related reactive attitudes are compatible with determinism. But they claim that arguing, as Strawson does, that these ordinary practices can be entirely insulated from philosophical concerns about determinism is too simple and easy a route to compatibilism. Compatibilists, these compatibilists argue, cannot insulate themselves entirely from the philosophical debates. They must engage with these debates and offer further arguments that, for example, the freedom to do otherwise in senses related to ordinary practices is in fact compatible with determinism or that moral responsibility does not require the freedom to do otherwise in any senses that are threatened by determinism.

I now want to explain why I believe compatibilist arguments for these further claims, including the more sophisticated ones of recent vintage, ultimately fail to be convincing.

3.8. Compatibilist Responses (Part I): Conditional Analyses of Power

The most common strategy to show that freedom and responsibility are compatible with determinism employed by compatibilists in the modern era—from Hobbes and Locke, to Hume and Mill, and well into the twentieth century—has been to acknowledge that moral responsibility *does* require the freedom or power to do otherwise *in some sense*, but then to go on to defend *conditional* or *hypothetical* interpretations of the freedom or power to do otherwise that turn out to be compatible with determinism.

According to these *classical compatibilist* strategies, as they are sometimes called, what we mean when we say that agents were "free or had the power to do otherwise" or "could have done otherwise" is that "they would or might have done otherwise *if* the past (or the laws of nature) had been different in some way." If, for example, persons had had different beliefs or desires, or had reasoned differently, they would or might have acted differently. And saying persons would or might have acted differently, if the past or laws had been different in some way, it is then argued, is consistent with saying that the agents acting as they did was determined, given the past and the laws as they actually were.

I believe this standard compatibilist strategy is deeply flawed. Kant, as is well known, called it a "wretched subterfuge" and William James a "quagmire of evasion"; and I think they were right. A number of cogent objections have been made against such conditional interpretations of the freedom to do otherwise of these kinds since the mid-twentieth century; and even many compatibilists today reject them. I have discussed at length many of these common objections to such conditional analyses in other works (including *The Significance of Free Will*, chapter 4) and will not repeat them all here. Instead, I want to state in summary fashion why I agree with Kant and James that such classical compatibilist strategies evade rather than resolve the real issues.

(P73) It may be true that persons would have done otherwise, if the past or the laws had been different in some way. But the problem is that the actual past was not different in some way; it was as it was. Likewise, the actual laws were not different; they were as they were. *Our freedom and responsibility must be exercised in the world that actually is, not in some hypothetical or merely possible world that might have been, but never actually was.* And if determinism is true of this actual world in which we live and act, then acting otherwise than we do *in the circumstances in which we actually find ourselves* would always be causally impossible.[15] It is not exonerating to be told that persons would or might have acted otherwise in some merely hypothetical or possible worlds that never actually existed, if their acting otherwise in this actual world in which they do live and act was causally impossible.

Imagine a sixteenth-century incarnation of a modern classical compatibilist who took it upon himself to correct Luther when Luther said, "Here I stand. I can do no other." "You were mistaken, sir, when you said, 'I can do no other,'" this classical compatibilist might say to Luther. "For all we mean when we say, 'I can now do other(wise)' is simply that in some possible worlds in which the past or the laws were different in some ways—in which, for example, you had different beliefs or reasons or purposes—you would or might have done otherwise. And this may well have been true of you, sir, at the time you said, 'Here I stand,'" this compatibilist might have said to Luther. "So, you see, sir, you were mistaken to say that you could *not* have done otherwise at that moment."

Luther would likely have replied, "Get thee gone, sophist! What I meant when I said, 'I can do no other' is that in the *actual world where I found myself at that moment* with all the beliefs, reasons, and purposes I had actually acquired in my long difficult journey to that point, my doing otherwise would have been impossible. What is it to me that I would or might have done otherwise in some merely possible world that did not actually exist at the time." And Luther would likely have indignantly added something else crucial here to his responsibility in response to his critic:

(P74) "Moreover, it was to some important degree the result *of my own past choices and actions* by which I made myself the person I was at that moment, that the actual world which did exist and in which I acted at that moment *was* a world in which I could not then have done otherwise. So, what you are claiming not only distorts what I was saying. It devalues my own contribution to making that actual world in which I was acting, *given the kind of person I had made myself*, into the kind of world in which I could not then have done otherwise."

3.9. Compatibilist Responses (Part II): Frankfurt-Style Examples

Many traditional arguments for compatibilism about moral responsibility, like the preceding, have tried to show that the power to do otherwise required for moral responsibility is not really incompatible with determinism. But a different and more direct strategy has become popular in recent philosophy. It is to argue more radically that the power to do otherwise is not required for moral responsibility at all. The most common and sophisticated versions of this strategy in recent philosophy involve appealing to so-called Frankfurt-style examples (FSEs), named for Harry Frankfurt, who formulated the first of these influential examples in a 1969 paper.

Frankfurt's aim in formulating the first of these examples was to refute a principle he called the Principle of Alternative Possibilities (PAP): *agents are morally responsible for their actions, only if they could have avoided performing them or could have done otherwise when they performed them*. To refute this principle, Frankfurt imagined the following scenario:

> A controller, Black, has direct control over the brain of another man, Jones, and wants to allow Jones to do only what Black wants him to do. Black prefers, however, to allow Jones to act on his own whenever possible and so will only intervene if Jones is about to do something that he, Black, does not want.

Given this scenario, Frankfurt asks us to consider situations in which Jones is about to do what the controller Black wants, so that Black does not intervene. In such situations, Frankfurt argues, Jones could be morally responsible for acting as he does, since he would have acted on his own, from his own motives and for his own reasons, and nothing and no one (including Black) would have interfered with or prevented him from doing what he chose to do. Yet Jones in such situations could not have done otherwise. For if he had given any indication of doing otherwise, Black would have prevented him from doing so. Thus, this Principle of Alternative Possibilities or PAP, Frankfurt concluded, is false: it is not true that agents can be morally responsible for their actions, only if they could have avoided performing them or could have done otherwise when they performed them.

Now the first thing to be said about this line of argument is that it should not surprise us at this point that this PAP of Frankfurt's is false. For we have already seen from the discussion of the Luther example and other examples that agents can be morally responsible for actions that flow from their wills at the time they acted and are such that they could *not* have done otherwise *at that time*. Agents can be responsible, in other words, for many "will-settled" actions like Luther's "Here I stand," even if the agents could not have done otherwise than perform them when they were performed.

In short, *we don't need to appeal to unusual examples involving Frankfurt-style controllers to establish that Frankfurt's PAP is false*—to establish, namely, that it is not true that agents can be morally responsible for their actions *only if* they could have avoided performing them or could have done otherwise when they performed them.

(P75) It is one thing, however, to argue that PAP is false from Frankfurt-style examples (FSEs) and other examples. It is another thing to argue from that fact to the conclusion that alternative possibilities and the power to do otherwise are not needed *at all* for moral responsibility. Those who make this further step, in my view, are guilty of a subtle fallacy of composition: from the fact that *some*, even many, actions in the lifetimes of agents may be such that the agents can be morally responsible for them even though they could not have done otherwise at the time they were performed, it does not follow that *all* actions in the lifetimes of agents could be like this. It does not follow if agents are ever to be responsible for their wills being set the way they are when they act. For this to be the case, agents would have to be capable, *at some times* in their lives, of "will-setting" or "self-forming" choices or actions (SFAs) for which the agents had the power to willingly (voluntarily and intentionally) perform them and also the power to willingly (voluntarily and intentionally) do otherwise.

(P76) As a consequence, while Frankfurt-style examples and many other examples may show that Frankfurt's PAP is false, they fail to show the falsity of a more complex principle that might be stated as follows and may be called (WILL-SETTING) "Agents are ultimately responsible for having the wills (characters, motives, and purposes) they express in action only if, at some times in their lives, they are capable of performing 'will-setting' or 'self-forming' choices or actions (SFAs) with respect to which the agents have the power to willingly (voluntarily and intentionally) perform the actions and the power to willingly (voluntarily and intentionally) do otherwise."

(P77) These reflections are particularly interesting in regard to Frankfurt-style examples. For it can be shown that whenever the choices and actions of agents are under the control of Frankfurt controllers or mechanisms, there could *be* no such "self-forming" choices or actions of the kinds described in this principle WILL-SETTING. In other words, in the presence of Frankfurt controllers, there could be no will-setting of the kind required at some points in the lives of agents for the agents to be responsible for having the quality of wills they do have.

(P78) This is the case because, in all FSEs, including all the more sophisticated versions proposed since Frankfurt's original one, there is one thing that Frankfurt controllers can never allow. They can never allow a process of deliberation or an effort on the part of the controlled agent to go to completion, if that process of deliberation or effort-making might end in the agent's making a choice *the controller does not want*. Even if the unwanted outcome of the process (the unwanted choice) is *undetermined*, so that it might or might not occur, the controller or some implanted mechanism of the controller must intervene beforehand or at the time of choice to *ensure* that the unwanted choice does *not* occur and the choice wanted by the controller does occur. And if the controller or mechanism does intervene either beforehand or at the time of choice to ensure that the unwanted choice does not occur, then the choice would no longer *be* a self-forming one. For the essence of a self-forming choice is that *the agent, and no one or nothing else*, can determine how such a self-forming choice will turn out when it is performed.

This is the case I will now argue for all FSEs, not only the original one of Frankfurt but also for newer FSEs that allow for indeterminism and other nuances. Consider Frankfurt's original example first.

If the controller Black sees that the controlled agent Jones is about to do what he, Black, wants, Black does not interfere and lets Jones act on his own. In such situations, Jones *can* be morally responsible for what he does, as conceded earlier. Indeed, if he acts on his own, he could be responsible *in both dimensions of responsibility* considered in this chapter. This would be the case to the extent that (i) Jones's action satisfies the usual compatibilist conditions for moral responsibility (uncoerced, reasons-responsive, etc.) (first dimension of responsibility) and that (ii) he acts from a will that was to some degree his own free will in the sense of a will formed in part by prior will-setting or self-forming actions (second dimension of responsibility).

(P79) But what would not be true of Frankfurt's example is that Jones's action under such conditions could *itself* be one of these "will-setting" or "self-forming" actions, or SFAs. For Jones cannot do otherwise in the situation and certainly cannot *willingly* do otherwise. Black lets Jones act on his own only when Black has some reliable "prior sign" that Jones's will is "settled" on doing what Black wants. This is the only way, in Frankfurt's original examples, that Black, the controller, can *ensure* that Jones will do what he, the controller, wants, short of preventing the agent from doing what the controller wants at the moment of choice. And under such control, there could be *will-settled* actions, but no *will-setting* ones of the kind required for agents to be ultimately responsible for having the quality of wills they do have.

3.10. Newer Frankfurt-Style Examples (1): Blockage Examples

More recent FSEs have been put forward in an attempt to answer objections of this sort and others made to Frankfurt's original example and other examples like it. Many of these more recent FSEs were designed to address an objection that became a significant part of the subsequent literature after Frankfurt, an objection provoking more complex FSEs designed to answer it. This objection (often referred to as the "Dilemma Defense" of PAP) is an objection I myself made against FSEs in my first book on free will (*Free Will and Values*, 1985) and again in subsequent works. Other versions of this objection were later made with further nuances by David Widerker (1995), Carl Ginet 1996), James Lamb (1993), and Keith Wyma (1997), among others.

(P80) Briefly stated, the core of the argument put forward in my 1985 book was that Frankfurt-style examples would not work against libertarian views of free will that required some acts of free will, such as free choices, to be *undetermined* up to the moment they occurred. For in the case of such undetermined acts, a Frankfurt controller could not know in advance (there would be no reliable prior sign) which way the agents were going to choose before they actually did choose; and it would then be too late to prevent the agents from doing what the controller did not want. On the one hand, if the controller waited until the agents chose, he would no longer have control over which way they chose. And if, on the other hand, the controller did not wait, but intervened in advance to make the agents do what he wanted, then the controller would be responsible for the choice made, not the controlled agents, since the controller would have determined that this choice was brought about rather than an alternative. FSEs like Frankfurt's thus begged the question, I argued, against libertarian views of free will *that require indeterminism in the deliberation process up to the moment of choice.*

Among the newer FSEs proposed in the past several decades in response to objections of this kind, two kinds of examples have been most prominent, often referred to as "blockage examples" and "buffered examples." I will consider the most widely discussed examples in each category, to illustrate what I take to be the limitations of all examples of these kinds.

One of the most widely discussed FSEs of the blockage variety was proposed by Alfred Mele and David Robb in an influential paper (1998). Their paper was a response to the objection like that just stated in P80, as formulated by me and independently by David Widerker. (Mele and Robb thus designate it the "Kane/Widerker objection.") To show that FSEs need not beg the question against views of free will requiring indeterminism, Mele and Robb assume in their example for the sake of argument that the agent's deliberation process is indeterministic up to the moment of decision, as libertarians such as Widerker and I might require. They then propose the following scenario:

An agent, Bob, decides on his own to steal the car of a woman, Ann, on the basis of his own indeterministic deliberation about whether to steal it, and his decision has no deterministic cause. Unknown to Bob, however, a controller, Black, has initiated a certain deterministic process in Bob's brain with the intention of thereby causing Bob to decide to steal Ann's car *unless* Bob decides on his own to steal the car or is incapable of making a decision. This deterministic process (implanted in Bob's brain by the controller) is in no way sensitive to any "prior sign" of what Bob will decide and in no way does it influence the indeterministic decision-making process that actually issues in Bob's decision. But if Bob had not decided on his own to steal the car, the controller's (implanted) process would have deterministically issued in Bob's deciding to steal the car anyway.

Mele and Robb claim it is plausible to assume that Bob could be morally responsible for his decision in this scenario *if* he makes the decision on his own and the controller's process does not have to be actually involved. Yet Bob could not have done otherwise. For if he had not decided to steal the car as a result of his own indeterministic deliberative process, the controller's deterministic process would have "preempted" Bob's own decision process and brought about Bob's decision to steal the car anyway.

Mele and Robb concede that *if* the preemption by the controller's deterministic process *had* occurred, Bob would not have been morally responsible for the outcome. The controller would have been responsible. But, as with all FSEs, they ask us to focus on what actually occurs in their example. What actually occurs is that Bob decides to steal the car as the result of his own indeterministic deliberative process and the controller's process does not intervene. In such a case, they argue, Bob can be responsible for doing so in a sense that libertarians ought to concede, *even though* he could not have done otherwise because the controller's process would not have let him.

But the example is as yet under-described, as Mele and Robb concede. In order to explain how the preemption and other features of the example might actually work, Mele and Robb spell it out in more detail. They ask us to suppose "that there are 'decision nodes' in Bob's brain," such that

> The "lighting up" of node N1 represents [Bob's] deciding to steal the car, and the "lighting up" of node N2 represents his deciding *not* to steal the car. Under normal circumstances and in the absence of preemption, a process's "hitting" a decision node in Bob "lights up" that node. If it were to be the case both that the controller's process hits N1 and that Bob's own process does not hit N1, then the controller's process would light up N1. If both processes were to hit N1, Bob's indeterministic deliberative process . . . would light up N1 and the controller's process would not. (1998, p. 104)

They then add,

> Of course, readers would like a story about why it is that, although Bob's process would preempt [the controller's process] in the former situation, [the controller's process] would preempt Bob's process in the latter. Here is one story. By [the time the choice occurs, the controller's process] has "neutralized" all the nodes in Bob for decisions that are contrary to the decision to steal Ann's car (for example, a decision not to steal anyone's car and a decision not to steal anything at all). In convenient shorthand [by the time of the choice, the controller's process] has neutralized N2 [the node representing Bob's choosing *not* to steal the car] and all "cognate decision nodes." (1998, pp. 105–6)

This "neutralizing" of alternative decision nodes was called *blockage*. And so Mele and Robb sum up the description of their example in a later paper by saying that while the controller's process "ensures that N1 will light up" at the time of choice, "blockage assures that the other relevant nodes will not light up" at the time of choice (2003, p. 129)

(P81) We see here a general feature of Frankfurt-style examples of this blockage variety. They involve two distinguishable features: occurrent *preemption*, on the one hand, and *blockage*, on the other. Both features are necessary. For the controller's implanted process must not only preempt the agent's own decision-making process at the time of choice if the agent does not himself decide as the controller wishes. The controller's process must also neutralize or block all alternative outcomes of the agent's own decision-making process other than the decision to steal Ann's car. The controller's deterministic process must not only light up the node N1 (representing the choice to steal the car) if Bob's own indeterministic decision process does not light up N1. The controller's process must also block any alternative node (such as N2 for the choice not to steal the car) that Bob's own indeterministic decision process *might* have otherwise issued in, if it did not issue in N1.

(P82) Such FSEs involving "blockage" thus also show that Frankfurt's PAP is false. Bob could be responsible for the choice to steal the car in this example if he made the choice on his own by virtue of his own indeterministic decision-making process and the controller's deterministic process did not intervene. Yet Bob could not have done otherwise because the controller's process would not have let him.

Such examples also show (through the addition of some complexities) that PAP could be false even when the actions involved are undetermined choices of the kinds libertarians require for free will. Indeed, Bob's choice to steal the car, if made on his own in this way in the example, might have even been an ultimately responsible choice in the (libertarian) sense described here in earlier steps, *if* the will from which it was made had been formed to some degree by Bob himself by virtue of *earlier* will-setting or self-forming actions, or SFAs, that were not Frankfurt controlled.

(P83) But what would not be true of this example is that Bob's choice to steal the car under such conditions could *itself* be one of these "will-setting" or "self-forming" choices, or SFAs. For *Bob cannot do otherwise in the situation and certainly cannot willingly do otherwise.* The controller's implanted process will not let him do otherwise than choose to steal the car.

(P84) We can thus say of Frankfurt-style examples of this blockage variety what was said of Frankfurt's original example. Such examples may show that PAP is false: agents can be responsible for actions even when they could not have done otherwise than perform them. But such examples do not show that *all* our morally responsible actions in the course of our lifetimes could be like this, if we are to be ultimately morally responsible to any degree for the state or quality of our present wills. Such examples thus fail to show the falsity of the more complex principle stated earlier (called WILL-SETTING): "Agents are ultimately responsible for having the wills (characters, motives, and purposes) they express in action only if, at some times in their lives, they have the power to willingly (voluntarily and intentionally) perform certain ("will-setting" or "self-forming") actions (SFAs) and the power to willingly (voluntarily and intentionally) do otherwise."[16]

3.11. Newer Frankfurt-Style Examples (2): Buffered Examples

Turn now to another very different class of new FSEs introduced in an attempt to respond to objections that such examples beg the question against libertarian views of free will by failing to account for free choices that may be undetermined. These other new FSEs, called "buffered" or "necessary condition" examples,[17] do not rely on occurrent preemption, as do blockage examples. Instead, these buffered examples return to a feature of the original examples, such as Frankfurt's, that rely on *prior signs* to indicate to the controller or implanted mechanism what the agent is going to do. But the unique feature of these buffered examples is that the prior sign, which signals to the controller or mechanism the need to intervene and preempt the agent's own deliberative process, is only a *necessary* condition for what might happen, not a *sufficient* or *determining* condition.

To see this difference and what it might mean, let us turn to perhaps the most widely discussed Frankfurt-style example of this buffered or necessary-condition variety, which nicely illustrates their general nature. The example is that of Derk Pereboom (2003):

> *Tax Evasion 2*: Joe is considering whether to claim a tax deduction for the substantial local registration fee that he paid when he bought a house. He knows that claiming the deduction is illegal, [but] that he probably won't be caught. . . . [Suppose] in addition, it is causally necessary for his failing to choose to evade his taxes in this situation that he attain a certain level of attentiveness to [his] moral reasons [for not doing so]. He can secure this level of attentiveness voluntarily. However, his attaining this level of attentiveness is not causally sufficient for his failing to choose to evade his taxes. If he were to attain this level of attentiveness, Joe could with his libertarian free will either choose to evade taxes or refrain from so choosing (without the intervener's device in place). More generally, Joe is a libertarian free agent. (2003, pp. 193–95)

Pereboom then imagines a Frankfurt-style controller in the form of a neuroscientist who wants to ensure that Joe chooses to evade his taxes. But, in the manner of such controllers, he prefers that Joe make this choice on his own and will only intervene if Joe might choose other than he, the neuroscientist, wishes.

The neuroscientist also knows that Joe *will* surely choose to evade his taxes on his own (as the neuroscientist wants) if Joe does *not* attain a certain level of attentiveness to his moral reasons for not doing so at an earlier time. The neuroscientist thus implants a device in Joe's brain that will sense whether Joe has or has not attained this level of attentiveness. If Joe has not attained this level of attentiveness to his moral reasons, the device will remain idle and will allow Joe to choose to evade his taxes on his own. If, on the other hand, the device senses that the required level of attentiveness has been attained, the device will electronically stimulate Joe's brain so that he would choose to evade taxes anyway. Pereboom concludes the example in the familiar manner of FSEs generally, by saying that we are to assume that

> In actual fact, Joe does not attain this level of attentiveness, and he chooses to evade taxes while the device remains idle. In this situation, Joe could be morally responsible for choosing to evade taxes despite the fact that he could not have chosen otherwise [because he did it on his own and the controller's device did not intervene]. (2003, pp. 195)

The choice in this buffered Frankfurt-style example can also be a libertarian choice, Pereboom argues, because the *prior sign* which signals to the controller's device to intervene—that is, Joe's attaining a certain level of attentiveness to his moral reasons—is only a necessary, and not a sufficient condition for Joe's failing to choose to evade his taxes. That is, if Joe were to attain this certain level of attentiveness to his moral reasons, it would not automatically follow (in the absence of the controller's device) that he would choose on the basis of those moral reasons not to evade his taxes. What would follow is rather that Joe *might* choose for those moral reasons not to evade his taxes, or he *might* choose to evade his taxes anyway for his self-interested reasons; and it would be undetermined which he would do.

(P85) Indeed, *in the absence of the controller and the controller's device*, if Joe had attained the required level of attentiveness to his moral reasons, we might even imagine that the subsequent choice might have been a will-setting or self-forming choice: that is, *if contrary to fact, the controller and his device were not in the picture at all*, we might imagine that Joe may have *voluntarily* and *intentionally* chosen to evade his taxes at some time during his deliberation or he may have *voluntarily* and *intentionally* chosen not to evade his taxes at some time during his deliberation; and it would be undetermined which he would do or whether or not he would do either one.

(P86) Thus we can draw the same conclusion about these "buffered" FSEs, as we did of those involving "blockage," and of Frankfurt's original example: *whenever the choices and actions of agents are under the control of*

Frankfurt controllers or mechanisms, there could be no such "will-setting or "self-forming" choices or actions of the kinds required at some points in the lives of agents for them to be responsible for having the quality of wills they do have.

(P87) This is the case because in all FSEs, including these buffered ones, the controllers never allow the agents an opportunity to bring to completion will-setting or self-forming choices such that the agents might willingly (voluntarily and intentionally) make them and also might willingly do otherwise. The controllers must intervene in some way or another to prevent the possibility of such will-setting choices from occurring so that *they* themselves, the controllers and not the agents, can *ensure* the agents *always* do what the controllers want them to do.

(P88) Note further that all such FSEs, including these buffered examples, rule out the possibility of such will-setting or self-forming choices, given the mere *presence* of the Frankfurt controllers or mechanisms even when the controllers or mechanisms do not actually intervene. For the mere presence of the controllers in the examples, whose implanted mechanisms are prepared to intervene if the agents do not choose on their own to do what the controllers want, changes situations in which agents might otherwise have been able to make will-setting or self-forming choices to situations in which they are no longer able to make such choices.

We can thus say of Frankfurt-style examples of this buffered variety what was said of other Frankfurt-style examples considered. They show that Frankfurt's PAP is false: agents *can* be responsible for actions even when they could not have done otherwise than perform them. But such examples do not show that *all* our morally responsible actions in the course of our lifetimes could be like this, if we are to be ultimately morally responsible to any degree for the state or quality of our wills. For the mere presence of the controllers in the examples and their implanted mechanisms change situations in which agents might otherwise have been able to make will-setting or self-forming choices to ones in which they are no longer able to make such choices. Such examples thus fail to show the falsity of the more complex principle stated earlier (P70, P74): "Agents are ultimately responsible for having the wills (characters, motives, and purposes) they express in action only if, at some times in their lives, they are capable of performing will-setting or self-forming choices or actions (SFAs) in which the agents have the power to willingly (voluntarily and intentionally) perform the actions and the power to willingly (voluntarily and intentionally) do otherwise."

3.12. Conclusion

In conclusion, it is worth noting that the arguments of this chapter have been relevant to both the Significance and Compatibility Questions about free will. I have not disagreed, for example, with P. F. Strawson's contention in "Freedom and Resentment" that our ordinary practices of holding persons morally and legally responsible, and the reactive attitudes related to them (such as blame, resentment, indignation, and moral approval) are *significant* features of any distinctively human "form of life," as he puts it.

What I *have* argued against is rather Strawson's further thesis that these significant practices and related reactive attitudes can be entirely "insulated" from traditional philosophical and metaphysical concerns about free will and determinism. I have also argued against a variety of other compatibilists, who may reject the insulation thesis, but who argue on other grounds either (i) that the power to do otherwise required for moral responsibility is in all relevant instances compatible with determinism or (ii) that moral responsibility does not require exercise of the power to do otherwise at any times in the course of our lives.

4
The Intelligibility Question (Part I)

4.1. An Ancient Dilemma

It is one thing to offer arguments attempting to show that free will is not compatible with determinism. It is quite another to address questions about whether an incompatibilist free will requiring ultimate responsibility is *intelligible* or *possible* at all and whether it can be reconciled with modern scientific views of humans and the cosmos. This is what I have called the "Intelligibility Question" about libertarian free will, and it is in many ways even more difficult than the Compatibility Question.

The culprit here is not determinism, but indeterminism. The Intelligibility Question, as noted earlier, is related to an ancient dilemma: if free will is not compatible with determinism, it does not seem to be compatible with indeterminism either. Arguments have been made since ancient times that undetermined events would occur spontaneously and hence could not be controlled by agents in the way that free and responsible actions would require. Undetermined events occurring in brains or bodies, it is argued, would not seem to enhance freedom and control over, and hence responsibility for, actions, but rather to diminish freedom, control, and responsibility. Arguments such as these and many others have led to often-repeated charges that undetermined choices or actions would be "arbitrary," "random," "irrational," "uncontrolled," "mere matters of luck," or "chance" and hence not free and responsible actions at all.[1]

It is little wonder that libertarians have often looked for some deus ex machina to solve these problems, while their opponents have cried magic or mystery. Indeterminism might provide causal gaps in nature, libertarians have reasoned, but that was only a negative condition for free will. Some additional form of agency or causation was needed that went beyond familiar modes of causation in the natural order to "fill" those causal gaps in nature. And thus, we had historical appeals to "extra factors," such as noumenal selves, immaterial minds, uncaused causes, and nonevent agent causes, to account for an otherwise undetermined free will. Tempting ways

THE INTELLIGIBILITY QUESTION (PART I) 59

to think, perhaps, but also prompting charges such as Strawson's of "panicky metaphysics."

As noted in Chapter 1, I long ago became disenchanted with such appeals. Avoiding them, however, requires a whole new look at the Intelligibility Question: Can one make sense of a libertarian or incompatibilist free will without reducing it to mere chance or luck, on the one hand, *or to mystery*, on the other, and can such a free will be reconciled with modern scientific views of the cosmos and of human beings?

4.2. Indeterminism: Empirical and Philosophical Questions

First, let us be clear that it is an empirical and scientific question whether any indeterminism *is* there in nature in ways appropriate for free will—in the brain, for example. No purely philosophical theory can settle the matter. As the Epicurean philosophers said centuries ago, if the atoms don't "swerve" in undetermined ways and in the right places, there would be no room in nature for free will.

Christoph Koch is a distinguished neuroscientist and a tough-minded one at that. He argues that "there is no evidence that any components of the nervous system—a warm and wet tissue strongly coupled to its environment—display quantum entanglement" (2009, p. 40). But Koch goes on to say that "what cannot be ruled out is that tiny quantum fluctuations deep in the brain are amplified by deterministic chaos" so that they might have non-negligible nondetermined effects on neural processing and thereby affect human decision-making (2009, p. 40) Koch does not endorse this idea, but says that it cannot be ruled out, given what is currently known about the brain. And such a role for indeterminism is all that would be needed for the theory to be presented here.

(P89) In the most recent edition of *The Oxford Handbook of Free Will* (2011), Robert Bishop agrees with Koch and cites a number of other neuroscientists and philosophers who have made similar suggestions. If minute quantum indeterminacies occurred at the intra-neural or synaptic levels of the brain, Bishop argues, affecting the timing of firing of individual neurons, these indeterminacies, however minute, could be amplified, due to sensitivity to initial conditions, so that they had non-negligible effects on neural processing. Bishop goes on to point out that one need not even have to appeal to chaos to get these effects. For, as he notes "the exquisite sensitivity needed for the sensitive dependence arguments in the normal amplification of quantum effects is a general feature of nonlinear dynamics and is present whenever nonlinear effects are likely to make significant contributions to the dynamics of a system" (2001, p. 91). And it is generally agreed, Bishop adds, that nonlinear dynamics is pervasive in the functioning of human brains.

Other scientists, not mentioned by Bishop, have also made suggestions about the possible role of indeterminism in the brain in recent years, including, interestingly, its potential evolutionary significance. They include neuroscientist Peter Ulric Tse, who has made detailed and highly original suggestions about these topics in a recent book (2013), as well as neuroscientists Paul Glimcher (2005) and Michael Shadlen (2014), biologists Bjorn Brembs (2011) and Martin Heisenberg (2013), astrophysicist Robert Doyle (2011), physicists G. F. R. Ellis (2009) and John Polkinghorne (2009), psychologist Dean Simonton (2004), and philosopher Nancey Murphy and neuroscientist Warren Brown (2007), to name just a few.[2] I will be referring to some of these figures and others in later discussions.

(P90) But our question at present is a philosophical one that has boggled people's minds since the time of the ancient Stoics and Epicureans: What could one *do* with indeterminism, assuming it was there in nature in the right places, to make sense of free will as something other than mere chance or randomness and without appealing to mystery? If minute quantum indeterminacies in the firings of individual neurons were amplified so that they introduced some indeterminism into the larger-scale processing in deliberation and decision-making, how could this help to make sense of free choice as something other than mere chance? Addressing such questions requires adding further pieces to the discussions of previous chapters.

4.3. Initial Pieces: Self-Formation, Efforts, Willpower, Volitional Streams

Before continuing, let me say that those familiar with my past work will notice further alterations and refinements in the pieces to follow that have been

THE INTELLIGIBILITY QUESTION (PART I) 61

developed in recent years in response to the critical literature. In this regard, I owe a debt to many critics and other writers on these subjects. In the spirit of Plato's intimation mentioned in the opening chapter, the search for Truth in his ideal sense is something we must participate in with others from our necessarily limited perspectives.

Let us begin by recalling what was said in P27–P29, that indeterminism does not have to be involved in all actions done "of our own free wills." Indeterminism need be involved only in those choices or acts by which we make ourselves into the kinds of persons we are, with the wills we have. These are the "will-setting" or "self-forming" actions, or SFAs, of earlier pieces.

(P91) I argue that these self-forming actions occur at those difficult times in life when we are torn between competing visions of what we should do or become; and they are more common in everyday life than one may think. Perhaps we're torn between doing the moral thing or acting from ambition, or between present desires and long-term goals, or we are faced with difficult tasks for which we have aversions, or have to make important life choices or have to exert willpower to keep prior commitments and resolutions rather than break them. In all such cases and many others, we may be faced with competing motivations and have to strive or make an effort or exert willpower to overcome the temptation to do something else we also strongly want.

(P92) At such times, the tension and uncertainty we feel about what to do, I suggest, would be reflected in some indeterminacy in our neural processes themselves. This would be in the form of amplified background neural indeterminacy as described in the previous section—*"stirred up," one might say, by the conflicts in our wills*. The uncertainty and inner tension we feel at such soul-searching moments of self-formation would thereby be reflected in some indeterminacy in our neural processes themselves. *The experienced uncertainty would correspond physically to the opening of a window of opportunity that temporarily screens off complete determination by the past.*

(P93) A further piece of this tapestry, then, involves noting that in most such cases of self-formation, where we are faced with competing motivations, whichever choice is made will require an effort of will or exercise of willpower to overcome the temptations to make an alternative choice. I thus postulate, in such cases, that different goal-directed cognitive processes (*volitional streams*, we might call them) would be involved in the brain, corresponding to these exertions of effort or willpower. These cognitive processes would have different goals corresponding to the different choices that might be made (e.g., a moral choice or a self-interested choice).

(P94) Crucially, however, *it is not being claimed here (as I once did) that these efforts or exercises of willpower aimed at different choices would be occurring at the same time during deliberation. Nor will they be occurring throughout the entire deliberation. Rather, different efforts or exertions of willpower may be initiated at different times, depending on the course of the agent's reasoning.*

To illustrate, consider a familiar example of van Inwagen's of a would-be thief, call him John, deliberating about whether or not to steal from a church poor box. Suppose John is deeply torn because, on the one hand, he is desperately in need of money and knows that no one is usually in the church on weekday afternoons, so he can likely steal without being caught. On the other hand, he has serious moral qualms about doing so, made even stronger because he knows the money in the poor box is used to help other people who are in need, some of whom may need help as much as, or more than, he does.

We might then imagine that in the course of John's deliberation, various thoughts, experiences, and memories come to mind, various thoughts, desires, and possibilities are assessed, so that his considered reasons incline him to choose to steal the money rather than not to steal it.

(P95) Of crucial importance, however, if this is a self-forming choice in the sense described in prior pieces, we must say that the reasons motivating the choice to steal the money merely *incline* John to make that choice at this time rather than the alternative. These reasons are not "decisive" or "conclusive," nor do they determine he will do so. To use a traditional expression of Leibniz ([1686] 1991), his reasons "incline without necessitating." If a choice is thus to be made in accord with these inclinations, effort would have to be made or willpower exerted to overcome the still-existing resistance in his will. This resistance would be coming from his motives to make the contrary choice, which motives also remain important to him.

(P96) Though the reasons merely incline and are not decisive or conclusive, nonetheless when it is the case that the agent judges that they incline to one choice to a degree that might justify making that choice at the time, an effort would be initiated to make that choice and thereby to overcome the still-existent resistant motives in the will. This is where indeterminism would enter the picture as well. For, in the manner described in P92, the conflict in John's will would "stir up" indeterminism in the effort to make the choice to which he is currently inclined, making it uncertain the effort will succeed in attaining its goal. If the effort to choose to steal does succeed, despite this indeterminism, the choice to steal to which John is presently inclined would be made and the deliberation would terminate.

(P97) Note that if this should happen, the choice to steal would have been made by John purposefully and in accordance with his will since it would have been the result of a goal-directed cognitive process (the effort or exertion of willpower) to make just this choice at this time rather than an alternative. Moreover, the choice would have been made for the reasons inclining him toward that choice at the time rather than the alternative. Thus, it wouldn't have been a mere accident that the choice occurred, *even though its occurrence was undetermined*. The choice would have been brought about voluntarily and on purpose, for these inclining reasons, as a result of the success of the goal-directed effort of the agent that might have failed due to the indeterminism, but did not fail.

But what would happen if, due to the indeterminism involved, the effort to choose to steal from the poor box did *not* succeed at that time and the choice had not been made? Many critics of a free will requiring indeterminism assume that if a choice is undetermined, the agent would be able to make a different choice, for example, to steal or not to steal, given exactly the same deliberation leading up to the moment of choice, including exactly the same desires, beliefs, thoughts, and prior reasoning.

These critics then argue that, given this assumption, it would follow that if John failed in his effort to choose to steal from the poor box at this time, due to the indeterminism involved, he would instead have chosen *not* to steal from the poor box at that same time instead. And this is problematic, these critics commonly argue, given that his deliberation would have been exactly the same leading up to the different choices. What would explain the difference in choice?

(P98) This commonly made assumption, however, which was made in some of my own prior writings, is *not* made in the account of self-forming choices being given here, as made clear in P94. It is not assumed, nor need it be assumed, on this account, that if a choice is undetermined, the agent might make different choices, for example, to steal or not to steal, given exactly the same deliberation, including exactly the same desires, beliefs, inclinations, and reasoning, leading up to the choice. All that follows on this present account from the assumption that a self-forming choice, or SFA, is undetermined is that the effort to make it may succeed *or may fail* at a given time in overcoming the resistance in the will to making it. And from this, it does *not* follow that if the effort fails, an alternative choice would be made at that same time instead.[3]

(P99) *To the contrary, failure would rather be a signal to the agent not to choose too hastily in terms of the presently inclining reasons.* Failure would say in effect: think more about this. The resistant motives for the alternative choice still matter to you and they should not be dismissed too readily.

(P100) These resistant motives are the causal source of the indeterminism in the effort to choose to steal in the first place, making it uncertain that the effort will succeed here and now. The stronger these resistant motives are, the greater the probability the effort may fail, due to the indeterminism to which the resistant motives give rise.

(P101) In sum, a distinction needs to be made between John's *not choosing to steal* at a time and his choosing *not to steal* at that time. What is assumed if, due to the indeterminism, John fails in his effort to choose to steal at the time is not that he would have made the contrary choice, not to steal, but rather that no choice at all would have been made at that time. The deliberation would either continue until a potential reassessment of the motivating reasons led to another later effort to make the choice to steal or a potential reassessment led to a later effort to make the choice not to steal. Or the deliberation might terminate without any decision being made, if this is possible in the circumstances and the agent is so inclined.

(P102) John, we may imagine, if he fails to overcome the resistance in his will to making the choice to steal at a time, might reconsider his motivating reasons. Then, moved by his moral qualms about stealing money from a poor box used to help others, he may be inclined seconds or minutes later to choose *not* to steal and make an effort to choose in accord with that inclination. The success of this later effort would also be undetermined, but if the effort succeeds in overcoming the conflict in his will, the choice *not* to steal would be made.

(P103) Or John may find on reconsidering that he really needs the money and makes a further effort at a time later to overcome his moral qualms. This later effort may also in turn fail, but if it succeeds despite the indeterminism, he will make the choice to steal at this later time. Or the deliberation may terminate without any decision being made. John may leave the church planning to think more about it, perhaps berating himself for his indecisiveness.

(P104) Note that in any of these possible scenarios, if John does succeed at a time in an effort to make whatever choice he is inclined to make at that time, he will have brought about that choice and will have done so voluntarily and intentionally and for the motivating reasons that inclined him toward that choice at the time. For he would have succeeded in an effort whose goal was to make that very choice *rather than* the alternative *for* those inclining reasons; and this would be the case *even though the occurrence of the choice, if he succeeds, would have been undetermined.*

(P105) Indeterminism would have been involved in the effort, but it would not be the cause of the choice if the effort succeeds. For the effort would have succeeded, *despite* the indeterminism and not *because* of it. The cause of the choice would have been the agent whose effort or exercise of willpower it was.

(P106) Note also that the indeterminism that is ingredient in the agent's effort to make the choice to which the agent is then inclined *is not an accidental feature of the situation.* This indeterminism does not just "happen" to be present. Its presence is rather a causal consequence of the conflict in the agent's will and of the resistant motives that are a feature of this conflict—resistant motives of the kind that have to be overcome by effort, if the choice is to be made.[4]

(P107) The idea is thus to think of the indeterminism involved in self-forming choices, not as a cause *acting on its own,* but as an *ingredient* in larger *goal-directed* or *teleological* activities of the agent, in which the indeterminism functions as a *hindrance* or *interfering* element in the attainment of their goals. The choices that result would then be *achievements* brought about by the goal-directed activities (the efforts of will or exercises of willpower) of the agent, which might have failed given the indeterminism ingredient in them, but one or another of which may succeed in attaining its goal, despite this indeterminism.

(P108) Moreover, if such processes aimed at different goals may occur at different times in the course of deliberation (in the conflicted circumstances of an SFA), *whichever choice may be successfully made will have been brought about by the agent's volitional striving to make that particular choice rather than the other at that time,* despite the possibility of failure due to the indeterminism.

4.4. Indeterminism, Responsibility, Will-Setting, and Inner Complexity

A further significant consequence of this way of looking at things concerns responsibility:

(P109) When indeterminism functions in this manner as an obstacle to success of goal-directed activities, the *indeterminism does not preclude responsibility, if the activities succeed in attaining their goals,* despite the indeterminism. This may be seen by further reflecting on what were earlier called Austin-style examples in P18–P19—examples introduced into modern discussions of agency by J. L. Austin, Elizabeth Anscombe, and others.

An Austin-style example of such a kind discussed in section 2.8 was of an assassin who is trying to kill a prime minister from a distance with a high-powered rifle when, owing to a nervous twitch in his arm, he fails to hit his target. Another example of this kind I have used is of a husband arguing with his wife, who in anger swings his arm down on her favorite glass tabletop intending to break it. In each of these cases, as Austin suggests, we could imagine that an element of genuine chance or indeterminism is involved. Perhaps the nervous twitches in the arms of the assassin that lead to missing the target—or the reduced momentum in the swing of the husband's arm that might lead to his failing to break the tabletop—were the result of undetermined quantum events in their brains or nerve pathways.

> (P110) In the earlier discussion of such Austin-style examples, it was assumed that, due to the indeterminism, the agents *failed* to do what they were intending and trying to do. But now we must look at the other side of the picture. Let us now suppose that, despite the indeterminism in their nerve pathways, the assassin *succeeds* in his goal of killing the prime minister and the husband in breaking the tabletop. In such cases, both the assassin and the husband would be *responsible* for their actions, because both would have succeeded in doing what they were intending and trying and making efforts to do, *despite the indeterminism involved.*

Thus, it would be a poor excuse for the assassin to plead in a courtroom that he was not guilty of killing the prime minister because due to the indeterminism in his nerve pathways it was undetermined, and hence a matter of chance, that he succeeded in hitting his target. It would also be a poor moral excuse—should he succeed in hitting his target despite the indeterminism—for him to plead that he was only responsible for attempting to kill the prime minister, while it was indeterminism that did the killing. It would be equally absurd for the husband to offer the excuse to his wife that, since it was undetermined that his arm swing would break the tabletop, the breaking of the tabletop was a matter of chance and so he was not responsible for it. She would not be impressed, and rightly so.

> (P111) There was indeed a "chance" these agents would fail in doing what they were trying to do. But if they succeeded nonetheless, chance would not have been the cause of the prime minister's death or the table's breaking. *They*, the agents, would have been the causes, by virtue of the fact that they would have succeeded in doing what they were intending and trying to do. In other words, when indeterminism thus functions as an obstacle to the success of goal-directed activities, the indeterminism does not preclude responsibility, *if the activities succeed in attaining their goals, despite it.*

(P112) So it would be as well with self-forming choices, or SFAs, as described in preceding pieces, but with an important difference: *whichever choice the agents should make* in the course of a deliberation in a self-forming choice situation, they will have succeeded in doing what they were making an effort to do at that time, despite the indeterminism involved in their neural processing.

If John, for example, chooses to steal from the poor box at any time during his deliberation, it will be due to the success of his effort to make that choice at that time, thereby overcoming resistance in his will to doing so. And if he chooses not to steal from the poor box at some other time in the course of the deliberation, it will be due to the success of his effort to make that other choice *not* to steal, thereby overcoming the resistance in his will to doing that.

(P113) Whichever choice is thus made in such self-forming choice situations, the indeterminism involved would not be a cause acting on its own, but an ingredient in a larger goal-directed cognitive activity of the agent that would have succeeded in attaining its goal, despite the indeterminism (P91). The agents would then be responsible for the choices made by virtue of the fact that they would have succeeded in doing what they were intending and trying to do (P94); and this would be the case in such an SFA situation whichever choice should be made (P95).

(P114) A further consequence of these pieces worth noting is that, while Austin-style examples teach us something important about the relation of responsibility to indeterminism, *Austin-style examples do not themselves amount to self-forming choices or SFAs*. For, in Austin-style examples, unlike self-forming actions, it is *not* true that whatever the agents should do would be done in accordance with their wills (voluntarily, intentionally, and rationally) *either way* they should act. The assassin's failing to kill the prime minister and the husband's failing to break the tabletop are not things they do voluntarily, intentionally, and for reasons. They are *mere failures*—unintended and unwanted, occurring merely by accident or mistake.[5]

(P115) Moreover, this difference—that Austin-style examples do not themselves amount to self-forming actions—is importantly related to the fact that, in Austin-style examples, the indeterminism is *an accidental feature of the situation with no significant connection to the agent's will*, whereas in self-forming choices, the indeterminism that is ingredient in the agent's effort is not an accidental feature of the situation. Its presence is rather a causal consequence of the conflict in the agent's will and the resistant motives that are a feature of that conflict—resistant motives that have to be overcome by some effort, whichever choice is made (P83, P88, P89).

(P116) This difference is related in turn to the fact that Austin-style examples are what were earlier called "will-*settled*" actions, whereas self-forming actions, or SFAs, are "will-*setting*" (P23–P24). The assassin's will is already *set* on killing the prime minister, not on failing. Thus, if he fails, it will not be voluntarily or intentionally, but merely by chance. Whereas in SFAs, the agents' wills are not already set one way before they choose. When one or another of their efforts to choose succeeds, they *set* their wills one way or another then and there and do so voluntarily and intentionally, whichever choice should be made.

(P117) To sum up, I have argued thus far that self-forming actions, or SFAs, occur at those difficult times in life when we are torn between competing visions of what we should do or become. On such occasions of self-formation, agents are, as is often said, *of two minds*. Yet they are not two separate persons. They are not dissociated from either of their conflicted states of mind.

Consider a young woman, call her Claudia, who is about to graduate with honors from a law school and who is deliberating about which of two attractive job offers to accept. One is with a large corporate law firm in a big city, the other a smaller, up-and-coming, but less prestigious firm in a smaller city near where she grew up and hence to her family and many friends. She is torn because each firm has features that are deeply attractive to her. On the one hand, people at the smaller firm are more friendly. On the other hand, she is extremely ambitious and the chance to be part of this prestigious firm in a large city is very attractive to her. She is a small-town person with big-time ambitions.

(P118) The young woman, Claudia, of this example is a complex creature, torn inside by different visions of who she is and what she wants to be, as we all are from time to time. *But this is the kind of complexity needed for genuine self-formation and hence free will rather than merely freedom of action.* And when agents, like this young woman, decide in such circumstances, and the indeterminate efforts they are making become determinate choices, they *make* one set of competing reasons or motives prevail over the others then and there by deciding. They thereby voluntarily and purposefully commit themselves to a particular option into the future; and this will be the case whichever choice they should make.

4.5. Initial Questions and Objections (Part I): Indeterminism and Chance

A host of questions and potential objections naturally arise about this view as so far presented. Addressing them will lead to further pieces of the view, the account of which is far from complete. Many of the most obvious objections rest on intuitions people have that if choices are undetermined, they *must* happen merely by chance—and so must be "random," "capricious," "uncontrolled," "irrational," and all the other things usually charged. Such intuitions are deeply rooted. But if we are going to understand free will, I think we have to break habits of thought supporting such intuitions and learn to think in new ways.

> (P119) The first step is to question the intuitive connection in people's minds between "indeterminism's being involved in something" and "its happening merely as a matter of chance or luck." "Chance" and "luck" are terms of ordinary language that have the connotation of "something's being out of one's control." So, using them already begs certain questions, whereas "indeterminism" is a technical term that merely rules out deterministic causation, not causation altogether. Indeterminism is consistent with nondeterministic or probabilistic forms of causation, where outcomes are caused, but not inevitably. It is thus a mistake (one of the most common in the history of debates about free will) to assume that *undetermined* must mean (or imply) *uncaused*.[6]

> (P120) Another source of misunderstanding is the following: suppose our young law graduate Claudia decides to join the larger firm in the big city.

THE INTELLIGIBILITY QUESTION (PART I)   71

If her decision is undetermined up to the moment when it occurs, one may have the image of her first making the effort to overcome the still-important competing motives (to join the smaller firm) and then at the last instant "chance takes over" and decides the issue for her. This image, however, is misleading. On the view presented, *one cannot separate the indeterminism and the effort*, so that first the effort occurs *followed* by chance or luck (or vice versa).

(P121) Rather, the efforts or exercises of willpower are temporally extended goal-directed processes of the agent (P88–P89), and the indeterminism is an ingredient in these larger processes (P89), not something separate that occurs after or before them. The neural networks that realize the efforts in the brain are circulating impulses, and there is some indeterminacy in the timings of firings of individual neurons in these circulating impulses. But these processes as a whole are her efforts, and they persist right up to the moment when the decision is made. *There is no point at which her effort stops and chance "takes over."* She decides as a causal result of her effort, even though she might have failed due to the indeterminism ingredient in that effort.

Similarly, the husband breaks the table as a causal result of his effort, even though he might have failed because of the indeterminacy. This is why his excuse "Chance broke the table, not *me*" is so lame when he succeeds.

4.6. Initial Questions and Objections (Part II): Phenomenology and Rationality

Yet another frequently made objection is that we are not introspectively or experientially aware of making efforts and performing multiple cognitive tasks in self-forming choice situations. This objection would have considerable force if the efforts to make different choices were being made at the same time, as in my previous view. But this is not the case on the view developed here.

(P122) What we are experientially aware of in self-forming choice situations on the view developed here is that our will is torn, so that if we are to make a particular choice to which we may be inclined at a given time, then resistance in our wills, whose source is in our motives for making an alternative choice, must be overcome. Consider John, who is torn between stealing money from the church poor box for self-interested reasons and his moral qualms about doing so. He must overcome these moral qualms if he is to choose to steal the money. Or consider Claudia, who is torn between the attractions of choosing to join the larger firm in the big city and the very different attractions of choosing a smaller firm near her friends and family. If she is inclined to make one of these choices, she must overcome the resistance in her will coming from the attractions of the alternative choice.

(P123) Overcoming resistance in the will in this manner requires an exercise of *striving will*, in the form of effort-making, trying, endeavoring, exerting willpower, etc. This effort-making need not always be conscious, but it can and often will be. While we would not be experientially aware of making simultaneous efforts to make different choices at the same time, as on my previous view, we could be experientially aware of making a single effort to make a particular choice at a time, to which we may be inclined, when there is resistance in our wills to doing so that must be overcome if the choice is to be made. And when one such effort succeeds in attaining its goal in such circumstances, we also may have the experience of having succeeded in bringing about the particular decision aimed at for the reasons favoring that decision by overcoming resistance in our wills to doing so. This is an important feature of the power and control we experience ourselves having as agents over our free decisions or choices.

An additional, frequently made, objection is that it is irrational to make efforts to do incompatible things.

(P124) I agree that it would be irrational, if the efforts to make incompatible choices (say, to steal or not to steal) were being made at the same time, given exactly the same trajectory of reasoning up to that time. But this is no longer being assumed in the case of self-forming choices as described here. Rather, one or another of these efforts or exercises of willpower may be initiated at different times, depending on the trajectory of the agent's reasoning up to that time (P84–P85), when agents judge that their considered reasons incline them to making one choice rather than another to a degree that would justify making that choice then and there (P86–P89).

It is not irrational to make an effort to make a choice in such situations in terms of one's presently inclining reasons, though it would be irrational to also make an effort at this same time to make an opposing choice, given these same inclining reasons.

(P125) It is important in this regard to recognize the uniqueness of such self-forming choice situations. For our normal intuitions about efforts are formed in everyday situations in which our wills are already "set one way" on doing something, where obstacles and resistance have to be overcome. We want to open a door which is jammed, so we have to make an effort to open it. Such ordinary situations are what were earlier called "will-settled" situations, where our wills are already settled on doing what we are making efforts to do.

I am making an effort to open a jammed closet door to get what is inside. There is no resistance in my *will* to doing so, no reasons to do otherwise: I need what is in the closet for my day's activities. The resistance that has to be overcome by effort thus has an *external source*, in the conditions of the door and door frame. *The resistance is not coming from my own will.*

(P126) By contrast, self-forming choices, as we have seen, are "will-setting," not already will-settled. Our wills are *not already* settled on doing what we may be making one or another effort to do. The resistance that has to be overcome by effort is thus not coming from an external source such as the jammed closet door. It is coming from our own wills. We "set" our wills one way or the other only in the act of choosing itself, when an effort we are making succeeds in overcoming the resistance in our will to making the choice in question.

We may reconsider at a later time whether or not we should act on the intention thus formed, especially when new considerations come to light. But if the will remains conflicted when such reconsideration takes place, a further self-forming choice may be required for its resolution.

(P127) This feature of will-setting choices—that the resistance to making them is coming from our own will, not from an external source—is related in turn to the fact that the reasons motivating the efforts to make such choices merely "incline" without necessitating. The reasons motivating an alternative choice, which still matter to the agent, must be overcome by effort, if the choice to which the agent is presently inclined is to be made. It is thus rational to make an effort in such circumstances in terms of one's presently inclining reasons if the resistance in one's will is to be overcome. What would not be rational would be to make an effort to make a contrary choice at this same time, given these same inclining reasons.

(P128) It would also be irrational to make *no* effort at all to overcome the resistance in one's will to making the choice to which one is inclined, but rather to leave the outcome to "chance" and "hope" the choice to which one is inclined "wins" out. *Self-forming choices as described here are not a matter of certain motivations* "winning out" over others "on their own." Rather self-forming choices involve the *agent bringing it about that one set of motivations wins out* over another by making an effort to do so and succeeding in that effort. That is why self-forming choices can be said to be "will-setting" or "self-forming" choices.[7]

(P129) Because most efforts in everyday life, such as the effort to open the jammed closet door, are made in will-settled situations where our wills are already settled on doing what we are trying or making efforts to do, we tend to assimilate all effort-making to such situations. But we thereby fail to consider the uniqueness of *will-setting, which is of a piece, in my view, with the uniqueness of free will.*[8]

4.7. Causation, Probability, and Agency

Another common intuition lying behind many objections to an undetermined free will is the following: if free choices must be undetermined up to the moment they occur, then indeterminism, and not the agent, would be the *cause* of whether one choice occurs rather than another at that moment. This familiar worry was partially addressed earlier (in P88, P90). But to fully address it, more needs to be said about the consequences of viewing the indeterminism involved in free choice as an ingredient in larger goal-directed activities of the agent, in which the indeterminism functions as an interfering element in the attainment of the goals.

(P130) If indeterminism plays this kind of interfering role in goal-directed processes leading to choice, it will not be appropriate to say, when these processes succeed, that the indeterminism was a *cause* of the choices that are actually made. This follows from a general feature of probabilistic causation. A vaccination may hinder or lower the probability that one will get a certain disease, so it is causally relevant to the outcome. But if one gets the disease despite it, the vaccination is not a cause of one's getting the disease, though it was causally relevant, because its role was to *lower* the probability of that effect. The causes of one's getting the disease would be those causally relevant factors (e.g., the infecting virus) that *enhanced* or *raised* the probability of getting the disease. If one gets the disease anyway, it is *because* of the infecting virus, but *despite* the vaccination.

(P131) Similarly, in the case of the young law graduate, Claudia, the causes of the choice she does make (e.g., to join the large law firm in the big city) are those causally relevant factors that significantly raised the probability of making that choice from what it would have been if these factors had not been present. These factors include the reasons and motives inclining her at the time to make that choice rather than the alternative, her awareness of these reasons, and, importantly, her deliberative efforts to overcome the motives in her will to make the contrary choice. By contrast, the presence of the indeterminism lowers the probability that this choice would result from these reasons, motives, and efforts from what that probability would have been if there had been no competing motives or reasons and hence no interfering indeterminism.

(P132) Moreover, since those causally relevant features of the agent, that can be counted among the causes of the Claudia's choice, are *her* reasons or motives, *her* conscious awareness, and, crucially, *her* efforts or exercises of willpower, we can also say that she, the agent, Claudia, is the cause of the choice. *She* brought it about *by* making an effort to do so *for* those reasons and by succeeding in that effort. The indeterminism or chance (like the vaccination) was causally relevant to the outcome, but it was not itself the cause of the choice, if the effort succeeded, despite the indeterminism.

76   THE COMPLEX TAPESTRY OF FREE WILL

This again explains why the husband's excuse, "Chance broke the table, not me," was so poor. The chance, in the form of indeterminism, was a hindering factor, not the cause. *He*, by virtue of his succeeding in the effort, was the cause.

4.8. Micro- vs. Macro-control

But is it not the case, one might ask, on the view proposed that whether agents succeed in making a choice A in such circumstances (i) depends on whether certain neurons involved in their cognitive processing fire or not (perhaps within a certain time frame); and is it not the case that (ii) whether or not these neurons fire is undetermined and hence a matter of chance; and hence that (iii) the agent does not have control over whether or not they fire? But if these claims are true, it seems to follow that the choice merely "happened" as a result of these chance firings and so (iv) the agent did not have control over whether the choice of A was made rather than not and (v) the agent was not responsible for making the choice made rather than the alternative.

For many persons, this line of reasoning clinches the matter. It looks like the outcome *must* be merely a matter of chance or luck after all. Yet they reason too hastily. For the really astonishing thing is that

(P133) Even though agents do not have control over whether or not the undetermined neurons involved in their cognitive processing fire or not, it does not follow that the agents do not have sufficient control to be responsible for the choices ultimately made. This does not follow when the following three things are also true: (i) the choosing of A rather than B (or B rather than A) was something the agent was striving or trying to bring about; (ii) the indeterminism in the neuron firings involved in this striving or trying was a hindrance or obstacle to the achievement of that goal; and (iii) the agent's striving or trying nonetheless succeeded in achieving the goal despite the hindering effects of the indeterminism.

(P134) For consider the husband swinging his arm down on the table. It is also true in his case that (i) whether or not his endeavoring or trying to break the tabletop succeeds depends on whether certain neurons in his nervous system fire or do not fire. It is also true in his case that (ii) whether these neurons fire or not is undetermined and hence a matter of chance and (iii) is not under his control. Yet even though we can say all

THE INTELLIGIBILITY QUESTION (PART I) 77

this, it does not follow that (iv) the husband did not break the tabletop, and that (v) he is not responsible for breaking it *if* his endeavoring or trying to do so succeeds. And, importantly, each of these things (i)–(v) would be true in the case of a self-forming choice, whichever choice should be made. Astonishing indeed! Yet this is the kind of surprising result one gets when indeterminism plays an interfering or hindering role in larger goal-directed activities of agents that may succeed or fail.

(P135) It is well to meditate on this: we tend to reason that if an action (whether an overt action of breaking a table or a mental act of making a choice) depends on whether certain neurons fire or not (in the arm or the brain), then the agent must be able to make those neurons fire or not, if the agent is to be responsible for the action. In other words, *we think we have to crawl down to the place where the indeterminism originates (in the individual neurons) and make them go one way or the other. We think we have to become originators at the micro-level and "tip the balance" that indeterminism leaves untipped if we (and not indeterminism) are to be responsible for the outcome.* And we realize we cannot do that. But we do not have to. It is the wrong place to look. We do not have to micromanage our individual neurons individually to perform purposive actions and we do not have such micro-control over our individual neurons even when we perform ordinary actions such as swinging an arm down on a table.

(P136) What is needed when we perform purposive activities, mental or physical, is *macro-control* of processes involving many neurons—processes that may succeed in achieving their goals despite the interfering or hindering effects of some recalcitrant neurons. We do not *micro*manage our actions by controlling each individual neuron or muscle that might be involved. But that does not prevent us from *macro*managing our purposive activities (whether they be mental activities such as practical reasoning, or physical activities, such as arm-swingings) and being responsible when those purposive activities attain their goals.

4.9. Control and Responsibility

But if indeterminism does not take away control altogether, does it not at least *diminish* the control agents have over their actions? Is it not the case that the assassin's control over whether the official is killed (his ability to realize his purposes or what he is trying to do) is lessened by the undetermined impulses in his arm—and so also for the husband and his breaking the tabletop?

(P137) Their control is indeed lessened by the indeterminism. But a further surprising thing worth noting is that *diminished control in such circumstances does not entail diminished responsibility, when* agents succeed in doing what they are trying or making efforts to do. The assassin is not less guilty of killing the official if he did not have complete control over whether he would succeed because of the indeterminism; nor is the husband less guilty of breaking the table if he succeeds, despite the indeterminism involved.

(P138) Suppose there were three assassins, each of whom killed an official. Suppose one of them (an older assassin contemplating retirement) had a 50 percent chance of succeeding because of the indeterministic wavering of his arms, another had an 80 percent chance, and the third (a young stud) nearly a 100 percent chance. Is one of these assassins less guilty than the others, *if they all succeed*? It would be absurd to say that one assassin deserves a hundred years in jail, the other eighty years, and the third fifty years. The diminished control in the assassins who had an 80 percent or a 50 percent chance does not translate into diminished responsibility when they succeed.

(P139) There is an important further lesson here about free will in general. We should concede that indeterminism, wherever it occurs, does diminish control over what we are trying to do and is a hindrance or obstacle to the realization of our purposes. But recall that in the case of the young law graduate Claudia mentioned earlier (and self-forming actions, or SFAs, generally), the indeterminism that is admittedly diminishing her control over the choice she may be trying to make (to join one law firm or another) is coming from her own will. It is coming from the motives she has for making the opposing choice (to join the competing firm).

(P140) In each case, the indeterminism is functioning as a hindrance or obstacle to her realizing one of her purposes—a hindrance or obstacle in the form of resistance within her will which has to be overcome by effort. If there were no such hindrance—if there were no resistance in her will—she might indeed in a sense have "complete control" over one of her options. There would be no competing motives standing in the way of her choosing it and therefore no interfering indeterminism. But then also, she would not be free to *rationally* and *voluntarily* choose the other purpose (to choose otherwise) at another time in the course of the deliberation, because she would have no good competing reasons to do so.

(P141) Thus, *by being a hindrance to the realization of some of our purposes, indeterminism opens up the genuine possibility of pursuing other purposes*—of choosing or doing otherwise *in accordance with, rather than against, our wills*. To be genuinely self-forming agents (creators of ourselves)—to have free will—there must at times in life be obstacles and hindrances in our wills of this sort that we must overcome.

Compare Evodius's question to St. Augustine (in Augustine's classic work *On the Free Choice of the Will* (1993, p. 27) of why God gave us free will, since it brings so much conflict and struggle into the world. Of relevance here as well is an image from Kant's *Critique of Pure Reason* ([1781] 1999, p. 47) that I have used before. It is of a bird that is upset by the resistance of the air and the wind to its flight and so imagines that it could fly better if there were no air at all to resist it. But, as Kant notes, the bird would not fly better if there were no air to resist it. It would cease to be able to fly at all.

(P142) So it is with indeterminism in relation to an ultimately responsible free will. By being a hindrance or obstacle to the realization of some of our purposes, it opens up the genuine possibility of doing otherwise in accordance with, rather than against, our wills. To be genuinely self-forming agents, there must at times in life be obstacles and hindrances in our wills of this sort that we must overcome. Free will is a gift, but it is also a struggle, and an achievement.[9]

5
The Intelligibility Question (Part II)

5.1. Agency, Complexity, Disappearing Agents

Another question that has had a hypnotic effect on modern free will debates, reflecting deeply rooted intuitions, is the following: Do we not have to postulate an additional kind of "agent causation" over and above causation by states and events to fully capture libertarian free choices, given that such choices must be undetermined by prior states and events? There is a residual fear underlying questions of this kind that the "agent's causing" will somehow "disappear" from the scene if we describe the agent's capacities and their exercise, including free will, in terms of causation by states and events of the agent alone.[1] This fear is understandable. But for reasons suggested in the previous chapter—reasons that must now be further explored—I believe it is a fear that is ultimately misguided.

(P143) A continuing substance (e.g., an agent) does not absent the ontological stage because we describe its continuing existence—its life, if it is a living thing—including its capacities and their exercise, in terms of states, events, and processes involving it. One needs more reason than this to think that agents do not cause things, only events cause things. For my part, I should confess that I am a substance ontologist and indeed something of an Aristotelian when it comes to thinking about the nature of living things and the relation of mind to body. Human agents are continuing substances with both mental and physical properties. But there is nothing inconsistent in saying this and being a "teleological intelligibility" theorist about free will who thinks that the *lives* of agents, their capacities, and the *exercise* of those capacities, including free will, must be spelled out in terms of states, processes, and events involving the agents.

(P144) In short, *one does not have to choose between agent (or substance) causation and event causation in describing freedom of choice and action.* One can affirm both, as I would.[2] In the case of self-forming choices or

SFAs, for example, it is true to say both that "the agent's deliberative activity, including her effort, caused or brought about the choice," and to say that "the agent caused or brought about the choice." Indeed, the first claim *entails* the second. Such event descriptions are not meant to deny that agents, qua substances, cause their free choices and actions. Rather the event descriptions spell out in more detail *how* and *why* the agents did so."[3]

Note, however, that if event-causal descriptions are to have these implications, the event causes they describe must be "agent-involving" in a special manner.

(P145) Relevant to explaining this special manner is a peculiarly modern scientific way of understanding human agency and causation by agents that has roots in the ancient view of Aristotle just mentioned. Agents, according to this modern conception, are to be conceived as *information-responsive complex dynamical systems*. "An agent's causing an action" is to be understood as "an agent, *conceived as such an information-responsive complex dynamical system*, exercising *teleological guidance control* over some of its own processes" (see, e.g., Kane 2011b, pp. 396ff.). (Hence the relevance of the "teleological intelligibility" label for the view that I have long favored.)

(P146) *Complex dynamical systems* are understood in this context in the manner of "dynamical systems theory." Such systems (now known to be ubiquitous in nature and which include living things) are systems in which emergent capacities arise as a result of greater complexity. When the emergent capacities arise, the systems as a whole or various subsystems of them impose novel constraints on the behavior of their parts. Alicia Juarrero, whose informative book on the nature and significance of complex dynamical systems in the sciences, *Dynamics in Action* (2010), calls these emergent novel constraints on the behavior of parts of the system "context-sensitive constraints."

(P147) Such complex systems exhibit *teleological guidance control* (TGC) when they tend through feedback loops and error correction mechanisms to converge on a goal (called an attractor) in the face of perturbations. Such control, as neuroscientist Marius Usher argues (2006), *is necessary for any voluntary activity*, and he interprets it in terms of dynamic systems theory, as I would as well. Neuroscientists E. Miller and J. Cohen (2001) argue that such cognitive (guidance) control in human agents stems from the active maintenance of patterns of activity in the prefrontal cortex that represent goals and the means to achieve them. These patterns provide signals to other brain structures whose net effect, as Miller and Cohen describe it, is to guide the flow of activity along neural pathways that establish the proper mappings between inputs, internal states, and outputs (Kane 2011b, pp. 403–4).

5.2. Deviant Causation

(P148) An important consequence of understanding the agent causation involved in free agency and free will in this way is that the causal role of the agent in intentional actions of the kind needed for free agency and will is not *reducible* to causation by mental states of the agent alone. That would leave out the added role of the *agent*, qua complex dynamical *system*, exercising teleological guidance control over the processes *causally linking* mental states and events to actions.

The significance of this requirement can be shown by considering examples of "deviant causation" by mental states, such as desires and beliefs, in debates about action and free will. Consider Donald Davidson's (1963) well-known example of such causal deviance, which was put forward as a problem for Davidson's own influential account of intentional action in terms of causation by beliefs and desires. The example is of a mountain climber who lets go of his rope, allowing his companion to fall. The climber *desires* to save his own life and *believes* he can do so in the present situation by letting go of his rope. But in the example, he does not intentionally let go of the rope. Rather, this desire and belief so unnerve him when he thinks of their consequences, that they cause him to *accidentally* let go of the rope.

(P149) What is lacking in such examples of deviant causation is the agent, understood as a dynamical system, exercising teleological guidance control over the *manner* in which the mental states cause the resulting events (by guiding "the flow of activity along neural pathways that establish the proper mappings between inputs, internal states, and outputs" and being able to alter those pathways in response to new information). In the absence of this *systemic control* by the agent, qua information-responsive dynamical system, over the manner in which the mental states cause the resulting events, the causation by mental states would be "deviant" and the outcomes would not be intentional actions of the agent, but accidental occurrences.

(P150) A further significant consequence of understanding causation of free actions in this way, as Marius Usher (2006) points out, is that, while teleological guidance control (TGC) of the kind required for voluntary action is compatible with determinism, it is also compatible with indeterminism. A complex dynamical system, he argues, can exhibit teleological guidance control, tending through feedback loops and error correction to converge on a goal, even when, due to presence of indeterminism, it is uncertain whether the goal will be attained. Such teleological guidance control is thus available to libertarian theories of free will as well as to compatibilist ones.

To sum up, one does not have to choose between agent (or substance) causation and event causation in accounting for free agency, libertarian or otherwise. You can, indeed you must, affirm both. And the agent or substance causation involved is not reducible to event causation by mental states and events alone for the reasons given. There is thus no "disappearing agent" problem as well.

5.3. Agent-Causal/Event-Causal

These pieces lead to the further significant refinement in my view anticipated in Chapter 1, where I said this refinement would be explained in more detail later. That time has come.

(P151) As a consequence of the commitments spelled out in P144–P150, the view developed here differs from traditional *agent-causal* and *noncausal* views of libertarian free will. But *it also differs from what are usually designated event-causal views in the current literature*. It differs from what are usually designated event-causal views in rejecting claims that libertarian free actions can be adequately explained merely by claiming they are indeterministically caused in appropriate ways by beliefs, desires, intentions, and other mental states of agents. It turns out that the "appropriate ways" must bring in references to agents, qua substances, understood as complex dynamical systems, exercising teleological guidance control over some of their own processes, thereby allowing us to say that the agents *brought about* the action *for* these motivating mental states. And such references are not reducible to mere causation by mental states or events of agents alone, *which otherwise might be deviant*.

(P152) The view developed here also differs from traditional *agent-causal* libertarian views in ways noted in Chapter 1 and spelled out in more detail in previous pieces: (1) The view developed here does not involve a "sui generis" or "metaphysically primitive" notion of causation by an agent or substance (P133–P137). (2) Nor does it require a notion of causation by agents that is not also required by compatibilist accounts of free agency (P139), nor (3) one whose *exercise* does not essentially involve causation by states, processes, and events (P133). (4) Nor does the view developed here require postulating a special kind of causation by an agent or substance that is, in principle, incapable of being itself caused by prior events, either deterministically or indeterministically (P133–P134). (5) Nor does the view developed here require a special kind of causation by an agent that is not subject to or governed by laws of nature of the natural sciences (P133); (6) nor does it require a special kind of causation that requires appeals to immaterial substances, noumenal selves, transempirical power centers, uncaused causes, or other examples of what P. F. Strawson called the "panicky metaphysics" of libertarianism (P130–P137).

(P153) In sum, (7) the irreducible agent causation involved in the view presented here is not of a kind that is *only* needed for libertarian free will. It is needed for any kind of voluntary agency, whether compatibilist or incompatibilist; and (8) it is consistent with determinism or indeterminism. Its irreducibility to causation by mental states and events alone is thus not a *sufficient* reason for saying, as many traditional agent-causal theorists have contended, that it is not compatible with determinism or that its exercise does not *involve* event causation.

(P154) Given these differences, I have come to believe that to avoid numerous potential misunderstandings in current debates about free will, we should distinguish, in addition to the familiar three kinds of libertarian theories—noncausal (NC), agent-causal (AC), and event-causal(EC)—a fourth kind that might appropriately be called an agent-causal/event-causal, or AC/EC, view. My view, as indicated in Chapter 1, has always been of this fourth kind. It differs from traditional agent-causal views in ways just summarized in P152–P153 and from views usually designated event-causal in ways summarized in P151. And it differs from noncausal views in the obvious sense of not requiring that basic libertarian free actions be uncaused.

I regret that too often over the past few decades I have accepted without qualification the designation of my view as simply "event-causal." This designation did not originate with me, and I don't know where and from whom it did originate. There was certainly some justification for it. When new libertarian views, including my own, came on the scene in the 1970s and 1980s, a new designation seemed required to distinguish these new views from the existing noncausal and agent-causal views that were prevalent at the time among libertarians; and "event-causal" seemed an appropriate designation, since causation by states, events, and processes, mental and physical, played an essential role in these new views.

But the designation "event-causal" has also led to misunderstandings of my view; and it has led to what I take to be misguided objections, such as those considered here concerning deviant causation and disappearing agents. These objections have usually been directed specifically against what came to be called "event-causal" libertarian views, including my own.

The simple designation "event-causal" has also misleadingly suggested to many that one must choose between saying libertarian free actions are caused by agents *or* by events. It has always seemed to me that such a choice, aside from being misguided, has given an unfair advantage to agent-causal theories among libertarians. For, given a choice between saying that free and responsible human actions are caused *either* by agents *or* by events but not both, most persons who are libertarians, it seems to me, would say agents. But, in fact, no such choice is required.

(P155) To avoid these misunderstandings, it now seems appropriate to distinguish four kinds of contemporary libertarian views rather than three and to insist (as does P154) that my own view is of this fourth, AC/EC, kind. (I first began using this designation in Kane 2014, though some features of the view it designates go back to the beginning of that decade; see, e.g., Kane 2011a.) In *The Significance of Free Will* and other writings, I also referred to this fourth kind of view as a "teleological intelligibility" view, and that title also remains appropriate for reasons explained in P148, according to which an agent's causing an action is to be understood as an agent, conceived as an information-responsive complex dynamical system, exercising *teleological guidance* over some of its own processes.

There are more than enough objections, as it is, to be dealt with in defending such a view—as we have seen in the previous chapters and will see more of in this and subsequent chapters. But if there should be libertarians out there whose views also differ from event-causal libertarian views in the manner summarized in P150, and from agent-causal libertarian views in the manner summarized in P151–P152, and from noncausal views in the manner cited in P153, they might also consider this fourth AC/EC designation a more accurate designation of their view as well. I'd be happy not to have to drink alone at this establishment.[4]

5.4. Regress Objections (Part I): The First SFAs and Character Development

Let us turn now to a very different set of objections that are also frequently made against all views of free will requiring ultimate responsibility, including this one. According to views requiring ultimate responsibility (UR), if a choice issues from, and can be explained by, an agent's present will (character, motives, and purposes), then to be ultimately responsible for the choice, the agent must be at least in part responsible by virtue of choices or actions voluntarily performed in the past, that is, self-forming actions (SFAs), for *having* the will he or she now has.

But it has often been argued that this leads to a vicious regress. For in order to be ultimately responsible for these earlier self-forming actions by which we formed our present wills, would we not have to be responsible in turn for at least some of the character traits, motives, or purposes from which these earlier self-forming actions issued? And would this not require still earlier self-forming actions by which we formed these earlier character traits, motives, or purposes?

We would thus be led backward to the earliest choices of childhood, when the wills from which we chose were not formed by us at all but were entirely the product of influences outside ourselves, parents, social conditioning, heredity, genetic dispositions, and so on. It may thus appear that all responsibility for later choices in life would go back to the earliest choices of childhood when we seem to have far less freedom and responsibility than we have later in life, which is absurd.[5]

The first response to make to this familiar worry is to note the following:

(P156) Ultimate responsibility for choices in later life need not have its source entirely in choices of childhood. This would be true only if we made no subsequent SFAs in later life. Whereas, to the contrary, the account of self-forming actions given in preceding pieces implies that, *if SFAs are possible for agents at all, they would normally occur throughout our lives and more so as we mature and life becomes more complex* as we may become more self-aware.[6]

(P157) For it is the complexity of our lives, and of our wills and motivations, that gives rise to conflicts in our wills and to self-forming actions in the first place; and this complexity does not abate, but normally grows, as we develop beyond childhood. In making self-forming actions as we mature, we would be constantly forming, but also reforming, our existing characters, motives, and purposes as we go along, in ways that, while influenced by our prior characters, motives, and purposes, would not be determined by our prior characters, motives, and purposes.

(P158) I therefore argue, in partial agreement with philosophers, such as Aristotle, who talk about the development of "character," that responsibility for our *wills* (characters, motives, and purposes) accumulates over time.[7] Putting the matter in terms of the present theory: by making many self-forming choices through a lifetime, we gradually *form* and *reform* our wills in ways influenced by our past, but not determined by our past.

(P159) It would follow that, with regard to most of the self-forming choices we make, our responsibility has a twofold source: first, in the self-forming choices themselves made at the time, between our conflicting motives and purposes and, second, in the conflicting motives and purposes themselves from which the choices are made, many of which motives and purposes may have had *their* source in earlier self-forming actions by which we gradually formed our present wills over time.

The exceptions, of course, would include the very earliest self-forming actions of childhood when it *is* normally true, if we go back far enough, that the motivations among which we choose all come from sources outside ourselves, parents, society, genetic inheritance, etc.[8] I have discussed these first self-forming actions of childhood in a number of writings[9] and have a distinctive view about them, which may be spelled out as follows.

> (P160) In the earliest SFAs of childhood, our responsibility, so far from being the source of all later responsibility, *is* very limited, precisely because there is as yet no backlog of self-formed character. That is why we hold children less responsible the younger they are.

> (P161) I further argue that the earliest SFAs of childhood have a probative (or probing or learning) character to them.[10] Young children are often testing what they can get away with (the limits) and what consequences their behavior will have on them and others (one of many reasons why childrearing is so exhausting). Their character is thus slowly built up by how they respond to the responses to these earliest probes. Character and purposes to which they commit themselves accumulate and they become more responsible for subsequent acts that flow not just from present efforts but from past formed character and purposes as well.[11]

> (P162) If a three-year-old is told not to take more than his share of cookies, but tries to do so anyway the next time, resisting his conflicting motives not to disobey his parents, then the child is responsible. But he is not as responsible as when he does it a second, third, or fourth time and it becomes a pattern of behavior. The wise parent will not punish him severely the first time, but may do so mildly, by withholding something he wants. But *the wise parent will also know that it is a mistake never to hold the child responsible at all for these earliest probes. For it is only by being so held responsible in however limited ways in our earliest years that we gradually become self-forming beings with wills of our own making.*[12]

5.5. Regress Objections (Part II): Efforts, Kinds of Freedom, and Dimensions of Responsibility

Yet another potentially vicious regress often mentioned by critics of the present view concerns the efforts or exercises of willpower that precede and give rise to SFAs.[13] If self-forming choices are brought about by the efforts or exercises of willpower of agents, then if these self-forming choices are to be ultimately *free* and *responsible* actions, it would appear that the efforts or exercises of willpower that bring them about must *also* be free and responsible actions. But if the efforts or exertions that give rise to self-forming choices are themselves to be free and responsible actions, do we not need to postulate earlier free self-forming actions to initiate each of these earlier efforts, and so on backward indefinitely?

The answer to this question is no. We do not need to postulate further SFAs to initiate each of the efforts or exercises of willpower that give rise to SFAs. The efforts or exercises of willpower might have been initiated by further self-forming choices in certain cases. Agents may sometimes be conflicted about whether even to begin to deliberate about a difficult choice they have an aversion to thinking about. But this need not always be the case and usually will not be the case.

(P163) The efforts or exercises of willpower preceding self-forming choices will normally occur in the context of deliberations initiated by the confluence of the agents' conflicted will plus the recognition of the situations they are in. Consider John, torn between his need for money and his moral qualms about stealing from a poor box meant to help others. When he sees the church is empty so that he has an opportunity to steal, that information is filtered through the present state of his will, including his conflicting motives. Deliberation thereby commences, causally initiated by his recognition of the situation he is in and his awareness of the conflict in his will. When, during the deliberation, he reaches a point where he believes that his motives incline him toward making one of the choices to a degree that would justify making the choice at the time, effort would be initiated to make that choice in terms of these inclining motives and thereby to overcome the still existing resistance in his will to doing so.

Such efforts or exercises of willpower thus initiated in self-forming choice situations would not themselves be SFAs. Yet if one or another such effort succeeds in attaining its goal, it would *bring about* an SFA. To see how this could be, we need to review what was said earlier about different *kinds of free acts* and different *dimensions of responsibility*.

Free acts, it was said (P34), may be (1) acts done voluntarily, on purpose and for reasons that are not coerced, compelled, or otherwise constrained or controlled; or they may be (2) acts (free in sense 1 that are also) done "of our own free will" in the sense of a will that we are ultimately responsible to some degree for forming; or free acts may be (3) "self-forming" or "will-setting" acts (SFAs) by which we form and reform the will from which we act in senses 1 and 2.

(P164) Efforts or exercises of willpower that may lead to self-forming choices would not themselves be self-forming actions, as noted, hence not free acts of kind 3. But such efforts must and would be free acts of kind 1, and many of them would also be free acts of kind 2. They must all be acts done voluntarily, on purpose and for reasons that are not coerced, compelled, or otherwise controlled, hence free acts of kind 1. And many such efforts would in addition be free acts of kind 2. For they would also be acts "done of the agent's own free will" in the sense of a will the agent was responsible for forming in part by prior undetermined self-forming actions.[14]

(P165) Such efforts or exercises of willpower thus initiated in self-forming choice situations would also be *responsible* actions in the first dimension of responsibility defined in P54–P55 (section 3.2): that is, agents making such efforts, in doing so, would be *expressing the will they had in action*, and doing so voluntarily and intentionally.

(P166) In addition, many such efforts (those that are also free acts of kind 2) would be responsible acts in *both* the first and second dimensions of responsibility: that is, agents making *such* efforts would be responsible both for *expressing the will they had in action* (the first dimension of responsibility) *and* for *having the will they were thus expressing in action* (the second dimension). These efforts would be responsible actions in both dimensions to the degree that the motivations for making them were formed in part by earlier undetermined self-forming actions.

(P167) Thus, the efforts or exercises of willpower initiated in self-forming choice situations would be *free* and *responsible* actions in significant senses. But these efforts would not *themselves* be self-forming actions and hence not free acts of kind 3. They would not themselves be self-forming actions, first, because they would be "will-settled" actions, not "will-setting" ones. For each such effort would have as its goal the making of a *specific* choice (e.g., to steal from the poor box) rather than any alternative choice. Moreover, the *initiation* of such efforts may be *determined* by

the trajectory of the agent's reasoning at the time they are initiated, in the manner described in P162.[15] Yet, if any such effort or exercise of willpower were to succeed in attaining its goal, it would *bring about* an SFA, hence a choice free in sense 3, that *was* both *will-setting*, not will-settled, and *undetermined*, not *determined*.
How can this be?[16]

(P168) The answer lies in the *context* of self-forming choice situations in which such efforts may be initiated. In particular, the answer lies in three features of this context. First, these efforts or exercises of willpower are goal-directed *processes* that take a time to occur. Second, the context in which they occur involves a conflict in the will, a conflict that is the reason why an effort is needed in the first place if one or another choice is to be made. Third, this conflict in the will is also the source of the indeterminism that is an ingredient in whatever effort is initiated, making its success uncertain.

(P169) As a consequence of these features, the following would be the case: while the *initiation* (and thus the *occurrence*) of such efforts or exercises of willpower may be *determined* by the trajectory of the agent's reasoning when the efforts are initiated, the *outcomes* of the efforts (the choices that may result) would *not* be determined by the conditions that led to the initiation of the efforts. This would be so because of the indeterminism ingredient in the efforts which makes it uncertain that their outcomes will be attained. In addition, while each effort or exercise of willpower would itself be a *will-settled* process with a specific goal (the particular choice aimed at), if any one such effort was to succeed in attaining its goal, thus overcoming the resistance in the will, it would "settle" the previously conflicted will in one direction rather than another. The choice thereby brought about by the effort would thus be a *will-setting* choice. Moreover, the effort would have brought about the choice *in a manner that was not determined* and might have failed, because of the indeterminism ingredient in the effort, even though the initiation, and hence the occurrence, of the effort may have been determined by the agent's prior reasoning which gave rise to it.

(P170) So any effort or exercise of willpower that succeeds in attaining its goal in the context of such a conflicted will, though this effort need not *itself* be a will-setting and self-forming choice, would nevertheless have *brought about* a will-setting and undetermined self-forming choice. For in bringing about such a self-forming choice, it would have *set* the agent's will in one direction rather than another.

5.6. Kinds of Control

(P171) Agents must of course exercise some kind of *control* over any effort or exertion of willpower that may thereby be initiated in self-forming choice situations. But the control agents must have over these efforts is not the same kind of control they must have over the self-forming choices that may result from the efforts. Rather the control required over each effort is what I have called, following neuroscientist Marius Usher, *teleological guidance control* (TGC). Such control is necessary for any voluntary activity and so it is necessary for the efforts that may be initiated in self-forming choice situations (P122–P124).

(P172) By contrast, the control agents must have over the self-forming choices that the efforts might bring about is what was earlier called *plural voluntary control* (PVC): agents have such PVC over a set of options (such as choices they may be deliberating about), when they have the power to bring about whichever of the options they will to bring about, when they will to do so, by successfully exercising teleological guidance control over an effort to bring about that particular option rather than any alternative; and they have the power to do this *voluntarily, intentionally,* and *rationally, whichever option* they may bring about (P28).

(P173) In self-forming choice situations, agents have such plural voluntary control over the choices that might be made by virtue of having the power to make either choice their will may incline them to in the course of the deliberation. Of course, any such effort may also *fail* to attain its goal due to the indeterminism involved in it. But any effort thus initiated might also succeed in attaining its goal, despite this indeterminism. And if any effort does succeed, the agent will have successfully exercised teleological guidance control to make the choice thereby brought about; and the agent would have done so voluntarily, intentionally, and rationally, whichever choice that effort was aimed at bringing about.[17] And this would be the case, even though the choice made would have been undetermined.[18]

(P174) These steps add a further twist to something also emphasized earlier, namely that incompatibilist or libertarian freedom and control presuppose compatibilist freedom and control (cf. P30, P). We cannot get to incompatibilist free will in one fell swoop in the real world. That is one leap too far. We must get there stepwise, by exercising compatibilist guidance control over cognitive processes aimed at making choices, that is, these efforts or exercises of willpower, and from there, in the context of a conflicted will (P157), to incompatibilist regulative control (PVC) over the choices (SFAs) that may result from one or another of these cognitive processes.[19]

(P175) Or, putting the matter in an evolutionary perspective, *we had to first develop the capacity for (compatibilist) teleological guidance control before we could develop—given the further cognitive or mental complexity needed to deal with conflicts in our wills—the capacity for (incompatibilist) plural voluntary control (PVC)*. No infinite regresses result because the efforts leading to self-forming actions do not have to be initiated by still earlier efforts or by still earlier self-forming actions. These efforts or volitional streams would normally be initiated by the confluence of the agents' awareness of the conflicts in their wills plus the agents' recognition of their situations when they come to believe that their inclining reasons may be sufficient to justify making a choice in terms of those reasons and thereby to attempt to overcome the still existing resistance in their wills to doing so.[20]

5.7. A Further Objection: Plural Voluntary Control, Power, Ability, and Opportunity

A further objection regarding the plural voluntary control involved here naturally arises for the present account of undetermined self-forming choices, an objection that may have occurred to many readers and must now be considered. This objection can be answered. But it is a significant objection because answering it reveals something more about the present account of self-forming choices and especially about the essential role that indeterminism and other features play in that account.

Consider John again, when his initial reasoning inclines him to choose to steal from the poor box, so that he makes an effort to set his will on doing so. The effort might fail due to the indeterminism involved coming from the resistant motives in his will in the form of his moral qualms. But suppose the effort succeeds in overcoming his still-significant moral qualms. He thus "settles" his will on stealing the money and proceeds to do so.

(P176) One may question in this circumstance whether the agent, John, really did have *plural* voluntary control over his options. For plural voluntary control implies the power to voluntarily make one choice in the course of a deliberation *and* the power to voluntarily make an alternative choice in the course of that same deliberation. Moreover, having this *power* to voluntarily make either choice does not merely imply having the *ability* to make either choice. It also implies having the *opportunity* to make either choice in the course of the deliberation. Yet, as we are now imagining, if John's *first* effort to make one of the choices *succeeds* in making that choice, despite the indeterminism, it would appear there would be no opportunity for him to make the alternative choice in the course of this same deliberation. If the initial effort to choose to steal had failed, John would have had the ability and opportunity to reconsider his reasons and motives and make a later effort to refrain, which might have succeeded. But if the initial effort to steal succeeds, it would seem that he would never have the ability plus opportunity to voluntary make the alternative choice in the course of this deliberation, as plural voluntary control would seem to require.

Such is the objection I now want to consider against this account of plural voluntary control of undetermined self-forming choices. Note that this objection does not apply to my previous (abandoned) account of such choices, according to which the efforts to make alternative choices were being made *simultaneously* prior to choice by the agent. In such a case, the opportunity existed that either effort might win out at the moment of choice. Yet it was also the case that, for this earlier account, indeterminism was a more serious problem, since it seemed to imply that there was no adequate explanation for why one of the competing efforts won out *rather than* the other *at a given time*. This was, of course, one of the main reasons why I abandoned that earlier account. (More will be said about these reasons in Chapters 6 and 7.)

(P177) In answer to the above objection (just stated in P176) to the revised account of this book, the first thing to note is the following: we must concede that, if John succeeds in his initial effort to steal the money, it is indeed true that he no longer has the opportunity to choose to refrain from stealing in the course of this deliberation. But this is because, if he succeeds in his initial effort to choose to steal the money, *the deliberation itself he was engaged in thereby terminates* and there is no longer any opportunity to choose anything else in the course of that deliberation. The general point of relevance here is that if *any* effort an agent makes in the course of a deliberation succeeds in making a choice to which the agent is then inclined, *the deliberation itself thereby terminates at that moment*. The deliberation continues only when efforts fail. When an effort succeeds and the deliberation terminates, the agent may reconsider the decision at a later time, and thus may have an opportunity to make an alternative decision at this later time. But that opportunity would be present in a different, later deliberation with a (perhaps different) outcome.

(P178) What cannot be said however is that there *never was* an opportunity to do otherwise than choose to steal in the original deliberation. To the contrary, there would have been such an opportunity that would have existed *throughout* the deliberation *until* the agent, John in this case, actually succeeds in *some* effort to make one of the choices and the deliberation is thereby terminated. This would have been the case because even if efforts were made earlier, if these efforts had not succeeded, the deliberation would either continue with the possibility that John might reconsider his reasons and motives and make an effort to make an alternative choice, or the deliberation might terminate without any choice being made. In sum, the general point that needs to be recognized is that *the opportunity to voluntarily do otherwise* than choose to steal *would continue to be present throughout the deliberation*, as plural voluntary control would require, *until such time as the deliberation terminates*, either with John's making the choice to steal or the deliberation terminates without any choice being made.

(P179) It is important to note finally how crucial the appeal to *indeterminism* is in getting this result. The effort to make any choice (e.g., the choice to steal the money) in a self-forming choice situation such as John's, involves indeterminism and hence might fail to succeed. *It is because of this possibility that the power (ability plus opportunity) to make an alternative choice remains present throughout the entire deliberation* until the moment when one or another of the agent's efforts does succeed and the deliberation is thereby terminated (or the deliberation terminates without any decision being made). In sum, it is the indeterminism ingredient in the efforts that allows it to be the case that the power (ability *plus opportunity) to voluntary do otherwise persists throughout the deliberation, as the condition of plural voluntary control requires*, until the moment the deliberation terminates in a successful effort or terminates without any decision being made. By contrast, if it was determined and hence "will-settled" at an earlier time that a particular effort would necessarily succeed, then the ability plus opportunity to voluntarily do otherwise would cease to exist at this earlier time before the deliberation itself terminated (perhaps even before it began).

5.8. The Explanatory Luck Objection: Authors, Stories, Value Experiments, and Liberum Arbitrium

These reflections lead us to one of the most common and powerful variants of the luck objection that has been made against nearly all libertarian theories during the past three decades. The objection, which has been called the "Explanatory Luck Objection," is paraphrased below based on the writings of Alfred Mele (1998, p. 583), one of its most astute and persistent defenders:

> If [as indeterminism would seem to imply] different free choices could emerge from the same past of an agent, there would seem to be no explanation for why one choice was made rather than another in terms of the total prior character, motives, and purposes of the agent. The difference in choice, i.e., the agent's choosing one thing rather than another, would therefore be just a matter of luck.

This objection in various formulations is now so widely cited and affirmed by critics of libertarian views of free will that it is often referred to as "the" luck objection in the literature. And many philosophers assume it is decisive. I think they are mistaken. But I also think the objection has the power it has because it teaches us something important about free will.

THE INTELLIGIBILITY QUESTION (PART II) 97

(P180) The first obvious thing to be said in response to this luck objection is the following: in the case of self-forming choices as described here in prior pieces, it is not true to say, as this objection does, that "different free choices could emerge from the same past of an agent." This is not true, if it means the agent could make opposing choices—for example, to steal or not to steal—given exactly the same prior reasoning leading up to the moment of choice. All that follows, as argued here, from the fact that a self-forming choice is undetermined is that it might be made at a given time or might *fail* to be made at that time. It does *not* follow if it fails, that the opposing choice—not to steal—would be made at that same time, given exactly the same reasoning leading up to the choice to steal. And this would be true whichever choice is made in a self-forming choice situation.

(P181) Moreover, the following things would also be true *whichever choice should be made* in a self-forming choice situation: (a) The agent would have caused or brought about that choice by succeeding in a teleologically guided cognitive process (an effort) to bring it about, thereby overcoming resistance in the will to doing so. (b) The agent would have knowingly made that choice *rather than* the alternative. (c) The agent would have had the power to bring about the choice made and would have successfully exercised that power when it was made. The power was not unlimited, since the effort through which it was exercised might have failed, due to the indeterminism ingredient in it. But if the effort succeeded in reaching its goal, despite this indeterminism, the agent's power to make the choice would have been successfully exercised. (d) The choice would then have been made for reasons that inclined (without necessitating) the agent to make that choice at that time rather than the alternative—reasons that the agent then and there chose to act upon. (e) The agent would have brought about the choice rather than the alternative *voluntarily* (without being coerced against his or her will) and (f) the agent would have done so *intentionally* or on purpose, not merely accidentally, by succeeding in a teleologically guided effort aimed at bringing about that very choice rather than an alternative for the inclining reasons for that choice.

If saying "the agent's choosing one thing rather than the other is just a matter of luck," as this objection does, is meant to deny any of these things (a)-(f) about such self-forming choices, then saying that the outcome was just a matter of luck seems to be the wrong conclusion to draw. And if one were to say that "just a matter of luck" is meant to be consistent with all these things, this argument from luck would seem to lose much of its traction.

Ah, but not quite all traction; and this is where things get interesting. With powerful arguments in philosophy, it is not enough to show that their conclusions do not necessarily follow from their premises. One needs also to show why they seem to have such power. The luck objection in this popular form does not show that libertarian free choices must be "just a matter of luck," if that entails denying any of the claims (a)–(f) of P181. But this luck objection does show that there is something to the often-repeated charge that such self-forming choices would be *arbitrary* in a certain sense.

(P182) A residual arbitrariness seems to remain in all self-forming choices because the agents cannot in principle have *sufficient* or *overriding* ("*conclusive*" or "*decisive*") prior reasons for making one option and one set of reasons prevail over the other.[21] Therein lies the truth in this explanatory luck objection: an undetermined free choice *cannot be completely explained by the entire past*, including past causes or reasons; and I think it is a truth that reveals something important about free will.

(P183) I have argued elsewhere that such arbitrariness relative to prior reasons tells us that *every undetermined self-forming choice is the initiation of a novel pathway into the future*, a "value experiment," as I have elsewhere called it, *whose justification lies partly in that future and is not fully explained by the past* (1996, pp. 145–46). In making such a choice we say, in effect, "I am opting for this pathway. It is not required by my past reasons but is consistent with my past reasons and is one branching pathway my life can now meaningfully take. Whether it is the right choice, only time will tell. Meanwhile, I am willing to take responsibility for it one way or the other."[22]

(P184) Of special interest here, as I have often noted, is that the term "arbitrary" comes from the Latin *arbitrium*, which means "judgment"—as in *liberum arbitrium voluntatis* ("free judgment of the will"—the medieval designation for free will since the time of Augustine). Imagine a writer in the middle of a novel. The novel's heroine faces a crisis, and the writer has not yet developed her character in sufficient detail to say exactly how she will act. The author makes a "judgment" about this that is not determined by the heroine's already formed past, which does not give unique direction. In this sense, the judgment (*arbitrium*) of how she will react is "arbitrary," but not entirely so. It had input from the heroine's fictional past and in turn gave input to her projected future.

(P185) In a similar way, as I have often emphasized, *agents who exercise free will are both authors of and characters in their own stories at once.* By virtue of "self-forming" judgments of the will (*arbitria voluntatis*) (i.e., self-forming actions), they are *"arbiters" of their own lives, "making themselves" out of a past that, if they are truly free, does not limit their future pathways to one.*

(P186) If we should charge such agents with not having sufficient or conclusive prior reasons for choosing as they did, they might reply: "True enough. But I did have 'good enough' reasons for choosing as I did, which I'm willing to endorse and take responsibility for. If they were not sufficient or conclusive reasons, that's because, like the heroine of the novel, I was not a fully formed person before I chose (and I still am not, for that matter). *Like the author of the novel, I am in the process of writing an unfinished story and forming an unfinished character who, in my case, is myself."*

5.9. Rollback and Replay Objections

Two other kinds of objections frequently made against theories of free will requiring indeterminism are related to this explanatory luck objection just discussed. The first of these further objections (to be considered in this section and the next), appeals to thought experiments involving *"rollbacks"* or *"replays"* of events preceding undetermined choices. The second kind of objection, to be considered in the final section, concerns *"contrastive explanations."*

A well-known "rollback" thought experiment, introduced by Peter van Inwagen in an essay entitled "Free Will Remains a Mystery" (2000), was originally introduced to show that agent-causal libertarian theories of free will fail to explain how free will can be compatible with indeterminism. However, numerous authors have pointed out that rollback or replay thought experiments, like van Inwagen's, can be used to develop general rollback versions of arguments from luck against all libertarian theories of free will requiring indeterminism. (See, e.g., Seth Shabo 2011 and Christopher Franklin 2018, among others.)[23]

In van Inwagen's thought experiment we are asked to consider an agent, Alice, who is deliberating about whether to lie or tell the truth. She freely decides to tell the truth at a time t and her choice is undetermined, as libertarian theories would require. We are then asked to imagine by van Inwagen that God has caused the world to "rollback" to the exact state of the universe at a moment before Alice made her choice, then letting the world evolve to the point of the choice, so that we are able to observe this "replay." If the choice is undetermined, van Inwagen says, in some replays she might choose to tell the truth, in others she might lie. He asks us to suppose God rolls the universe back in this way 1,000 times. After watching 726 replays, he says, we find that in about half of these replays, Alice tells the truth. In the other half, she lies. In the light of watching each of these replays, van Inwagen then says,

> We shall be faced with the inescapable impression that what happens in the seven-hundred-and-twenty-seventh replay will be due simply to chance.... What other conclusion can we accept about the seven-hundred-and-twenty-seventh replay (which is about to commence) than this: each of the two possible outcomes ... has an objective, "ground floor" probability of .5—and there is nothing more to be said? And this surely means that, in the strictest sense imaginable, the outcome of the replay will be a matter of chance.... And if it was a mere matter of chance which of these things she did, how can we say that ... she was *able* to tell the truth and *able* to lie. How could anyone be able to determine the outcome of a process whose outcome is a matter of objective, ground-floor chance? (2000, pp. 15–16)

A number of arguments have been made both for and against such rollback or replay objections to views of free will requiring indeterminism.[24] I will focus here on the answer provided by the view developed in these chapters.

(P187) The first relevant thing to note about the implications of the view of self-forming choices developed here for rollback objections like the above is the following: if Alice makes an undetermined choice to tell the truth at a time t and it is a self-forming choice, it would *not* necessarily be the case, if we consider many replays (such as a thousand), that in about half of them she would tell the truth at t and in the other half she would lie at t. This key assumption fails for several reasons.

(P188) The most important reason (emphasized in many previous pieces) is this: from the fact that a self-forming choice made at a time t (such as Alice's choice to tell the truth) was undetermined, it does not follow that if this choice failed to be made at t, an alternative choice (to lie) would be made at that same time t. What *is* assumed, if Alice failed in her effort to choose to tell the truth at t due to the indeterminism, is rather that no choice at all would have been made at t (P92–P93). The deliberation would either continue until a potential reassessment of the motivating reasons that inclined to one choice or the other led to a later effort to make the choice to tell the truth or a potential reassessment led to a later effort to make the choice to lie. Or the deliberation might terminate without any decision being made.

In other words, in some percentage of rollback scenarios, Alice would tell the truth at t, as she does in the actual world; and in the other rollback scenarios, she would make no choice at all at t.

(P189) In addition—and this is crucial—in those scenarios where no choice at all was made by her at t, we would simply not know what might transpire *after t* in each rollback by knowing what happened in the real world after t where she *did* choose to tell the truth. In some of these rollback scenarios where no choice at all was made by her at t, she might have thought more about it and later made a choice to lie or thought more about it and later made a choice to tell the truth after all, or the deliberation might have terminated with no choice being made.

(P190) Note also that on all these possible rollback scenarios, when a particular choice (e.g., to tell the truth) fails to be made at a time t, if either choice (to tell the truth or to lie) should be made later in the deliberation, its occurring would *not* be (to use van Inwagen's words) "a mere matter of chance." For if any choice might occur later in the deliberation, it would be brought about voluntarily, intentionally, and rationally by the agent, as a result of the agent's succeeding in an effort at that later time to make *that* particular choice rather than the alternative for the reasons or motives inclining the agent to that choice at that time. And if the deliberation should terminate without any choice being made, it will also not be the case that one or another choice will have occurred as "a mere matter of chance," because it would not be the case that one or another choice will have occurred.

(P191) In summary, for self-forming situations as described here, if any choice should be made at any time during the deliberation, it will not be the case that its being made at the time would have been, in van Inwagen's words, "due simply to chance." In a certain percentage of the replays, Alice will also succeed in her effort to tell the truth at t. In another percentage of replays, she will fail in her effort to tell the truth at t; and in these replays, a number of different things might then transpire. In some, she may succeed in a later effort to tell the truth; in others she may succeed in a later effort to lie, overcoming motives in her will to tell the truth. In still other replays, she may fail in later efforts as well. And in some of these replays, the deliberation may terminate without any choice being made at all.

(P192) But in none of these replays, for reasons spelled out in P184–P187, will it have been the case that if one or another choice is made at any time during the deliberation, its being made at that time rather than the alternative was "a mere matter of chance." If any choice is made in any of these scenarios, it will have been brought about by the agent voluntarily, intentionally, and rationally rather than the alternative as a result of the agent's succeeding in a teleologically guided process (an effort) to bring about that particular choice; and otherwise, no choice at all would be made.[25]

5.10. Indeterminism, Probabilistic Causation, and Agency

In stating this rollback objection, van Inwagen says that if we assume that Alice's choice to tell the truth at a time t is undetermined, then, after watching many (e.g., 726) replays, we would find that in about half of these replays, Alice tells the truth at t, while in the other half, she lies. In response, I noted that if the choice in question was a self-forming choice as understood here, this assumption would not be true for several reasons. The most important reasons were spelled out in the previous section in P187–P192.

But there is one other reason worth considering because it throws further light on the roles of indeterminism and the will in self-forming choices. If Alice's choice is a self-forming choice, there is another reason why it would also not necessarily be the case that in half the replays she would choose to tell the truth at t and in the other half she would fail to make any choice at all at t.

(P193) This other reason has to do with the fact that whether or not the choice is made at t in a self-forming choice situation would be a matter of probabilistic causation; and the probability of the choice's occurring at t need not be .5. The probabilities of success or failure of the effort to make a self-forming choice at a time would depend upon the strength of the motives inclining the agent to make the choice at that time, on the one hand, and the strength of the resistant motives in the will against making that choice at that time, on the other. And these probabilities may vary depending on the trajectory of the agent's reasoning and circumstances at the time of choice. They will not always be .5.

(P194) To say the outcomes are undetermined in such contexts is to say that the outcomes are not certain, as they would be if they were determined. But this does not imply that whether a particular choice occurs at a given time is merely a matter of luck or chance. If any particular choice occurs, it would be caused by the agent in accordance with the agent's will. To say the causation would be probabilistic, not deterministic, would not imply that the probabilities of a choice's occurring or failing to occur at a time would be equal. For these probabilities would depend respectively on the strengths of the inclining motives for making the choice and the strength of resistant motives against it, which strengths may vary depending on the trajectory of the agent's reasoning and circumstances at the time of choice.

It is worth recalling what was said earlier (P110) about the intuitive connection in people's minds between "indeterminism's being involved in something" and "its happening merely as a matter of chance or luck." "Chance" and "luck," it was said, are terms of ordinary language that have the connotation of "something's being out of one's control," whereas "indeterminism" is a technical term that merely rules out deterministic causation, not causation altogether. Indeterminism is consistent with probabilistic forms of causation, where outcomes are caused, but not inevitably.

One might argue further, however that, while *success* of an effort in bringing about a choice in self-forming choice situations is an act of *agency*, *failure* of these efforts, due to the indeterminism, is not an act of agency.[26] It is a *failure of agency*. This is true.

(P195) But it is also worth noting that in SFAs, such failure in the effort to make a choice also has its source in the *will* of the agent. The proximate source of failure is the indeterminism in the effort. But the causes of this indeterminism are the resistant factors in the will of the agent (such as traits of character, motives, and purposes) that stir up indeterminism in the effort of the agent, lowering the probability that the choice will be made. Indeterminism is the *means* by which these resistant factors in the will lower the probability of success of the effort the agent may be making. So, while failure of the effort is *not* something the agent *does*, it *is* nonetheless caused by something the agent *wills*, namely, these resistant motives. Unlike cases such as that of the jammed closet door where the obstacle to be overcome by effort has an external source and is not in the agent's will, the obstacles to be overcome in self-forming choices are resistant motives in the agent's will.

With this in mind, return to the example of probabilistic causation used earlier. A vaccination may lower the probability that one will get a certain disease, so it is causally relevant to the outcome. But if one gets the disease despite the vaccination, it is not the cause of one's getting the disease. The causes of one's getting the disease are those causally relevant factors (e.g., the infecting virus) that *enhanced* or raised the probability of getting the disease. If one gets the disease, it is *because* of the infecting virus, but *despite* the vaccination. If one fails to get the disease, by contrast, it might be *because* of the vaccination (which raised the probability of *failure*) and *despite* the infecting virus.

Similarly, in self-forming choices, the resistant motives in the will lower the probability that the agent's effort to make a choice to which the agent is then inclined will succeed. So these resistant motives are causally relevant to the outcome. But if the agent is successful in the effort to make the choice nonetheless, the causes of the choice are not these resistant motives, but rather those factors that raised the probability of success, such as the motives that inclined the agent to make this choice and the agent's effort to make this choice for those inclining motives. If the choice is made, it is *because* of these inclining motives and the agent's effort, but *despite* the resistant motives, whereas, if the choice *fails* to be made, it would be *because* of these resistant motives in the will of the agent, *despite* the inclining motives and effort of the agent.

5.11. A Recent Luck Objection: Haji

In a recent issue of the Iranian *Journal of Philosophical Theological Research*, Ishtiyaque Haji (2022) has introduced a luck objection directed at this new view of mine, which I had introduced in a condensed form in an earlier issue of this same Iranian journal (Kane 2021). Haji explains his objection in terms of van Inwagen's example of John, who is torn between choosing to steal the money in the church poor box and choosing not to do so for his moral reasons.

He asks us to imagine that at a time t in the actual world, W_1, John's reasons and motives incline him to make an effort to choose to steal from the poor box. But the effort fails and the choice to steal is not made at that time. Haji then asks us to consider that in some other possible world, W_2, John's reasons and motives also incline him at t to make the choice to steal, and he makes the same effort to choose to steal, which succeeds in his making the choice to steal at that time. It seems, Haji says, that "the explanatory luck objection is still with us." For nothing about John's past, including his reasons and motives and the effort itself, is any different in the two worlds to explain the difference in outcome.

But it does not follow on the present account that because any particular effort made in the course of a self-forming choice situation might fail to attain its goal that "the explanatory luck objection is still with us." The explanatory luck objection says that "the agent's choosing one thing rather than another is just a matter of luck" because "there is no explanation for why one choice was made rather than another in terms of the total prior character, motives, and purposes of the agent" (Mele 1998, p. 134). And this is not true of the present view. On this view, if any free choice is made at a certain time in the course of a deliberation (say to steal, in John's case) it would be because the agent succeeded in an effort to make that choice voluntarily, intentionally, and for the reasons inclining the agent to that choice at that time. And if a different free choice had been made by the agent (say, not to steal) at a different time, it would have been because, at that different time in the course of the deliberation, the agent succeeded in an effort to make that other choice voluntary, intentionally, and for different reasons inclining the agent toward that other choice at that different time.

The key point here is that the role of indeterminism in self-forming choices, which has its source in the conflict in the agent's will, is to make it merely *probable*, and not certain, that *particular* efforts made to resolve conflicts in the will succeed in attaining their goals, without eliminating the possibility of any such particular effort doing so. To say the outcomes are undetermined in such contexts is to say that the outcomes are not certain, as they would be if they were determined. But this does not imply the outcomes are merely matters of luck or chance. If they occur, they would have been caused by the agent in accordance with the agent's will, though the causation would be *probabilistic*, not deterministic (P194).

(P196) Putting the matter in another way, what the indeterminism does is to *diminish* the (one-way) *teleological guidance control* (TGC) agents have over *particular* choices they might make to resolve conflicts in their wills. But in doing so, the indeterminism makes possible to agents a more than one-way, or *plural voluntary control* (PVC), the power to make either one of different choices in the course of a deliberation, voluntarily, intentionally, and rationally, whichever choice they should make. And such PVC at certain points in their lives is what agents need to have free will in a sense that requires ultimate responsibility. Moreover, while the indeterminism may diminish teleological guidance control over the outcome of particular efforts, it need not eliminate such control altogether in deliberations concerning self-forming choices. For when agents exercise PVC, they do so by *successfully* exercising teleological guidance control over one or another of their efforts.

(P197) There are thus causal influences on the outcomes of particular efforts, on the view defended here, causal influences coming from the *conflicting motives in the wills of agents*. But these causal influences are not determining regarding the success or failure of particular efforts (probability of 1) nor necessarily merely random or equiprobable (.5 for success or failure of the efforts). They may at times make success or failure of the resulting efforts uneven to varying degrees (e.g., 70 percent for success, 30 percent for failure) and that may causally influence whether the effort succeeds or fails in bringing about a choice in particular cases. Moreover, there is another interesting way in which *failure* of an effort may causally influence the probabilities of success or failure of subsequent efforts. Failure may make the agent realize that the motives for the competing choice, which are the source of the failure, should be given more attention, thus influencing the agent's subsequent reasoning and the probabilities of success or failure of subsequent efforts for one choice or the other. But while these causal motives in the will of the agent can thus influence the agent's reasoning and the outcomes of particular efforts, they do not *determine* those outcomes, which is important for the presence of PVC in libertarian free choices. For it shows that the possible failure of *particular* efforts is not the end of the story of free will on this account, but only a part of the story. Thus, the takeaway of this objection of Haji's is this: limiting the probabilities of success of agents' (one-way) teleological guidance control over some of their mental processes (efforts of will) is necessary at some points in their mental lives if they are to have (more-than-one-way or) plural voluntary control over some of their choices, decisions, and other mental acts.

Putting the matter in yet another way, on this view *failure of an effort does not mean that which choice is made is out of the agent's control*. Failure of an effort just means that which choice is made *has not been decided yet*. The agent needs to think further about it. And if and when it is decided, and whichever way it is decided, *it will be the agent who decides it* by *succeeding* in an effort to decide it in that way rather any other way. This in fact is what is meant by PVC. And such control is consistent with some efforts to choose failing to succeed.

The failure of these efforts has its source in the competing motives in the wills of agents that are sending a signal: think more about this before you commit to one thing or another. In the case of Haji's imagined agent whose effort to decide in terms of these inclining reasons *fails*, this agent will *not* thereby make a conflicting choice at that time. Rather, no choice will be made at that time. Failure will be a signal to this agent to reconsider his or her motive, which may lead to a reassessment of the inclining reasons and to a later effort to make a conflicting choice or a later effort to make the original choice, either of which may succeed later. If none succeed, the agent may terminate deliberation without any choice being made and may conclude that it would not necessarily have been a good outcome if his or her *initial* effort had succeeded since that wouldn't have been the best choice. In any of these cases the agent will have PVC over any *reassessment of the inclining reasons* or *later efforts to make a conflicting choice* or to make *the original choice* or *to terminate the deliberation without settling the matter at this time*. For any of these outcomes will have been brought about by the agent voluntarily, intentionally, and for reasons the agent then and there endorses. (We will also see later in Chapter 7, sections 7.14–7.15, that assessments and reassessments of reasons in these and other contexts can be further examples of self-forming actions.)[27]

We may put this response to Haji in the following way, which brings out the role of indeterminism in libertarian free will as conceived here in an enlightening way:

> (Addendum to P197) To have *freedom of will*, over and above mere freedom of action, one must at times in life successfully exercise PVC over some of one's own choices or other actions (SFAs), where every successful exercise of such PVC is a successful exercise of *teleological guidance control* (TGC) over a choice or action *that might have failed, but did not in fact fail*. The possible failure of such an exercise of TGC is what makes PVC and hence freedom of will *possible*, and the success of such an exercise of TGC, despite the possibility of failure, is what makes PVC and hence freedom of will *actual*.[28]

5.12. Contrastive Explanations

A further set of commonly made objections against views of free will requiring indeterminism that are closely related to the explanatory luck objection and to replay objections are objections concerning "contrastive explanations." A contrastive explanation is an explanation for why one thing occurred *rather than* another. In the case of free choices, it would be an explanation in terms of an agent's prior character, reasons, or motives for why the agent made one choice rather than another.

The objections in this case take the following form: if a self-forming choice (e.g., between A and B) is undetermined up to the moment when it is made, it may be argued that there could be no adequate contrastive explanation for why the choice was made rather than the alternative choice. For the fact that the choice was undetermined would mean that either choice (A or B) might

THE INTELLIGIBILITY QUESTION (PART II) 109

have occurred, given the totality of the agent's traits of character, motives, and reasoning preceding the moment of choice. There thus could not be an explanation for why one choice was made rather than the other at that moment in terms of the totality of the agent's character, motives, and reasoning prior to choice.

(P198) The first thing to be said in response to this familiar argument is similar to the first thing said in response to the explanatory luck objection and to rollback objections: in the case of self-forming choices as understood here, it is not true to say, as the objection does, that either choice (A or B) might have occurred at a time, "given the totality of the agent's traits of character, motives, and reasoning preceding the moment of choice." All that follows from the fact that a self-forming choice (e.g., the choice A) is *undetermined* at a given time is that it might be made at that time or might fail to be made at that time. It does *not* follow, if the choice (A) fails to be made at that time, that an opposing choice—(B)—would be made *at that same time*, given exactly the same reasoning that led to the choice A.

But those who make this objection concerning contrastive explanation to views of free will requiring indeterminism usually have a further assumption in mind that also needs to be addressed. They often assume as well that for an explanation of a free choice to be adequately contrastive in the sense they require, the following would have to be the case: if making the choice that was made rather than any alternative was the rational or reasonable thing to do, given the totality of the agent's reasons or motives, then making any alternative choice during that same deliberation, given the totality of the agent's reasons or motives, would *not* have been rational or reasonable. If making an alternative choice during this deliberation might also have been a rational or reasonable thing to do, we would not have an adequate contrastive explanation, in the sense these critics would require, for why one choice was made *rather than* the other in terms of the agent's reasons and motives.

(P199) But if this is what contrastive explanations would require, then there is an instructive reason why there could not be contrastive explanations in the sense these critics require of SFAs. For it is an essential feature of self-forming choices that no *such* strong contrastive explanations could be given for them. This is the case because in addition to being undetermined, self-forming choices must satisfy *plurality conditions* for free choice: the power to make them and the power to do otherwise (e.g., to make some alternative choice) *either way*, voluntarily, intentionally, *and rationally*. And this rules out the requirement that any other choice that might have been made in the course of a deliberation, other than the choice actually made, would have been unreasonable or irrational.

(P200) Moreover, this feature is not a defect of self-forming actions, according to the account given, but rather it is a consequence of their power. For it is precisely because agents have the power to make such choices and the power to do otherwise, voluntarily, intentionally, *and rationally* either way, that makes it possible for such choices to be *will-setting* rather than *will-settled*. And the power to make will-setting choices at some points in our lives is what makes it possible for us to be makers or creators to some degree of our own wills rather than to be always acting from wills already formed.[29]

(P201) It is also important to emphasize, however, that while agents who make such will-setting or self-forming choices may not have conclusive or decisive reasons for making the choice that is made rather than any other, such agents do nonetheless have reasons for choosing that are "good enough" to render the choices they do make reasonable and rational ones, given their total reason sets when they choose. Some formal decision theorists speak in this connection of *satisficing reasons*—reasons that are good enough to justify a choice or action even though they are not sufficient to render any possible alternative choice or action that might have been made in the course of this deliberation unreasonable or irrational. Reasons for will-setting or self-forming choices are satisficing reasons in this decision-theoretic sense.

(P202) Moreover, the fact that the reasons for self-forming choices are satisficing in this sense is related to something significant about free will spelled out in P183. It is related to the fact that *every undetermined self-forming choice is the initiation of a novel pathway into the future, whose justification lies partly in that future and is not fully explained by the past*. In making such a choice it is appropriate to say, "I am opting for this pathway.

It is not *required* by my past reasons but is consistent with my past reasons and is one branching pathway my life may now meaningfully take."

This "narrative" conception of self-formation, as we might call it, is nicely captured in an important recent book by John Doris, *Talking to Ourselves: Reflections on Selfhood, Agency, and Responsibility* (2015). In a section of this book in which Doris talks about my views of agency and responsibility, he notes (p. 162) that in my defense of libertarian free will, I "develop the intriguing suggestion that ambivalence" about what one's true values are "and its resolution in action" is not contrary to responsible agency, but is essential to responsible agency. It is so, at least at some points in our lives, when we are torn between conflicting values.

(P203) At such times, Doris says, when on my view, as he correctly describes it, we are engaged in self-formation, it is possible that more than one path into the future could represent our "true values," and it would be "up to us" which path we will take. We decide then and there which of our *possible* true values our actions will express. If we were never ambivalent in this way—ambi-valent as I have sometimes put it—we could not be self-creating beings, since our choices and actions would always be expressing what we *already* were, the formed will we already had.

At this point in his book where Doris references these views of mine on conflicting values and ambivalence, he also discusses the example of Huckleberry Finn—an example that has played such a prominent role in contemporary philosophical writings on agency and ethics. On one telling of the Huck story, Doris says, "Huck held values favoring *both* the conventional course of action," that he should turn his friend and companion Jim, a black man who had escaped from slave owners, over to the authorities and, on the other hand, "the course [Huck] actually followed," of not turning Jim over. In sum, Doris says, "Huck's values *conflicted* . . . he suffered a kind of *ambivalence*" (2015, p. 161).

(P204) That, I believe, is how Mark Twain himself tells the story. Huck is growing and developing as a self or agent. In deciding not to turn Jim in, Huck is not merely *expressing* what sort of a self he already is; he is also *deciding* what sort of a self he is going to be, by deciding from among the conflicting values he has which ones he will follow. He is thereby not merely engaged in self-*expression*, but in self-*formation*, of the kind I believe *freedom of will* and not mere *freedom of action* sometimes requires. Such conflicts in the will and their resolution or lack thereof (as my wife, a writer, continually reminded me) are the stuff of most great literature and drama, Huckleberry Finn, Madame Bovary, Hamlet, Anna Karenina, you name it.

6

The Libertarian Spectrum (Part I)

Deliberative or Non-centered Views

6.1. Deliberative Libertarian Views

In an important critical survey of contemporary libertarian views (*Libertarian Accounts of Free Will*, 2003), Randolph Clarke makes a useful distinction between what he calls "centered" libertarian views and "deliberative" or "non-centered" libertarian views. Centered views place the indeterminism in the making of choices themselves that conclude deliberations. Deliberative or non-centered views place the indeterminism earlier in the deliberation process, at various times prior to decision.

Clarke criticizes such deliberative or non-centered views, arguing that, while they may provide some of what is needed for an adequate libertarian account of free will, they fall short of providing all that is needed. I agree with such criticisms and have made similar objections myself in earlier works. In *The Significance of Free Will*, for example, I made deliberative or non-centered views a *part* of the overall account of libertarian free will developed there. But I also insisted that such deliberative or non-centered views could only be a part of an adequate libertarian view (pp. 162ff). To get the full picture, one would also have to add centered accounts of "self-forming" or "will-setting" choices or actions of the kinds terminating deliberations developed in that work (and further developed with modifications in this book).

In this chapter, I first explain in more detail how deliberative views might play a role in the overall account of libertarian free will developed here, and second, why I believe they can only be a part of such an account. In doing so, I also consider, third, how the role of self-forming-actions developed thus far may be expanded beyond their crucial "centered" role in terminating deliberations. Fourth, and finally, I explore important connections, suggested by these topics, between libertarian free will, on the one hand, and human evolution and creative problem-solving, on the other. Reflecting on these topics allows us to expand further the account of free will presented thus far.

6.2. Clarke on Deliberative Libertarian Views: Dennett, Mele

As a starting point, it will be useful to consider Clarke's criticisms of some deliberative libertarian views. He focuses on three well-known deliberative accounts suggested respectively by Daniel Dennett (1978), Alfred Mele (1995), and Laura Ekstrom (2000). I will focus on his criticisms of the deliberative views suggested by Dennett and Mele and will consider Ekstrom's view in the next chapter, where other libertarian views are considered. Ekstrom distances her view somewhat from the deliberative views suggested by Dennett and Mele in ways that will be discussed.

In a 1978 paper entitled "On Giving Libertarians What They Say They Want," Dennett approvingly quotes the French poet Paul Valéry's assertion that the essence of invention is intelligent selection from among chance-generated candidates. Dennett goes on to suggest a model of decision-making based on this "Valerian" idea (p. 294). He asks us to imagine this account:

> When . . . faced with an important decision, a consideration-generator whose output is to some degree undetermined produces a series of considerations, some of which may . . . be immediately rejected as irrelevant by the agent (consciously or unconsciously). Those considerations that are selected as having more than negligible bearing on the decision then figure in a reasoning process, and if the agent is in the main reasonable, those considerations ultimately serve as predictors and explicators of the agent's final decision. (p. 295)

On such a view, Dennett says, "an intelligent assessment and selection procedure determines which microscopic indeterminacies get amplified . . . into important macroscopic determiners of choice and ultimate behavior" (p. 295). He adds significantly that libertarians should *not* want indeterminism to occur when the final decision was made "after all rational deliberation had terminated." Indeterminism occurring in such a manner, he adds, would make the final choice a mere matter of chance. Only the coming-to-mind of various considerations earlier in the deliberation, he argues, should be required to be causally undetermined. It should be allowed that the selection and assessment of these considerations and the subsequent decision that results be causally determined by the prior deliberation process (p. 295).

Dennett suggests that such a model might serve the needs of libertarians by allowing a role for indeterminism. But he is skeptical it would give them everything they want. Moreover, as a compatibilist, Dennett is also deeply skeptical, as we have seen, about whether "all that libertarians want" is really "worth wanting" (and he is also of course skeptical about whether all that libertarians want is attainable). He thinks one can get all the freedom worth wanting without the need for indeterminism at all.

Mele (1995) suggests a similar deliberative view that he calls "modest libertarianism." Like Dennett, Mele requires indeterminism in this modest view only earlier in the deliberative process (p. 214). The indeterminism would be involved in the coming to mind of certain beliefs, "whose coming to mind is not something [the agent] would control even if determinism were true" (p. 216). The indeterminism might also be involved in the coming-to-mind of various desires, and on which beliefs or desires an agent may attend to at a given time; and it might continue up to the point where an evaluative judgment is formed about which choice should be favored (p. 217). But like Dennett, Mele also argues that indeterminism coming *after* such an evaluative judgment would be undesirable. He recommends a "compatibilist" account of the relation between the making of an evaluative judgment and the subsequent choice, an account that would allow (though not require) deterministic causation of the subsequent choice.

Like Dennett, Mele does not claim that such a "modest" libertarianism would give libertarians all they want. But, unlike Dennett, Mele is agnostic about whether libertarianism or compatibilism is true. His goal, he says, is to try to formulate the best account of each view that one can. And in later writings (notably his *Free Will and Luck*, 2006) he suggests (also without endorsing) other stronger libertarian views, some of which would allow indeterminism up to the moment of choice. The stronger of these other suggested libertarian views of Mele's will also be assessed in the next chapter, where further recent alternative libertarian views are examined.

As noted, Clarke argues that these deliberative views fall short of what libertarians want and need for free will. What libertarians need, he argues, is that in some cases of "acting freely, agents make a difference, by exercising active control, to how things go" (2003, p. 64). By contrast, "on Dennett and Mele's [deliberative] views" Clarke says (p. 63), "it is allowed that once the agent has made an evaluative judgment" favoring one decision rather than another, the agent "is not able to do otherwise than make the decision" favored by that evaluative judgment if the final choice is to be a rational one.

Yet it is also assumed on these views, Clarke adds, that the evaluative judgments themselves may be caused or brought about by the undetermined comings-to-mind of various considerations, which undetermined comings-to-mind are not under the agent's active control. The agents may be said to exercise a kind of active control in the forming of the evaluative judgments. But the agents must form the evaluative judgments that are favored by the considerations brought about by the prior undetermined comings-to-mind if the evaluative judgments are to be rationally or reasonably formed. The agents are also able to exercise a kind of active control over the decisions subsequently made. But this would also be merely a compatibilist kind of control, Clarke argues, since the agents must decide in accordance with the evaluative judgments previously formed and cannot rationally or reasonably decide otherwise.

6.3. The Libertarian Dilemma and Deliberative Responses

I agree with these criticisms of such deliberative views, as indicated. But what I now want to do is expand on these criticisms and their implications in terms of the account of free will developed thus far in Chapters 1–5. Doing so will allow me to explain how deliberative views might play a role in an overall account of libertarian free will, but also why I believe they can only be a part of such an account.

> (P205) To begin, it will be helpful to return to Borges's image of the garden of forking paths. It seems that at times in life there are branching paths into the future either of which may be taken, and it is "up to us" which of these paths will be taken. We feel we are able at such times to "set" our wills in one way or another by choosing or deciding which of these possible paths we will take. Moreover, in saying it is "up to us" which path is chosen at such times, we clearly do not intend that only one of the paths may be chosen by us voluntarily, intentionally, and rationally and the other only involuntarily (e.g., as the result of coercion) or unintentionally (e.g., by

accident or mistake) or irrationally (without reasons favoring that choice over the alternative).

(P206) In other words, if the path chosen at such times is to be an expression of our freedom of will, it must be the case that *whichever* path is chosen would be chosen *in accordance with our wills* and *not against our wills*. This is an important consideration that gives point to the expression free *will*.

(P207) This consideration also accounts for how indeterminism gets into the picture. Indeterminism is not wanted by libertarians for its own sake. What is wanted if we are to be ultimately responsible for forming or shaping our own wills and the kinds of persons we become is rather what P205–206 suggest: the power at some points in our lives to choose different paths into the future and to be able to do so in accordance with our wills (i.e., voluntarily, intentionally, and rationally), whichever path is chosen (P54). Such a plural power was earlier called "plural voluntary control" (P26); and exercising such a power seems to require indeterminism in some manner. For if the choice made at such times was determined, it would not have been causally possible to have made an alternative choice, and a fortiori, not causally possible to have made an alternative choice voluntarily, intentionally, and rationally.

Yet it is also difficult to see how it might be that which choice is made on such occasions could be *undetermined*. For we normally do not have such plural voluntary, intentional, and rational control over the occurrence or non-occurrence of events whose occurrence or non-occurrence is undetermined. Imagine, for example, that whether the ball in a spinning roulette wheel lands in a red slot or a black slot is genuinely undetermined. Suppose, in addition, that a certain agent should have a special (psychokinetic) power to voluntarily and intentionally *make* the ball land in a red slot rather than a black slot, or vice versa; and suppose the agent should exercise this power to make it land in a red or black slot on a certain occasion for a lucrative payoff. Then, on that occasion, the ball's landing on a red slot rather than a black one or vice versa would no longer *be* an *undetermined* event.

It is not difficult to see from such examples (which could be multiplied) why it is so commonly believed that no choices or other actions *could* be *both* undetermined *and* such that their occurring one way rather than another was under the voluntary, intentional, and rational control of an agent, whichever way they should occur. If their occurring one way rather than another is undetermined, it may easily seem to be a matter of chance or luck which way they occur. Such is a version of the "libertarian dilemma" introduced at the beginning of Chapter 4 that has inspired so many familiar objections to libertarian views through the centuries. It also throws light on the motivations for deliberative or non-centered libertarian views.

(P208) *Deliberative libertarian views represent a particular kind of libertarian response to this familiar dilemma.* The deliberative response is to separate the indeterminism from the final choice in the process of deliberation: that is, require the indeterminism only at earlier stages in deliberation, for example, in the undetermined comings-to-mind of various considerations over which the agent lacks voluntary control. These undetermined comings-to-mind would then give rise to evaluative judgments favoring one choice or another and the agent would only *then* exercise active and voluntary control in bringing about the choice favored by the evaluative judgment thus formed.[1] But this active and voluntary control in making the final choices is allowed to be a compatibilist kind of control. For it would not *require* indeterminism; and if indeterminism should be involved at this final stage, these deliberative theorists, like Dennett, insist, it would diminish rather than enhance the agent's voluntary control over which choice was made.

6.4. Squaring the Circle

(P209) Note that, on such deliberative views, at no stage of the deliberative process is it required that the very same events (whether final choices or formations of evaluative judgments) be *both* undetermined *and* such that their occurring one way rather than another is under the voluntary, intentional, and rational control of agents, whichever way they should occur. To require this would be to reinstate the libertarian dilemma that such deliberative views are meant to avoid.

But how, it might be asked, *could* a free choice or other action be *both* undetermined *and* also such that its occurring in one way *rather than* another would be under the voluntary, intentional, and rational control of an

THE LIBERTARIAN SPECTRUM (PART I)   119

agent, whichever way it should occur? An answer to this question was given in preceding chapters. It will be helpful to review some key features of this answer that throw light on the questions of how deliberative theories might play a role in the theory developed here without being the whole story.

The first thing to note about this answer of earlier chapters is that we do not have to suppose that indeterminism is involved in all actions done "of our own free will." Indeterminism need be involved only in those choices or acts by which we make ourselves into the kinds of persons we are with the wills we have, namely, the "will-setting" or "self-forming actions" of earlier pieces (P27–29, P75–76). We considered John, for example, desiring to steal money he sorely needs from a poor box and yet being conflicted about stealing the money for moral reasons. We imagined that in the course of his deliberating about this, various thoughts, experiences, and memories come to mind, various desires, possibilities, and consequences are assessed, so that his considered reasons incline him to make one choice rather than an alternative choice (P77).

(P210) Note that there are similarities here to the early stages of deliberation that are also required by deliberative theories. But there are also differences. For one thing, it is not required in the account given here of self-forming choices that indeterminism be involved in these earlier stages of deliberation, in the comings-to-mind of various considerations. Indeterminism *might* also be involved there, so this aspect of deliberative theories could be accommodated in this account of self-forming choices, as we shall see. But indeterminism is not required in these earlier stages of deliberation. For the pivotal indeterminism in the account of self-forming choices comes in other places and in a different way.

What is crucial if John's choice is to be a self-forming one is that the reasons motivating the choice to steal the money that emerge from these initial stages of deliberation merely *incline* John to make that choice at this time. If a choice is to be made in accord with these inclining reasons, effort would have to be made or willpower exerted to overcome the still-existing resistance in his will coming from his motives to make the contrary choice (P86–87). These resistant motives are the causal source of the indeterminism in the effort to make the choice to which the agent is then inclined, making it uncertain this effort will succeed (P76, P79–P80). If the effort should fail, due to this indeterminism, it does not follow that an alternative choice would

120   THE COMPLEX TAPESTRY OF FREE WILL

be made instead at that same time (P82–P84). The deliberation would either continue until a potential reassessment of the motivating reasons that inclined to one choice or the other led to another later effort to make the choice to steal, or a potential reassessment led to a later effort to make the choice not to steal. Or the deliberation might terminate without any decision being made (P84–P85).

(P211) The key point to notice about this account for present purposes is the following: if *either* effort were to *succeed* in the course of such a deliberation, despite the indeterminism involved in it, the agent would have brought about the resulting choice (to steal or not to steal) and would have done so voluntarily and intentionally and for the reasons that inclined the agent toward that choice at the time (P86). Moreover, this would be the case even though the choice's occurring at that time rather than not *would have been undetermined*, due to the indeterminism ingredient in the effort or exertion that made its success at that moment uncertain. And this would be true of the resulting choice if either effort were to succeed and hence if either choice were to be made at any point in the course of the deliberation.

An answer is thus provided to the question at the beginning of this section: *How could a free choice or other action be both undetermined and such that its occurring one way rather than another would be under the voluntary, intentional, and rational control of an agent, whichever way it should occur?*

(P212) The answer lies in locating the source of the indeterminism *in the will of the agent*, in a conflict in the agent's will (P78, P82). It further involves thinking of the indeterminism, whose source is in the agent's conflicted will, not as a cause acting on its own, but as an ingredient in larger goal-directed or teleologically guided activities of the agent (the efforts or exertions of willpower) in which the indeterminism functions as a hindering or interfering element in the attainment of their goals (P88).

(P213) Putting these two things together yields the following result: if either of these teleologically guided activities should succeed in attaining its goal at some time in the course of the deliberation, the resulting choice would have been brought about voluntarily, intentionally, and rationally by the agent rather than any alternative at that time. Yet it would also have been the case that the choice's coming about at that time would have been *undetermined* due to the indeterminism in the effort that had made its success uncertain (P100–P101, P176).

(P214) Thus, in the context of such self-forming choices, indeterminism, by being a hindrance to the realization of some of our purposes, opens up the genuine possibility of pursuing other purposes, of choosing or doing otherwise *in accordance with our wills* either way, rather than against our wills (P122); and this is what libertarians need at some points in the lives of agents if the agents are to be ultimately responsible to some degree for forming their own wills in one way or another (P122–P123).

Why must it be the case, if agents are to be ultimately responsible for forming their own will, that at some points in their lives they have the power to choose different possible paths their lives may take and to do so in accordance with their will, whichever path is chosen? A detailed answer to this question was given in Chapter 2 (P17–P32) by appeal to the following notions: (i) plurality conditions for free will, (ii) the distinction between will-setting and will-settled actions, (iii) the need for something more than merely indeterminism plus alternative possibilities to account for libertarian free will, (iv) Austin-style examples, (v) a distinction between sufficient *causes* and sufficient *motives* for action, and finally, (vi) by appeal to what was called the "dual regress of free will" (P30–P32).

I will not repeat the details of these arguments here. But it is worth repeating the conclusion drawn from them which was summed up in P33: often we act from a will already formed, but it is "our *own* free will" by virtue of the fact that we willingly formed it by other choices or actions in the past (self-forming actions) for which we *could* have *willingly* done otherwise. If such choices or actions did not occur at some points in the course of our lives, there is nothing we could have ever *willingly* done differently in our entire lifetimes to make our wills different than they are.

6.5. Kinds of Agential Control and Power

We have also seen in previous chapters that making sense of an incompatibilist or libertarian free will in this way requires distinguishing different *kinds of freedom* (P31), different *dimensions of responsibility* (P65–P69), and different notions of *will* (P41–P46). We may now add the following in the light of the immediately preceding pieces and earlier ones:

(P215) To make sense of how indeterminism may be compatible with free will, it is also necessary to distinguish different *kinds of (agential) control or power*. Indeterminism *does* rule out what I have elsewhere called (1) *antecedent determining control*, the *power* to *determine* which of a set of outcomes (e.g., choices) will occur *before* it occurs. But indeterminism does *not* thereby rule out a kind of (2) *direct control* or *power* to determine in self-forming choice situations which of a set of outcomes (such as one or another competing choice) occurs, *when* or at the time it occurs. Indeterminism makes it uncertain whether any particular exercise of this direct power will succeed at a given time. But indeterminism does not rule out the possibility of a successful exercise of this power at some time in the course of a deliberation to bring about one choice rather than another at that time. We have also seen that indeterminism rules out (3) a *micro-control* (over individual neurons) (P114–P115). But indeterminism does not thereby rule out (4) a *macro-control* over complex goal-directed cognitive processes involving many neurons, such as the efforts or exercises of willpower involved in self-forming choices (P115–P116).

(P216) We have also seen that indeterminism *diminishes* a kind of (5) *teleological guidance control* (TGC) over particular goal-directed cognitive processes such as these efforts, making it uncertain they will attain their goals (P101–P102, P118). But, by doing this, in the manner spelled out in P174–P176, indeterminism makes possible (6) a *plural voluntary control* (PVC): the power at some points in our lives to choose from among different possible paths our lives may take and to be able to do so in accordance with our wills, whichever path is chosen (P26, P54). By diminishing a "one-way" voluntary control (TGC) over certain goal-directed cognitive processes, indeterminism thereby makes possible a "plural" voluntary control (PVC) over the outcomes of these cognitive processes—an enhanced control of the kind that libertarians believe is necessary at some points in our lives, if we are to be ultimately responsible for forming our own wills.

6.6. Expanding Self-Forming Actions (Part I): Deliberative Theories Revisited

Return now in the light of all this to deliberative libertarian theories. Three stages were distinguished in such theories. In the first stage—the indeterministic comings-to-mind—there is indeterminism, but no agential control. In the third stage—the making of the final choice—there is agential control, but indeterminism is not required and would merely diminish agential control if it did occur, since the final choice must be made in accordance with the prior formed evaluative judgment if the final choice is to be rational.

The most interesting stage of these deliberative views, however, and the one I want to focus on for present purposes, is the second stage—the formation of evaluative judgments concerning *which* choice should be made in the final third stage. Agential control of a sort is assumed in this second stage as well. For there must be reasoning on the part of the agent to assess which evaluative judgments should be formed, given the considerations that have indeterministically come to mind in the first stage. But it would seem to suffice on these deliberative theories, as Clarke points out, that the agential control in this second stage was also a compatibilist kind of control. For the agent must form the evaluative judgment implied by the prior comings-to-mind and cannot do otherwise if the judgments are to be rationally formed.

But perhaps not. It is possible to imagine a different conceivable scenario for this second stage of the deliberative process in deliberative views.

(P217) Suppose the considerations that indeterministically come to mind in the first stage, on such deliberative views, do not definitively "settle" which evaluative judgment should be formed. In other words, these considerations leave the agent with a conflicted will. The reasons that emerge from the comings-to-mind in the first stage, we may imagine, may incline the agent to form one of these evaluative judgments rather than another, but they only *incline*. They are not decisive and do not definitively resolve the conflict in the agent's will. If an evaluative judgment is thus to be made in accord with these inclining reasons, effort would then have to be made or willpower exerted to overcome the still-existing resistance in the agent's will coming from the motives to make a contrary evaluative judgment.

But if this should be the case, it would follow that

(P218) If either competing evaluative judgment was formed in such manner in this second stage of the deliberative process in order to resolve the resulting conflict in the agent's will, the formation of that evaluative judgment would be a *self-forming action* of the kind described in previous chapters. For if either competing evaluative judgment was formed in such a manner, that judgment so formed would have resolved a conflict in the will of the agent by the agent's overcoming resistance in the will coming from the motives to make a contrary evaluative judgment.

(P219) If this were the case, it would not then matter if the final choice made in the third stage of the deliberation, in accord with this evaluative judgment, could not have been otherwise made, if it was to be a reasonable choice. Nor would it even matter if the final choice was determined by this prior formed evaluative judgment. For the crucial indeterminism would have come earlier in the deliberation, in the agent's successfully *forming* this evaluative judgment by overcoming resistance in the will to doing so.

(P220) What we see here is that self-forming actions need not occur only as the final choices in deliberation. Self-forming actions may also occur at various stages earlier in the deliberation, as in this case of forming evaluative judgments (and in other ways to be discussed in the following sections). In other words, self-forming actions may be centered or noncentered. *It is not where self-forming actions occur in the practical lives of agents* that matters for free *will, but how they occur.* Wherever they occur, self-forming actions must resolve conflicts in the will of agents; and the agents must be able to resolve these conflicts in accordance with their will, whichever way they are resolved.

For further insight into why it is important that agents be able to resolve conflicts in their will and to do so in accordance with their will, whichever way they are resolved, it is instructive to return once again to deliberative theories.

(P221) Suppose the indeterministic comings-to-mind in the first stage of deliberation in these deliberative theories did *not* leave the agent with a conflicted will, as we have just imagined. Suppose instead that these comings-to-mind definitively "settled" which evaluative judgment should be rationally formed. The agent would then not be able to willingly (voluntarily *and rationally*) form any other evaluative judgment at that point. If this were the case, the formation of an evaluative judgment in such circumstances would then have been what was earlier called a "will-settled" action, rather than a "will-setting" or "self-forming" action (P27–P29). The agents might have done otherwise by chance or accident or mistake, unintentionally or involuntarily (as in the case of Austin-style examples), but they could not have willingly (voluntarily and rationally) done otherwise.

(P222) In such cases, where agents' wills are already settled on doing what they might do, in order to establish that the agents are ultimately responsible in the sense of UR for the resulting actions, one must establish that the agents are responsible *for their wills being settled the way they are* by virtue of some earlier voluntary actions that were not also will-settled when they occurred, but rather "will-setting" (P30–P32). If all actions in our lifetimes were already will-settled when we performed them and none were will-setting, then our wills being set the way they are at any time would never have been something in our power to have *willingly* made otherwise.

A general conclusion of some significance that may be drawn from this is thus the following:

(P223) We become *self-forming* beings with wills that are to some degree of our own *making* by resolving conflicts in our wills through such will-setting actions that are under our plural voluntary *control*, and *not by merely allowing such conflicts to be settled by chance*—for example, by flipping coins or spinning roulette wheels *or* by the outcomes of undetermined comings-to-mind over which we lack voluntary control. We actively *form* our wills in one way rather than another, not letting the formation of our wills merely "happen" one way or another outside of our control.

In support of these claims of P221–P223, it is worth citing once again John Doris's comments on my views about such will-setting or self-forming actions quoted in P169: he says there that, on my view of such actions, "it is possible that more than one path into the future could represent our 'true values,' and it would be 'up to us' which path we will take. We decide then and there which of our *possible* true values our actions will express. If we were never ambivalent in this way, we would not be beings who formed their own wills, since our choices and actions would always be expressing *the formed wills we already had*."

6.7. Expanding Self-Forming Actions (Part II): The Significance of Free Will

By thus reflecting on deliberative theories, we see that self-forming actions need not occur only as the final choices in deliberation. They may also occur earlier in deliberation in the formation of evaluative judgments; and they may occur in other ways as well. In *The Significance of Free Will*, I mentioned a variety of other ways in which self-forming actions may play a role in the practical lives of agents in addition to their "centered" roles in terminating deliberations.

One of these other ways was noted earlier here in Chapter 5, section 5.5: "Agents may sometimes be conflicted about whether even to begin to deliberate about a difficult choice they have an aversion to thinking about." In such a case, a self-forming action may also be required to resolve a conflict in the will one way or the other (to decide now or put off a decision for a future time); and effort or willpower may be required to overcome resistance in the will either way such a conflict is resolved.

Another context in which self-forming actions play a role in *The Significance of Free Will* involves what I call there "efforts sustaining purposes" (1996, pp. 152–67): our efforts of will, it was said, need not only be directed at forming new intentions or purposes by making choices. Exertions of effort or willpower may also be aimed at sustaining or carrying out intentions or purposes already formed in the presence of obstacles to their realization (p. 152).

> (P224) Free will was defined in *The Significance of Free Will* (1996, p. 4) as it has been defined here earlier in P2, as the power of agents to be the ultimate creators *and sustainers* of their own ends or purposes. And it was noted there that, while we create ends or purposes through choices or decisions, we may also *sustain* purposes by making efforts to carry out these choices or decisions in the face of impediments and countervailing inclinations. When these impediments are coming from the agents' own will and they allow for countervailing efforts, then whether agents succeed or fail to sustain purposes when faced with countervailing inclinations can be further examples of self-forming actions (1996, pp. 152–54).

This category of efforts sustaining purposes would include efforts involved in activities—for example, in arts, crafts, work, sports, games, meditation, or rational inquiry—requiring efforts to counteract inclinations to laziness or lack of focus as well as efforts to carry out tasks or projects for which one has aversions, fears, or dislike. This category would also include heroic and courageous acts that require overcoming fears and anxieties (1996, p. 153). Not all such efforts sustaining purposes would amount to self-forming actions. The conflicting desires may not always be resistible due to compulsion or other causes. Or the agents may not will themselves to fail when they fail, but rather fail because of impediments that are unwilled and beyond their control (p. 154).

(P225) For these reasons, it is tempting to argue that all failures to sustain purposes must be unwilled and beyond our control in this manner, and that *willed* failure to sustain purposes is not possible. Such arguments are akin to traditional arguments going back to the ancient Greeks that akrasia, or weakness of will, is always a matter of lack of control or power so that one can never *freely* and *voluntarily* act against one's better moral and prudential judgments (the very terms "akrasia" and "weakness of will" suggest as much). According to such arguments, when we fail to act in accord with our better moral or prudential judgments, it must be because we are "overcome" by contrary desires. I believe these traditional arguments oversimplify our practical lives, and I have argued against them in other writings, including in *The Significance of Free Will* (1996, pp. 132–33, 154–57).

(P226) It is one thing to say that immoral or imprudent actions may often be due to lack of control or being overcome by contrary desires; it is quite another to say that agents can never freely and voluntarily *will* to act against their better moral or prudential judgments. Similarly, it is one thing to say that failure to sustain or carry out purposes previously formed may often be due to lack of control or to being overcome by contrary desires. But it is another to say that agents can never freely and voluntarily *will* to fail to carry out purposes in the face of obstacles and countervailing inclinations. Effort or willpower may indeed be needed to overcome resistance in our wills to acting morally or prudentially. But it may also be needed to overcome resistance in our wills to acting from self-interest or for immediate pleasures in opposition to our moral or prudential judgments.

This was the case, as we saw, for John when he was torn between stealing from the poor box for self-interested reasons, on the one hand, and his moral motives for not doing so, on the other.

(P227) Similarly, one may be torn between sustaining purposes previously formed and abandoning them for competing reasons or motives in the face of obstacles to their realization. In such cases, sustaining purposes or abandoning them for competing reasons or motives may be further examples of self-forming actions.

(P228) To be sure, what is generally called weakness of will in the presence of moral or prudential better judgment is *from one point of view* motivationally perverse and irrational. But (and here is a crucial point) in all cases of self-forming actions, agents are experiencing conflicts between *competing internal motivational points of view*. They resolve these conflicts by making one of these internal points of view prevail over the other: morality versus self-interest, prudence versus present desires, prior formed purposes versus present fears, aversions, difficulties, and other impediments to carrying them out. From one internal point of view (e.g., the moral one) it *is* irrational to act against one's better (moral) judgment. But from another internal point of view (e.g., a self-interested one) it may be rational to do so. There is moral rationality and self-interested rationality. Or, as noted earlier, persons conflicted in this way are of "two minds," though they are not thereby two separate persons.[2]

(P229) This kind of motivational ambivalence is a price to be paid for free will, as suggested in the earlier quotation from Doris. I also expressed this thought in *The Significance of Free Will* (1996, p. 155) in the following way: "Those who have free will are no longer motivationally simple creatures but are capable of either nobility or perversity. They live somewhere east of Eden, having gained the power of self-determination, but lost innocence."

(P230) Finally, several other ways are mentioned in *The Significance of Free Will* (p. 167) in which efforts and self-forming actions may be involved in practical reasoning, which can also be accommodated in the present theory. These include, for example, efforts to resolve conflicts one way or another (1) between temptations to decide immediately in terms of present inclinations, on the one hand, and not wanting to choose too hastily, on the other; or (2) between temptations to decide in terms of present inclinations, on the one hand, and the belief that one should consider more of the possible consequences of such a decision before making it, on the other hand; or efforts to resolve conflicts (3) between wanting to consider all relevant considerations and wanting to suppress some considerations one may be resistant to thinking about, or (4) between tendencies to self-deception or rationalization about the relevance of certain considerations, on the one hand, and motives to resist such tendencies to self-deception and rationalization in making a decision, on the other. Wherever effort or willpower is needed to resolve these conflicts in the will, whichever way they are resolved, their resolution one way or the other would be a self-forming action.

(P231) In summary, self-forming actions need not occur only as final choices or decisions terminating deliberations. They may play many other roles in other places of our practical lives: in initiating deliberations or in forming evaluative judgments in the course of deliberations (P213–P215), in resolving conflicts in the will arising during deliberations of the diverse kinds just listed in P230, and in the sustaining or failing to sustain intentions or purposes that may have been formed by prior deliberations (P223–P227). Yet other roles self-forming actions may play will be considered in subsequent chapters.

6.8. Practical Deliberation, Evolution, and Creative Problem-Solving

I said earlier that if indeterminism was involved in the forming of evaluative judgments or the making of final choices, as suggested here, indeterminism would not also have to be involved in the comings-to-mind of various considerations in the first stage of deliberation as proposed by these deliberative theories. But I added that indeterminism *might* be involved in these earlier stages of deliberation as well, so that this aspect of deliberative views could also play a role in the account of free will given here. If indeterminism only played a role in these earlier stages of deliberation, however, in the manner of most deliberative theories, it could not be the whole story of libertarian free will, for reasons given earlier. But it might be a part of that story.

It's worth exploring this possibility further. For, as argued in *The Significance of Free Will*, if indeterminism also occurred in the earlier stages of deliberation in the manner supposed by deliberative theories, it would suggest some significant connections between free will, on the one hand,

and creative problem-solving and natural evolution, on the other. For, as I said there,

> (P232) Practical deliberation and creative problem-solving have much in common. Both may involve trial-and-error processes requiring thought experimentation concerning possible outcomes and their consequences. The similarities suggest that if indeterminism were to play roles in practical deliberation, one of these roles might be like that of inspiration for the creative thinker. Undetermined occurrences might influence the conscious and unconscious cognitive processing of the reflective agent, suggesting new options, new consequences of the options, and new ways of viewing the consequences.

> (P233) Inspiration in creative problem-solving is not totally within the control of the reflecting agent. Yet its effects need not undermine the rationality of the process, since the agent must interpret the effects of inspiration and accept or reject them as guides to further reasoning. Undetermined influences in the conscious and unconscious cognitive processing of reflective agents might play a similar role in practical deliberation (*Significance of Free Will*, p. 160).

Some philosophers who have suggested the possibility of deliberative libertarian theories have noted such connections to creative problem-solving. As we have seen, Dennett is a prime example of someone who does this quite explicitly in referencing French poet Paul Valéry's assertion that the essence of invention is intelligent selection from among chance-generated candidates. Another thinker who has more recently developed a deliberative libertarian view, Robert Doyle (2011), an astrophysicist who has also made contributions to computer science as well as to free will debates, emphasizes the connections described here between deliberative libertarian views and creative problem-solving.[3]

A further connection between creative problem-solving, conceived as in P232–P233, and natural evolution, is also suggested in my earlier work on *The Significance of Free Will* (1996, pp. 161–62) in the following way.

> (P234) Viewed in the manner of P232–P233, practical deliberation would be conceived as a further development of the evolutionary process allowing analogues of genetic mutations to occur in the mind and then to be subject

to selection within the mental environments of deliberating agents. The result would be a qualitative change in the evolutionary process, by which ways of living and acting within a single species would be indefinitely multiplied and the importance of individuals of the species in the selection process (each with his or her own *internal* rational environment) would be immeasurably enhanced. Ways of living and acting could be tested and rejected internally without requiring actual experimentation and possible harm or death to the individual.

(P235) This may be viewed as an extension of the idea of what I have elsewhere called a "value experiment" or, in John Stuart Mill's expression, an "experiment in living." In this connection, it was said earlier in P164 that every self-forming choice is the initiation of such a value experiment, or experiment in living, whose full justification partly lies in the future and is not fully explained by the past. In making such a self-forming choice, as described in P165–P168, we say in effect, "I am opting for this pathway. It is not required by my past reasons but is consistent with my past reasons and is one branching pathway my life can now meaningfully take." What is added here in P234–P235 is that such value experimentation can take place "in the mind" as well as in action, through practical reasoning before being tried in reality, thus allowing a qualitative change in the processes of evolution by which ways of living and acting are tested and selected.

These evolutionary themes in relation to deliberative libertarian theories of free will are anticipated by a number of modern thinkers. Doyle traces them back to William James (1956), the American pragmatist, and to Henri Poincaré (1952), the great mathematician and physicist. Poincaré, Doyle says, was the first thinker following James to propose what Doyle calls a "two stage" model of decision-making (which Doyle himself defends)—a process of random or chance alternatives arising in the mind followed by rational selection of one choice or another. Later thinkers cited by Doyle who also suggested such a two-stage view include mathematician Jacques Hadamard (1945) (who also quoted the poet Paul Valéry, as did Dennett later), also Nobel Prize–winning physicist Arthur Holly Compton (1935), and philosopher of science Karl Popper, in Popper's provocative Arthur Holly Compton Memorial lecture "Of Clouds and Clocks" (1972).

The problem for indeterminists, according to Popper, was to explain "how freedom is not just chance, but rather the result of a subtle interplay between *something almost random or haphazard* and *something like a restrictive or selective control*" (1972, p. 237). But, to Popper, that is the problem of evolution and life itself. Random or chance mutations are trial balloons subjected to the selective control of the environment, and "each organism is all the time engaged in problem solving by trial and error" as it reacts to new and old problems by trials that are eliminated if unsuccessful."

Of course, this randomness or chance might not require an underlying physical indeterminism. It may be based on algorithmic random search procedures such as those created by researchers in artificial intelligence in designing intelligent machines capable of creative problem-solving.[4] But the randomness or chance would be no less effective in creative problem-solving and deliberation if the randomness had its source in amplified (and hence non-algorithmic) quantum indeterminism in the brain, as a growing number of scientists have recently argued, including Doyle himself, as well as neuroscientists Peter Ulric Tse (2013), Paul Glimcher (2005), and Michael Shadlin (2014), biologists Bjorn Brembs (2011) and Martin Heisenberg (2013), and astrophysicist David Layzer (2022), among others.[5] After all, as many of these figures note, nature is not a computer scientist writing algorithms for random search procedures in machines. If this were done by nature, they reason, it would likely be by allowing for amplified quantum processes in the brains of living organisms.

6.9. Evolutionary Themes and Free Will

I want to conclude this chapter by suggesting that these evolutionary themes have broader significance for understanding free will beyond their relevance for deliberative theories. In the earliest stages of evolution of living organisms, as Popper says, random or chance mutations are trial balloons subjected to the selective control of the environment, and "each organism" is all the time engaged in problem solving by trial and error as it reacts to new and old problems by trials that are eliminated if unsuccessful.

In support of this view, biologist Martin Heisenberg, citing his own groundbreaking research on primitive organisms in an article in *Nature* (2009), says that "evidence of randomly generated action" affording evolutionary advantages "can be found in the most primitive of unicellular organisms." (Martin Heisenberg is the son of Werner Heisenberg, one of the founding figures of quantum physics. Martin did not follow his father into physics, but instead became a distinguished biologist focusing his study on the behavior of primitive organisms. My thoughts on these matters have been influenced by correspondence with him and discussions with him at various conferences.)

Consider, Martin Heisenberg says, the way the unicellular "bacterium *Escherichia coli* moves. It has a flagellum that can rotate around its longitudinal axis in either direction: one direction drives the bacterium forward, the other causes it to tumble at random so that it ends up facing in a new direction ready for the next phase of forward motion. This 'random walk' can be modulated by sensory receptors, enabling the bacterium to find food and the right temperature" (Heisenberg 2013, pp. 98–99). Such randomizing processes, enabling the bacterium to find food and the right temperature, Heisenberg adds, have obvious evolutionary advantages for survival. Other scientists, including neuroscientist Paul Glimcher (2005), have noted further biological contexts in which randomized behavior occurring in organisms and animals has evolutionary advantages for survival, notably in making it difficult for predators to learn and predict how their prey will react when threatened.

As described in P234–P235, a higher stage of evolution is reached in humans in which a further development of the evolutionary process allowing analogues of genetic mutations to occur in the mind and then to be subject to selection within the mental environments of agents. This higher stage of evolution also allows agents to exercise a certain kind of *control* over their own behavior that was earlier called *teleological guidance control* (TGC). Agents exhibit such teleological guidance control over some of their own processes when they tend through feedback loops and error correction mechanisms to converge on a goal in the face of perturbations. Such control, as noted, is necessary for any voluntary activity and is the basis for the evolution of freedom of agency.

(P236) What I now want to suggest from the point of view of the evolution of *free will* is that a still higher stage of evolution in human beings arises when their inner rational environments reach a stage of complexity that allows them to have conflicts in their wills about what to do and how to act. This further stage of evolution of their inner rational environments allows human agents to exercise not merely a compatibilist *teleological guidance control* (TGC) over their own behavior—the ability to exercise control over their pursuits of certain goals or ends. It also allows them to exercise incompatibilist *plural voluntary control* (PVC) over which goals or ends they choose to pursue when their wills are conflicted about which ends to pursue. This further development of the internal rational environments of human agents amounts to a further evolution from freedom *of action* to freedom *of will*.

It is worth recalling here what was said about these matters in P174–P175 of the previous chapter:

> We cannot get to incompatibilist free will in one fell swoop in the real world. That is one leap too far. We must get there stepwise, by exercising compatibilist guidance control over cognitive processes aimed at making choices, that is, these efforts or exercises of willpower, and from there, in the context of a conflicted will . . . , to incompatibilist regulative control (PVC) over the choices (SFAs) that may result from one or another of these cognitive processes. . . . Or, putting the matter in an evolutionary perspective, *we had to first develop the capacity for (compatibilist) teleological guidance control (TGC) before we could develop—given the further cognitive or mental complexity needed to deal with conflicts in our wills—the capacity for (incompatibilist) PVC.*

We will see the further significance of these claims when discussing other libertarian accounts of free will in subsequent chapters.

7
The Libertarian Spectrum (Part II)
Event-Causal Views, Centered and Non-centered

7.1. Introduction

(P237) My view is usually depicted in the current literature as both an *event-causal* and a *centered* view of libertarian free will. But, as argued here, it is not (and has never strictly been) either one. For reasons explained in Chapter 5, it was never strictly an event-causal view, but rather an agent-causal/event-causal, or AC/EC, view of the kind described there. For reasons spelled out in the Chapter 6, the view was also not strictly speaking a "centered" view. Undetermined self-forming free actions need not occur *only* in terminating deliberations, but in many other places in the practical lives of agents as well, cited in Chapter 6, and in yet other places to be discussed.

Relevant to all this is a general theme that will play an important role in this chapter and subsequent ones, a theme that was summed up in the conclusion of

(P220) Undetermined self-forming actions may be centered or non-centered. *It is not where undetermined self-forming actions occur in the lives of agents that matters for free will, but how they occur.* Wherever they occur, self-forming actions resolve conflicts in the wills of agents; and the agents must be able to resolve these conflicts in accordance with their wills, whichever way they are resolved.

In this chapter, I discuss further *event-causal* (EC) libertarian views of differing kinds, some centered, some non-centered, comparing them to the view developed in this book. Doing so throws additional light on this view and free will issues generally. In the next chapter, I do the same for agent-causal and noncausal libertarian views.

7.2. Torn Decisions and L-Freedom: Balaguer's *Free Will as an Open Scientific Problem*

Mark Balaguer's book *Free Will as an Open Scientific Problem* (2010), makes important contributions to contemporary debates about free will. He says explicitly that the view he develops is an EC view: "It doesn't involve any sort of irreducible agent causation, but it does hold that undetermined L-free [i.e., libertarian free] decisions are (ordinarily) causally influenced by—indeed probabilistically caused by—agent-involving events, most notably events having to do with the agent having certain reasons and intentions" (p. 67). His view, he says, is also *non-Valerian* (or non-deliberative): "The important indeterminacy is located at the moment of choice, rather than prior to choice, as with Valerian views" (p. 67).

He adds that "this general sort of view was hinted at by Wiggins (1973) and later developed by Kane (1985, 1996, 1999), Nozick (1981) and Ekstrom (2000)." Of these, he adds, "my view is most similar to Kane's, but, as we'll see, it is also importantly different from his view" (2010, p. 67). Indeed, I would add that there are similarities in our views, but also differences, which are, in certain respects, even more substantial than he suggests. Discussing both these similarities and differences throws light on the views involved, as well as on contemporary debates about libertarian free will generally.

Central to Balaguer's view is the notion of a "torn decision," which he defines as "a decision in which the person ... (a) has reasons for two or more options and feels torn as to which set of reasons is strongest, that is, has no conscious belief as to which option is best and (b) decides without resolving this conflict, that is, the person has the experience of 'just choosing'" (p. 71). He says that "this notion of a torn decision," as he has defined it "is similar to Kane's (1996) notion of a *self-forming action* (SFA)" (p. 73). But he adds that there are four differences worth noting.

"First," he says, Kane's "SFAs are by definition undetermined, and so it is an open question whether there actually exist any such things. What I call torn decisions, on the other hand, are not defined as being undetermined. They are defined in terms of their phenomenology; thus, it is clear that there do exist torn decisions—we know this by our experiences" of being torn (2010, p. 73). This difference between his torn decisions and my self-forming actions is worth pointing out. I sometimes speak of self-forming actions as "torn decisions," and this is correct phenomenologically, in terms of how we experience them. But whether they are undetermined, I have always emphasized, is an empirical question that cannot be settled merely phenomenologically, as Balaguer rightly says of his torn decisions.

"A second difference between torn decisions and Kanean SFAs," Balaguer says, "is that the former need not involve what Kane calls *efforts of will.* Now this isn't to say," he adds, "that efforts *can't* play a role in torn decisions, and indeed, I think that some torn decisions do involve something like efforts of will (think, for instance of someone who is trying to quit smoking and who, at some specific moment, badly wants a cigarette but is trying to resist). . . . But all torn decisions don't *have* to involve efforts of will" (2010, p. 74).

It is interesting that he concedes a role for efforts here, and interesting as well that the examples he gives where efforts play a role are ones that have significance to the agent's character- and will-building. For these are ones that matter in my view to an adequate account of "self-formation." This is so because self-formation, on my view, is usually a long-term process, only rarely a one-off occurrence. There may also be, as Balaguer suggests, phenomenologically torn decisions in his sense, that are not character- or will-forming in significant ways, and do not involve efforts, such as whether to have one dessert or another at a restaurant. On the other hand, if one is trying to lose weight, and one of the choices of desserts one really likes is especially fattening, effort may indeed be involved. The key point here, and one to which I'll return, is that effort is involved where character- and will-building are involved, in other words, in self-*formation*.

On the third difference between his torn decisions and my self-forming actions, Balaguer says, "*some* of our torn decisions are momentous events in our lives," for example, "where we will live, who we will marry, what careers we will pursue. . . . But on my view," he adds, "we make numerous torn decisions and most of these decisions are pretty insignificant" (2010, p. 74).

The initial point to be made clear here in response to this suggested difference is that it doesn't contradict the important statement just made about self-forming actions, which bears formally repeating.

(P238) Self-formation is usually a long-term process, only rarely a one-off occurrence. With regard to the momentous decisions he mentions, like when and whom to marry, what career to pursue, and others, many further self-forming actions also involving efforts will inevitably be involved in carrying them out—for example, in making marriages work over time (or not), in making careers successful (or not), and so on. In general, self-formation is a process that usually requires multiple self-forming actions.

Some self-forming actions are pivotal, like these momentous ones he mentions, because they set us on new paths in life. But the self-formation is not just in choosing these paths, it is also in pursuing them and carrying them out.

I would also not deny Balaguer's claim here that some of our *phenomenologically* torn decisions may be insignificant. We might quibble about just how many are significant and how many are not. But I would argue that the significant ones, so far as free will and ultimate responsibility are concerned, are those that involve conflicts in our wills, where some effort is required to overcome resistance in our wills to making them. For these are ones in which character- and will-building, and hence self-formation, are involved. How impactful any such actions will be on our future lives is also an empirical question and will vary greatly on my view as well.

The fourth difference Balaguer mentions between his torn decisions and my self-forming actions is that "in order for a decision to count as a torn decision," in his sense, the agent "has to be more or less neutral between her various live options," whereas a decision can be an SFA on my account, he says, even if the agent is "leaning toward" one or more of her live options (2010, p. 74). This is correct about self-forming actions on my view since the reasons for the choices made may merely be "inclining" without necessitating. But Balaguer himself thinks this difference is not "theoretically important" since he will later argue that decisions involving "leanings" of this sort can still be L-free decisions in his sense.

Yet he refuses to call such decisions involving leanings "torn decisions," and this I find odd. For, as I've argued, you can often be "torn" even when at various times in the course of a deliberation your reasons incline or lean you to one choice rather than another without being conclusive or necessitating, so that there remains resistance in the will that must be overcome by effort if the favored choice is to be made. More will be said about this as we consider Balaguer's argument for his view.

7.3. Balaguer's Argument

Having noted these differences between his torn decisions and my self-forming actions, Balaguer's account of libertarian freedom (or L-freedom, as he calls it) of torn decisions, proceeds as follows:

> If an ordinary human torn decision is *wholly undetermined*, then it is L- (or libertarian) free—that is, (a) it is not just undetermined but also *appropriately nonrandom* . . . and (b) the indeterminacy in question increases or procures the appropriate nonrandomness. (2010, p. 78)

All this requires explanation. By saying a torn decision is "wholly undetermined" he means that given the agent's reasons for the competing decisions, the probabilities that either decision might be made are about even. And no other causes besides the agent's reasons are significantly causally relevant to which of the options is chosen. All the causes that matter, in other words, leave the probabilities that either choice might be made about equal.

The other crucial notion, "appropriate nonrandomness," requires more attention: "In order for a decision to be L-free, it has to be authored and controlled by the agent in question; that is, it has to be *her* decision, and she has to control which option is chosen." But that is not enough, he adds.

> In connection with torn decisions, *appropriate nonrandomness* also requires what Kane has called *plural authorship and control*, which can be understood as follows: If an agent . . . is trying to decide between multiple options . . . and if [the agent] eventually chooses A in a torn decision sort of way, then, in order for the choice to be plurally authored and controlled . . . , it must be the case that . . . there was at least one other option, say B, such that if [the agent] had chosen B, then that choice would also have been authored and controlled by [the agent]. Moreover, appropriate nonrandomness also seems to require . . . at least in connection with torn decisions, *plural rationality*. Either choice would have to be a rational one in some sense to be defined. (2010, p. 83)

This looks like my requirement of *plural voluntary control* for self-forming actions. But a closer look will reveal some significant differences, as we'll see.

With this account of torn decisions in hand, Balaguer then argues as follows: "If our ordinary torn decisions are wholly undetermined in the sense defined," that is, if the probabilities that either decision might be made are about even, and no other causes besides the agent's reasons are significantly causally relevant to which of the options is selected, "then the decisions are *appropriately nonrandom*" and "*we have as much authorship and control over them as we could possibly have*" (2010, p. 93, italics mine). In arguing for these claims, he uses, as illustration, an example of a fellow, Ralph, who is torn between staying in his hometown of Mayberry, North Carolina, accepting a job as manager of a small local business and marrying his childhood sweetheart, or moving to New York City, where he has been offered a part in an off-Broadway play. Ralph finally decides to move to New York "but not because," Balaguer adds, "he came to believe his reasons for moving to New York outweighed his reasons for staying in Mayberry. He was unable to come to a view either way on that question and in the end, he *just decided to go*. Period" (p. 72). With this example in mind, Balaguer then argues a follows:

> The fact of the matter is that, if Ralph's decision is a torn one in the sense I have defined, Ralph's conscious reasons do not pick out a unique best option; but he does have reason to make *some* choice, that is, for not remaining in a state of indecision. Thus, it seems clear that Ralph has good reason to *just pick* from among his tied for best options (that is, to pick randomly or arbitrarily). Given this, it seems that the most we could hope for here, vis-à-vis authorship and control, is that it is *Ralph* who does the just-picking, that is, who makes the random selection from among his tied for best options. (pp. 96–97)

7.4. Responses to Balaguer

I find these claims problematic in a number of ways. On the view of self-forming actions developed in this book, it is also the case that if either choice is made at a time, it will be undetermined that it is made at that time. But it is *not* the case that the agent's making one of the choices amounts to "just picking" that particular option randomly. Nor is it true on my view that "the most we can hope for," in a self-forming choice situation regarding "authorship and control," is that it is the agent "who does the just picking" by making a "random selection from among his tied for best options."

First, we need to remind ourselves that the options, on the view of self-forming decisions developed here, need not be equally probable or "tied for best." The probabilities can vary depending on the course of the agent's reasoning, and they have to do with the relevant strength of the agent's competing reasons at a given time for making different decisions. These reasons may differ in strength and thus may imply different probabilities for the respective decisions. But a second and more important difference is the following:

(P239) When a particular undetermined decision is successfully made in a self-forming decision situation, on my view, it is brought about by the agent rather than the alternative decision, *not* by the agent's "just picking" one or another outcome randomly, as Balaguer says of his torn decisions. To the contrary, the decision made in the case of self-forming decisions is brought about by the agent with the specific *goal* or *purpose* of bringing about *that particular* decision *rather than* any alternative at that time for reasons that incline the agent to make that particular decision at the time. And this will be the case *whichever* decision should actually be made in the course of the deliberation if the decision is a self-forming one in my sense. As a consequence,

(P240) Just picking or randomly selecting an alternative is *not*, as Balaguer says, "the most we can hope for as regards authorship and control" of a libertarian free decision where the decision made must be undetermined at the time it is made. For we can also say that whichever decision is made in a self-forming situation would be the causal result of the agent's successfully exercising teleological guidance *control* (TGC) over a goal-directed cognitive process (an effort or exercise of willpower) whose goal or telos was to make *that particular decision rather than* any alternative. Moreover, we can say this whichever decision should be made; and we can say it even when it was undetermined that the decision was made at the time it was made. For what would be undetermined is not *which* decision would be made at that time, but *whether* an agent's teleologically guided cognitive process did or did not succeed in attaining its goal (making the particular decision it was aiming at) at that time, thereby overcoming resistance in the will to doing so.

(P241) The agent would thereby have the power to make either decision in a self-forming decision situation by successfully exercising such teleological guidance control (TGC) over a cognitive process whose goal was to make that particular decision rather than an alternative for the reasons favoring that decision. This plural power is more control than one would have by "just picking randomly" which undetermined choice is made. And this plural power is what I mean by plural voluntary control.

Now, as noted earlier, Balaguer does allow that some L- (or libertarian) free decisions may involve "leanings" or inclining reasons like my self-forming actions or SFAs, and emphasizing this is to his credit. But then, as also mentioned, he refuses to call such decisions involving leanings "torn decisions." And he further insists that what he defines as torn decisions give us as much control as we could hope for concerning authorship and control for undetermined decisions, namely, that the agent "makes a random selection from among tied for best options."

> (P242) By contrast, I believe that refusing to call decisions involving "leanings" or "inclining reasons" "torn decisions," as Balaguer does, leaves out an important possibility: namely, that reasons may incline agents to one decision rather than another even when the agents remain "torn" to some degree about what to decide and have to make efforts to decide in terms of the inclining reasons by overcoming the still-existing resistance in the will to making the decision to which they may incline (without determining) the agent.

> (P243) It is also a problem, I believe, having narrowed the scope of "torn decisions" in this way, to then insist that torn decisions so defined give us "the most we could hope for" concerning authorship and control for undetermined decisions, namely, that the agent "makes a random selection from among tied for best options." To the contrary, in the manner spelled out in P237–P238, choices or decisions involving leanings or inclining reasons allow agents to have *more* plural control and power over *which* decision is made when they are torn about what to decide. For decisions involving leanings or inclining reasons give agents the power to make whichever decision is made by successfully exercising a teleologically guided cognitive process whose goal or telos is the bringing about of a particular decision *rather than* any alternative, *for the reasons favoring* that decision at that time. And this is more power and control than one would have if "the most one could hope for" in the case of undetermined decisions in the way of authorship and control was making "a random selection from among tied for best options."

Balaguer's book involves many subtle arguments and makes important contributions to current debates about libertarian free will. I have focused only on those that bring out the differences between my libertarian view of self-forming actions and his view of torn decisions, which are important differences in our views bearing on issues of authorship and control over undetermined free choices or decisions. Of particular importance among the parts of his book I have not discussed is his fourth and final chapter, where he argues that whether or not any of our phenomenologically torn decisions are actually undetermined is a scientific question that cannot be settled by introspection or philosophical argument alone. In this final chapter, he also offers cogent arguments that whether or not phenomenologically torn decisions are actually undetermined is an "open scientific problem" which is far from being settled one way or the other by contemporary science. I am in agreement with these claims and have learned much on these matters and other matters relating to free will from Balaguer's book.[1]

7.5. Daring Libertarianism: Mele's *Free Will and Luck*

All the authors cited and discussed in this book, whether I agree with them or not, have had an important influence on my thinking about free will—but none more than Al Mele. Our interactions go back many years to when he invited me to speak at Davidson College in North Carolina. I stayed in his home with his family, and we took nightly walks discussing many issues about free will, moral responsibility, agency, and other topics.

Mele remains agnostic about whether compatibilism or libertarianism is true, as noted in the previous chapter. His goal in most of his writing on the subject, he says, has been to formulate the best versions of each view that he can. Initially, he focused on compatibilist views, since he was deeply skeptical about the two most prominent libertarian views on offer at the time—noncausal (NC) and agent-causal (AC) views. It was partly his encounter with my early work on free will in the 1980s, he has said (particularly my *Free Will and Values* [1985], and the article "Two Kinds of Incompatibilism" [1989]), that led him to believe that a coherent libertarian view might be possible that was neither noncausalist nor (nonevent) agent-causalist. He had reservations about my view itself, but it suggested to him that some less extravagant event-causal libertarian view consistent with the empirical sciences might be possible.

His initial foray in this regard was to develop a view that placed the indeterminism earlier in the deliberative process in the undetermined comings-to-mind of various considerations that subsequently influence choice. This was, of course, the deliberative libertarian view discussed in Chapter 6 that he dubbed "modest libertarianism." Mele believed this modest view gave libertarians some of the things they wanted, but he was quite explicit in noting that it did not give them everything they wanted, particularly regarding responsibility (hence the "modest" designation). And he subsequently explored the possibility of stronger libertarian views in later works, including his *Free Will and Luck* (2006), some of which stronger views allowed for indeterminism up to the moment of choice.

The strongest of these further views, and the one he says comes closest to mine, is what he calls his "Daring Libertarian View." He defends this view against mine in *Free Will and Luck* (2006) and in other writings (e.g., Mele 2014), including a more recent paper entitled "Two Libertarian Theories: Or Why Event-Causal Libertarians Should Prefer My Daring Libertarian View to Robert Kane's View" (2017b). In this latter paper he says:

> My Daring Libertarian view (in *Free Will and Luck*) is similar to Kane's view. The main difference is that where Kane postulates concurrent competing indeterministic efforts to choose, I postulate [one] indeterministic effort to decide (or choose) what to do. That effort can result in different decisions, holding the past and the laws of nature fixed. (2017b, p. 51)

To illustrate this difference, he uses an example, originally used in *Free Will and Luck*, of an agent, Bob, who faces a choice between cheating and doing what he thinks is the right thing, that is, not cheating. Mele says:

> In Bob's story, as I tell it, there are no concurrent competing efforts to choose. Instead, there is a possible world in which Bob's effort to decide what to do . . . issues in a decision to cheat, and in another world with the same past up to t and the same laws of nature, that same effort [to decide] issues at t in a decision [not to cheat]. Bob has competing reasons at the time, and the decision he makes—whether it is the decision to cheat or to do the right thing—is made for reasons that favor it. The cross-world difference at t in what Bob decides seems to be a matter of luck. But it does not seem to be any *more* a matter of luck than a cross-world difference that I identified in [Kane's] version of Bob's story in which Bob is trying to choose to cheat while also trying to choose to do the right thing: namely, the difference between the former effort succeeding and the latter effort succeeding. (2017b, pp. 52–53)

In the conclusion of this paper, Mele then summarizes, in the light of these remarks, the reasons why he argues that his Daring Libertarian View should be preferred to my view.

"When the agent's choice-making occurs in a way that fits Kane's concurrent efforts view, the cross-world difference in which of his efforts to choose wins out is no less a matter of luck or chance" (2017b, pp. 56–57) than is the cross-world difference in what the agent chooses on my Daring Libertarian View. Yet, while

> ordinary experience supports the claim that normal human agents sometimes make an effort to decide what to do, the same cannot plausibly be said for the claim that agents sometimes make concurrent efforts to choose of the kind featured in Kane's view. And, to the best of my knowledge, there is no direct evidence of any kind that normal agents ever make Kane-style concurrent efforts to choose. (2017b, p. 59)

Thus,

> Kane's concurrent efforts view has a significantly heavier burden—and therefore carries a significantly higher cost—on the empirical front . . . while having no advantage over my Daring Libertarian View on the [crucial] issue of cross-world luck at the time of choice or decision. (2017b, p. 59)

7.6. Responses to Mele (Part I): The Development of My View

I have no intention of disputing this particular conclusion of Mele's because I have come to agree with it. His arguments against what he calls my "concurrent efforts" view, along with arguments of others, have convinced me to reject the appeal to simultaneous or "concurrent" efforts in my recent thinking, as reflected in this book.[2] My reasoning on this matter evolved as follows:

> (P244) In the past decade, I came to realize that the problem to which Mele and other critics of my view of plural efforts have drawn attention, was not in the postulation of plural efforts alone, but rather in two further mistakes made about them. The first of these mistakes was to assume that

competing efforts to make different choices would have to be occurring simultaneously, or "concurrently," as Mele puts it. I now reject this assumption, and it is not made in the view presented in this book.
I further came to realize over the past decade the following:

(P245) This first mistake—of assuming that competing plural efforts would have to be occurring simultaneously or concurrently—was based on a second and more fundamental mistake that has bedeviled libertarian views of free will historically, down to the present time. This second mistake was the assumption that if some choices must be undetermined up to the time when one or another choice is made, then *either one* of the opposing choices (e.g., to cheat or not to cheat, to steal or not to steal, to stay in Mayberry or go to New York) might be made *at that same time, given exactly the same past*, including exactly the same past desires, beliefs, and other motives and reasoning of the agent up to that time.

Note that, if one rejects this second assumption, there is no further need to assume that efforts to make either of the competing choices would have to be occurring simultaneously or concurrently preceding the time when one or another choice is made. For it no longer needs to be assumed that opposing choices might be made at that same time. Hence, the alterations in my view that were summarized earlier:

(P94) It is not being claimed here (as I once did) that these efforts or exercises of willpower aimed at different choices might be occurring at the same time during deliberation. Nor will they be occurring throughout the entire deliberation. Rather, different efforts or exercises of willpower may be initiated at different times, depending on the course of the agent's reasoning.

Among the consequences of these changes, the following is especially worth noting for present purposes:

(P246) On the view developed here, in the light of these changes, at no point in the course of a deliberation leading to an undetermined self-forming choice would it be the case that opposing choices (e.g., to cheat or not to cheat) might be made at a time, given exactly the same past up to that time, including exactly the same past motives and reasoning of the agent. To the contrary, if opposing choices might be made in the course of such a deliberation, the past would be different when those different choices might be made.

(P247) To illustrate, consider again John deliberating about whether or not to steal from the poor box. If he chooses to steal at any point in his deliberation, it would be because he had come to believe that his reasons inclined him to make that choice to steal at that time rather than the alternative. He would also at that time have succeeded in making an effort to make the choice to steal in terms of these inclining reasons, thereby overcoming the remaining resistance in his will to doing so. If, on the other hand, he had chosen *not* to steal from the poor box at any other time during the deliberation, it would have been because he had come to believe at *that* time that his reasons inclined him to make that different choice *not* to steal, and he would have successfully made an effort to make the choice not to steal at that time, overcoming resistance in his will coming from his motives to choose to steal.

(P248) In sum, if different choices had been made, *the pasts preceding each of those different choices, including the agent's reasoning and efforts leading up to them, would not have been the same.* Yet it would still be true that whichever choice was made would have been undetermined by the past preceding it; and it would still be true that whichever choice was made would have been brought about by the agent rather than the alternative, voluntarily, intentionally, and for the reasons inclining the agent to make that particular choice rather than any other at that time.

It is these consequences of the present view that also allow one to answer many other common objections to libertarian views, such as explanatory luck objections, rollback and replay objections, and objections concerning contrastive explanations, as we have seen in earlier chapters.

7.7. Responses to Mele (Part II): Three Powers

In the light of this, let us now compare Mele's Daring Libertarian View to the view presented in this book in which the appeal to simultaneous competing efforts is not made. It will be enlightening to make this comparison in terms of a distinction between different powers and kinds of control that may be involved in making undetermined free choices.

> (P249) In the view developed in this book, there are at least three powers that might be involved in exercising agential power and control over undetermined self-forming choices. These powers may be described in terms of a general notion of *control* introduced earlier—namely, teleological guidance control (TGC)—the exercise of which, as neuroscientist Usher and others have pointed out, is necessary for any voluntary activity.
> (1) The power to exercise TGC over a cognitive process (of deliberation) to decide or choose what to do, whose goal or telos is making one or another possible decision or choice, for example, a choice A or a choice B.
> (2) The power to also exercise TGC over a cognitive process (in this case, an effort or exercise of willpower) whose goal or telos (in the context of such a more general process of deliberation) is specifically to make one of the choices, for example, the choice A *rather than* the alternative choice B.
> (3) The power to exercise TGC over a cognitive process (an effort or exercise of willpower) whose goal or telos (in the context of such a process of deliberation) is specifically to make an alternative choice, choice B *rather than* choice A.

Mele's Daring Libertarian View gives agents the first of these three powers and kinds of control, but it does not give them the second two powers and kinds of control.

> (P250) By contrast, the view developed here gives agents all three of these powers and kinds of control in the making of undetermined self-forming choices. It gives agents the power to exercise TGC over the larger process of deliberation itself, as does Mele's Daring Libertarian View. But it also gives agents the powers to exercise TGC over additional subprocesses of this larger process at different times in the course of that general deliberation, each of whose goals is to bring about one of the decisions being deliberated about rather than the alternative.

(P251) Having all three of these powers and kinds of control, I contend, is having more power and control than merely having the first of these powers. For having all three powers allows one to say that *whichever* decision is made in the course of the deliberation would be the causal result of the agent's successfully exercising TGC over a goal-directed cognitive process whose goal was to bring about *that particular decision* made *rather than* any alternative at that time for specific reasons for that decision rather than any alternative. And this is more power and control over undetermined decisions than the Daring View provides in merely postulating a power to exercise guidance control over a single process of deliberation that may result in different decisions, given exactly the same past and laws leading up to the decision.

(P252) Moreover, this further power and control is something we *do* sometimes recognize experientially. Mele says that "ordinary experience supports the claim that normal human agents sometimes make an effort to decide what to do." But he adds that it does not support the claim "that agents sometimes make concurrent efforts to choose of the kind featured in Kane's view." This is true. Yet ordinary experience *does* also support the claim that normal human agents sometimes make efforts to make particular decisions to which they may be inclined where they must overcome still-existing resistance coming from motives in their wills to make an opposing decision. When an effort succeeds in attaining its goal in such circumstances, we have the experience of having succeeded in bringing about the particular decision aimed at for the reasons favoring that decision by overcoming resistance in our wills to doing so.

(P253) To actually get this further power and control, it is not sufficient to postulate a *single* process (deliberation) with *multiple* possible goals (making decision A or decision B). One must also allow for the possibility of multiple *subprocesses* (efforts of will, which are *exercises of TGC* that involve overcoming obstacles in the wills of agents if they are to succeed). These efforts may occur at different times in this general process of deliberation, such that each subprocess has a *specific* goal of making one of the decisions *rather than* the other for the reasons favoring that decision at the time. Any decision thus made would indeed be caused by the general process of deliberation of the agent. But it would also be caused by a subprocess also under the (teleological guidance) control of the agent which is a part of that general process of deliberation and involves the agent causing the particular decision made rather than the alternative for the reasons inclining the agent at the time to make that particular decision.

(P254) In addition, we need not (and should not) assume that these subprocesses that might be aimed at different decisions would be occurring at the same time during deliberation. Rather we need only assume, in the manner summarized in P92, that different efforts may be initiated at different times, depending on the course of the agents' reasoning, when their reasons incline them to one decision rather than the other and resistance in their wills must be overcome if they are to make the decision to which they are then inclined.

There are indeed more things postulated on this view than on Mele's Daring Libertarian View (P247–P251). But the additions are not superfluous.

(P255) These additions give agents more power and control over undetermined free choices than the Daring View allows. The Daring View postulates a power to exercise guidance control over a general process of deliberation whose goal is making one decision *or* another, where either decision might occur given exactly the same reasoning and motives of the agent up to the moment of the decision. By contrast, in the case of self-forming decisions these additions give agents further active powers to "form" or "set" their wills in one direction rather than another by also exercising TGC over which particular decision is made at a time rather than another in the course of a deliberative process. These additional powers do this without requiring that an alternative decision might have been made at that same time, given exactly the same reasoning and motives of the agent up to the moment of decision (P240–P243).

(P256) Importantly, in doing this, these additional powers also allow one to give a stronger account of its being "up to the agent" *which* decision is made as the result of a deliberation, without denying that the decision made was *undetermined*.

Mele's writings over many years have made numerous important contributions to free will debates from which I have learned a great deal and many of which I agree with. Even the differences discussed here between his

Daring Libertarian View and my present view are the result of my coming to realize the limitations of my concurrent efforts view through his writings and the writings of others.

Importantly, I did not appeal to *concurrent* competing efforts to choose in *The Significance of Free Will* (1996) or in any earlier works. I came up with the idea of concurrent efforts a couple of years after *Significance* in response to various objections. I remember first suggesting it at the World Congress of Philosophy meeting in Boston in 1998. After one of the sessions I was at a dinner with Mele and the respected Finnish action theorist Raimo Tuomela, along with others. Al and Raimo were pressing me with objections about my view when I announced in response to an objection by them that I was contemplating a new twist to my view involving simultaneous dual efforts. I recall that Al, who was sitting beside me in the restaurant booth, reared back and said, "Hmm, this *is* new." Indeed, it was. It was not assumed in my *Significance of Free Will* or other earlier works. Al was suspicious of the idea from the start but recognized it as a new twist to the debates that would have to be dealt with. Ultimately, I became convinced that his suspicions of this idea and the suspicions of others about it were justified.

In numerous writings over the years, Mele has made many other important contributions to aspects of free will debates that have influenced my thinking. His criticisms (in two books, 2006, 2009, and many articles) of Benjamin Libet, Daniel Wegner, and other neuroscientists and psychologists who argue that the apparent causal power of conscious willing is an illusion are among the most thorough available criticisms of these influential views; and I find them convincing. Similarly insightful are Mele's discussions in books and articles of such topics as weakness of will (2006, 2009), manipulated agents (1995, 2006, 2017), Frankfurt-style examples (1995, 2006, 2017a), and other topics. He is also alert in all his writings to the importance of the historical dimensions of issues about free will and responsibility—that is, how we historically got to be the kinds of persons we are with the wills (reasons, motives, etc.) we do have—something I emphasize as well.

7.8. A Minimal Libertarianism: Franklin on Event-Causal Libertarianism and Agency Reductionism

The third event causal (EC) libertarian view I want to consider here, which is of more recent vintage, has important further things to teach us about the dialectic of recent EC libertarian accounts of free will. It is Christopher Evan Franklin's *A Minimal Libertarianism: Free Will and the Promise of Reduction* (2018). This book is carefully argued, replete with fine distinctions, and contains more than a few novel arguments in defense of an EC libertarian view. For all these reasons it is a significant contribution to recent debates that deserves to be read by anyone interested in these debates.

Franklin's event-causal account of free action makes two related assumptions. The first is what he calls the *Causal Theory of Action*, according to which an agent's causing an action "is nothing over and above mental states and events [e.g., desires and beliefs] involving the agent causing or bringing about the action" (2018, p. 14). The scope of this Causal Theory of Action, he adds, "is limited to basic action and is silent about the nature of other kinds of agency, such as free or self-determined action" (p. 14). By contrast, the second assumption he makes which is related to this Causal Theory of Action is more general. He calls it *agency reductionism* and defines it as "the view that the causal role of the agent in all agential activities (from nonintentional to autonomous action) is reducible to the nondeviant causal activity of appropriate mental states and events involving the agent" (p. 14).

This notion of agency reductionism is pivotal to Franklin's "minimal" EC libertarian view in the book. And it is the feature of his view that I will take issue with, despite agreements with much else that he argues for in his book. Interestingly, Franklin himself argues in his final full chapter that there are "unsolved challenges" to this notion of agency reductionism. He adds that, since the minimal EC libertarianism he defends in the book depends on agency reductionism, "the tenability of agency reductionism in general, and event-causal libertarianism in particular," is problematic and uncertain (2018, p. 172). With this conclusion I am in agreement, as we'll see.

Franklin's case against agency reductionism is developed in terms of what he calls the "It Ain't Me Argument." In introducing this argument, he says

> The best way to appreciate this [reductionist] worry about agency is to consider cases of self-determination, where we seem to experience ourselves as sources of activity over and above the activity of our motivations. This experience is most vivid in the case of motivational conflict. Consider the classic case of conflict between duty and desire, such as when I know I should be more attentive to my children but am exhausted. Duty pulls one way, desire

another. Suppose I make an effort to turn my attention to my children and succeed in this endeavor. In this case, it does not seem that my decision was merely a function of my desires and beliefs. These attitudes were in conflict, after all, and I myself had to decide how to resolve the conflict, or so it seems. It is this seeming experience of myself as playing a causal role over and above the causal role of my desires and beliefs that suggests I exercised the power of *self*-determination. (p. 182)³

In line with these thoughts, Franklin says the It Ain't Me Argument "contends that, if the causal etiology of my actions is exhausted by states and events, then 'it ain't me' that causes my decision and thus I do not *self*-determine what I do." For I, as an agent, am "not identical to any state or event or any bundle of states and events" (2018, p. 183). Franklin considers possible responses EC libertarians might make to this It Ain't Me Argument and finds them all wanting. He thus draws the following conclusion on the final page of his book:

It remains an open question whether event-causal libertarians can in fact secure a valuable kind of freedom and responsibility unavailable to compatibilists, but only because it remains an open question whether agency reductionism is true. If it is true, then minimal event-causal-libertarianism is true. If it is false, then libertarians must reject event-causal libertarianism and locate free agents outside the natural order, but so also must compatibilists. Therefore, the ultimate tenability of event-causal libertarianism remains uncertain. (p. 200)

7.9. Responses to Franklin (Part I)

(P257) I agree that agency reductionism, as Franklin understands it, is problematic. I also agree that if agency reductionism is false, we must reject the kind of (minimal) event-causal libertarianism defended in his book. But I do not also agree that if agency reductionism is false and we reject such an event-causal libertarianism, "libertarians must . . . locate free agents outside of the natural order, [and] so also must compatibilists." (As we shall see, Franklin himself seems to reject this assumption in subsequent writings.)

(P258) For there is, on my view, a *non-reductive* account of agency that is available to libertarians and compatibilists alike that is consistent with what is known about human agency in the neurosciences and other natural sciences and does not require locating free agents outside the natural order.

(P259) This non-reductive account of agency is the view defended in previous chapters according to which "an agent's causing an action is to be understood as an agent, conceived as an information-responsive complex dynamical system, exercising *teleological guidance* over some of its own processes" (P155; Kane 2011b, 396ff.). The causal role of the agent in causing action on this account is *not reducible* to causation by mental states and events of the agent alone, for reasons spelled out earlier (P149). The teleological guidance control that is required by agency, so defined, is not only necessary for any voluntary activity, as neuroscientists such as Usher argue, but also compatible with indeterminism as well as determinism. Such teleological guidance control is thus available to libertarian theories of free will as well as to compatibilist theories (P151).

(P260) Moreover, agency understood in this way is very much a part of the natural order and does not require locating "free agents outside of the natural order." There are historical lessons relevant here about the rise of EC libertarian views generally over the past forty-plus years and the connection of such views to agency reductionism. For EC views, as noted earlier, were generally a reaction to existing noncausal and AC views, previously common among libertarians. Moreover, EC views were especially a reaction to the most popular of these alternative libertarian views, namely, AC views, which typically appealed to special forms of agent causation that were not subject to natural laws, or not capable of being caused in turn by events, either deterministically or indeterministically, and not also required by compatibilist views of agency. Some of these AC views located free agents outside the natural order altogether, though not all of them did.

(P261) In reacting to such AC views, however, EC libertarian views, as I see it, were often tempted to go too far in the opposite direction, maintaining that causation of actions by agents could be entirely reduced to causation by states and events, such as desires, beliefs, and intentions, of the agent, and wholly consisted in such causation by such states and events. What was needed to avoid this reaction was an account of agent causation that was consistent with what is known about human agency in the natural and human sciences and yet was not reducible to causation by states and events alone, including mental states and events; and such a view was available by appeal to complex dynamical systems and TGC.

(P262) Not only was such a view of complex dynamical systems and teleological guidance control consistent with what is known about human agency in the sciences. But agent causation understood in this way, as I argued, would also not be *reducible* to causation by mental states or events of agents alone. For such a reduction would leave out the added role of agents, as such complex systems, exercising guidance control over the processes *causally linking* mental states and events to the actions they cause (P149).

As indicated earlier, I have never held an agency reductionist view like that presupposed by the minimal event-causal view of Franklin's book. That is one of the main reasons why I was always uneasy about the designation of my view as "event-causal" in the current literature and preferred to call my view in many of my own writings, such as *The Significance of Free Will*, a "teleological intelligibility" view of free will.

It is also why I came to believe over the past decade that we need to distinguish at least four kinds of libertarian views of free will rather than the familiar three, adding to NC, AC, and EC views a fourth kind that I've designated as an agent-causal/event-causal, or AC/EC, view (P151–P152).

(P263) Event causes, including mental states and events of the agent, *do play an essential causal role on such an AC/EC view in the etiology of libertarian free actions*. But the agent conceived as a complex dynamical system also plays an essential, and importantly, an *irreducible* causal role in that etiology as well.

(P264) Looked at in this way, the "minimal libertarianism" defended in Franklin's book may be viewed as an example of what we might think of as a purely event-causal or EC libertarian view, as distinguished from such an AC/EC view. Interestingly, if viewed in this way, the difference between the views would indeed largely have to do with what Franklin calls "agency reductionism." According to agency reductionism, he says, "agents' settling which of two causally possible decisions they make *wholly consists* in the decisions being non-deviantly caused by apt mental states and events involving them." This, he adds, "is simply what exercising the power to settle" would amount to on such a minimal event-causal theory (2018, p. 180).

(P265) By contrast, on the AC/EC view developed here, agents' "settling" which of two or more causally possible decisions they make also involves causation by the agents in a special and non-reducible way. The appropriate mental states or events would not cause the decision to be made on their own, so to speak. Rather it would be the agent who *brings it about that* the appropriate mental states or events cause the decision by guiding the flow of activity along neural pathways that establish the proper mappings between inputs, internal states, and outputs and being able to alter those pathways in response to new information (P151).

I should add that Franklin, to his credit, in a number of recent writings since his book was published has himself abandoned agency reductionism and has argued that an irreducible role for agents must be made in libertarian views of free will. I'll return to this point at the end of the next section.

7.10. Responses to Franklin (Part II)

I have not yet addressed Franklin's specific critique of my libertarian account of free will in chapter 4 of his book, where he considers what he refers to as four "counterintuitive" features of my view. The first such feature he discusses is that the way in which efforts of will occur in my theory makes the efforts seem redundant. He argues that if agents are trying or making efforts to choose to do something they want to do and want to try to do, there is a sense in which their wills are "already settled on this course of action though, due to temptation, it is still possible that [they] will fail to follow through" (2018, p. 101). The effort of will that is needed, he argues, would therefore not be to make the decision to do that thing, but rather to carry out the decision already made. To suppose an effort is needed to *make* the decision in addition to carrying it out in such a context would be "redundant."

This worry involves a misinterpretation of my view, albeit a common and revealing one.

(P266) When agents make efforts in self-forming choice situations, it is because their wills are still conflicted about what they should *choose* or *decide* to do, or what they should "settle" their *wills* on doing. Their reasons may incline them at the time to one choice rather than another, but their reasons do not yet "settle" that this choice will, or has been, made at the time, as the objection contends. To settle their wills on doing what their reasons may presently incline them to do, the agents must make an effort to overcome the conflicting and resistant motives in their wills for not making the choice in question.

Relevant here is the distinction, introduced in Chapter 2 (2.10), between *will-setting* and *will-settled* actions. Actions are will-setting when the wills of agents are *not* already set one way when they act (P29–P30). They settle their wills in one way rather than another in the performance of the actions themselves. Choices or decisions that are self-forming actions are will-setting in this sense. The agents' wills are not already set one way before they choose or decide, but they set their wills one way or the other, voluntarily, intentionally, and rationally, in the act of choosing or deciding.

This objection of Franklin's assumes that if you are making an effort to choose or decide to do something you want to do and want to try to do, then your will is already settled or decided on doing that thing. There are reasons why such an assumption may be tempting, reasons that were discussed in Chapter 4 (section 4.6). They have to do with the fact that our normal intuitions about efforts are formed in everyday situations in which our wills are already settled on doing something, where obstacles and resistance have to be overcome. We want to open a closet door which is jammed, so we have to make an effort to open it. Such ordinary situations are what were earlier called "will-settled" situations, where our wills are already settled on doing what we are making efforts to do (P123).

By contrast, self-forming choices being "will-setting," our wills are not already settled on doing what we may be making one or another effort to do. The resistance that has to be overcome by effort is not coming from an external source such as the jammed closet door. It is coming from our own wills. We "settle" our wills one way or the other only in the act of choosing itself, when an effort we are making succeeds in overcoming resistance in our will to making the choice in question (P128). The idea here was summed up in

(P131) Because most efforts in everyday life, such as the effort to open the jammed closet door, are made in will-settled situations where our wills are already settled on doing what we are trying or making efforts to do, we tend to assimilate all effort making to such situations. But we thereby fail to consider the uniqueness of *will-setting, which is of a piece, in my view, with the uniqueness of free will.*

The second counterintuitive feature of my view that Franklin considers in his Chapter 4 concerns my postulation of *concurrent* efforts of will prior to self-forming choices. His concerns here are similar to those expressed by Mele and other critics of my concurrent efforts view. And since I have granted the cogency of such concerns and no longer defend such a view in this book, I will move on to what Franklin regards as the third counterintuitive feature of my view. He says,

> The third counterintuitive feature of Kane's account is that his location of indeterminism makes indeterminism an obstacle to agents carrying out their goals, and, in this sense, diminishes their control. . . . Kane's argument . . . was that while indeterminism diminishes one kind of control, it enhances another kind of control. But even if that is true, it does not obviously follow that agents who satisfy Kane's theory have, all things considered, more control than they would have if they satisfied only compatibilist theories. Compatibilists . . . must concede that, on their accounts, agents do not have plural voluntary control, but they can counter Kane by arguing that their accounts allow that all free agents' efforts guarantee success. That is, they can allow that all free agent's efforts to perform [certain actions] deterministically bring about [those actions]. (p. 103)

Indeed, compatibilists *can* allow this. But what they cannot allow, as Franklin himself concedes, is the kind of control made possible on my account, namely plural voluntary control, which is an enhanced kind of control that most libertarians believe is necessary at some times in their lives over their free choices or decisions. For such plural voluntary control is the power to make either one of a set of competing possible choices or decisions, and to do so *in accordance with one's will*, whichever choice or decision should be made. This kind of control requires that the choice or decision that is made was not determined by the agent's existing will at the time. If all choices or decisions were determined by the agent's existing will at the time they were made, as compatibilists would allow, it would have been causally impossible for agents to have had the power to have *willingly* chosen or decided otherwise than they did. This power, which is incompatible with determinism, is what most libertarians, myself included, want to affirm for freedom of *will*.

About the fourth problem Franklin identifies with my view he says,

> The final counterintuitive element of Kane's theory I want to highlight is that his account entails that a *directly* free action and for which [the agent] is *directly* morally responsible must be a *nonbasic action*. But this does not seem possible. An agent's nonbasic action is a derivative action: it is an action ultimately in virtue of a basic action the agent performs. (p. 105)

This objection requires further explication. The "*directly* free" and "*directly* morally responsible" action he refers to is in my view the self-forming choice itself that results from deliberation when the will is conflicted. It turns out as a consequence, he argues, that this directly free and responsible action (the self-forming choice) must, on my view, be a *nonbasic action*. That is, it must be an action that is *brought about by some other action*, namely, an effort of will.

Franklin argues that it is desirable to get a simpler and more attractive EC view in which *directly* free and responsible actions turn out to be *basic* actions, not nonbasic actions. To get such a simpler view, he says:

> I have discarded, or at least demoted, efforts of will and am now envisioning free agents' basic action as choice. Somewhat ironically, then, on both Kane's and my theory it will be choice that is undetermined. However, on my proposed revision, free agents do not bring about their directly free undetermined choices by performing some other action, such as an effort of will. Rather, their directly free choices are brought about by *nonactional* states or events involving them, such as their reasons. (p. 107)

The desire to get a simpler theory is laudable. But I think something is lost by making this kind of move to a simpler theory.

> (P267) For the role of efforts of will in my picture was to account for how the *agent* could exercise *control* over *which* undetermined choice was made for the reasons supporting that particular choice, rather than an alternative. And given such efforts of will, the causal role of the agent would not be *reducible* to causation by "nonactional" mental states or events of the agents alone. Free choices would not simply be "brought about by *nonactional*

states or events involving the agents, such as their reasons," which is the problem with all purely event-causal views. For it leaves out the added role of the agents, as complex dynamical systems, exercising guidance control over the cognitive processes causally linking the nonactional mental states and events to the choices or decisions they cause (P148–P149).

As a consequence,

(P268) The appeal to efforts of will also allows one to make room for an irreducible causal role for the agent in bringing about a particular choice. And importantly, as a result, *it thereby allows one to counter the problem of agency reductionism which, if true*, as Franklin himself argues, would undermine the kind of minimal event-causal libertarianism he wishes to defend in his book. Simplicity is not always a good thing. Sometimes it may leave important things out.

But Franklin raises a further frequently made objection at this point to the appeal to efforts of will for this purpose. If agents are free and responsible with respect to their choices in such cases, he argues, the agents must also be free and responsible with respect to the efforts that give rise to the choices. But then, he says, "the threat of an infinite regress looms . . . requiring the effort of will to be undetermined and raising the problem of luck, now, at the level of the prior effort of will" (2018, p. 105).

This is a common regress objection to postulating efforts of will that has often been raised; and it is an objection I addressed at length in Chapter 5 (sections 5.4–5.6; P162–P170). I will not try to repeat the entire argument of the relevant section of Chapter 5 here, which appeals to distinctions defined earlier between different kinds of freedom (Chapter 2, section 2.12; P37–P40) and different dimensions of responsibility (Chapter 3, section 3.5; P53–P54). But a few key themes from this section of Chapter 5 are important to answering Franklin's objection to efforts of will at this point and are worth reviewing.

Efforts or exercises of willpower that may lead to self-forming choices would not themselves be undetermined self-forming actions, hence not free acts of kind 3. But such efforts must and would be free acts of kind 1: they must be acts done voluntarily, on purpose and for reasons that are not coerced, compelled, or otherwise controlled. And many of these efforts of will would also be free acts of kind 2, acts "done of the agent's own free will" in the sense of a will that the agent was responsible for forming in part by prior undetermined self-forming actions (P162).[4] Efforts of will that were free acts of kind 1 would also be responsible actions in the first dimension of responsibility: agents making such efforts would be *expressing the will they had in action*, and doing so voluntarily and intentionally (P167). Efforts that were also free acts of kind 2 would be responsible actions in both the first and second dimensions: agents making them would be responsible both for *expressing the will they had in action* and *for having the will they were expressing in action* (P168).

But, importantly, while efforts or exercises of willpower that may lead to self-forming actions may be free and responsible acts in these senses, *it is not required that the occurrences of these efforts or exercises of willpower be themselves undetermined*, like the self-forming actions to which they may give rise. The reason for this lies in the *context* of self-forming choice situations in which such efforts are initiated (P170). First, the efforts are goal-directed *processes* that take a time to occur. Second, the context in which they occur involves a conflict in the will that is the reason why an effort is needed in the first place. Third, this conflict in the will is also the source of the indeterminism that is ingredient in the trajectory of whatever effort may be initiated, making its success uncertain.

As a consequence of these features, the following would be the case, as summed up in the following condensed version of:

(P169) While the *initiation* and hence the *occurrence* of such efforts of will may be *determined* by the trajectory of the agent's reasoning when the efforts occur, the *outcomes* of these efforts (the choices that may result from them) would *not* be determined by the conditions that led to the occurrence of the efforts. This would be so because the indeterminism ingredient in the efforts, whose origin is in the agent's conflicted will, would have made it uncertain that the outcomes of the efforts would be attained. Thus, while each effort or exercise of willpower would not itself be such that its occurring was undetermined, if it did occur and was to succeed in attaining its goal, overcoming the resistance in the will, it would bring about a self-forming choice whose occurrence was undetermined and yet successfully probabilistically caused.

Return now to the familiar worries about infinite regresses of past efforts and the reappearance of luck at the level of prior efforts, to which Franklin appeals here.

(P269) There is no threat of an infinite regress in this case because there is no requirement that the initiation and hence the occurrence of the efforts of will be undetermined like the occurrence of the self-forming actions to which those efforts may give rise. Nor does a problem of luck reappear "at the level of the prior effort of will," for it is not a mere matter of luck that such efforts of will occur. They occur when the agents' reasons incline them to make a particular choice that can only be made by making an effort to overcome resistance in the will to making it; and they are initiated voluntarily and intentionally by the *agent* when the agent's reasoning reaches such a point.

One of the many contributions of Franklin's book is that he has done us a service in bringing out the importance of the relation of agency reductionism, on the one hand, and the "It Ain't Me Argument," on the other, to current debates about libertarian views of free will and to the viability of purely EC libertarian views. In the concluding paragraph of his chapter 7 (2018, p. 196), he says, "The real problem for event-causal libertarianism is the tenability of agency reductionism itself. Does the theory afford the self a robust enough role in action to account for the power of self-determination?"

(P270) As I've argued here, postulating efforts of will addresses both related problems of agency reductionism and the "It Ain't Me Argument," which (if he is right, as I think he is) are two major unsolved problems faced by pure event-causal libertarian views of the kind his book defends. The addition of such efforts of will (i) allows one to say that the role of the agent in bringing about libertarian free actions is not reducible to causation by nonactional states or events involving the agent alone; and the addition of efforts of will as teleological or ends-directed actions under the guidance control of the self or agent (ii) affords the self a robust enough role in action to account for the power of *self*-determination. The addition of such efforts understood in the manner described here thus addresses the two major unsolved problems that Franklin rightly identifies as being faced by pure EC views of libertarian free will. They do so, however, by making clear that an irreducible causal role of the agent is critical to understanding the causal role of mental events in libertarian free actions (hence AC/EC).

7.11. Franklin on the Failure of Agency Reductionism

As noted earlier, in further writings since his book appeared, Franklin himself has argued that agency reductionism fails and that an irreducible role of the agent is in fact needed to account for libertarian free will. Prominent among these more recent papers is "The Heart of Libertarianism: Fundamentality and the Will" (2019).[5] In this paper, he argues that "cases of motivational conflict reveal the limits of event-causal theories" of free will (p. 74). It is "this idea of motivational conflict" that EC theories cannot account for and that require a fundamental role for the agent (p. 3).

I agree with these claims, which are supported in my previous writings, including my earlier books *Free Will and Values* (1985) and *The Significance of Free Will* (1996): in these works, agency reductionism is not assumed, and an irreducible role of the agent is in fact needed to account for libertarian free will. Moreover, the need for such an irreducible role for the agent is revealed, among other things, by reflecting on motivational conflicts in the wills of agents. These were in fact reasons I did not designate my view as simply "event-causal" in these earlier writings and now wish to designate it as an agent-causal/event-causal (AC/EC) view, to avoid further misunderstandings. I thus applaud Franklin for these developments in his more recent writings. But still there are significant differences in the way these ideas are developed in our views that are instructive and need to be considered.

As a result of rejecting agency reductionism and assuming an irreducible role for the agent in libertarian free will in these recent writings, Franklin refers to his revised view as an agent-causal theory. But because he continues to hold that motives or reasons also play a causal role in libertarian free choices, he adds the following: "I adopt," following Randolph Clarke, what Clarke calls an "integrative" agent-causal theory in which "some of the agent's motivations are always joint causes with the agent when he exercises his will" (2019, p. 9). Clarke's integrative agent-causal view will be considered in the next chapter, where a variety of other AC views are considered. But it is worth noting here that Clarke himself has since criticized AC views of free will in general, including his own integrative view, and he no longer endorses a libertarian view of free will at all. Nonetheless, I believe we can say of Franklin's endorsement of Clarke's integrative agent-causal view what I will say, both positively and negatively, of Clarke's integrative view in the next chapter:

(P271) Clarke's suggestion of an "integrated agent-causal account" of libertarian free will is a step in the right direction. For it points to the need for both an irreducible role for agent causation and an irreducible role for event causation in an adequate libertarian account of free will. As a consequence, it would bring AC views closer to the kind of AC/EC view I have been defending in this book.

(P272) But, perhaps surprisingly, I would also argue that Clarke's suggested integrated agent causal view, here adopted by Franklin, *does not give enough of a role to agent causation* to provide an adequate account of libertarian free will. Franklin follows Clarke in saying that, on such an integrated agent-causal view, a libertarian free choice or action is caused by an agent and at the same time it is "co-caused" by certain mental states and events of the agent (2019, p. 9; Clarke 2011, p. 345). This is true on the AC/EC view I defend as well. But it does not capture all that is true about the causal role of the agent on this AC/EC view. What is also true on this AC/EC view is that it is the *agent* qua complex dynamical system who *causes* or *brings it about that* the *particular* mental states and events that "co-cause" the choice or action, do in fact play the co-causal roles they do. Agents do this, qua complex dynamical systems, by exercising teleological guidance control over the cognitive processes *causally linking* the mental states or events that provide the reasons for the choice or action to the choice or action itself.

(P273) *Indeed, efforts of will on my account are particular cases of agents' exercising teleological guidance control over processes linking mental states or events that provide reasons for a choice or decision, particular cases which occur in those special situations where there is resistance in the will that has to be overcome to bring about the choice or decision in question.* In sum, *efforts of will are effortful exercises of teleological guidance control*

(P274) This allows one to also answer a common objection sometimes made to both EC views and to integrated agent-causal views. The objection in question points to the fact that agents may have different reasons or motives for making a particular choice or performing a certain action, only some of which reasons or motives may have actually played a role in motivating and causing the choice or action on a particular occasion. What would account for this difference? The answer on the agent-causal/EC view would be that those reasons or motives which actually motivate a particular choice or action on a given occasion are those that are *causally linked* to the choice or action *by* the teleological guidance control exercised by the *agent* as a complex dynamical system on that occasion.

It thus follows:

(P275) Both the reasons or motives, on the one hand, and the agent, on the other, are causally involved in free actions on this AC/EC view, as on Franklin's revised view. But it is the agent who *does* something (exercises TGC) *to bring it about* that these *particular* reasons or motives play the causal roles they do, whereas other possible reasons or motives that might be reasons for the same choice on other occasions may not be causally involved in this instance. The reasons or motives that are causally involved do not just "happen" to be causally involved. They are so because the agent actively "sees to it that" they are causally involved.

Another significant difference between Franklin's revised view and the AC/EC view defended here concerns his treatment of contrastive explanations. A common objection considered earlier (Chapter 5, section 5.11) against libertarian theories requiring indeterminism is that they cannot adequately account for contrastive explanations, that is, explanations in terms of an agent's prior character, reasons, or motives for why the agent made one choice *rather than* another. Franklin deals with this objection in his revised view in the same way he deals with it in his book.

He considers van Inwagen's example of an agent I've called John, who is conflicted about stealing from a church poor box. On the one hand, John has strong reasons for stealing the money (his desperate need for the money) but also strong reasons for not doing so (his promise to his late mother to act morally and avoid stealing money meant to help others). Franklin, appealing to Christopher Hitchcock's (2012) influential work on such explanations, argues that if John chooses to steal the money, we *can* give a contrastive explanation of why he did so. We can do so by simply citing the reasons he had for choosing to steal the money (his desperate need for the money) *rather than* his reasons for not doing so (his promise to his mother). And if he had chosen not to steal the money, we could cite his reasons for not doing so (his promise to his mother) *rather than* his reasons for doing so. Franklin calls this a "type 2" contrastive explanation.

Critics of libertarian views requiring indeterminism, however, would not find such a contrastive explanation adequate, as Franklin is well aware. They argue that, for a fully adequate contrastive explanation, if John chose to steal the money, one would also want to know not merely what reasons he had for doing so rather than doing otherwise, but also why he chose *for the reasons he had* for stealing the money *rather than for the reasons he had* for *not* stealing the money, or vice versa. To be sure, we could cite reasons he had for either choice, if it is made. But this wouldn't tell us why this particular choice was made for its reasons *rather than* the alternative choice for its reasons; and it wouldn't tell us why the choice was made for certain reasons the agent had for this choice rather than for other reasons the agent might have had for this same choice. Franklin argues that on libertarian views requiring indeterminism, one cannot give this stronger kind of contrastive explanation (which he calls a "type 1" contrastive explanation). But it doesn't matter, he argues, because in practice we simply cite the reasons the agent had for the choice made and that is good enough.

But I agree here with those critics of libertarian views who say that this is *not* good enough. One should and can do more to account for contrastive explanations of type 1 as well as type 2, even granting that whatever choice is made would be undetermined. I explained how this might be done in the context of the AC/EC view in Chapters 4 and 5. To summarize, in cases of self-forming choices which involve such "motivational conflict," and of which John's choosing to steal the money is an example, we must first imagine that the reasons motivating the choice to steal the money merely incline the agent to make that choice at this time rather than the alternative. These reasons are not decisive or conclusive, nor do they determine he will do so. If a choice is to be made in accord with these inclinations, effort would have to be made or willpower exerted to overcome the still-existing resistance in his will (P91–P95).

Though the reasons merely incline and are not decisive, when it is the case that the agent judges that they incline to one choice to a degree that might justify making that choice at the time, an effort would be initiated to make that choice and thereby to overcome the still-existent resistant motives in the will. Indeterminism would enter the picture here, but it would not just happen to occur. Rather, the conflict in the will of the agent would "stir up" indeterminism in the effort to make the choice to which the agent is currently inclined, making it uncertain the effort will succeed in attaining its goal. If the effort does succeed, despite this indeterminism, the choice to steal to which John is presently inclined would be made and the deliberation would terminate (P96).

(P276) Note that if this should happen, we would have a strong (type 1) contrastive explanation for John's stealing the money as well as a weaker (type 2) explanation. We could do more than simply cite John's reasons for stealing the money rather than doing otherwise (by citing his strong desire and need for the money) (type 2). We could *also* say why, in these circumstances, he chose *for these reasons he had for stealing the money rather than* for other reasons he also had for *not* stealing the money (type 1). We could say the following: his reasons for stealing the money in these circumstances inclined him to a degree that would justify making an effort to make the choice to steal at this time, thereby overcoming his resistant motives for choosing not to steal. If *he succeeded in that effort*, despite the possibility of failure due to the indeterminism stirred up by the conflict in his will, his making this choice at the time *rather than* any other, would not be *unexplained*, even though it would be undetermined.

Franklin in his revised view continues to reject appeals to efforts of will in making sense of libertarian free will. He thinks that by rejecting the need for efforts to resolve motivational conflicts we get a simpler theory, with no losses that matter. But, as I've argued, there are significant losses incurred. By appealing to efforts in cases of motivational conflict, we can give agents a greater causal role in resolving motivational conflicts in their wills. For such appeals allow us to say (P272–P273) that it is the agent who *does* something (exercises TGC) over processes (efforts of will) whose goal is *to bring it about* that certain *particular* reasons or motives play the causal roles they do in motivating a choice, whereas other possible reasons or motives that might have been reasons for the same choice on other occasions may not be causally involved in this instance. The reasons or motives that are causally involved are so because the agent actively "sees to it that" they are causally involved by making efforts to choose in terms of them.

We thus see how such appeals to efforts of will provide a stronger reply to critics who argue that libertarian theories of free will cannot adequately account for contrastive explanations.[6] We've also seen earlier (Chapter 5) how appeals to efforts of will would help to answer other common objections to libertarian accounts of free will, such as explanatory luck objections and rollback objections.

(P277) Regarding rollback objections, for example, on the libertarian view presented here involving efforts, the following would be the case: if we rollback to a time just before an undetermined free choice, A, was made and replayed the scene up to the moment of that choice, it would not be the case that we might see a different choice (B) emerge from exactly that same past in such a rollback. It would not be the case that B might emerge from the same past, that is, if B were to be a voluntary, intentional, and rational choice, as a free libertarian choice would require, rather than a mere accident. For the past in which the choice of A occurred would have involved an effort of will to make the choice of A for the reasons motivating that choice rather than any alternative choice, an effort that might have failed because its outcome was undetermined, yet succeeded in bringing about the choice of A. If an alternative choice B were to occur as a voluntary, intentional, and rational choice, it could not occur as a result of that same past, but would have to occur at some other time in the deliberation and would be preceded at that other time by an effort of will to make that choice B rather than the choice of A for the reasons motivating the choice of B rather than the choice of A.

In summary, in recent writings beyond his book, Franklin has made some important further steps that bring his view closer to mine. I welcome these further steps, for there was already much in his book and earlier writings that contributes to making sense of libertarian free will that I also agree with. His emphasis on the irreducible role of agents brings his view even closer to my AC/EC view, despite the remaining differences noted.

7.12. Preferences: Ekstrom's Event-Causal Libertarianism

Laura Ekstrom's EC libertarian view is often treated as a deliberative or non-centered view, and this is correct insofar as she places the required indeterminism earlier in the deliberative process rather than at the end in the final decision itself. But she distances her view in a number of interesting ways from other deliberative views considered in Chapter 6, such as Dennett's Valerian view and Mele's modest libertarianism, that make her view worth considering separately.

On Ekstrom's view, the notion of *preference* plays a central role, rather than the notion of *evaluative judgment*, as in the deliberative views suggested by

Dennett and Mele. She says that an act (including a choice terminating deliberation) "is free just in case it results by a normal causal process from a preference for the act," where the preference is a desire "formed by a process of critical evaluation with respect to one's conception of the good" (2000, p. 106; 2011, p. 373). She requires indeterminism only in the production of these preferences, allowing that free decisions may be causally determined by prior formed preferences favoring those decisions. The considerations that come to mind and lead to the formation of preferences may also be undetermined, but they do not have to be. On these points, she departs from Dennett's and Mele's suggestions as well, which require indeterminism in the coming-to-mind of various considerations that influence evaluative judgments. For Ekstrom, while indeterminism may occur earlier in this way, the only required indeterminism is in the formation of the preferences themselves.

She also faults Dennett's and Mele's deliberative views on the grounds that neither provides an account of the self. The self, on her view, is the agent's preferences and reflectively formed beliefs, together with her faculty of forming these by reflective evaluation with respect to her conception of the good (2000, pp. 106, 137). The preferences in question must have what Ekstrom calls *undefeated authorization*: they must be noncoercively formed and maintained and must be caused but not determined by the inputs to the agent's deliberative process (2011, p. 373). Preferences understood in this way, she says, are "key components in the identity of the self" (2014, p. 66).

Critics of Ekstrom's view such as Clarke, Pereboom, and Franklin have focused, as one might expect, on the undetermined formation of these preferences. About this, she says:

> At the point in time of the deliberation over the various factors relevant to what to decide to prefer to do . . . the free agent's decision might terminate in one way, and it might terminate in another way, instead. The resulting decision output, the preference, when indeterministically caused and noncoercively formed, is authored by the agent since it is formed by her for reasons that justify or explain it, and its claim to being authentic is not defeated by the objection that she formed it [in a manner that] was causally necessitated [or determined] by the past and the natural laws. The preference, that is, has undefeated authorization. (2011, p. 373)

The first thing to be noted here is this: if the formation of a preference in such manner must be undetermined, so that it "might terminate in one way, and ... might terminate in another way, instead," then it seems that different preferences (e.g., to cheat or not to cheat, to lie or tell the truth) might be formed given exactly the same past and laws, including exactly the same reasoning processes of the agent up to the moment of formation of one preference or another. What then would explain why one preference was formed at that time rather that another?

An initial answer consistent with her view might be that the preference decided upon would have been favored "by a process of critical evaluation with respect to the agent's conception of the good," whereas any other preference that might occur would not have been so favored by such a critical evaluation process. But then the presence of indeterminism in the formation of preferences would seem to diminish the agent's control by making it possible that the preference formed might not be the one favored by the prior process of critical evaluation, but rather some other preference not favored by such a critical process that just happened to occur instead because of the indeterminism.

Compatibilists and free will skeptics could thus argue, and many have argued, that requiring indeterminism in this manner at the point of formation of the preference would merely diminish the agent's rational control over which preference was formed rather than enhance that rational control. Compatibilists could further argue that the agent would have *more* control if the preference formed was *determined* by the preceding process of critical evaluation with respect to the agent's conception of the good, so that no other preference not satisfying these conditions could be formed instead.

To this objection one might respond by saying that if the preference favored by the prior process of critical evaluation failed to be formed because of the indeterminism, it would not be the case that an alternative preference might be formed instead that was not favored by this critical process. Rather, if the preference favored by the prior critical process failed to occur due to the indeterminism, no preference would be formed at all at the time. But to this, compatibilists could respond in turn, with some justification, that requiring indeterminism at the point of formation of the preference would in this case also merely diminish the agent's rational control over the outcome rather than enhance that rational control. For the agent would have *more* control, compatibilists could argue, if the preference favored was *determined* by the preceding process of critical evaluation, so that the preference favored by that critical process could not fail to be formed due to the indeterminism.

7.13. Preference Formation, Will-Setting, and Self-Formation: Further Comments on Ekstrom

What seems to have been lost sight of in the preceding dialectic is the role indeterminism is supposed to play in libertarian accounts of free will, a role that could not be satisfied if determinism were true. Indeterminism is supposed to make it possible, as determinism would not, for agents to have the power at some points in their lives to "settle" their will in one direction or in a different direction, and to do so *in accordance with their will*, in *whichever* direction they may settle their will (P54, P197–P199).

This "will-settling" or "will-setting," to be sure, need not occur only in making choices or decisions that terminate deliberation. It can also occur in other places earlier in deliberation, as we found in Chapter 6, such as in the formation of evaluative judgments in the deliberative views of Dennett and Mele, among other places.

> (P278) We might now add that such "will-setting" could also occur earlier in deliberation in the formation of preferences, as in Ekstrom's view. But for this to be the case, certain further assumptions would have to be made analogous to those made in the formation of evaluative judgments and other cases of "will-setting" earlier in deliberation. For example, in order to capture the requirement that different preferences might be voluntarily, intentionally, and rationally formed by the agent, the processes of critical evaluation leading to preference formation must not always *decisively* or *deterministically* "settle" the agent's will on the goodness or rightness of forming a particular preference rather than any alternative. These processes of critical evaluation would have to sometimes leave the agent with a conflicted will about which goods should be favored and hence which competing preference should be formed.

> (P279) In such cases, the processes of critical evaluation leading to preference formation might incline the agent to form one preference rather than another, but they would only incline. They would not be decisive or determining and would not definitively resolve the conflict in the agent's will if the formation of the preference was to be undetermined. If a preference were to be formed in accord with these inclining reasons, effort would thus have to be made or willpower exerted to overcome this conflict in the will coming from the motives to form an opposing preference. It would

not then matter if the final decision terminating deliberation was determined by this prior formed preference. For the crucial indeterminism would have come earlier in the agent's successfully forming this preference rather than any alternative, by overcoming resistance in the will to doing so (P211–P213).[7]

The crucial takeaway here is that for instances of preference formation to be "self-forming" in this way, agents' "conceptions of their good" must be more complex than Ekstrom's account seems to suggest. Consider, for instance, Balaguer's Ralph deciding whether to form a preference to stay in Mayberry, become a manager at a small local business, and marry his childhood sweetheart, or to go to New York to be in an off-Broadway play. He is conflicted about *which* aspect of his "conception of the good" ought to prevail in this circumstance. Or consider Claudia, the law school graduate trying to decide whether she prefers to join the large law firm in the big city or the smaller, up-and-coming firm nearer home. She is conflicted about which aspects of her "conception of the good" ought to prevail in forming such a preference. Or consider John trying to decide whether to form a preference to steal the money he desperately needs or a preference to refrain from taking the money intended for the good of others. Or Huck Finn, trying to decide whether his notion of the good (his "true values," as Doris puts it) favor forming a preference to turn his friend Jim over to the authorities or favor forming a preference not to do so.

Among the lessons in these examples is that the "conception of the good" of beings capable of such self- and will-formation is complex, not simple, multifaceted, not monolithic, and capable of change, not static. In addition, one's conception of the "good" in such contexts of self- and will-formation doesn't necessarily have to mean the "moral" good. It's not clear that a special account of the good, such as the moral good, is what Ekstrom actually has in mind by an agent's "conception of the good." But if this were what she has in mind, the resulting view of libertarian "free will" would be problematic. For it would imply that we could only act freely and responsibly in a libertarian sense when we decide to form moral preferences, never when we decide to form self-interested or immoral ones (not to mention people having different views about what the moral good may be in many circumstances). Likewise, if one's conception of the good included only what was prudentially good, then one could only act freely and responsibly in a libertarian sense when one did the prudent thing or formed the prudent preference, never the imprudent one.

Claims that one would only be acting freely and responsibly if one acted morally or prudently are problematic. For those who have free will, as I have said, live somewhere east of Eden, having gained the power to settle their wills in different ways, but having lost innocence in the process, so that they may sometimes settle their wills on immoral or imprudent preferences. Or they might settle their wills on one or another set of competing goods they may be seeking, for example, which future path in life they would prefer to take; and they could also be acting freely and responsibly when settling their will either way in such circumstances.

(P280) In summary, three things need to be avoided in postulating indeterminism at the time of the formation or creation of preferences (as with choices). (1) One must avoid its being the case that, due to the indeterminism, a preference might just happen to occur that is not the one favored by the agent's prior process of critical reasoning and evaluation. (2) One must also avoid the possibility that the teleologically guided process leading to the creation of the preference allows it to be the case that *one or the other* of *opposing* preferences might be formed as a result of that very same teleologically guided process, where it is undetermined which one is formed. This *would* be the case if the only teleologically guided process that produced the preference was the deliberation itself and the outcome of that deliberation was undetermined. (3) One must also avoid its being the case that the indeterminism merely plays a role in diminishing the guidance control over the formation of the preference, without as a consequence thereby enhancing the agent's power to form one or another of different preferences in the course of deliberation, in accordance with the agent's will, either way.

(P281) Note that postulating efforts of will, as in the view developed here, at various points in deliberation when the agents' processes of critical evaluation incline them to form a particular preference, allows one to avoid each of these consequences. (1) It rules out the possibility that, due to the indeterminism, some other preference not favored by the agent's prior process of evaluation might have been formed at the time when the favored preference was formed. If the favored preference fails to be formed, no preference would be formed at all at that time.

(P282) In addition, postulating efforts of will, as in the view developed here, rules out (2) the possibility that, due to the indeterminism, the teleologically guided process leading to the creation of the preference (namely, the effort of will) might allow that either one of opposing preferences might be formed, voluntarily, intentionally, and rationally, as a result of that same teleologically guided process, whose goal was to form a particular preference *rather than* any opposing preference.

(P283) Finally, postulating efforts of will in this manner (3) allows one to avoid its being the case that the indeterminism merely plays a role in diminishing the guidance control over the formation of the preference, without thereby also enhancing the agent's power to form either one or another of different preferences in the course of a deliberation, in accordance with the agent's will, either way. By being a hindrance or obstacle to the success of an effort of will to form a particular preference, the indeterminism would thereby open up the genuine possibility of forming some alternative preference at some other time in the course of deliberation, also in accordance with, rather than against, the agent's will. To be a genuinely self-forming agent (a creator of one's own will)—to have free will—there must at times in life be obstacles and hindrances in one's will of this sort that one must overcome (P143–P144).

(P284) In sum, allowing the possibility of different efforts of will under the teleological guidance control of agents is not superfluous in making sense of libertarian free will. Doing so allows one to avoid the preceding problems posed by requiring indeterminism in accounts of free will. And, as we have seen earlier, allowing the possibility of such efforts also allows one to avoid the problems posed by "agency reductionism" and the "It Ain't Me Argument."

Ekstrom is right, however, that such will-setting and self-formation *could* also occur in deciding to form one preference rather than another in the course of our processes of practical reasoning. She is right as well that such preference formation might play a crucial role in the formation of the self—in becoming the kinds of persons we are with the wills (characters, motives, purposes, *and* preferences) we have. We can thus accommodate preference formation as yet another of the ways in which *self*-formation may enter into the practical lives of agents in the account of free will given here—though preference formation would only be one, and not the only, significant way in which undetermined actions could play a role in the formation of the self.

7.14. A Modified Nozickian Event-Causal View: Lemos

John Lemos's initial philosophical writing focused on philosophy of science, especially biological sciences, and culminated in a book, *Commonsense Darwinism: Evolution, Morality and the Human Condition*, published in 2008. During that time, Lemos also became interested in issues about free will. He was attracted to a libertarian position on free will that would be consistent with the sciences and he took a particular interest in my view. There followed a series of articles (beginning in 2007) defending a view like mine against various criticisms, but also raising some questions about it. This work culminated in an important book, *A Pragmatic Approach to Libertarian Free Will*, published in 2018. On the initial page describing the aims of this book, he says,

> This book argues that the kind of free will required for moral responsibility and just desert is libertarian free will. It is a source of great controversy whether such a libertarian free will is coherent and whether we should believe we have such a free will. This book explains and defends Robert Kane's conception of libertarian free will while departing from it in certain respects. It is argued that a suitably modified Kanean model of free will can be shown to be conceptually coherent.[8]

The two objections to my previous view of simultaneous plural efforts that he believes have not been adequately addressed in my prior writings are what I have called the phenomenological and irrationality objections. About the first, phenomenological, objection, he says that if these simultaneous competing plural efforts that I propose to make opposing choices occur completely unconsciously, then "it is hard to see how an agent can have the conscious control over them that is necessary to be responsible for" the self-forming actions that may be caused by them (2018, p. 77). On the second, irrationality, objection, he says that "to exert effort to do two different actions which cannot both be performed is irrational" (p. 77).[9] Lemos's support for these objections against my previous simultaneous competing efforts view over the past decade have played a further role in leading me to change this view—particularly because he was otherwise sympathetic to my approach to free will and had insightfully defended many other aspects of my view in his writings over this period.

As indicated, I no longer appeal to concurrent competing efforts in my view, as a result of these criticisms and similar criticisms of others, including others, like Mele, discussed in this chapter. Instead, on the view defended here, a single effort is made when the agent's reasons incline the agent to make a particular choice rather than another and when resistance in the will must be overcome to do so. It is not irrational, as I've argued, to make a single effort in this manner to overcome resistance in one's will.[10] We are aware of the need for such effort making when we are experientially torn in this manner about what to do and have to overcome resistance in our will if one choice rather than another is to be made (P242).[11]

Having made these objections in his book, Lemos goes on to suggest alternative views that he believes would avoid the problems he sees with the appeal to concurrent efforts. It is instructive to compare the most important of these alternative views to the revised view of this book, which was not fully developed when his book was being written. The alternative view he suggests that I believe is the most important is what he calls a "modified Nozickian" view of libertarian free will.

Robert Nozick was one of the philosophers mentioned earlier who, along with me in the 1970s and 1980s, suggested alternative models of libertarian free will that might be compatible with contemporary science, and were unlike the noncausal and AC libertarian views prevalent at the time. Nozick's view was suggested in a chapter of his 1981 book, *Philosophical Explanations*, a large work that dealt in interesting ways with a great variety of philosophical issues. About the view of free will suggested by Nozick in this book, Lemos says,

> Nozick holds that our causally undetermined free decisions occur when we make torn decisions, when certain reasons make the choice of one option, A, attractive and certain other reasons make another option, B, attractive. Nozick believes that when we make a decision in such situations our reasons cause our decision, but it's not necessarily the case that they deterministically cause it.... Furthermore, he says that when we make such undetermined choices, in choosing we assign greater weight to one set of reasons. In choosing, we [thereby] establish which considerations are of more value to us.... In this way, these undetermined decisions we make

contribute to shaping our hierarchy of values, making the decisions similar in certain respects to Kane's SFAs. (2018, pp. 106–7)

Lemos then adds, however, that Nozick's view, as stated, "suffers from problems similar to other event-causal views." (As examples of other EC views with similar problems, he mentions Balaguer's view, Mele's Daring View, and various deliberative EC views). Lemos then says,

> The problem with Nozick's view is that there is not enough agential involvement in the deliberation process in the moments leading up to choice to make sense of the agent's control over and responsibility for *which* choice gets made in basic undetermined free choices. . . . In contrast, on Kane's view since the agent exerts an effort to choose A prior to the choice of A and since the choice is indeterministically caused by this effort, it is the agent that makes the choice of A happen. And, of course, since the agent simultaneously makes an effort to choose B, then had he chosen B, he'd have been responsible for that choice instead. (p. 107)

Since Lemos has argued that my appeal here to simultaneous competing efforts has problems of its own, he suggests as an alternative account of agential involvement, a "modified" version of Nozick's view of "assigning weights to reasons."[12] To make the idea of assigning weights to reasons useful for this purpose, he says we need to reconceive the timings of these "weightings" of reasons postulated by Nozick.

Nozick says that at the moment of decision, in choosing one course of action over another, we assign greater weight to the reasons in favor of that action (1981, pp. 296–P297). But suppose we move the assigning of weights to reasons back prior to choice and suppose that the weight we assign to the reasons is not causally determined. Suppose as well that once the weights are assigned to the reasons, this then typically dictates in a determined way which choice gets made. For instance, suppose I am torn between doing A or B and have good reasons to do A and good reasons to do B, and thus I'm deliberating about which to do. Suppose that during deliberation, I do in a causally undetermined way assign greater weight to the reasons for A—that is, I assign greater value to those reasons than the reasons for B—and this leads me to choose A instead of B (Lemos 2018, p. 107).

Lemos then considers a number of objections to this "modified Nozickian view," the most important objection of which is similar to the objection he made to Nozick's original view. In Nozick's original view, since it is undetermined which decision is made at the time of decision by the totality of the agent's prior reasoning up to that time, there is nothing in the theory to explain why greater weight was assigned at the moment of decision to the reasons for one decision rather than the other.

The problem is that a similar objection would also seem to apply to the modified Nozickian view that Lemos himself suggests, in which the assignment of weights to reasons comes earlier in deliberation. For, on this modified view, it would also be undetermined by the totality of the agent's prior reasoning up to this earlier time *which* competing reasons would be assigned greater weight at this earlier time.[13] To establish the agent's control over the "causally undetermined weighting," Lemos says, "it will not suffice to note that the agent meets compatibilist criteria for assigning these weights. For even though such criteria are met, the weighting [of one set of reasons rather than another] may still be a consequence of [the indeterminism] over which [the agent] has no control. Whereas on Kane's view of SFAs in making a choice either way, the agent will succeed at something she was antecedently trying to do, and thus she will be responsible either way" (2018, p. 110).

In response to this objection, Lemos argues that this is less of a problem if the indeterminism comes earlier in the deliberation than if, as on Nozick's original view, it comes at the moment of decision. But it's not clear that this is the case. For, either way, whether the weighting comes at the time of decision or earlier, the agent would lack control over which competing reasons were assigned greater weight at that time, and this assignment in either case would determine which decision was ultimately made.

7.15. Further Expanding the Account of SFAs and Lemos's Nozickian View

What I now want to argue, however, is that this problem of agential involvement can be addressed if this modified Nozickian view of weighting reasons of Lemos is related to the view of this book. This would include the changes suggested in this book that allow one to avoid appeals to simultaneous competing efforts and thus allow one to avoid the phenomenological and irrationality objections he sees with such appeals. Interestingly, and perhaps more surprisingly, given these changes to the concurrent efforts view made here, I believe Nozick's original view of weighting reasons as well as Lemos's modifications can also be accommodated in the view of this book.

Consider Nozick's original view first. He holds that our causally undetermined free decisions occur when we make torn decisions, when certain reasons make the choice of one option, A, attractive and other reasons make another option, B, attractive. In making an undetermined decision in such situations, according to Nozick, we assign greater weight to the reasons favoring that decision. The problem Lemos sees with this original view of Nozick's is that since it must be undetermined which reasons are assigned greater weight at the moment of decision, given exactly the same reasons and reasoning process prior to the decision, there isn't enough agential involvement in the deliberation in the moments leading up to the decision to explain why the agent assigned greater weight to one set of reasons rather than another at the time of decision.

To address this problem in the manner suggested by the view of this book, the first change to be made would be to eliminate the requirement that greater weights might be assigned to different sets of reasons favoring one or another competing decision *at the same time* in the course of a deliberation, given exactly the same process of reasoning up to that time. Making this change would eliminate the need to postulate simultaneous competing efforts to make different choices at the same time.

The second change would be to add to Nozick's original view the assumption that in the reasoning process preceding a decision, the reasons considered by the agent would only *incline* without necessitating the agent to favor making that decision. These inclining reasons would not yet be conclusive, so that effort would have to be made to overcome the still-existing resistance in the agent's will coming from the reasons to make the alternative decision.

(P285) Given these additions, if this effort succeeds and the decision (say, A) is made, one can then interpret Nozick's view that greater weight is thereby assigned to the reasons for the decision A at the time of, and by, the making of the decision itself. For the reasons for making the decision A would have been assigned *greater weight* at the moment of decision, as Nozick requires, *by virtue of the fact that*, while they were only *inclining reasons before the decision*, they would have been made *decisive reasons by the making of the decision itself in terms of them*.

(P286) This transition from inclining to decisive reasons would have been brought about by the agent's successful effort to make the decision A favored by the inclining reasons, thereby overcoming resistance in the will. There would thus be "enough agential involvement in the deliberation process in the moments leading up to choice" to explain why it was the agent who assigned greater weight to a particular set of reasons rather than another in making the decision itself. The agent would have done so by succeeding in a goal-directed cognitive process (an effort or exercise of willpower) whose goal was to make the particular decision to which the agent's reasons then inclined, thereby assigning greater weight to those reasons by making them, not merely *inclining*, but *decisive*.

(P287) In addition, as Nozick also requires, the assignment of greater weight to one set of reasons rather than another in making the decision would have been caused by the agent, but *not deterministically caused*. This would be the case because of the indeterminism ingredient in the effort, whose source was in the conflict in the agent's will, which made it uncertain and undetermined that the effort would succeed and hence that the decision would be made assigning greater weight to the reasons for that decision. The indeterminism would not just luckily "happen" to be present at the moment when one decision was made rather than another. The assigning of these greater weights at the moment of decision would then be a *self*-forming action.

Turning now to Lemos's modified Nozickian view in which the assignment of greater weight to the reasons for one decision rather than another occurs earlier in deliberation, we can say similar things about the assignment of weights at this earlier time.

(P288) When the agent's deliberation reaches a certain point where the reasons for one decision, A, incline the agent to making that decision without yet being conclusive, an effort could be initiated to assign greater weight to those reasons by overcoming resistance in the will to doing so. If that effort succeeds, greater weight would be assigned to these reasons at this earlier time, so that they would become conclusive reasons, and the subsequent decision made in terms of them would be "will-settled." The assigning of greater weight to those reasons at this earlier time would also then be a self-forming action. Recall from (P92) that it is not *where* self-forming actions occur in the practical lives of agents that matters, but *how* they occur. Wherever they occur, *they "settle" the agent's will in one direction or another* and do so in accordance with the will, whichever way they settle it.

Indeed, I would suggest we could now say more radically the following:

(P289) (1) All self-forming actions, wherever they occur—at the moment of decision, or earlier in deliberation, or elsewhere—could be viewed as involving an assignment of greater weight to one set of reasons rather than others, making the set of reasons to which greater weight was assigned *decisive* when those reasons had only previously been *inclining*. (2) In addition, the assignment of greater weight to one set or reasons must be the result of a process under the teleological guidance control of the agent whose goal or telos is to assign decisive weight to one particular set of reasons rather than any other. (3) This teleologically guided process of the agent that assigned greater weight to one set of reasons rather than another would be an exercise of *striving* will, that is, an effort or exercise of willpower or striving to attain this goal against resistance, in this case resistance in the agent's own will. And (4) assigning greater weight to certain reasons in this manner would then be an integral feature of self-forming action wherever self-forming actions might occur in the practical lives of agents.[14]

With these additions made, I believe Lemos's modified Nozickian account of assigning greater weights to reasons as well as Nozick's original account could be accommodated in the view of this book.[15] In the process, something important would be added, namely, that self-forming actions *wherever* they occur would involve assigning greater weight to the reasons for the choice or other action settled upon. I would welcome this addition as well.[16]

8
The Libertarian Spectrum (Part III)
Agent-Causal and Noncausal Views

8.1. Agent-Causal Views (I): O'Connor

Timothy O'Connor has been a leading defender of an agent-causal, or AC, libertarian view of free will for the past several decades. In an earlier writing, he has said that "agent-causal views postulate a *sui generis* form of causation by an agent" that is not reducible to causation by events of any kinds involving the agent, physical or mental (1995, p. 7). In recent years, however, his view has undergone some refinements, as has mine, leading to a number of interesting convergences between our views that fall short of identity but are revealing about contemporary free will debates.

O'Connor himself nicely describes some of these convergences in a collection of essays edited by David Palmer (2014a) in which ten authors critically examine my views and I respond. O'Connor writes there,

> I agree with . . . Kane's basic orientation to the problem of free will, on which metaphysical freedom consists in being the ultimate, reasons-guided causal source of an intention to act in the face of alternative possibilities. . . . Over the years, he has developed and refined a complex analysis of what the exercise of such an ultimate causality consists in . . . intended to contrast with "agent-causal" accounts that take it as a conceptual and metaphysical primitive. I . . . argue, however, that when we draw out [the] metaphysical assumptions to which Kane's account is plausibly committed, we can easily be led to an account that is just a particular version of something like the primitivist agent-causal theory itself. . . . Kane's theory and the agent-causal theory are much closer than has so far been recognized. (p. 28)

The convergences in our views O'Connor mentions are many:

> (P290) (i) We both reject noncausalist views of free will, and (ii) eliminative reductionist views of the mental. (iii) We also both hold that substance dualism is not required to make sense of free will of the "ultimate, reasons guided causal kind" that libertarians require. (iv) We also both believe the exercise of free will requires emergent capacities or powers of some kinds. Though it's not clear, as he notes, that our accounts of emergence are exactly the same. (v) Yet we do both hold, he adds, that the emergent capacities and powers needed to account for free will need not be, in his words "spooky" and "not amenable to empirical investigation"; and (vi) we both relate the emergent capacities needed for libertarian free will to important new research on what have come to be called complex dynamical systems. Finally, (vii) we both espouse what he calls a neo-Aristotelian account of human agency, according to which explanations of human actions must include references to something akin to Aristotelian *formal* and *final* causation as well as *efficient* causation. (p. 30)

I do hold all these things. The Aristotelian connections are particularly interesting. They were noted in discussions of the teleological features of my view and in the role of complex dynamical systems and teleological guidance control in that view.[1]

In the light of these convergences, one might well ask what the differences are. One important difference emerges near the end of his essay where O'Connor asserts that "all causation is substance causation." This has been a theme of some agent-causationists in recent years, notably E. J. Lowe (2008), among others, though it is not accepted by all agent-causationists.[2] O'Connor arrives at it by way of a discussion of the metaphysics of causation in which he rejects neo-Humean and counterfactual theories of causation. I'm sympathetic to the critique of these theories of causation. But it hardly follows from this critique that all causation is substance causation; and I find this strong thesis highly implausible if it implies, as it seems to, that there is no such thing as causation by events or that causation by events plays no essential role in accounts of free agency and free will.

In my response to his essay, I note that earthquakes, for example, are events and they cause houses to collapse and much other damage. One might say geological plates cause earthquakes and they are substances. Yes, but also in addition, and more specifically, it is the *movement* of geological plates and the *slippage* between them that cause the quakes; and these are events. One can say an airplane caused one of the Twin Towers to collapse; and the airplane is a substance. But one can also say that the airplane's crashing into the upper stories of one of the Twin Towers caused the whole tower to collapse; and those are events. The event causes here are substance-involving events, to be sure. They involve geological plates and an airplane causing things. But the event descriptions give us more information about *how* and *why* the substances in question caused what they caused, more information than is given simply by saying that the substance (e.g., the airplane) caused what it caused (the collapse of the tower).

The same is true, I would say, of agents as causes of their choices or other actions. I do not deny that agents, like other substances, can be causes. However,

> (P291) It is a central thesis of my view that one doesn't have to choose between agent or substance causation, on the one hand, and agent-involving event causation, on the other, in describing human action and free will. You can, and should, affirm both. And, importantly, *neither is reducible to the other*. On the one hand, such agent-involving event-causal descriptions of action give us more information about *how* and *why* agents caused the choices or actions they caused, information that is not given simply by saying that "the agent caused this action at this time."

> (P292) On the other hand, accounts of the causal role of the *agent* in acting are also not reducible to accounts of causation of the action by events involving the agent alone, including mental events. That would leave out the role of the agents qua dynamical systems exercising guidance control over how and why certain events, including mental events, cause the actions. The agents do this "by guiding the flow of activity along neural pathways that establish the proper mappings between inputs, internal states, and outputs" (P147–P149). Thus, agency *reductionism* of the kind postulated by purely event-causal accounts of agency and free will, such as the minimal event-causal view of Franklin's book, also fails for reasons that Franklin himself notes and develops in more recent writings.

Hence the designation of the view developed here as an agent-causal/event-causal view rather than simply an AC or simply an EC view. Since O'Connor says many things that would seem to accord with the claims just made in P289–P292, might it be that agent-causal/event-causal is a better description of his view as well? It is difficult to say for sure.

One would have to ask what he would say about the following claims mentioned earlier that have played roles in one or another traditional AC account of free will (P154–P155). Would he say, for example, that his present view of agent causation: (1) involves a "sui generis" or "metaphysically primitive" notion of causation by an agent or substance, as he has sometimes said in the past? (In a preceding quotation, for example, he does say that my view was "intended to contrast with 'agent-causal' accounts that," like his view, take causation of free actions by agents "as a conceptual and metaphysical primitive" (Palmer 2014a, p. 28)). (2) Would he also say that his view of agent causation requires a notion of causation by agents that is *not* also required by compatibilist accounts of free agency? (3) Or that it requires a notion of causation by agents whose exercise does not essentially involve causation by states, processes, and events involving the agent? (4) Or that it requires a special kind of causation of free actions by an agent or substance that is, in principle, incapable of being itself caused by prior events, either deterministically or indeterministically?

He clearly does say that his view does not postulate "a special kind of causation" that requires appeals to immaterial substances, noumenal selves, transempirical power centers, and other such "spooky" things, as he calls them, that traditional and some modern AC theorists have claimed. (5) But would he also say that the irreducible agent causation involved in free agency is not of a kind that is *only* needed for libertarian free will—that it is not also needed for any kind of voluntary and free agency, compatibilist or incompatibilist? (6) And would he say its irreducibility to causation by mental states and events alone is not by itself a sufficient reason for saying, as many traditional AC theorists have said, that it is not compatible with determinism or that its exercise does not involve event causation? If he would not affirm any one of (1)–(4) and would affirm either one of (5) or (6), then our theories would indeed be very "much closer than has so far been recognized." This would be a significant development.

Yet there is more to be said about possible similarities and differences. In recent writings, O'Connor advocates an ontology of "powers" to account for agent causation, as have some other recent agent causalists (e.g., E. J. Lowe). In my AC/EC, view, of course, I also talk about agential powers that are required for a fully adequate account of free agency and free will. But there may be differences here as well. The two most important agential powers involved in my AC/EC account of self-forming actions are what I have called teleological guidance control (TGC) and plural voluntary control (PVC). TGC is a power that is needed for any *voluntary* action, while PVC is an agential power needed at some times in the lives of agents if they are to be capable of "will-setting" and "self-forming" actions that are not determined.

> (P293) To secure such a power of PVC over choices that are undetermined, I believe that in addition to the exercise of powers of Rational Will such as deliberation or practical reasoning, there must also be subprocesses (namely, efforts or exercises of willpower), within these larger processes of *Rational Will*. These subprocesses would be exercises of powers of *Striving Will* on the part the agent to resolve conflicts in the will, in such manner that the agent may be said to have resolved or *settled* the conflict in the will by bringing about one particular outcome rather than another, voluntarily, intentionally, and rationally, whichever way they are resolved.

Would O'Connor give a similar role to the powers of Striving Will as well as those of Rational Will in his account of *free* will? If so, there would be further reason to say our views are much closer than is usually assumed; and I would welcome such an outcome. For, as I said, I'd prefer not to have to drink alone at this establishment.[3]

8.2. An Integrated Agent-Causal View: Clarke

Randolph Clarke's *Libertarian Accounts of Free Will* (2003) is another work that has had a significant impact on the development of libertarian views of free will and controversies about them in the twenty-first century. Clarke criticizes *noncausal* (NC) libertarian views (Chapter 2) in ways that will be considered later in this chapter. He then discusses and criticizes *event-causal* (EC) accounts in four chapters (3 to 6) of his book. In Chapter 4, he argues against the "Deliberative" libertarian views suggested by Dennett and Mele (criticizing them in ways discussed earlier in Chapter 6 of this book) and against the deliberative view of Ekstrom (considered here in Chapter 7). In Chapters 5 and 6 of his book, Clarke turns to "centered" libertarian EC views that place the indeterminism at the moment of choice terminating deliberation, focusing much of Chapter 5 and some of Chapter 6 on a critique of my previous view.

In Chapters 7–9 of his book, Clarke then turns to AC libertarian views. He argues that if there is to be any hope for a successful libertarian account of free will, it would have to be an AC account of some kind. But he is skeptical that traditional AC accounts, as well as more recent AC accounts, give us all that is needed for libertarian free will. A major problem for traditional and contemporary accounts of agent causation, he argues, concerns "whether an agent-causal account can adequately provide for reasons and reason-explanation" (2003, p. 135). He then argues that EC views, by contrast, despite the inadequacies he has noted in them, do provide us with accounts of the causal role of reasons in the explanation of actions, accounts that AC views might exploit. He says,

> A credible case can be made for the tenability of event-causal accounts of reason explanation. In the context of an agent-causal libertarian view... we could exploit the success of event-causal accounts of explanation by requiring that [the making of a choice or decision and hence] the acquisition of... an intention be caused *by the agent and nondeterministically caused by her having certain reasons.* This would give us an *integrated agent causal account.* (p. 143, italics mine)

Clarke goes on to defend such an "integrated" AC account of free action and free will in Chapters 8 and 9 of his book, arguing for its superiority over other purely AC accounts, on the one hand, and over purely EC accounts, on the other.

But, interestingly, in the final chapter of his book, he considers objections to all AC accounts of free will, and concludes that some of these objections also "carry significant weight" against his integrated agent-causal view (2003, p. 209): "Objections concerning the temporality of causation, the influence that causes can have on the probabilities of their future effects and the structured nature of entities that are directly in time count against the possibility of substance causation," in the sense postulated by AC views, including the integrated version he has defended. He adds that it seems to him that "although none of these considerations is individually decisive, collectively they incline on balance against" AC accounts of free will in general, including his integrated account (p. 209). As a consequence, in subsequent writings Clarke no longer defends an incompatibilist or libertarian view of free will at all, remaining agnostic on the issues dividing compatibilist and libertarian views (see, e.g., Clarke 2011).

(P294) Nonetheless, I would argue, as I have in the previous chapter, that Clarke's suggestion of an "integrated agent-causal view" is a step in the right direction for AC views of libertarian free will. For it points to the need for both an irreducible role for agent causation and an irreducible role for event causation in an adequate libertarian view and would thus bring AC views closer to the kind of AC/EC view I have been defending (P273–P274). But I would also argue, as I did in the previous chapter, that Clarke's suggested integrated agent-causal view *does not give enough of a role to agent causation* to provide an adequate account of libertarian free will. For while it says that libertarian free choices are "co-caused" by agents and certain mental events, it does not say that agents play a special role of causing or bringing it about that the particular mental events that co-cause the choices or actions play the co-causal roles they do. Agents do this by exercising TGC over the cognitive processes causally linking the mental states or events that provide the reasons for the choices or actions to the choices or actions themselves (P275).

This, as I also argued, allows one to answer a common objection sometimes made to both EC views and integrated AC views, namely that agents may have different reasons for making a particular choice or performing a certain action, only some of which reasons may have actually played a role in motivating and causing the choice or action on a particular occasion. The reasons which actually motivate the particular choice or action on a given occasion would be those that are causally linked to the choice or action by the TGC exercised by the agent on that occasion (P274). The reasons that are causally involved would thus not just "happen" to be causally involved. They would be so because the agent actively "sees to it that" they are causally involved (P275).

Perhaps Clarke would say this as well about his integrated AC view, in which case that view would also be closer to the AC/EC view defended here than might have earlier been realized; and I would welcome this outcome as well.

8.3. Other Agent-Causal Views: Griffith and Others

Meghan Griffith, who is another defender of an AC account of libertarian free will, has provided us with a useful critical survey of recent AC views

(2017).[4] Among the essential features of agent causation, Griffith says, are the following:

> Agent causation is *irreducible substance causation*. The agent, the person, is a metaphysical substance whose causal activity grounds autonomous agency (and responsibility). According to the agent-causalist, exercises of free will require something other than the usual causal story about actions flowing from mental states or events. . . . Another central feature of agent causation is realism about causation. . . . When an agent agent-causes, there is a real bringing about of a genuine exercise of causal power. Agent-causation, then, is nonreductive in more ways than one. There is no reduction to event-causation and no reduction to noncausal processes. (2017, pp. 73–74)

It is obvious and significant that all these things are also true of the AC/EC view defended here. The causal role of the agent, qua substance, on this AC/EC view, also grounds autonomous agency and responsibility and is also irreducible to causation of actions by mental states or events alone (as in EC views) or to noncausal processes (as in NC views). So, if there are differences between this AC/EC view and agent-causal views, as Griffith understands them, we must look elsewhere for the differences.

AC views, she also says, are consistent with Cartesian dualism, but do not require mind/body dualism: "An agent-causalist," she adds, "could hold, for example, that agents are psychological substances with both mental and physical 'processes'" (2017, p. 75). She cites too prominent recent agent causalists, E. J. Lowe (2008) and Helen Steward (2012),[5] who hold this. Griffith holds this as well. She defends a naturalistic "constitution" view according to which "a person can have the causal powers of agency as understood by the agent causalist, while still being fully constituted by the physical" (2017, p. 75). Kevin Timpe and Jonathan Jacobs (2015) are also cited by Griffith as defenders of such a naturalistic view of agent causation.

(P295) There are also obvious convergences on these points between AC views so conceived and the AC/EC view developed here. Causation of action by agents on this AC/EC view also does not require mind/body dualism and is also consistent with a naturalistic view of agent causation. Griffith further adds that, while most agent causalists are libertarians about free will, "at its core agent causalism is a position about the irreducibility of the relation between an agent and her behavior." Thus, she says, "it does not require an initial commitment to libertarianism and there are agent-causalists who are compatibilists" (2017, p. 76). (As examples of the latter she mentions Ned Markosian [1999, 2012] and Dana Nelkin [2011].) There are also no obvious differences on these points with the AC/EC view I have been defending. I have made it clear that causation of action by agents on this AC/EC view is also consistent with compatibilist as well as incompatibilist accounts of free agency and thus "does not require an initial commitment to libertarianism."

What then, one may ask, are the differences, if any, between AC views, as Griffith understands them, and the AC/EC view developed here? I think we get some clues by considering some recent criticisms of purely agent-causal or AC libertarian views. Consider, for example, the criticism of Derk Pereboom in *Free Will, Agency, and Meaning in Life* (2014):

> The unavailability of an explanation to the agent-causal libertarian for why the subject agent-causes her decision by contrast with agent-causing a refraining from the decision leaves us in the dark about what the mechanics of agent-causation might be.... The agent-causal libertarian might reply by claiming that the ability to substance-cause a decision and in the same causal context to substance-cause a refraining from that decision instead, is a simple and fundamental power the agent-as-substance has, and this power and its exercise have no further explication. The concern for this suggestion is that the agent-causal libertarian is trading in inexplicable powers at the very core of her theory, which renders the position obscure.... When causal powers at as high and apparently complex a level as human agency are claimed to be fundamental and inexplicable, doubt begins to set in. (2014, p. 65)

Similar concerns are expressed by many other critics of AC libertarian views, including among others, Mele (2006), Ishtyaque Haji (2009, pp. 200–201, 207–8), Neil Levy (2011), Gregg Caruso (2012), and Clarke (when Clarke turns to criticizing AC views). For example, Mele says:

> Suppose someone claims that exercises of agent-causation are exercises of a kind of control such that to exercise control of that kind is to satisfy all freedom relevant conditions for basic moral responsibility. Then it should

be asked what is it about control of this [special agent-causal] kind in virtue of which this is true. (2006, p. 76)

(P296) What these and other critics of AC views are asking for is some more detailed account of just *how* agents agent-cause their *undetermined*[6] free decisions on an agent-causal view, such that *whichever* decision agents make from among different possible undetermined decisions, would be made in accordance with their wills and for reasons favoring that decision rather than any alternative at the time it is made. Agent causalists argue that the special kind of causation by an agent they posit has the power to do this, but they need to say more, these critics are insisting, about how exactly it is done and indeed how it is possible, given the fact that whichever decision is made must be undetermined. It's not good enough to say the exercise of the agent-causal power to do this is irreducible and hence inexplicable in terms of any other kinds of causation.

8.4. Agent Causation, Complex Systems, and Teleological Guidance Control Revisited

(P297) Putting these criticisms in another way, the irreducibility of agent causation to other kinds of causation should not be treated as an *excuse* for not giving an explanation of agent causation in more detail of the kind critics such as Pereboom, Haji, Mele, Levy, Caruso, and others are asking for: How could it be that agents can exercise the causal power to "settle" which of competing undetermined choices or decisions will occur at a given time rather than any alternatives? And how is it possible for the agents to do this in accordance with their will, whichever way they exercise this power at the time?

Rather than merely appealing to the irreducibility of agent causation here, I would argue that if an adequate explanation of how agents can exercise such causal power over undetermined events is to be given, such an explanation would, among other things, explain why the exercise of agent-causal power in this way was irreducible to other forms of causation, such as causation by mental states and events alone.

This is one of the things the AC/EC view defended here is specifically meant to do. It begins by insisting on the following:

(P298) You don't have to appeal to esoteric or "conceptually or metaphysically primitive" accounts of agent causation to make the case that the agent causation involved in libertarian free will is irreducible to causation by mental states and events of agents alone. Nor do you have to claim that all causation is substance causation. For there is an account of agent causation of actions that will get these results, an account that has become available through developments in the natural sciences themselves in the latter part of the twentieth century and into this century. This account first appeals to the developing science of complex dynamical systems.

As noted in P146, "such systems (now known to be ubiquitous in nature and which include living things) are systems in which emergent capacities arise as a result of greater complexity. When the emergent capacities arise, the systems as a whole or various subsystems of them impose novel constraints on the behavior of their parts."

(P299) Alicia Juarrero, whose book was referenced earlier on the nature and significance of such complex dynamical systems in the sciences, *Dynamics in Action* (1999), says that "as research increasingly uncovers context-dependent mutualist feedback in the brain (Edelman 1993; Freeman 1999), we can posit the dynamical self-organization of a neurological hierarchy. Progressively higher levels of neural organization self-assemble, each exhibiting novel properties and greater degrees of freedom. In turn the higher levels impose . . . constraints on the lower ones." She adds that "this is what self-consciousness and intentional action are all about" (p. 143). Such higher-order contextual constraints "are also the ongoing structural mechanism whereby Aristotle's formal and final causes are implemented" (p. 143).[7]

A further feature of the account of agent causation appealed to in this AC/EC view that has also become available through recent developments in the natural sciences comes from the neuroscientists. It was described earlier:

(P147) Such complex systems exhibit *teleological guidance control* when they tend through feedback loops and error correction mechanisms to converge on a goal (called an attractor) in the face of perturbations. Such control, as neuroscientist Marius Usher argues (2006), *is necessary for any voluntary activity*, and he interprets it in terms of dynamic systems theory.... Neuroscientists E. Miller and J. Cohen (2001) argue that such cognitive (guidance) control in human agents stems from the active maintenance of patterns of activity in the prefrontal cortex that represent goals and the means to achieve them. These patterns provide signals to other brain structures whose net effect, as Miller and Cohen describe it, is to guide the flow of activity along neural pathways that establish the proper mappings between inputs, internal states, and outputs.

Putting these pieces together yields the account of agent causation that is central to the AC/EC libertarian view defended here, according to which "an agent's causing an action" is understood as "an agent, conceived as *an information-responsive complex dynamical system*, exercising *teleological guidance control*, over some of its own processes" (P145).

Since agent causation conceived in this way, however, is compatible with determinism as well as indeterminism (P150), more is required to explain how it might be involved in a *libertarian* account of free will, where the actions caused (such as choices or decisions) must sometimes be undetermined. Usher (2006) suggests some of the further things that may be required for this from a neuroscientific perspective where indeterminism might be involved. He says,

> The property of attractor dynamics does not apply constantly over time. (If it did, people would be much more predictable, and boring, than they are!). Rather [in reasoning leading to intentional action] one typically finds a process that involves successive stages of attraction (where perturbations are absorbed) and bifurcations (where they are amplified). While the attraction stages correspond to goal states [such as intentions]... that reliably predict (and guide) behavior, at bifurcation points the agent's behavior is less predictable and shows a higher sensitivity to the input of reasons.... Such fluctuations can appear in two important ways in the genesis of free actions. First, they take place when the agent is faced with a choice between conflicting courses of action, each of which is supported by some reasons the agent endorses. Second, bifurcation processes [may also be involved]... in a slower process related to character formation where conflicting sources of information are interpreted). (2006, pp. 206–7)[8]

While such bifurcation dynamics are consistent with determinism, Usher argues that they may in such situations, also involve indeterminism and the presence of "noisy input." A simple way to take such factors into account (standardly used in neurocomputational models of choice) is to add a source of noise on top of the dynamics of the choice microstate (for example, quantum indeterminism may lead to minute stochastic fluctuations in synaptic transmission events). (Usher 2006, p. 208)

This is the kind of role I suggested for indeterminism in self-forming actions in earlier writings, including *The Significance of Free Will* (1996)—without appealing to the neuroscientific details Usher introduces here. In fact, at this point in his article, he cites both me on self-forming actions and Balaguer on torn decisions, relating the account of agency he is considering to our views:

At [such] bifurcations . . . the agent's will is divided. If the agent has competing reasons for two courses of action, no matter which of these reasons she chooses to act on, the agent [can have] authorship over the action. . . . Thus in agreement with Kane and Mark Balaguer . . . I believe that indeterminism [need] not undermine the fact that when an agent performs an action and this action is probabilistically caused by her . . . (for reasons consistent with the agent's character, motivation, and so on), the agent [can bear] responsibility for her action. (Usher 2006, p. 208)

Importantly, however, at this point Usher also distances himself from my view and other libertarian views such as Balaguer's, by introducing some familiar criticisms of these views frequently made by compatibilists and free will skeptics. He does so as follows:

Nevertheless, as Kane admits, although probabilistic causation explains the action as a causal outcome of the agent's mental states, it cannot explain why the agent chose A *rather than* B. Since such *contrastive* explanation is unavailable, the fact that the agent chose A *rather* than B remains random. . . . [Thus] if we inquire about [what Kane calls] the agent's UR—that is, her responsibility for having the character and motives she has—I agree with the compatibilist critics that the lack of contrastive explanation is likely to become problematic: [for] at birth there is little mental repertoire to ground responsibility for indeterministic decisions, and if the developing character depends on them (as Kane requires), the way this character turns out may well be considered to be a matter of luck. (pp. 208–9)

8.5. Agent Causation, Irreducibility, and Explanation

These objections about luck, also made by many others, are significant, and I have attempted to address them in earlier chapters, notably Chapters 4 and 5. Doing so required adding further pieces to the AC/EC view developed in these earlier chapters. By briefly reviewing some of these relevant further pieces, I now want to argue for something further:

(P300) The additional pieces of the AC/EC view, when added to the neuroscientifically based account of agent causation discussed in the previous section, also provide a more detailed explanation of agent causation that critics of *agent-causal or AC libertarian views*, such as Pereboom, Haji, Mele, and others, say is wanting on such views: an explanation, that is, of *how* agents can exercise the causal power to "settle" which of competing choices or decisions occur at a given time in accordance with their wills, whichever way they exercise this power, when it is also the case that whichever choice occurs at a given time is undetermined.

(P301) Agent causalists typically say that agents, qua substances, have special powers to do this. But they do not say enough about how agents do this and how these special powers are exercised. Pereboom sums up this worry when he says that "the concern is that the AC libertarian is trading in inexplicable powers at the very core of her theory, which renders the position obscure. . . . When causal powers at as high and apparently complex a level as human agency are claimed to be fundamental and inexplicable, doubt begins to set in."

I agree that "causal powers at as high and apparently complex a level as human agency" require more explication. Here is a brief summary of some of the further relevant pieces of the AC/EC view developed here that address these concerns.

First, if either of competing *undetermined* choices could be made in accordance with the agent's will, the will must be divided, so that, as Usher says, the agent would have conflicting and competing reasons for making either of the competing choices that might be made (P91–P92).

Second, this being the case, the choice that is made would have to be made for only a subset of these reasons the agent has, namely, reasons favoring this particular choice rather than any other competing choice at the time; and this would have to be the case whichever choice should be made (P95–P96).

Third, taking into account the previous neuroscientifically inspired discussion of an agent's causing an action, the following would also be the case: the choice that is made would have been the goal or telos of a cognitive process under the teleologically guided control (TGC) of the agent, since such agential control would be necessary for any voluntary and intentional action (P97–P98).

Fourth, this cognitive process under the teleologically guided control of the agent would, among other things, causally link the subset of reasons or motives favoring the choice made to the specific goal of making this particular choice, thereby rendering the outcome rational as well as voluntary and intentional (P102–P104).

Fifth, these reasons or motives in the form of mental states and events would thus also play a causal role in causing the particular choice made, as in "integrated" agent-causal views, such as Clarke's and integrated views of other AC theorists mentioned by Griffith. But the reasons or motives involved would not just "happen" to be "co-causes" of the choice along with the agent. For it would be the agent who would bring it about, or cause it to be the case, that these particular mental states and events rather than any others *are* causally involved and do contribute to causing the choice made (P143–P147).

Sixth, to do this, the agent, qua complex dynamical system, would have to exercise a kind of (teleological) guidance control over the causal processes linking these particular mental states and events favoring this choice to the occurrence of the specific choice which is the goal or telos of this process. If the goal of this teleologically guided process should be attained, the agent would thereby *voluntarily* and *intentionally* cause the *particular* choice aimed at *rather than* any competing choice. The agent would do so *for* the motivating reasons or motives causally linked to that choice by this teleologically guided process rather than for any reasons or motives the agent may have had for any competing choice (and rather than for any other reasons or motives the agent may have had for the choice made that were not reasons or motives the agent acted upon in making this choice on this occasion) (P148–P150, P171).

Seventh, the causal role of the agent under these conditions would be *irreducible* to causation by the mental states or events of the agent alone, unlike what would be required on purely EC libertarian views. For without this causal linkage between the reasons for the choice and the choice itself provided by the guidance control of the agent, the causation of the action by the reasons would be "deviant" and the outcomes would not be a voluntary and intentional actions of the agent (P151–P155).

Eighth, if it is also to be the case that either of competing undetermined choices could be made in accordance with the agent's will, the will must be divided (as emphasized in the first point made above). The agent would have conflicting and competing reasons or motives for making one or another of competing choices, so that if any one of the choices is to be made, the reasons or motives favoring any competing choice must be resisted and overcome. Thus, a further role of the agent's teleologically guided process of making a particular choice in such circumstances of a conflicted will would be overcoming resistance in the will coming from the reasons or motives for making any competing choice (P171–P175).

Ninth, this being so, the teleologically guided process involved in settling such cases of a conflicted will would have to be an instance of *striving will* (an effort of will or exercise of willpower, a trying or striving, etc.) whose goal of making a particular choice could be attained only by overcoming resistance in the will coming from motivations for making any competing choice (P44–P45, P99–P100). Note that, as emphasized in P273–P274, these efforts of will would be instances of TGC where the guidance control would have to overcome resistance in the will if it is to succeed.

Tenth, efforts or other instances of striving will are required in acting whenever attaining a goal requires overcoming resistance of *some* kind. In most cases, the resistance that may require effort has an external source, such as a jammed closet door. But it may also come from the will; and the resistance in such cases of a divided will is from the will of the agent, not from an external source (P195).

Eleventh, it is this resistance in the will that also makes it *undetermined* and hence *uncertain* that the teleologically guided process (the effort or exercise of willpower) to make a particular choice rather than any other will attain its goal. Its causation of the goal, if it does succeed, will be probabilistic and not certain. As a consequence, the indeterminism involved in such libertarian free choices (i.e., self-forming choices) doesn't just happen to be present. It has its causal source in the (conflicted) will of the agent (P105–P107).

Twelfth, to actually get this further agential power and control in the presence of indeterminism, it is not sufficient to postulate a *single* process (deliberation) with *multiple* possible goals (making decision A *or* decision B). One must in addition allow for the possibility of *multiple* subprocesses of striving will (efforts or exercises of willpower) which may occur at different times in this general process of deliberation, such that each subprocess has a *specific* goal of making one of the decisions rather than the other for the reasons favoring that decision at the time (P247).

Thirteenth, these subprocesses that might be aimed at different decisions would not be occurring at the same time during deliberation. Rather we need only assume that different efforts may be initiated at different times, depending on the course of the agents' reasoning, when their reasons incline them to one decision rather than another and the remaining resistance in their wills must be overcome if they are to make the decision to which they are then inclined (P123–P128).

(P302) These additional pieces of this AC/EC view, when added to the neuroscientifically based account of agent causation discussed in the previous section, provide a more detailed explanation of agent causation that critics of *agent-causal (AC) views*, such as Pereboom, Haji, Mele, and others, say is wanting on such views: an explanation, that is, of how agents can exercise the causal power to settle which of competing choices or decisions occur at a given time *in accordance with their will, whichever way they exercise this power*, when it is the case that whichever choice occurs at a given time must be undetermined (P287). Agent causalists typically say that agents have special powers to do this. But, according to their critics, with whom I agree, they do not say enough about how agents do it and how these special powers are exercised, given that the choices occurring at any given time must be undetermined.

The above is a brief review of some of the relevant pieces of the AC/EC view developed in this book that address this particular concern. If agent causalists reject these pieces, they need to give an alternative account to explain what these special powers of agent-causes might be and how they are exercised, given that the choices that result from them on a libertarian view must be undetermined. If, on the other hand, there should be agent causalists who find the account given here plausible in some respects, then my AC/EC view and their AC view would indeed be, in O'Connor's words, "very much closer than is usually assumed." I would welcome this outcome as well, as I said.

8.6. Agent-Causal Views: Final Thoughts (My Place in the Narrative)

One thought that has become more and more evident to me in recent years as I review traditional and recent arguments in favor of and against AC libertarian views is a thought made evident in Griffith's overview. Central to all AC views, she says, is the *non-reducibility* of the causal role of the agent in libertarian free action. The causal role of the agent according to AC views is not reducible to causation by states and events alone, as in EC libertarian views, or to noncausal processes, as in NC views. Franklin provides additional support for such claims from an EC perspective when he argues that the major problem facing purely EC libertarian views of the kind he wishes to defend in his book is what he calls "agency non-reductionism"—the irreducibility of the causal role of the agent in libertarian free action to causation by states and events alone involving the agent. The arguments for such agency non-reductionism, Franklin contends, are strong and perhaps irrefutable, thus constituting a major obstacle to accepting purely EC libertarian views. I agree with him on this important point.

(P303) These thoughts have a particular significance when one considers that over the past forty to fifty years of debate about libertarian free will, only three possible views were generally thought to be in the running: event-causal (EC), noncausal (NC), and agent-causal (AC). Thus, it seemed that if the causal role of the agent in libertarian free agency was not reducible either to states and events involving the agent or to noncausal processes, then EC and NC views would be out of the running and AC views would seem to be the only available option for libertarians.

(P304) I think this is a major reason why AC views have continued to be popular among contemporary libertarians about free will. Of course, many contemporary agent causalists have frequently disowned some of the more extravagant claims of traditional AC views, such as requirements of mind-body dualism, or "immanent" causation (as in Reid [1788] 1969 and Chisholm 1966) that have led to charges of obscurantism and mystery, as Griffith suggests. But most contemporary AC theorists have held on to the idea that the agent causation involved in libertarian free will is something special that can't be reduced to any other forms of causation.

(P305) When I look at my own place in this recent historical narrative, I find that I am in agreement, and have always been in agreement, with this mantra of contemporary AC views, namely, that the causal role of the agent in libertarian free agency is not reducible either to causation by states and events or to noncausal processes. As a consequence, I came to realize that the "event-causal" label usually put on my view had always been misleading and should be corrected. But at the same time, a purely AC label for the view I had held would have been misleading as well, since I had always held in earlier works that the causal roles of the *agent* qua substance *and* of agent-involving mental states and events were both necessary to account for libertarian free agency; and neither was reducible to the other. Hence the AC/EC designation for my present view.

This brought my view closer to "integrated agent-causal views," like Clarke's, but with a difference, noted earlier (P285–P296). The causal role of the agent in this AC/EC view plays an even more consequential causal role than in most integrated AC views like Clarke's. To explain this required going beyond claims made by traditional defenders of purely AC views, including integrated ones, in ways spelled out in the summary of the previous section.[9]

As Griffith's overview also makes clear, many modern writers who identify as AC theorists also reject at least some of these implications of traditional AC theories. So the extent to which these new AC views may converge with the AC/EC view remains an open question. Nonetheless, what even new AC views fail to provide, as many of their critics have argued (and which *makes* this an open question), is more detailed accounts of just how the special causal powers that agent-causes are supposed to exercise over undetermined free actions are exercised and the details of in what these special causal powers consist.[10]

8.7. Noncausal Views (I): Ginet, McCann, and Others

Noncausal libertarian views of free will have failed to receive widespread support among libertarians and are often summarily dismissed in the literature. But there is something to be learned by considering what motivates their advocates and why such views have been considered wanting by their critics.

Noncausal libertarians argue that exercises of the power of self-determination need not be caused or causally structured. We control our self-determined choices or volitions, they say, simply in virtue of their being ours, their occurring in us. They are intrinsically active events. We can explain why they were done in terms of motivating conditions or reasons (the kinds of conditions that fall under what I have called Motivational Will—beliefs, desires, etc.). But these reasons or motivating conditions, noncausalists contend, while they may *explain* why the choices or actions are performed, do not *cause* the choices or actions. Using Aristotelian terminology (as recent noncausalists, such as Thomas Pink [2004, 2017], Stuart Goetz [2009] and David Palmer [2021] have done), they say reasons or motivating conditions may function as *formal* and *final* causes of action, but they do not function as *efficient* (and much less as *material*) causes of action.

Carl Ginet, one of first contemporary philosophers to mount a lengthy defense of an NC libertarian view (beginning in Ginet 1966), argues that "what distinguishes each basic action [such as a volition or choice] from non-active mental events is an 'actish phenomenal quality'" which he characterizes as "its seeming to the agent as if she is directly producing, making happen or determining, the event in question" (1996, p. 13). Hugh McCann, another well-known defender of an NC view, in a recent survey of such views, citing Ginet, says that "although acts of will [such as decisions] are caused neither by agents nor by other events, they are still explainable teleologically in terms of the agent's reasons" (1998, p. 87).

In rejecting causal views of both EC and AC kinds, McCann adds, "it should not be supposed that exercises of free agency can have no explanation... for the exercises of active willing do have teleological explanations.... My act of deciding can be explained teleologically as directed toward a specific end... i.e., what I decide to do" (1998, pp. 92–93). It follows, according to McCann and other noncausalists, that if acts of will such as decisions are teleologically explainable in this manner but are not antecedently caused "either by agents or by events," then such acts also cannot be *determined* by antecedent causes. That they are undetermined follows from the very nature of these acts.

A criticism of such NC views made by many critics, both incompatibilists and compatibilists, is nicely expressed by Clarke. It concerns the issue of "active control," which is regarded by most philosophers as an essential feature of responsible agency. Citing Ginet's claim that what distinguishes basic actions, such as volitions or choices, from nonactive mental events is an "'actish phenomenal quality'—i.e., its seeming to the agent as if she is directly producing, making happen, . . . the event in question" (Ginet 1996, p. 88), Clarke says that

> the mere feel of a mental event—the way it seems to one undergoing it—although it may be a (more or less reliable) sign of active control, cannot itself *constitute* the agent's exercise of such control (cf. O'Connor 2000b: pp. 25–26). To hold that it does is to render the exercise of active control wholly subjective. . . . The point here is reinforced by Ginet's observation (1990: p. 9) that an event with the actish phenomenal quality could be brought about by external brain stimulation, in the absence of any relevant desire or intention on the part of the "agent." . . . An event produced in this way and in these circumstances hardly seems to be an exercise of agency at all. (2003, p. 20)

Pursuing this concern about control further, Clarke (2003, p. 180) cites McCann as saying that the control exercised in acting "has to be spontaneous and active; it is a creative undertaking on the agent's part, to be accounted for by its intrinsic features, not by the operations of other denizens of the world. . . . It has a certain *sui generis* character that renders it incapable of being reduced to anything else" (McCann 1998, p. 92). Clarke responds to such claims, in a manner similar to many other critics of NC views (e.g., O'Connor, Mele, Pereboom), that "reducible or not," active control is "a phenomenon that stands in need of explication." McCann rejects both EC and AC construals of it, but "because he offers no substantive alternative," Clarke adds, "the exercise of active control remains a mystery" on NC views like his and others (2003, p. 21).

Pereboom expresses similar criticisms of NC views in an alternative way. He quotes Ginet as saying: "It was up to me at a time T whether the event [such as a volition or decision or other action] would occur only if I *made it the case that it occurred* and it was open to me at T to keep it from occurring" and hence open to me to *make a difference* whether it happened at T or did not (Ginet 1990, p. 245). Pereboom responds that one may rightly object here "that the making [happen] relation is just the causal relation (and the same is true for the keeping from happening relation). After all, isn't causation fundamentally just *making something happen* or producing something" and hence *making a difference* in whether something occurs or not at a given time (2014, p. 40). Pereboom quotes David Lewis's statement in this regard that "a cause is something that makes a difference, and the difference it makes must be a difference from what would have happened without it" (Lewis 1986, p. 95).

Turning to McCann, Pereboom says that McCann's view that a "basic action is a spontaneous, creative undertaking is suggestive of the agent's making it the case that the basic action occurs, which also risks invoking the causal relation. The same would be true," Pereboom adds, of McCann's invoking "the notion of intrinsic intentionality. For it wouldn't appear to make sense to say that a basic action is intrinsically intentional while denying it is made to occur by the agent or that the agent makes the difference whether it occurs" (2014, p. 41). This making happen relation and making a difference whether or not something happens, Pereboom adds, is in turn necessary for attributions of moral responsibility. Powerful arguments against noncausal theories along these lines are also made by Justin Capes in an important article (2017).

8.8. Noncausal Views (II): Goetz, Pink, and Palmer

Noncausalists can, and often do, respond to such objections by saying that making a choice or other basic action happen and making a difference whether it does or does not happen, simply consists in the agent's performing the basic action, that is, the agent's simply choosing or acting in this way rather than not. To assume that doing this must be spelled out in causal terms, according to noncausalists, simply begs the question against them. This response is developed further by Goetz and Pink. Its most recent embodiment is in a forthcoming book by David Palmer, *Free Will without Causation*.

Palmer's book offers a new and comprehensive defense of the NC libertarian view, which accepts some of the views of Goetz and Pink, but adds further arguments and insights. Specifically, it argues for the version of the view on which for a person to act freely, her action *must* be uncaused. The first part of Palmer's book develops a new argument in favor of this position, explaining why free will is incompatible with causation. The second part defends the view against common objections, developing NC accounts of action, control, and reasons, and addressing the puzzle of uncaused events more generally. What emerges is a novel case for this controversial view of free will that should be considered by critics of NC accounts when it is published.

While I am sympathetic to objections about control and responsibility raised to NC views by Clarke, Pereboom, and other critics and do not believe

204   THE COMPLEX TAPESTRY OF FREE WILL

they are question begging, I would like to add another kind of argument that throws further light on these objections.

(P306) A pivotal claim by defenders of NC views is that it should not be assumed, as some of their critics do, that denying that free choices or volitions have *causes* implies that their occurring one way or another is lacking *explanations*. To the contrary, one can *explain* why a given choice was made teleologically as directed toward a specific end, what one decides to do, and in terms of motivating conditions or reasons *for* which the choice of this end was made. But these reasons or motivating conditions, noncausalists contend, while they may explain why the choices were made, do not *cause* the choices or actions. Rather, using Aristotelian terminology suggested by such teleological explanations, one can say the following (as some noncausalists, such as McCann, Pink, Goetz, and Palmer explicitly do): reasons or motivating conditions function in Aristotelian terms as *formal* causes of the choice, while the goal chosen functions as a *final* cause. But neither the motivating conditions nor the goals chosen, according to these noncausalists, function as *antecedent* causes in modern senses (*efficient* causes in Aristotle's sense) and much less as *material* causes in modern senses.

Thus, for example, whether John chooses to steal from the church poor box or chooses to refrain from doing so, we can explain his choice in terms of his motivating conditions. If he does choose to steal from the poor box (call this choice A) these motivating conditions would be his dire need for money for food and clothing. If he chooses to refrain, the motivating conditions would be his moral qualms about stealing from a poor box used to help others. In either case, there would be a satisfactory explanation of why choice A was made by him in terms of the motivating conditions for that choice or why choice B was made by him in terms of the motivating conditions for that choice. And this could be the case, these noncausalists argue, even though the choice, whichever one was made, was not caused, and hence not determined, by these motivating conditions but only motivated by, or explained by, them.

(P307) But a problem arises at this point. Yes, you may be able to explain for any undetermined choice why it was made at a time, *if* it is made, as teleologically directed toward a specific end, and in terms of motivating conditions for which it was made. But, given that *which* choice is made at the time, on NC views, must have been uncaused and hence undetermined by all past circumstances, what remains unexplained is why one of these choices, to steal the money or not to steal it, was made rather than the other when one of them was made. This is no minor or extraneous problem: it is essential for libertarian accounts of free will that require alternative possibilities *and* indeterminism at some points in the lives of agents that they explain this. And, as it happens, this is the very combination of requirements that has led to a variety of objections regarding luck and chance against other libertarian views, whether AC or EC.

Consider, for example, *explanatory luck objections* such as the one paraphrased here and earlier from Mele (1998, p. 582): "If different free choices could emerge from the same past of an agent, there would seem to be no explanation for why one choice was made rather than another in terms of the total prior character, motives and purposes of the agent. The difference in choice, i.e., the agent's choosing one thing rather than another, would seem to be just a matter of luck." Or *rollback objections*: if opposing choices could occur on different rollbacks, given exactly the same past up to the moment of choice, then the occurrence of one or the other choice on any particular rollback would seem to be a matter of chance.

Such objections were addressed in Chapter 5, and I attempted to answer them by appealing to *prior occurrences in the deliberative lives* of agents that play different *causal* roles in explaining why one possible choice was made at a given time rather than any opposing choice. Defenders of AC and EC libertarian views try to do this as well. I also tried to explain in subsequent chapters why I think AC and EC explanations for this fall short in ways that might be remedied by an AC/EC view. But whether or not these arguments are successful:

(P308) There is reason to believe *some* appeal to the antecedent causal circumstances leading up to undetermined libertarian free choices is necessary to explain why one undetermined choice is made at a given time rather than any opposing choice or why one forking path into the future is chosen rather than any other path, when it is undetermined which path will be chosen. As critics of NC views have often pointed out, the very notion that agents must exercise *control* over which undetermined choice is made at a time rather than any other suggests this. For as these critics of NC views have argued, *control* itself is a causal notion. It involves "making or bringing it about that something happens" and "making a difference" as to what happens. Pereboom rightly quotes David Lewis on causation in this regard.

(P309) In the AC/EC view, I put a name on the kind of control that is involved which, according to Usher and other neuroscientists, is a kind of control involved in all human action—namely, TGC. Its exercise involves *formal* and *final* causes to be sure, such as motivating conditions and a goal or end to be chosen, as NC theories rightly recognize. That is the *teleological* part of TGC. But the *guidance control* aspect of it is equally important. It involves appealing to agents as information responsive complex dynamical systems exercising guidance control over some of their own processes, thereby functioning as *efficient* causes, in Aristotelian senses, of action. And doing this amounts to introducing Aristotelian *material* causes as well. For, as neuroscientists Miller and Cohen describe such guidance control in human agents (P145), it stems from the active maintenance of patterns of activity in the prefrontal cortex that represent goals and the means to achieve them. These patterns provide signals to other brain structures whose effect is to guide the flow of activity along neural pathways that establish proper mappings between inputs, internal states, and outputs. This teleological guidance involves both efficient (antecedent) causes and material (neurophysiological) causes in Aristotle's senses.

(P310) In sum, *one needs the entire Aristotelian spectrum of causes to explain the human agency involved in human action*, not merely *formal* and *final* causes (though they are necessary), but in addition *efficient* and *material* causes. When it comes to explaining undetermined free actions of the kind libertarian free will requires, you also need a good deal more than such TGC alone affords. This good deal more is represented in part by the thirteen steps spelled out in section 8.5 and many other steps as well spelled out in previous chapters. These steps must be added to, and built upon, the neuroscientific accounts of TGC, I've argued, if an adequate account of libertarian free will is to be formulated and objections concerning luck and chance addressed.

Among the important lessons learned by considering NC accounts of libertarian free will is the importance of teleological explanations of human action to such accounts. Such explanations are not the whole story, but they are an important part of the story.

9

The Compatibilist Spectrum

9.1. Preliminaries

Compatibilist views of freedom and responsibility have proliferated and become more sophisticated to an astonishing degree in the last half of the twentieth century and into this century. My aim in this chapter is to discuss some interesting patterns in this proliferation that throw further light on the view developed in this book and on debates about free will and responsibility in general.

Begin by recalling the first two pieces of the tapestry in Chapter 2, which have been central to what has followed.

(P1) The first significant step on this freedom path involves recognizing that as the Compatibility Question is formulated in many modern discussions of free will—"Is freedom compatible or incompatible with determinism?"—the question is too simple. For *there are many meanings of "freedom"* (as one would expect from such a much-disputed and much-debated term) *and many of these meanings are compatible with determinism.*

Even in a determined world, we would want to distinguish persons who are free from such things as physical restraint, coercion, compulsion, covert control, political oppression, and many other things, from persons who are not free from these things; and we should acknowledge that these freedoms are significant ("worth wanting") even in a determined world.

(P2) Libertarians about free will (those who believe in a free will that is incompatible with determinism) should, I argue, concede this point to compatibilists. What libertarians should insist upon instead is that *there is at least one significant kind of freedom worth wanting that is not compatible with determinism*. This further freedom is freedom *of will*, which I define as "the power to be the ultimate source and sustainer to some degree of one's own ends or purposes."

We know that compatibilists and many others have been deeply suspicious of this "deeper" freedom of will that involves such a power to be the ultimate source of one's ends or purposes. They regard it as an incoherent and unintelligible ideal, the "best self-contradiction so far conceived by the human mind," as Nietzsche put it. And they have looked for accounts of freedom and responsibility that do not require it.

(P311) My theme in this chapter will be that the considerable complexity and subtlety of modern compatibilist doctrines of free will and moral responsibility are due in great part to an overriding factor. They are all trying by whatever means to give adequate accounts of moral responsibility and the freedom it may require, while avoiding, to the degree possible, such questions as "Was it ever causally possible for agents to have done anything differently in the course of their lives to have made their qualities of will any different than they are?" Contemporary compatibilists thereby hope to bypass or defuse any historical questions that may lead to concerns about ultimate responsibility (UR) that fuel incompatibilist views about free will and moral responsibility.[1]

9.2. Frankfurt: Hierarchical Motivation, Meshes, and Real Selves

One of the most influential of these modern compatibilists is Harry Frankfurt. In his important 1969 article, discussed earlier, where he introduced Frankfurt-style examples, Frankfurt argued that moral responsibility does not require alternative possibilities, or the freedom to do otherwise. In an equally influential article in 1971, he asked what freedom of will and moral responsibility *do* in fact require and introduced what has been called a "hierarchical motivation theory" to explain this.

Desires play a central role in this hierarchical motivation view. Frankfurt distinguishes between first-order and second-order desires. First-order desires have as their objects actions. Second-order desires have as their objects first-order desires. Some first-order desires do not actually move one to action, such as the desire to skip work today, when one knows that might mean being fired. But other first-order desires do move one to action.

(P312) Frankfurt identifies an agent's *will* with the agent's *effective* first-order desires, the ones (as he puts it) that move the agent "all the way to action" (1971, p. 84). He also distinguishes different sorts of second-order desires. Some second-order desires may be desires to have a certain first-order desire, but not *a desire* that this first-order desire comprise one's will. He uses the example of a psychotherapist who wishes to experience a desire for a drug in order to understand an addicted patient better. But the psychotherapist does not want such a second-order desire to be effective in leading her to action. She does not want it to be *her* will (1971, p. 84). Other second-order desires, however, are desires to have first-order desires that will be effective in action and thus constitute the agent's will.

(P313) Frankfurt calls such second-order desires that certain first-order desires be one's will *second-order volitions*. A defining feature of *persons*, he argues, is that they have such second-order volitions. They care about which first-order desires move them to action. He also suggests that there is no limit to how highly ordered one's desires might be. There may, for example, be a third-order desire that some second-order desire not play such a significant role in one's deliberations, and so on for higher-order desires.

The complexity here is mind-numbing, but Frankfurt attempts to make it clearer by examples, including examples of three different addicts. *Wanton addicts* have conflicting first-order desires. They desire both to take the drug to which they are addicted as well as not to take it. But they have no second-order volitions. They exercise no control over which of these desires "wins out." Wanton addicts in such situations do not act as persons and do not engage in *freely willed* actions. *Unwilling addicts*, by contrast, are also torn between conflicting first-order desires, but they *do* have second-order volitions that the first-order desires to take the drug *not* be their wills. Unfortunately, the addictive desires to take the drugs are irresistible and they do take the drug *unwillingly*. Finally, the third class of addicts, *willing addicts*, do have second-order volitions to take the drug to which they are addicted. In other words, they will to be as they are. Frankfurt says such willing addicts act of their own free wills since their wills *mesh* with what they want it to be.

(P314) In summary, on Frankfurt's view, agents act *of their own free wills* just in case their actions issue from wills (first-order desires) they want to act upon. In such cases, they have second-order *volitions* that those first-order desires be effective in action. It seems odd, on this view, that *willing* addicts act of their own free wills, even though, due to their addictions, they cannot do otherwise. But we must recall from his earlier 1969 paper on Frankfurt-style examples that Frankfurt does not believe the freedom of will required for moral responsibility requires the freedom to do otherwise or alternative possibilities. What matters is only that agents take ownership of the (first-order) desires that move them to action and do so by virtue of second-order volitions. They thus act of *their own* free wills. The desires that move them to action are theirs. They represent the agents' true or real selves.

Susan Wolf has thus rightly called Frankfurt's hierarchical view a *real self theory* (1990, p. 29). Others, such as John Fischer (1998, 2006) and Michael McKenna (2003, 2008b), also call it a *mesh theory*: when one acts of one's own free will, what one does meshes with what one wants to be, and one is "wholehearted" in so acting.

9.3. Assessing Frankfurt's View: Historical and Mesh Concerns

Much discussion and numerous objections have been devoted to this view of Frankfurt's. I will focus here on a prominent class of objections that have a bearing on the relation of his view to that of this book.

(P315) On Frankfurt's view, if freely willed actions for which an agent is morally responsible are merely a function of the relation of the agent's will to his or her second-order volitions, then it does not seem to matter in any way *how an agent came to have* that particular "mesh" between first-order and second-order desires. Many critics of Frankfurt's view have argued, to the contrary, that cases can be constructed in which it *does* matter for agents' free will and moral responsibility how they came to have the particular mesh between their first- and second-order desires (Gary Watson 1975; Don Locke 1973; Michael Slote 1982; Kane 1996; Fischer and Ravizza 1998; Haji 1998; Pereboom 2001; Mele 1995, 2006).[2]

(P316) Consider, for example, Frankfurt's own case of the willing addict. Suppose the addict's second-order willingness to take the drug is itself caused by the effects of the drug use, which may have impaired the agent's capacities to properly evaluate what he or she should desire. Or consider cases in which agents are brainwashed or manipulated to have different psychological preferences than they might otherwise have had. In such cases, according to these critics, Frankfurt seems committed to the view that such agents act of their own free wills and are morally responsible, *so long as they have the wills they want to have, no matter how it came about that they have the second-order volitions they do have.*

Many of the above-mentioned critics who make such objections to Frankfurt are themselves compatibilists of various sorts or at least agnostic about whether compatibilism or incompatibilism is true. For example, Gary Watson (1987) makes this objection in connection with his well-known discussion of the serial murderer Robert Harris on death row in California, whose upbringing was so horrendous that he may not have been able to resist becoming the kind of person he was. While Watson is sympathetic to Frankfurt's view, he nonetheless, like the other critics mentioned, cites the following kind of objection to it.

(P317) Frankfurt's compatibilist view makes no room for important *historical* dimensions to free will and moral responsibility that should be recognized, even by compatibilists. Our personal responsibility is a function not merely of what kinds of persons we are now and what we do now, but also to some degree on how we got to be the kinds of persons we are now, who would act as we now do. Are we responsible to some degree for becoming the kinds of persons we are with the quality of wills we have, or is this entirely due to conditions over which we lacked control?

Frankfurt, for his part, in later writings remains defiant in the face of such historical objections, fully embracing the nonhistorical view of both free will and moral responsibility he has espoused: "What we need most essentially to look at is rather, certain aspects of the psychic structure that is coincident with the person's behavior.... We are the sorts of persons we are; and it is what we are, rather than the history of our development, that counts" (2002, pp. 27–28).

If we are "wholeheartedly" committed to having and acting from the wills we have, according to Frankfurt, then we can act of our own free will and can be morally responsible for being the way we are and acting the way we do, no matter how we got to be that way.

Many years ago (I think it was in the 1980s or earlier) I wrote a letter to Frankfurt posing an objection to his nonhistorical view that is relevant here, and so far as I knew, had not been posed in the literature to that time. It went something like this:

> (P318) If, as you, Frankfurt, contend, to have free will in the sense needed for moral responsibility requires being wholeheartedly committed to having and acting on the will one has, rather than being ambivalent about one's desires, then *one could never get from ambivalence to wholeheartedness "of one's own free will." For one wouldn't have free will until one got there.*

Sometime later, I received a letter from Frankfurt (it was before the era of email) that was characteristically both gracious and bold. He began by saying,

> (P319) "Many philosophers think I'm crazy. . . . But I do believe we cannot get from ambivalence to wholeheartedness of our own free wills. We get there in many ways depending on our social environments and upbringings. But it is the having of wholeheartedness about our wills that is the great good, no matter how we got there."

I should add that this objection to Frankfurt did not come out of the blue. At the time of making it, I was developing a view of my own, according to which having a free will that would be required for ultimate moral responsibility would involve at some times in the course of one's life, making choices or decisions that were self-forming and hence *will-setting*, not already *will-settled*.

> (P320) When making choices or decisions that were self-forming in this sense, agents would be *ambivalent* (ambi-valent, as I put it) about which of their opposing desires or motivations in certain situations should move them to action. In other words, there would be "conflicts in their wills," and these self-forming or will-setting choices would resolve the conflicts in favor of one path into the future rather than another. The choice of

either path would be possible, so that neither choice would be determined by the agent's existing will. What we would thus be doing when engaged in self-formation, on such a view, would be precisely what Frankfurt insists would [not] be required for free will—*getting from ambivalence to wholeheartedness of our own free will, by overcoming ambivalence about which of competing desires should be our will.*

Frankfurt of course, as a compatibilist, would reject the possibility of such self-forming choices because they would require that we be able at such times to choose in different ways without being determined. But accepting the possibility of such self-forming actions would allow him to avoid saying something even many of his fellow compatibilists would reject, namely that "we can never get from ambivalence to wholeheartedness of our own free wills."

(P321) In this correspondence, I also conceded to Frankfurt that he was right to insist that many of the choices in our lifetimes are will-*settled* and not will-setting in this way. Such will-settled choices may still be made "of our own free wills" and we may be morally responsible for them *even though* we could not have done otherwise (did not have alternative possibilities) at the time they were performed. I conceded, in other words, that Frankfurt was right about the falsity of what he called the Principle of Alternative Possibilities ("Persons are morally responsible for what they have done only if they could have done otherwise"). But I argued that, if actions that were will-settled and determined in this way were to be done "of our own free wills," the quality of wills from which they were performed must have been wills we were to some degree responsible for forming by virtue of some free actions in the past (self-forming actions) that were not already will-settled and determined when we performed them and for which we could have done otherwise. And this, as a compatibilist, he could not accept.

9.4. The Reason View: Wolf

Susan Wolf is another compatibilist who rejects Frankfurt's view, which she calls, as noted earlier, a real self view. Her own view she calls a *reason view*. In her criticism of Frankfurt, Wolf adds an instructive dimension to the *historical* worries about Frankfurt's view. This comes in Wolf's much-cited example of a dictator's son she calls JoJo.

> JoJo is the favorite son of . . . an evil and sadistic dictator. . . . JoJo is given a special education and is allowed to accompany his father and observe his routine. In the light of this special treatment, it is not surprising that JoJo takes his father as a role model and develops values very much like his Dad's. As an adult he does many of the same sorts of things his father did, including sending people to prison or to death or torture chambers on a whim. He is not coerced in doing these things, he acts according to his own desires . . . that he wholly *wants* to have. . . . This way of life expresses a sort of power that is part of his deepest ideal. (1990, p. 153; see also Wolf 2002, pp. 153–55)

Wolf notes that JoJo is "wholeheartedly" committed to being the sadistic dictator he is, in Frankfurt's sense: he has "the will he wants to have," for his first-order desires are in conformity with his second-order volitions. Yet, despite this, Wolf argues that "in the light of JoJo's heritage and upbringing—both of which he was powerless to control—it is dubious at best that he should be regarded as responsible for what he does." And she adds: "It is unclear that anyone with a childhood such as his could have developed into anything but the twisted and perverse sort of person he had become" (2002, pp. 155–56). But compatibilists like Frankfurt—and Wolf—cannot accept this line of reasoning because it may lead to appeals to incompatibilist accounts of free will that are in their view nonstarters—impossible and unintelligible. As Wolf puts it, "Whether we are determined or undetermined, we cannot have created our deepest selves, as such an historical condition would require: literal self-creation is not just empirically, but logically, impossible" (2002, pp. 154).

(P322) Yet, if Wolf cannot accept an incompatibilist resolution of this problem, she also cannot accept Frankfurt's compatibilist solution. So she looks for another reason JoJo might be said to be unfree and not responsible, despite his being wholeheartedly committed to the will he has in Frankfurt's sense. What JoJo lacks, Wolf says, "is the power to do the right thing for the right reasons" or "to act in accordance with the True and the Good" (2002, p. 156). And this, she adds, is compatible with determinism. JoJo, she says, was not the way he is *simply* because he was determined. We may all have been determined by our upbringings. But if persons were determined by upbringing to act in accord with the True and the Good, they would nonetheless be free and responsible. And if they were determined by upbringing, like JoJo, *not* to act in accord with the True and the Good, they would be unfree and not responsible.[3]

(P323) Generalizing this line of reasoning, Wolf commits herself to an *asymmetry thesis* concerning responsibility, according to which praiseworthy action does not require the freedom to do otherwise, but blameworthy action does require this. If persons are psychologically determined so that they cannot but act in accord with the True and the Good, she argues, their inability to act otherwise does not threaten any freedom required for moral responsibility. But if an agent like JoJo is determined in such a way that he cannot act in accord with the True and the Good, it would be unreasonable to blame him if he could not have done otherwise. While praiseworthy behavior does not require the freedom to do otherwise, blameworthy behavior does require the freedom to do otherwise.

Various compatibilist critics of Wolf's view, including prominently John Fischer (1994) and John Fischer and Mark Ravizza (1998), have argued that Wolf's defense of this asymmetry thesis commits her to giving a compatibilist account of the ability to do otherwise, a commitment that views like Frankfurt's were precisely meant to avoid.

(P324) Fischer and Ravizza argue that one of the most important contributions of Frankfurt's and Frankfurt-style examples to the modern compatibilist cause is to have relieved compatibilists of the burden of giving accounts of the ability to do otherwise that are compatible with determinism. Frankfurt-style examples, they argue, show that moral responsibility does not require the ability to do otherwise at all. Yet Wolf's asymmetry thesis, by requiring the power to do otherwise for blameworthy actions, recreates that burden for many significant actions.

Wolf, for her part, is aware of this sort of criticism. Her key move in response is to argue that metaphysical determinism does not entail psychological determinism and it is only psychological determinism that undermines the ability to do otherwise needed for responsibility. But this is an unsatisfactory reply for reasons related to those I have argued for earlier (P52–P53).

What she calls metaphysical determinism, if relevant at all here, would be the doctrine that whatever occurs at any time, occurs of necessity, and its not occurring at that time would be metaphysically impossible. Causal determinism as advocated by many scientists would be one variant of this. It would follow that if metaphysical determinism in the form of causal determinism were true, anything you might have done differently in the course of your life to make yourself different than you are would have been causally impossible. Your character, your motives, your dispositions, your intentions, the quality of your will at any time—anything you might have done to make these things different about yourself at any time—would have been causally impossible. Would this not undermine the ability to do otherwise needed to avoid blameworthiness?

> (P325) Fischer and Ravizza thus argue, in the light of Frankfurt-style examples, that Wolf should reject her asymmetry thesis and move to a symmetry thesis, according to which *neither* praiseworthiness *nor* blameworthiness requires the ability to do otherwise. To show the need for such a move, they introduce a Frankfurt-style example of a vile character, Joe, who decides for his own perverse reasons to push a child off a pier so she will drown. Had Joe shown any sign of not acting on his decision to push the child, a Frankfurt controller, who had implanted a device in Joe's brain, would have caused Joe to acquire the decision to push the girl off the pier. But Joe decides on his own to push the child off the pier and the controller's device remains inactive. In such a case, Fischer and Ravizza argue, it is reasonable to say that Joe is blameworthy for deciding to do this *on his own*, though he could not in the circumstances have done otherwise because the controller's mechanism would not have allowed it. Given Frankfurt-style examples of this sort, they conclude, compatibilists should move to a symmetry thesis according to which neither praiseworthiness nor blameworthiness requires the power to do otherwise.

9.5. Reasons-Responsive Compatibilisms

The challenge for compatibilists such as Fischer and Ravizza, if this criticism is correct, would be to give an account of moral responsibility—for praiseworthy as well as blameworthy action—that does not require the power to do otherwise, yet escapes the problems with Frankfurt's own hierarchical view.

(P326) Building on Fischer's important earlier work (1994), Fischer and Ravizza (1998) attempt to do just that. They note that moral responsibility would require some kind of *control* over one's actions and they distinguish two kinds of control that might characterize our freedom. What they call *guidance control* is simply the ability to perform an action at a given time. It does not require the ability to do otherwise at that time. By contrast, what they call *regulative control* is the ability to perform an action at a given time and the ability to do otherwise at that time. Following Frankfurt, and in opposition to Wolf's asymmetry thesis, they argue that moral responsibility, for *both* praiseworthy and blameworthy action, requires only guidance control and hence does not require the ability to do otherwise. Since guidance control is compatible with determinism, so is moral responsibility.

The task for Fischer and Ravizza is to give a compatibilist-friendly account of guidance control. Fischer goes on to do this in terms of a theory of *reasons-responsiveness* (1998). It should be noted that reasons-responsive theories of one kind or another are very popular among modern compatibilists. In addition to Fischer and Ravizza, they have been proposed in one form or another by Dennett (1984), Haji (1998), Nelkin (2011), Brink and Nelkin (2013), McKenna (2013), Vihvelin (2013), and Sartorio (2016), among others.

(P327) According to such theories, an agent's reasons-responsiveness is understood in terms of the range of reasons to which an agent would be responsive at the time of action. This responsiveness could be spelled out in terms of how an agent *would* have acted if certain reasons had been salient that were not salient in the actual context of the agent's action. The truth of counterfactual propositions of this kind, expressing how an agent might have acted if certain reasons were salient, is consistent with determinism, since determinism is silent regarding how an agent would act were the agent's actual past or the laws of nature just a little bit different than they actually were.

(P328) Classical compatibilists, of course, also appealed to counterfactual propositions of such kinds to account for how an agent might have done otherwise, if the past or laws had been different in certain ways. But contemporary reasons-responsive theories add new twists and refinements. For example, by introducing counterfactuals about how agents may have responded or failed to respond to certain *reasons*, they can also identify a variety of freedom-defeating conditions that are *internal* to the psychic life of agents, such as compulsions, phobias, addictions, delusions, and the like, as well as external constraints such as physical obstacles, coercion, or lack of opportunity.

Yet the problem with all such counterfactual theories, whether classical or contemporary, if determinism should be true, is this: such counterfactual theories tell us how agents might have acted otherwise at given times *if* the agents' actual pasts or the laws of nature had been different in some ways than they actually were. But, if determinism was true, these counterfactual theories would not allow the possibility of the agents acting otherwise, *given that the past and laws are as they actually are* when the agents act.

(P329) Fischer and Ravizza, to their credit, are well aware of this problem. But they think Frankfurt can come to the rescue for compatibilists. What Frankfurt-style examples show, they argue, is that any freedom to do otherwise that would require indeterminism, is not the freedom to do otherwise that matters for *moral responsibility*. Moral responsibility can be understood in terms of a *reasons-responsive theory* according to which it *is* compatible with determinism. They call this view *semi-compatibilism*.[4]

There is a problem, however, that semi-compatibilists, like Fischer and Ravizza, must face if this strategy is to work. It may seem that agents in Frankfurt-style examples are not reasons-responsive. For if they were given different reasons to act otherwise, they would not respond to these reasons because the Frankfurt controllers would not let them. In response, Fischer, leading the way, asks us to consider the actual internal causal processes that caused the agents to act as they did *when the controllers did not intervene*. He refers to these internal processes as the *agent's mechanisms of action*. If we focus on the agent's mechanism of action, he argues, we can assess whether the agent would have been responsive to certain reasons *if there had been no Frankfurt controller in the picture*.

This so-called mechanism-based account of reasons-responsiveness has been subject to an extensive critical literature among compatibilists and others in recent years about how we are to identify and individuate mechanisms, what they should consist of, and so on. Fischer, its principal advocate, has responded by offering more and more sophisticated accounts of these mechanisms, distinguishing different degrees of reasons-responsiveness (weak, moderate, etc.), also distinguishing reasons-*responsiveness* from reasons-*reactivity* within the mechanisms, and so on. These criticisms and responses have in turn led to an ever-widening critical literature.

I will not be pursuing the details of these complex debates here, however, because, as an incompatibilist, I believe they divert our attention from the main problem, which is the following:

(P330) Reasons-responsive theories, whether they are mechanism-based or not, are *counterfactual* theories that tell us how agents might have acted otherwise at given times if their actual pasts or the laws of nature had been different in some ways than they actually were. If determinism was true, however, these counterfactual theories would never allow the causal possibility of the agents' acting otherwise, *given that the past and laws are as they actually are* when the agents act. Even more troubling, if determinism was true, such counterfactual theories would never allow the causal possibility that agents might have ever done anything *in their actual pasts* to have made themselves any different than they are.

The appeal to Frankfurt-style examples does not allow one to avoid these basic problems of counterfactual theories. Frankfurt-style examples may seem to do so by showing that moral responsibility does not require the power to do otherwise. But, as argued earlier in Chapter 3 (P75–P78), it is one thing to argue that Frankfurt's Principle of Alternative Possibilities is false from Frankfurt-style examples, quite another to argue from this fact to the conclusion that alternative possibilities and the power to do otherwise are not needed *at all* for moral responsibility. From the fact that *some*, even many, actions in the lifetimes of agents may be such that the agents can be morally responsible for them even though they could not have done otherwise at the time they were performed, it does not follow that *all* actions in the lifetimes of agents could be like this (P75). It does not follow if the agents are ever to be responsible *for their will being settled the way they are when they act*. For this to be the case, agents would have to be capable, *at some times* in their lives, of "will-setting" or "self-forming" choices or actions for which the agents had the power to willingly perform them and also the power to willingly do otherwise (P75–P77).

Despite these problems, a number of distinctions made by Fischer and Ravizza are important even for *incompatibilist* views of moral responsibility as well. Of particular importance is their distinction between two kinds of *control*: *guidance control*, the ability to perform an action at a given time, does not require the ability to do otherwise. *Regulative control*, by contrast, does require the ability to perform an action and the ability to do otherwise than perform it. I have disputed their claim that guidance control alone is sufficient to account for moral responsibility.

(P331) But I think it is also important to note that what Fischer and Ravizza call guidance control is *necessary*, if not sufficient, to make sense of free will and moral responsibility, even ultimate moral responsibility, in an incompatibilist sense. Their *guidance control* is in fact similar to what I have been calling *teleological guidance control*, a kind of control, I argued, that must be an important *part* of any overall theory of agency, whether compatibilist or incompatibilist. Such teleological guidance control is necessary for any voluntary action; and it *is* compatible with determinism. But I also argued that a fully adequate account of free and ultimately responsible agency must also include—at least for *some* responsible actions in our lifetimes—what Fischer and Ravizza call *regulative control* and what I earlier called *plural voluntary control*, which, as they emphasize, does require the power to do otherwise.

9.6. Strawsonian Compatibilisms

Another significant group of new compatibilists tries to defend the compatibility of moral responsibility (and the freedom it may require) with determinism by focusing on the *practices* of everyday life in which we hold each other responsible and the *attitudes* we take toward others as a result of these everyday practices. Such an approach is inspired by P. F. Strawson's 1962 essay "Freedom and Resentment," discussed in Chapter 3. Strawson argued that to regard persons as responsible agents is to be ready to treat them in certain ways, to adopt various "reactive attitudes" toward them, such as indignation, guilt, blame, approbation, etc. To be responsible, he argued, was to be a "fit" subject of such reactive attitudes. It was to be part of a "form of life" or moral community in which people can take such attitudes to one another and thus hold each other responsible. More controversially, Strawson argued that our human commitment to the reactive attitudes can be insulated from any philosophical worries about determinism.[5]

This view of Strawson's has had a significant influence on current debates about moral responsibility and the freedoms it might involve.[6] But what exactly is required for someone to be a "fit" subject of resentment, blame, and other reactive attitudes? On Strawson's view, we must look at ordinary practices of *holding* persons responsible to decide this. Yet when we look at such practices, we find that we often excuse persons from responsibility or blame when they "couldn't help" doing what they did and so could not have done otherwise. And this raises familiar worries about determinism and the power to do otherwise. As a result, as we saw earlier, many critics of Strawson, including prominently his son, Galen Strawson, have argued that ordinary practices of holding responsible and the reactive attitudes associated with these practices cannot be entirely insulated from philosophical worries about determinism that have engaged philosophers for centuries.

In Chapter 3, sections 3.2–3.5 (P51–P70), I offered extensive arguments in support of such criticisms of the elder Strawson's view. His essay, it was argued, does not provide a sufficiently developed account of ordinary practices of holding responsible to show why determinism poses no threat to them. But the story doesn't end there because there are contemporary compatibilists sympathetic to Strawson's view who have attempted to offer accounts of freedom and responsibility to show why determinism poses no threat to them. One such philosopher who offers a sophisticated account is R. Jay Wallace. In his *Responsibility and the Moral Sentiments* (1994), Wallace argues that if we look more closely at ordinary practices of *excusing* and *exempting* persons from responsibility and blame, we find these practices are not undermined by determinism, just as Strawson claims.

(P332) To make his case, Wallace focuses on reactive attitudes of a moral kind. For persons to be "fit" subjects of moral reactive attitudes such as resentment, indignation, and guilt, he argues, it must be *fair* to hold them responsible for what they have done or failed to do. And it is fair to hold them responsible only if they have violated a moral obligation we can reasonably have expected them to obey. Suppose Joan blames Henry for not picking her up on the way to a party. Henry responds: "I'm not to blame. No one told me I was supposed to pick you up." If he is telling the truth and there was no other way he could have known this, he has violated no obligation and has a valid excuse.

Wallace argues that even though it might *seem* that Henry is excusing himself by saying he could not have done otherwise in the situation since he did not know of Joan's expectations, this is not the reason we excuse him. The reasons we absolve persons of blame in cases of legitimate excuses, Wallace argues, is that the agents did not *choose* to do what they did. They did not do it *deliberately* or *on purpose*. In other words, it is the *attitudes* of persons that counts when we blame or excuse them, not whether they could have done otherwise or had alternative possibilities. In this connection, Wallace asks us to recall Strawson's claim that the reactive attitudes are about whether persons display ill will or goodwill toward us in their attitudes and actions.

(P333) Having considered excuses, Wallace turns to reasons why we *exempt* persons from responsibility for such conditions as childhood, retardation, insanity, and addiction. Here again, it is often the case that the persons could not have done otherwise. But that is not *why* we exempt them, according to Wallace. The reason is that such agents lack what he calls *reflective self-control*—"the power to grasp and apply moral reasons and to control their behavior in the light of such reasons." And satisfying this condition, he argues, also does not require the power to do otherwise. For we may have the power to understand what is morally required of us and to do it even when we could not have done otherwise. Wallace concedes that often when we excuse persons from blame, it turns out they could not have done otherwise. But that's not *why* we excuse them, he argues. The reason we excuse them is because they have not done anything wrong. They have not "violated a moral obligation."

Fair enough, say the critics. But isn't it the case that not being able to do otherwise is sometimes the *reason why* we say persons have not violated a moral obligation and so have not done anything wrong? Suppose an elderly man on a walk at dusk sees an assault taking place in an alley. He chooses not to come to the aid of the victim himself and he also chooses not to look for police or to seek help from others, not wanting to get involved. It is reasonable not to blame him for not coming to the aid of the victim himself, given his age and frailty. But it is also reasonable to blame him for not looking for police or seeking help from others. What accounts for this difference?

(P334) The principle at work in cases like this seems to be something like the following: *it is unfair to hold persons to obligations they could not reasonably have fulfilled and fair to hold them to obligations they could have reasonably fulfilled.* The elderly man did not have an obligation to stop the assault himself, but he did have an obligation to alert others of the attack and to seek help from police or others. Ishtiyaque Haji, in a critical discussion of Wallace's theory (2002, pp. 207–10), argues that this italicized principle is a plausible principle of our ordinary practices of holding persons to moral obligations and it entails that it is unfair to blame persons for failing to fulfill an obligation, if *they could not have done otherwise* than fail to fulfill it.

In response, Wallace concedes that if an event, such as a human action, is determined, it is *physically impossible* that it does not occur, given the facts and the laws of nature (1994, pp. 201–2). But he denies that mere physical impossibility in this sense constitutes an excusing condition in ordinary practices of holding responsible. I believe his view in this regard can be questioned.

(P335) Consider a construction foreman who blames his female crew chief for improperly fitting together two pieces of a building under construction. The crew chief pleads that she is not to blame because it was physically impossible (according to the facts and laws of nature) to fit these pieces together due to faulty construction. She then proceeds to prove this to the skeptical foreman by doing measurements and computer simulations. If she is right, it would be unfair to continue to blame the female crew chief for the failure to fit the pieces together. The principle operating here is that it is *unfair* to blame persons for failing to do something that is physically impossible for them to do (given the facts and laws of nature). And this is a point, I believe, about *ordinary practices* of holding persons responsible.

Wallace tries to meet objections of this kind by making a distinction between two senses of physical impossibility (1994, pp. 216ff.). The sense of physical impossibility that is at work in ordinary practices of excusing such as this one, he argues, is not the sense defined by determinism. The sense involved in ordinary practices of excusing has to do with the agent's "general powers"—"what is not possible for a person to do, given the laws of nature and the facts about the basic constitution and capacities of the person" (p. 217). By contrast, he argues, the physical impossibility defined by determinism is "relativized" to particular times and circumstances; it concerns the physical impossibility of exercising general powers at particular times in particular circumstances (p. 218).

But this appeal to "general powers" only in excusing agents, rather than also to the possibility of "exercising" these general powers in specific situations, has led to a common and serious objection to his view.

(P336) As stated by Paul Russell, one of the philosophers who has made this objection along with Haji: "On Wallace's account, it is fair to hold persons responsible for doing wrong even though they may have been unable to *exercise* their general powers of reflective self-control differently in the actual circumstances. All that is relevant to the question of the agent's responsibility, Wallace maintains, is that the agent possesses the relevant general powers" (2011, p. 210). Although Wallace worries over this (1994, pp. 182–86, 196ff.), Russell adds, "his position, in the end, reduces to his insistence that this further condition (i.e., that the agent can control how his general powers are actually exercised in specific situations) would simply 'give the game away' to incompatibilists" (2011, p. 211).

It would give the game away, he thinks, because an agent's moral responsibility for many specific acts might then depend on whether the agent could have done otherwise, or had alternative possibilities, on those occasions. And Wallace has already conceded that the power to do otherwise, and agents' having alternative possibilities, may well be threatened if determinism is true.

(P337) It is noteworthy that these criticisms appeal to Wallace's own addition to Strawson's view about our ordinary practices of holding responsible, an addition on Wallace's part that I believe to be correct and important: *for persons to be "fit" subjects of moral reactive attitudes such as resentment, indignation, and blame, it must be "fair" to hold them responsible for what they have done or failed to do.* I think this is right. But Haji, Russell, and other critics argue, also rightly I believe, that *it is fair* to hold agents responsible *only if they have violated a moral obligation they could have obeyed, that is, if they could have done otherwise in the situation.* And this seems crucial to our ordinary practices of holding persons responsible if those practices *are* to be *fair*.[7]

Another new compatibilist theory of responsibility that is broadly Strawsonian in nature has recently been put forward by Michael McKenna in his *Conversation and Responsibility* (2012). McKenna agrees with Strawson and Wallace that we cannot understand responsibility without reference to practices of holding responsible and that such holding responsible involves the reactive attitudes. But McKenna also believes we need a more nuanced account of the relation between "being responsible" and "holding responsible" which does not see one of them as prior to the other. The key to understanding this relationship and the symmetry it involves, McKenna believes, is to consider them in terms of the analogy between *responsibility* and *conversation*. Competent speakers must not only be able to express themselves, but also able to interpret and understand those who may reply to what they say. In a similar way, McKenna argues, responsible agents must be able to appreciate the significance of their acts and the quality of their wills from which they act; and this is possible only if they are able to interpret the way their acts are received and responded to by others.

McKenna uses this conversational model to elucidate our understanding of blame and desert. The basic point of blame is to communicate with wrongdoers; and accordingly blame is both public and directed at those who are blameworthy. The value of blame lies in several non-instrumental goods it secures, such as the good that is made clear in the blamer's commitment to morality and the generation of a "dialogue aimed at resolution and reconciliation" between the blamers and the subjects of blame. Blaming responses are "fitting" when they move this dialogue along and thus preserve the moral community.

9.7. Ultimacy Revisited

I agree with much that McKenna says here about blame and our ordinary practices of holding responsible as well as much that Wallace and the P. F. Strawson say about these practices. I also agree with much that compatibilists who defend *reasons-responsiveness*, *mesh*, or *reason* views have to say about the conditions of free and responsible action, including Fischer (2007, 2012) and Fischer and Ravizza (1998), T. M. Scanlon (2008), Dennett (1984), Kadri Vihvelin (2013), Wolf (1990), Hilary Bok (1998), David Brink and Dana Nelkin (2013), Carolina Sartorio (2016), and Haji (2002), among others.[8] But, of course, I disagree with all of them in their belief that everything significant that can be said about the conditions of free and responsible behavior and our ordinary practices of holding responsible is consistent with the truth of determinism. As noted in the opening section of this chapter:

(P338) These new compatibilist views are all trying by whatever means possible to give adequate accounts of moral responsibility, and the freedom it may require, while avoiding to the degree possible, questions about *how we got to be the kinds of persons we are with the qualities of wills or motivational structures we actually have.* They are trying to avoid such questions as "Was it ever causally possible for agents to have done anything differently in the course of their lives to have made their qualities of will any different than they are?" These contemporary compatibilists thereby hope to bypass or defuse any questions that may lead to concerns about our UR for having the qualities of will we do have that fuel incompatibilist views about free will and moral responsibility.

One of the compatibilists mentioned in the prior section who has tried to deal head on with concerns about ultimate responsibility without abandoning a compatibilist perspective is Michael McKenna. McKenna discusses my ultimate responsibility condition in several writings, including his contribution to a collection, mentioned earlier, edited by David Palmer (2014a) in which ten critics critically examine my views followed by my replies. In his contribution, McKenna (2014b) argues that compatibilists like him must reject my condition of ultimate responsibility, noting that, if the case for incompatibility (as he agrees) cannot be made on the condition of alternative possibilities alone, it could be made if ultimate responsibility were added. If agents must be responsible to some degree for anything that is a sufficient cause or motive for their actions, an impossible infinite regress of past actions would be required unless some actions in the agent's life history did not have sufficient causes or motives and hence were undetermined (2014b, pp. 83–84).

But while McKenna thinks compatibilists must reject UR, he also interestingly argues that it "would be a mistake" for compatibilists to deny that free will requires any notion of "ultimate sourcehood" altogether. In this connection, he says

> Compatibilists would be ill-advised to avoid a battle over ultimacy. An adequate theory of free agency should be able to make sense of a person's shaping her life.... And there is substance to the thought that sometimes, as one struggles with a hard choice, she settles not only what to do just then, but she also shapes what sort of a person she will become.... Kane's ... picture of free will, of the historical relation between actions done of one's own

free will and other self-forming actions in the shaping of a life, is not something that compatibilists should be prepared to give up. We want to capture the thought that for some features of our own agency we are, after all, their source. Thus, did we *freely* shape ourselves. (2014b, p. 84)

(P339) What compatibilists must do then, McKenna argues, is resist the move from ultimacy to the denial of determinism. They must argue that "an agent can be the ultimate source of her will and acts even if there is a deterministic explanation for them that traces back to factors for which she is *not* ultimately responsible" (2014b, p. 85). To do this, he suggests, compatibilists must appeal to the fact that accounts of origins or ultimate sources in everyday life are a "contextual" matter dependent on one's explanatory interests. Thus, he says, we speak of the ultimate source of Perrier drinking water as a spring in the South of France. If we were geologists, we might trace the origins of the spring back further to the formation of the earth's crust. But "in ordinary contexts," he says, "it would never dawn on us to think that whether the water in our glass *really* originated in France turned on whether determinism was true or not" (2014b, p. 85).

My response to this challenge in this festschrift was as follows:

(P340) I think McKenna is right to argue that a compatibilist view of ultimacy would have to be "contextual" in the sense he defines. That is, the search for origins would have to stop at some point where one's explanatory interests ran out. But in the "ordinary contexts" he describes to illustrate this point, something crucial is overlooked: we are not concerned with the *moral responsibility* of the spring in southern France or other such sources in producing what they do produce. By contrast, the specific context of UR (and free will) is that of *persons* or *agents* with *wills* (characters, motives, and purposes) who can in principle be held praiseworthy or blameworthy for being the sorts of persons they are, with the quality of wills they have. And in such contexts of responsible agency, it *does* matter whether the agents are personally responsible to some degree by virtue of some past choices or actions for becoming the sorts of persons they are with the quality of wills they have, or whether the formation of their wills was *entirely* traceable to factors the origins of which they had no role in producing or bringing about (Kane 2014, p. 182).

(P341) This is in fact my pivotal motivation for being an incompatibilist and it leads to the condition for ultimate responsibility or UR. It *does* matter in assessing the moral responsibility of agents whether the agents are personally responsible to any degree by virtue of past choices or actions for becoming the sorts of persons they now are with the quality of wills they have.

This leads to a key point about the theory presented in this book that is brought out by McKenna's comments on ultimacy.

(P342) To satisfy this condition of ultimacy, *one does not have to "backtrack" to the beginnings of the universe or to the Big Bang or anything so esoteric*. In that respect, the backtracking is contextual: what is required is only that there be some choices or actions (self-forming ones) *in the life histories of agents* that are *influenced* by, but not determined by, their formative circumstances at the time they are made. Such choices or actions are those in which agents settle their wills in one direction when it was causally possible for them to have settled their wills in different directions, voluntarily, intentionally and rationally, whichever way they settle them. The ultimacy required for free will and ultimate responsibility *arises in the lifetimes of agents and does not have to be traced back to the beginnings of the universe*, as some critiques of Libertarian free will have claimed.

9.8. Dispositional Compatibilism

Yet another significant class of contemporary compatibilists are the "new dispositionalists." They include Kadri Vihvelin (2004, 2013), Michael Smith (2003), Michael Fara (2008), and Dana Nelkin (2011), among others.[9] These new dispositionalists contend that agential powers and abilities can be understood as dispositions to act in various ways in different circumstances. But they try to give more nuanced accounts of the relevant dispositions than classical compatibilists were able to do, allowing them to affirm that agents do have abilities or capacities, conceived as dispositions, to do otherwise, in various circumstances that are compatible with determinism.

To illustrate the difference between the new dispositionalist accounts of the ability to do otherwise and that of classical compatibilists, consider an example suggested by McKenna and Justin Coates (2021, p. 14). A young woman, Danielle, is psychologically incapable of wanting to touch any blond-haired dog. On her sixteenth birthday, her father, unaware of her condition, brings her two puppies to choose from, one blond haired, the other black haired, and asks her to choose one for her birthday. She happily picks the black-haired puppy. Did she have the ability to do otherwise on this occasion, to pick the blond-haired puppy? Knowing her psychological condition, the inclination would be to say no. But according to the classical compatibilist analysis, she would have the ability to do otherwise if it were the case that "if she *wanted* or *chose* or *tried* to do otherwise, she would have done otherwise." And this conditional might be true, even though, given her psychological condition, she could not have wanted or chosen or tried to pick up the blond-haired puppy and so could not have done otherwise.

> (P343) According to these new dispositionalists, one needs a more nuanced appeal to abilities as dispositions to avoid such problems with classical compatibilism. Suppose a woman, Jane, speaks harshly to her husband on a certain occasion. Did she have the ability to do otherwise in this situation? To determine this, new dispositionalists argue, we must consider the underlying structure of Jane's disposition to speak harshly, including her internal motivational structure, and then consider a variety of counterfactual situations slightly different from this actual one in which this internal motivational structure might operate. Might Jane in a variety of these counterfactual situations have avoided speaking harshly to her husband? If the answer is yes, then we can say she had the ability to have done otherwise than speak harshly to him *on the present occasion* even if her doing so in that situation had been determined. Now consider Danielle again, the young woman who is psychologically incapable of wanting to touch any blond-haired dog. Even in counterfactual situations slightly different from this one, she would not have selected the blond-haired puppy for her birthday present. So she did *not* have the ability to pick the blond-haired puppy in this actual situation.

New dispositional analyses can capture this difference between Danielle and Jane better than classical compatibilist analyses. More generally, new dispositional analyses of abilities can deal more appropriately than classical analyses with various internal constraints upon agential abilities, such as compulsions, phobias, addictions, and the like, as in Danielle's case.

Nonetheless, these new dispositional analyses of abilities to do otherwise have themselves been subject to criticisms. One striking criticism concerns Frankfurt-style examples. Suppose a man, Allen, freely shoots another man,

Smith. If Allen were about to do otherwise, a counterfactual intervener, Black, would have caused Allen to do so against Allen's will. In accord with the standard line on such examples, when Allen shoots Smith on his own and Black refrains from interfering, Allen does so freely and is morally responsible, despite the fact that, due to the controller's presence, Allen was not able to do otherwise.

(P344) New dispositionists, however, reject this standard line (Vihvelin 2017; Smith 2003, p. 19; Fara 2008, pp. 854–65; Nelkin 2011). They would say Allen *did* have the ability to do otherwise and was free to do otherwise when he shot Smith on his own. For if we focus on the motivational structure that is causally involved in Allen's shooting Smith on his own and consider other possible worlds in which this motivational structure operates unimpeded, we will rule out possible worlds in which the counterfactual intervener Black is involved. We will then be able to specify a range of true counterfactuals in which the agent had some reason to do otherwise and did otherwise. And this would allow us to say that the agent *had* the ability or power to do otherwise *in the actual situation in which the intervener was involved*. This goes against what most defenders of Frankfurt-style examples contend, namely that in Frankfurt-style examples agents do not, at the time they acted, have the ability to do otherwise because the intervener would not allow them to do otherwise.

(P345) Note that on accounts such as this, an agent's having a certain ability to do otherwise in a situation does not require that the agent is able to *exercise* that ability in the situation. Against this, it has been argued by critics, as we have seen, that if the ability to do otherwise in a given situation is required to be morally responsible *for satisfying a moral obligation*, it is not sufficient for the agent to possess this ability if the agent cannot *exercise* the ability *in the specific situation*. If this were to be the case, the agent could not satisfy the moral obligation in the specific situation he or she is in.

For reasons such as this, it seems to me that the comments made earlier about views of free will and moral responsibility that appeal to conditional and counterfactual analyses of the powers to do otherwise also apply to new dispositional and other new compatibilist views that make such

232   THE COMPLEX TAPESTRY OF FREE WILL

appeals, despite the greater sophistication of these new views. For, as I've argued earlier:

> (P73) Our freedom and responsibility must be exercised in the world that actually is, not in some hypothetical or merely possible world that might have been, but never actually was. And if determinism is true of this actual world in which we live and act, then acting otherwise than we do *in the circumstances in which we actually find ourselves* would always be causally impossible. It is not exonerating to be told that persons would or might have acted otherwise in some merely hypothetical or possible worlds that never actually existed, if their acting otherwise in this actual world in which they do live and act was always causally impossible.[10]

9.9. Libertarian Compatibilism: Christian List

I want to consider finally a relatively new compatibilist alternative that has been ably defended by Christian List in recent articles, and most fully in a carefully argued and original book entitled *Why Free Will Is Real* (2019). These recent writings of List require us to consider some new twists to traditional debates about compatibilism and are therefore instructive.

I was first alerted to his new version of compatibilism when I was invited to speak to the Aristotelian Society at the University of London in 2013. Christian and his wife, Laura Valentini, who were both at the time professors of philosophy at the London School of Economics and Political Science, took me out to dinner at a London restaurant the night before the meeting; and among other interesting topics of conversation were the thoughts Christian was then developing on issues such we have been considering of free will and determinism. I was intrigued, but not entirely convinced. These ideas were to be included in some forthcoming papers (e.g., List 2014) and eventually in the 2019 book just mentioned.

Crucial to List's view is a distinction between "physical possibility" and "agential possibility." To his credit, he acknowledges and agrees that in a deterministic world, only one future sequence of events is *physically possible*. And his book and other writings include astute criticisms of historically influential compatibilist views that have attempted to reconcile such determinism with the possibility of doing otherwise, including traditional conditional and counterfactual interpretations of the power to do otherwise and more recent dispositional and other analyses considered earlier in this chapter, all of which he finds wanting in various ways.

Nonetheless, List thinks there is another way to reconcile physical determinism with agential possibilities of doing otherwise. He argues that there is a more "coarsely grained" way of describing human agents and their environments which can be consistent with more than one such physically possible sequence of events and thus can be "agentially possible." So we need to distinguish two different levels of "physical possibility" and "agential possibility" if we are to make sense of free will and responsible agency. Such "agential possibility" distinguished from "physical possibility," he then argues, is supported by our best theories of human agency in the psychological and social sciences. The descriptions that matter in such sciences for agency and responsibility are not the microscopic physical ones, but macroscopic psychological ones that are involved in advanced modern versions of psychological decision theory such as are found in economic psychology and cognitive sciences. As it happens, these are among the fields that List's prior research and writing has dealt with and to which he has made significant contributions.

He sums up this view in the following way:

> I have argued that free will and its prerequisites are supported by our best theories of the human and social sciences. Intentional agency, alternative possibilities, and causal control are all higher level phenomena which emerge from physical processes but cannot be captured in physical terms alone. In this respect they are in the company of many other higher-level phenomena: beliefs, desires, intentions; institutions, governments, and cultures; money, inflation, and unemployment. All of these emerge from some physical phenomena but cannot be captured in physical terms alone. And, of course, their reality is not in doubt. . . . The situation is no different with free will. It is a higher level phenomenon, but no less real for that. (2019, p. 150)

His arguments for this two-level approach are supported by some technical considerations not yet considered. They involve appeals to critical notions in the philosophy of mind, in general, including, crucially, *supervenience* and *multiple realizability*. Agential or mental states, he argues, supervene on underlying physical states of the brain. But the mental states are more coarse-grained than the physical states on which they intervene. This means that while there cannot be variations in the agential states without variations in some physical states on which they supervene, there can be multiple realizability: the same mental or agential state can in principle supervene on different physical states of the brain, so that the supervenience base of a mental or agential state may be different at different times.

To illustrate, he offers diagrams in which at a time t^1, a mental state of an agent, m^1, supervenes upon a physical state, p^1. The mental state m^1, however, is multiply realizable at t^1 in different physical states, p^1, p^2, p^3, though it is actually realized at t^1 in only one of these physical states, p^1. The other realizations are nonetheless possible ones. And had either one of them (p^2 or p^3) occurred, they would have given rise to different histories at subsequent times (t^2, t^3, t^4, etc.). These alternative mental or "agential" histories would not have actually occurred if the mental or agential state m^1 had supervened on the physical state p^1 at t^1, as assumed. But they would have been possible alternative "agential histories" of the kind that are assumed and required by "our best theories of human agency in the psychological and social sciences." What would matter in such sciences for agency and responsibility are not the microscopic physical histories, but macroscopic psychological ones that are involved in advanced modern versions of psychological decision theory such as are found in economic psychology and cognitive sciences. Such macroscopic psychological histories would be compatible with determinism at the physical level.

In assessing this view, note first that if determinism did obtain at the physical level, it would have been determined that the mental state m^1 supervened upon the physical state p^1 at the time t^1 and did not supervene upon other physical states p^2 or p^3 *at t^1*. Given multiple realizability, it would have been possible that the mental state m^1 supervened on a different physical state than p^1 at some other time. But it would not have been possible at t^1 if in fact the mental state m^1 had supervened on the physical state p^1 at t^1. And if determinism did obtain at the physical level, it would have been determined that the microscopic physical history of the brain after t^1 was consistent with the actual physical state of the brain, p^1 at t^1, and not with the possible physical states p^2 or p^3 at t^1. In general, even if we grant that macroscopic psychological histories of the psychological and social sciences may be multiply realizable in microscopic physical histories of the brain, the following would remain true: if the microscopic physical histories of the brain were *determined*, the macroscopic psychological histories which supervene upon the microscopic physical histories would also be determined. Supervenience and multiple realizability, in other words, will not protect the psychological and social sciences from determinism if it holds at the physical level.

List says the place to look for free will is at the agential level of explanation of human behavior, not at the physical level. But if what we find at the agential level *supervenes* on the physical level, then the physical level cannot be left out of the picture altogether if we are to have a complete picture of what is actually happening when agents act.

(P346) He also says that the psychological and social sciences can proceed on the assumption that there is indeterminism in human behavior in the form of multiple possibilities *at the agential level*, even if determinism is true at the physical level. Indeed they can. And this is an important point. But if determinism is true of the physical world, then the "agential possibilities" which List rightly assumes are presupposed by the psychological and social sciences would exist only *in merely possible worlds*, not in the actual world. This helps us to see that his libertarian compatibilism, though a novel and original view, is a form of compatibilism like some other traditional views, including counterfactual or conditional or dispositional compatibilisms. Like them, it interprets the ability to do otherwise in terms of what may have taken place in other merely possible worlds, but not what might have taken place in the actual world, given the actual past and the laws as they actually are. Yet List's version, involving a distinction between two levels of "physical possibility" and "agential possibility," is an original view that avoids some common objections to these other traditional views that appeal to merely possible worlds, as he himself argues in his book.[11]

9.10. Revisionist Views: Vargas and Others

Revisionist views of free will and moral responsibility have also played an increasingly significant role in debates about these issues since 2000. Revisionists concede that our ordinary understanding of free will and moral responsibility has some genuine incompatibilist strands as well as compatibilist strands. But revisionists are critical of the *incompatibilist* strands in ordinary thinking about free will and moral responsibility, suggesting they cannot be realized. They argue as a consequence that what we should do is *revise* our ordinary thinking about free will and moral responsibility in a compatibilist direction. In the process, we should expunge all elements that imply or seem to imply the necessity of incompatibilist views.

The best-known and most influential defender of such revisionist views, who is largely responsible for making them a significant part of current debates, is Manuel Vargas (2007, 2013). Vargas notes that strands of revisionism can be found in other thinkers. He mentions J. J. C. Smart (1961), Susan Hurley (2000), Ira Singer (2002), Henrik Walter (2004), Shaun Nichols (2015), and Victoria McGeer (2013), among others.[12] But he has developed the view in more detail than anyone else has done. A crucial distinction, Vargas argues, for understanding revisionist views, is between *diagnostic accounts* of free will and moral responsibility and *prescriptive accounts* of these notions. Diagnostic accounts characterize the kinds of commitments ordinarily had about free will and moral responsibility. Prescriptive accounts are proposals about the commitments that, all things considered, we ought to have (2005, p. 129). Revisionist accounts argue that we should abandon certain commitments in our ordinary thinking about free will and moral responsibility in our final prescriptive account of them. For Vargas and other revisionists mentioned, the commitments that must be abandoned because they cannot be coherently defended are the incompatibilist commitments.

His arguments, which are complex and subtle, proceed in several steps. The first step is to argue that contrary to the assumptions of conventional compatibilists, there are incompatibilist intuitions embedded in our common sense that are not the results of mere confusions or errors. These incompatibilist intuitions play a role, he argues, in certain well-known arguments for incompatibilism, such as the Consequence Argument, manipulation arguments, and others. The core idea of such arguments, he says, is that "if determinism is true, there is only one way, physically speaking, the world can turn out if we hold fixed the past and the laws of nature" (2000, p. 131). And this would hold of human actions themselves, none of which could turn out differently than they actually do, if determinism was true.

Vargas canvasses many well-known compatibilist responses to such arguments for incompatibilism, many of which compatibilist responses have been discussed in this chapter; and he argues they all fall short. But his arguments against such compatibilist responses are qualified in a significant way: what makes arguments for incompatibilism, like the Consequence Argument, seem powerful, Vargas says, "is not so much that they rule out the possibility of compatibilism, but rather that they show how easily incompatibilism seems to capture ordinary ways of thinking about our agency" (2005, p. 402).

He draws a similar conclusion when discussing the proliferation of recent work in "experimental philosophy," which shows that ordinary persons sometimes give compatibilist responses regarding the responsibility of agents in certain hypothetical scenarios, but many give incompatibilist responses in other differently described scenarios. Here again, Vargas argues, such experimental work does "not rule out the possibility of compatibilism," but it does "show how easily incompatibilist" intuitions also seem to be involved in much ordinary thinking about responsibility.

(P347) In Vargas's discussion of these various disputes, the difference emerges between his *revisionist* view of free will and moral responsibility and conventional *compatibilist* views. He does not have to show that what libertarians who defend incompatibilism mean when they talk about such notions as ability or power to do otherwise is really what some compatibilist interpretation or other says they mean and that incompatibilists are simply mistaken about what they mean. For he concedes that both compatibilist and incompatibilist views of free will and moral responsibility play a role in ordinary usage. But the incompatibilist interpretations are ultimately indefensible and must be expunged from any adequate revisionist view.

He offers two lines of argument to show why he believes libertarian views that require indeterminism should be rejected. The first is that indeterminism adds nothing essential to the control agents must have over their free and responsible actions. Indeed, indeterminism diminishes, rather than enhances, that control. The second line of argument appeals to the "empirical implausibility" of libertarian views that require indeterminism for free and responsible actions. Regarding the first line of argument, that indeterminism adds nothing essential to the control agents must have over free and responsible actions, he asks us to consider an agent he calls Max, who seems to satisfy all the ordinary requirements for control over his actions.

Like anyone reading this book, Max deliberates about what to do, decides some things are better and some worse, and decides to do some things rather than others. The only thing he is lacking is indeterminism. Were he suddenly to be bestowed with it (in whatever way the libertarian likes), this wouldn't change the way his deliberations appear to him. He would still be deciding between options. He would still (let us say) have just as much control as he had previously. And the mental elements out of which his control was constituted and out of which the indeterministic possibilities would be shaped would not suddenly become under his control if they were not already. So whatever freedom indeterminism bestows on Max, it is nothing that changes the way his deliberations will appear to him, and it does nothing to change the control he actually has. The work indeterminism does begins to seem ephemeral (Vargas 2000, p. 150).

The first thing I would ask in response to this picture from a libertarian perspective is this:

> (P348) What if we assumed that *determinism* was true of the world in which Max does all this deliberating? Whenever he deliberated and decided "to do some things rather than others" in this world, now or at any previous and subsequent times in his life, if determinism was true, it would have been causally impossible for him to have decided differently than he actually decided. He may have *believed* it was causally possible for him to decide on any of the options he was considering, but it was not in fact so. "The way his deliberations appeared to him" would not be the way they actually were. He would still be exercising control in choosing the option he chose, to be sure. But the control he exercised would have been more limited in scope than he may have believed.

This is only the first thing I would say in response to this revisionist argument. In order to give a positive accounting of the role of indeterminism, I would go on to recall the three kinds of freedom, or free acts, distinguished in Chapter 2, section 2.11 (P37). Free acts may be (1) acts done voluntarily, on purpose, and for reasons that are not coerced, compelled, or otherwise constrained and not subject to control by other agents, (2) acts (free in sense 1 that are also] done "of our own free will" in the sense of a will that we are ultimately responsible (UR) to some degree for forming, (3) "self-forming" or "will-setting" acts by which we form and reform the will from which we act in sense 2.

Acts of kind (1) are compatibilist free acts. Acts of kinds (2) and (3) are libertarian free acts. But interestingly, acts of kind (2), though free in a libertarian sense, may also be determined. What makes them libertarian free is that the will from which they flow was formed in part by earlier self-forming acts of kind (3) that were not determined. So, when Max "deliberates and decides what to do," he may be acting "of his own free will" in a libertarian sense, *even though his deliberating and deciding did not involve any indeterminism*. But this would be so only if the will from which this decision flowed was his own free will by virtue of having been formed to some degree by earlier acts that *were* will-forming and were not themselves determined.

Further steps in my response to this revisionist argument would then involve giving an account of how indeterminism functions in these self-forming actions to *enhance* the agent's control over *how the will is formed* when they occur. Indeterminism would indeed diminish the control agents might have without it, in the case of free acts of kinds (1) and (2). The control in question for these free acts is what I have been calling teleological guidance control, which is necessary for any voluntary activity. In self-forming actions of kind (3), however, the *control* exercised by the agent would be what I have called *plural voluntary control*, which involves indeterminism. By diminishing teleological guidance control over whichever choice might be made in such a self-forming choice situation, indeterminism would make it possible in such self-forming actions in the manner explained earlier for the agents to make either of alternative choices in the course of the deliberation voluntarily, intentionally, and rationally, whichever choice might be made. It would thereby make possible another kind of control, plural voluntary control, which libertarians regard as necessary at some times in our practical lives if we are to be ultimately responsible for having the qualities of will we do have.

This brings us to the second line of argument Vargas makes against libertarian theories. He argues that the appeal to indeterminism as a requirement for the freedom of will required for moral responsibility makes such theories more "empirically implausible" than alternative compatibilist or revisionist compatibilist theories:

> Libertarianism requires that indeterminism be present in our agency in a very particular way and at very particular times, in the process leading up to or in the decision about what to do. . . . All libertarian theories are thus committed to indeterminism showing up in the world at particular times and places. . . . In contrast . . . whether your favorite theory is a traditional form of compatibilism or the revisionist account I offer . . . these alternatives do not have this requirement. Moreover, what requirements

these alternatives to libertarianism (i.e., compatibilism and revisionism) have will typically be requirements that libertarians have no special reason to dismiss. (2007, p. 141)

I agree with some of what he says here. As I've made clear throughout, requirements for any adequate incompatibilist free will must include plausible compatibilist requirements of reasons-responsiveness, rational self-control, absence of external and internal constraints, and so on. I've also argued that most free actions in everyday life, even many done "of one's own free will" (in a sense of a will that was formed in part by past self-forming or will-setting actions) may be determined and do not require indeterminism. Only the self-forming or will-setting actions themselves by which we formed the wills to some degree from which we later act require indeterminism. And they do require, in Vargas's words, "indeterminism showing up in the world at particular times and places." But I've argued, in the manner just summarized, that indeterminism's showing up at these particular times and places is not arbitrary nor is it unconnected to the role these actions play in will-formation and hence the freedom of *will* required for moral responsibility.

In Chapter 4, I further cited neuroscientists and other scientists who have pointed out that current neuroscientific theory treats a number of microprocesses in the brain, including synaptic transmission, spike firing of individual neurons, and the opening and closing of ion channels, statistically or probabilistically; and these neuroscientists argue that it cannot be ruled out that quantum indeterminacies play a role at these microlevels.[13] The neuroscientists I cited further note that if minute quantum indeterminacies occurred at the intra-neural or synaptic levels of the brain affecting the timing of firing of individual neurons, these indeterminacies, however minute, could be amplified, due to sensitivity to initial conditions, so that they had non-negligible effects on neural processing (P89). Moreover, they point out that the sensitivity needed for the normal amplification of quantum effects is a general feature of nonlinear dynamics; and it is generally agreed, they add, that nonlinear dynamics is pervasive in the functioning of human brains.

So yes, I've argued that if indeterminism is to play a role in libertarian accounts of free will, it must "show up in the world at particular times and places." But I've also argued that its showing up at these particular times and places would not be arbitrary and would be connected to its role in will-formation and hence free will and moral responsibility. When it would show up, under conditions of conflicts in the wills of agents, such indeterminism would make it possible for agents to choose different paths into the future and to do so in accordance with their will (voluntarily, intentionally, and rationally) whichever path they choose. It would allow agents at such times to set their will in different directions in a manner that was not determined by their past.

(P349) Vargas argues that such an account is more "empirically demanding" than any compatibilist or revisionist compatibilist account of free will and moral responsibility. I agree. But that is because such an account attempts to capture aspects of our agency that allow us to say that we are ultimately responsible for *having* the qualities of will, whether ill will or goodwill, we do have and display in our actions. Compatibilist accounts, and revisionist accounts like that of Vargas, do not do this. They offer us views of free will and moral responsibility that could exist in a thoroughly determined world. And they ask us to accept the fact that all the free will and moral responsibility we could have is consistent with its *not* being causally possible for us to have done anything different in the course of our lives to have made ourselves and the qualities of our wills any different than they are.

My strategy is different from this. It is to hold on to these important incompatibilist features of free will and moral responsibility and to attempt to give as coherent an account of them as I can that would capture notions of ultimate responsibility and the power to form our will in different ways at certain points in our lives. The goal would also be to give an account of such a free will and moral responsibility in a manner that would be empirically possible given what we know about the natural world in the sciences, including the neurosciences. In doing so, the goal would also be to answer a host of objections of philosophers and others that such a view of free will would be unintelligible and must reduce to luck or chance or mystery or require some impossible account of self-creation.[14]

Having done all this, I would take my chances with such an incompatibilist view rather than go to some revisionist or other view before I have to. If future science should definitively show that everything in the universe is determined and/or that the brain is thoroughly determined and allows no role for quantum indeterminacies in relevant ways, I would have to give up my view. I would then consider embracing what I would take to be the most plausible compatibilist view on offer, or a revisionist view like that of Vargas or some other revisionist alternative, or perhaps some version of free will skepticism of one of the kinds to be discussed in the next chapter. But whatever I chose, in my view, would give us a good deal less in the way of freedom of will and moral responsibility than the view I had abandoned.

In a book entitled *Four Views of Free Will* (2007), cowritten by me and three other authors, John Fischer (defending his semi-compatibilist view), Derk Pereboom (defending free will skepticism), and Vargas (defending his revisionist view), Fischer posed the following challenge to my view: suppose, he said, "perhaps hundreds of years in the future a headline should appear in the *New York Times* and other papers which said: 'Scientists prove that everything in the universe is thoroughly determined.' Then Kane would have to give up his view of free will. But my semi-compatibilist view would still be standing." I responded as follows:

> If I do ever read Fischer's future headline and determine for myself that it is true, I would give up my libertarian view and perhaps go over to one of these or other views. I think empirical evidence matters. But I don't know which of these other views I'd go to. For someone with libertarian instincts like me, it would be like being asked whether I wanted to live in the desert, in the middle of the jungle, or at the South Pole. Well, I don't like any of the options. Do I have to choose *now*? Can I spend a few weeks in Hawaii while I think about it? (2007c, p. 181)[15]

9.11. Critical Compatibilism or Free Will Pessimism: Russell

One further path compatibilists could take here which throws additional light on the issues at stake is represented by the view of critical compatibilism or free will pessimism, developed in recent writings by Paul Russell. Russell's early research and first book, *Freedom and Moral Sentiment: Hume's Way of Naturalizing Responsibility*, discussed the views of David Hume and other sentimentalist writers of the eighteenth century, such as Adam Smith, on freedom and responsibility. He noted a connection between these eighteenth-century writers and contemporary philosophers, in the tradition of P. F. Strawson's "Freedom and Resentment," who relate issues of free will and responsibility to the "reactive attitudes" and to practical attitudes in general.

Russell argues that by immersing themselves in reactive attitudes and other practical dimensions of our thinking about freedom and responsibility, and in related contractual and consequentialist aspects of that thinking, modern compatibilist views have been able to illuminate many aspects of our thinking about traditional problems of free will and moral responsibility. But not all. And here is where his thinking takes a critical turn. He argues that modern compatibilists fail to take full account of what Bernard Williams (1986) has called "the morality system." The morality system has a practical dimension which is central to it, and contemporary compatibilists have illuminated in new ways much that is important about this practical dimension. But the morality system also has a "metaphysical dimension" where it turns out that free will and related notions of ultimate responsibility and ultimate desert are central concerns.

Where modern compatibilists, like traditional compatibilists, were right, however, Russell argues, is that this metaphysical dimension of free will and ultimate responsibility cannot be accessed. Kant, we might note, answered the sentimentalists of the eighteenth century by arguing that this metaphysical dimension of free will could not be found in the empirical world where causal laws and determinism held sway, as he believed, but could be realized somehow by our noumenal selves, which were outside this causal/phenomenological network. Modern advocates of this metaphysical dimension of free will and moral responsibility do not go down this Kantian road to mystery. But they also fail, according to Russell, in ways noted by Thomas Nagel (1986): their views of free will and responsibility, which require the falsity of determinism, fall prey to "moral luck" of varying kinds, constitutive, circumstantial, consequential, or antecedent.

But where modern compatibilists, like their traditional predecessors, go wrong, according to Russell, is in assuming that solving the practical dimensions of the free will problem is solving the whole problem full stop. That the metaphysical dimension of the problem is unsolvable does not imply that the metaphysical dimension is of no significance. The metaphysical dimension of the free will problem is something we can understand even if we cannot solve it.

(P350) That ultimate responsibility and ultimate desert cannot be realized in the causal-phenomenal world in which we exist is something we can understand, as did Kant, though we cannot solve it as Kant, and many other incompatibilists, would have us do. Thus, Russell argues for what he calls a *critical compatibilism* or *free will pessimism*. We should be compatibilists, he argues, but not complacent compatibilists who believe our compatibilism has put to rest all the dimensions of the free will problem, including the metaphysical dimensions. This critical compatibilist or free will pessimist view should *not* be regarded as a solution to the free will problem, he argues, but as a rejection of the assumptions and aspirations that often lie behind it. What we have in the free will problem is not a skeptical problem waiting to be solved, he says, but a troubling human predicament that needs to be recognized and acknowledged. (Hence the "pessimism" designation.)

I agree with Russell, Bernard Williams, Thomas Nagel, and many other philosophers that there are metaphysical dimensions of the free will problem which cannot be summarily dismissed from debates about it. There are indeed also practical dimensions of the problem that modern compatibilists have dealt with in illuminating ways (reasons responsiveness, reactive attitudes, etc.), and these practical dimensions must be accommodated by any adequate libertarian theory as well, as I've argued. But, for us libertarians, there is also a metaphysical dimension that one must try to accommodate. I have described it in earlier writings by appeal to the origins of the term "metaphysics."

(P351) When ancient scholars organized Aristotle's large corpus of writings on philosophy and science, they placed what came to be called his treatise on metaphysics after (*meta*) his book on physics. Hence the origin of the term "metaphysics." In that treatise (placed after his book on physics) Aristotle says its subject matter was to understand the ultimate causes and reasons (*archai kai aitiae*) of all things. In earlier writings, I have argued that the free will issue has a metaphysical dimension in this ancient sense, since it seeks to understand the ultimate causes and reasons (*archai kai aitiae*) of some things in the universe of particular concern to us, namely, our human wills and actions. Were the ultimate causes and reasons (*archai kai aitiae*) of our wills and actions to any degree "up to us," or were those ultimate causes and reasons for why we have the wills we do and act the way we do to be located entirely in features of the universe beyond our control?

Russell agrees that there is such a metaphysical dimension to the free will problem. But like other compatibilists, he believes its goals cannot be realized. Yet he also rejects the view that some compatibilist position or other solves all significant dimensions of the free will problem. He says that of his view:

> The correct understanding of "critical compatibilism" is . . . that it aims to *replace* the free will problem with an acceptance of free will pessimism, considered as a more truthful account of the human predicament. This predicament along with its distinct pessimistic implications is not a problem to be solved, but a predicament waiting to be recognized and acknowledged. . . . When we abandon the assumptions of the morality system [including assumptions of ultimate responsibility and ultimate desert] we do not solve the free will problem as much as cast it aside. (Russell article 2017, p. 28)

I agree with Russell that the metaphysical dimension of the free will issue is difficult to solve, but not that it is insoluble. We can make sense of it I believe, unlike Kant, within the physical, causal order of the universe in which we must act and live. Doing so, to be sure, requires acknowledging that various empirical and scientific questions about the human constitution and the brain must be answerable in certain ways for it to be possible; and this requires controversial input from the empirical sciences. But we don't have to assume like Kant that free will in a libertarian sense could only exist in a noumenal world outside space and time.

I recall in this regard a memorable encounter with one of the philosophers Russell appeals to in his arguments, Thomas Nagel. It was at a conference in 2010 at Boston University Law School in honor of Ronald Dworkin's then forthcoming book *Justice of Hedgehogs*. I was on a panel discussing the topic of free will and ethics, one of chapters of Dworkin's then forthcoming book.[16] Dworkin defended a compatibilist view of free will, as did two other prominent figures on this panel, T. M. Scanlon and Amartya Sen. I introduced myself as the token incompatibilist on this otherwise distinguished panel and defended my view against Dworkin's compatibilism. Nagel was sitting in the front row of the large auditorium where this conference was held, beside Dworkin, his longtime colleague and friend at New York University. After the conference session there was a gathering of the audience in an antechamber at which Nagel sided up to me and said: "They were all against you out there. But I was on your side. Unlike Ron and those others, I believe there is an incompatibilist dimension to the free will problem. Though of course I don't believe it has been solved and am unsure it can be solved." This was close to an expression of Russell's free will pessimism. But at the time and in the context, it lifted my spirits.[17]

10
Skepticism and Illusionism about Free Will and Moral Responsibility

10.1. Introduction

According to free will skepticism, we lack the kind of free will required for moral responsibility of the kind that is at issue in debates about free will. That kind of moral responsibility is called by Derk Pereboom, a leading contemporary defender of free will skepticism, moral responsibility in the "basic-desert sense." He says that such desert "is basic in the sense that the agent, to be morally responsible, would deserve blame or credit just because [the agent] performed the action, given sensitivity to its moral status, and not merely by virtue of consequentialist or contractualist considerations" (2001, p. 47; 2014, p. 62). The free will that is necessary for such basic-desert moral responsibility, according to free will skeptics such as Pereboom, is incompatible with determinism. Compatibilist views thus fail to capture it. But free will skeptics also argue that incompatibilist free will, such as libertarians defend, is incoherent or impossible or is ruled out by our best scientific theories.

As a consequence, what all varieties of free will skepticism share is the belief that it is not possible to have the free will needed to ground basic-desert moral responsibility and the practices associated with it—such as backward-looking praise and blame, punishment, and reward (including retributive punishment) and the reactive attitudes such as resentment and indignation. Versions of free will skepticism have historically been defended by Spinoza ([1677] 1992), Voltaire (1977), Diderot (1746), Schopenhauer ([1841] 1999], and Nietzsche (1989). In the past several decades, however, the view has been revived and given new sophisticated defenses by a number of philosophers, including Pereboom, Galen Strawson (1986, 2002), Bruce Waller (1990, 2011, 2014), Ted Honderich (1988), Sam Harris (2012), Neil Levy (2011), Gregg Caruso (2012, 2016), Tamler Sommers (2007, 2012), Thomas Nadelhoffer (2011), and Benjamin Vilhauer (2015).[1]

Traditional free will skeptics were usually determinists, and their view was sometimes called "hard determinism." Spinoza is a clear example. He says that "in the Mind there is no absolute, or free will, but the Mind is determined to will this or that by a cause which is also determined by another, and this again by another, and so to infinity" ([1677] 1985, p. 129). Interestingly, Spinoza also offers an explanation of why persons usually believe they have a deep free will even though they do not: "Experience itself, no less clearly than reason, teaches that persons believe themselves to be free because they are conscious of their own actions and ignorant of the causes by which they are determined" (p. 143). Unlike some other traditional hard determinists, Spinoza's view also has a religious dimension. Believing that everything that happens is necessitated by God's will is a good thing, he argues, because it liberates us from harmful emotions: this doctrine, he says, "contributes to communal life by teaching us to hate no one, to disesteem no one, to mock no one, to be angry at no one" (p. 490).

Contemporary free will skeptics do not usually defend their views on religious grounds, like Spinoza. Nor are they usually hard determinists, believing that determinism is true in all of nature. They are well aware of the twentieth-century developments of modern physics, including developments of quantum theory, and most remain, as a consequence, agnostic about whether determinism is true or whether some indeterminism may exist in the natural world. But it doesn't matter, they hold, since free will in the basic-desert sense required for true moral responsibility is impossible whether our actions are deterministically caused or not. In this chapter, I consider a number of these contemporary skeptical views, relating them to the views of this book.

10.2. Galen Strawson's Basic Argument

Galen Strawson is one such contemporary skeptic who has argued by way of his "Basic Argument" that the notion of moral responsibility at stake in the debate—which he calls "ultimate responsibility"—requires conditions on free agency that cannot be satisfied whether our actions are determined or undetermined. In Chapter 3, section 3.2, I mentioned Galen Strawson's (1986) critique of his father, P. F. Strawson's, view that ordinary practices of holding persons morally responsible could be entirely insulated from metaphysical concerns about determinism). But I did not discuss Galen's own skeptical view, embodied in his Basic Argument, which is defended in that work and in later writings; and I now want to do that. But first:

(P352) It is noteworthy that Galen Strawson calls the kind of basic-desert responsibility involved in his argument "ultimate responsibility" and emphasizes that it has an important historical dimension. For what I mean by ultimate responsibility (UR) also has a historical dimension and is very much like what Pereboom calls basic-desert responsibility. It involves not only being responsible for expressing in action the quality of will one has, but also being responsible for having the quality of will one expresses in action and being the kind of person one is (the two dimensions of responsibility defined in P66–P68, Chapter 3, section 3.5).

Strawson's Basic Argument against such ultimate responsibility proceeds as follows: when agents act, he says, they act as they do because of the way they are. To be ultimately responsible for acting, they must then be ultimately responsible for being the way they are, at least in key mental respects (including motives or reasons for acting as they do). But if the agents are to be morally responsible for being the way they are in those key mental respects, they must have been morally responsible for the way they were that resulted in those mental respects. We thus have an infinite backward regress, which implies that finite beings like us cannot satisfy the conditions of ultimate responsibility.

(P353) Consider first the initial premise of this Basic Argument: "When agents act, they act as they do because of the way they are in key mental respects." This is also true for self-forming actions (SFAs) on the view defended here. But in these SFAs, "the way agents are in key mental respects" sometimes involves motivational conflict in their wills, which gives rise to indeterminism, making it uncertain how the conflicts will be resolved. So, while agents do act at such times because of the way they are in key mental respects, these key mental respects do not determine *which way* they will act. Whichever choice is made, will result from effort on the part of the agents to overcome resistance in their wills coming from the motives for an alternative choice. If any such effort succeeds, despite this indeterminism, the agents, by exercising teleological guidance control over the effort, will be ultimately responsible for "setting their wills" in one way rather than another, in a manner that will have been influenced by, but not determined by, "the way they were in key mental respects."

(P354) Turn now to the second premise of this Basic Argument: "To be ultimately responsible for acting, agents must be ultimately responsible for being the way they are, at least in key mental respects (including motives or reasons for acting as they do)." This is true only in a qualified sense for self-forming choices or decisions as just described. To be ultimately responsible for such self-forming choices or decisions, agents do not have to be ultimately responsible for *having* the conflicting motives or reasons that are the sources of the conflicts in their wills. What agents are ultimately responsible for in such SFAs is *resolving* the conflicts in their wills in one way rather than another and doing so in a way that is influenced by, but not determined by, their existing wills. *Agents can thus be ultimately responsible for the outputs of SFAs, the choices or decisions made, whether or not they are ultimately responsible for the inputs (the motives that are the sources of the conflicts in their wills).*

(P355) The ultimate responsibility of agents for self-forming choices *may* also partly consist in the ultimate responsibility of the agents for having some of the inclining motives or reasons for which the choices are made. This will in fact often be the case. But it need not always be the case. It will not be the case, for example, for agents making many self-forming choices in the early stages of their self-formation; and it may also not be the case for some other self-forming choices later in their self-formation. On such occasions, agents may not be ultimately responsible for having the motives or reasons that give rise to the conflicts in their wills. But they will nonetheless be ultimately responsible for *settling* these conflicts one way rather than another and thus forming their wills going forward in one way rather than another.

(P356) Consider, finally, the remaining premise and the conclusion of this Basic Argument: "If agents are to be ultimately responsible for being the way they are in key mental respects, they must have been ultimately responsible for the way they were that resulted in those mental respects" (p. 58). We thus have "an infinite regress, which implies that finite beings like us cannot satisfy the conditions of ultimate responsibility." It follows from the preceding pieces that no such unending regresses are required on an account of ultimate responsibility that involves such self-forming actions. For the agents' ultimate responsibility on such an account goes back to all the varied self-forming actions agents performed in the course of their lives. If agents also happen to be ultimately responsible for some of the motives or reasons involved in these self-forming actions ("for being the way they are in key mental respects"), it will be because their ultimate responsibility for these motives or reasons also traces back to some other earlier self-forming actions. *All ultimate responsibility agents possess thus originates in self-forming actions, past and present, of the agents themselves and does not regress any further back beyond all their self-forming actions.*

(P357) Moreover, it is important to add that all ultimate responsibility of agents does not go back to the earliest self-forming actions of childhood or in general to self-forming actions where agents are not ultimately responsible for being the way they are in key mental respects when they perform them. This was made clear in (P156–P159, Chapter 5, section 5.4), where it was said that "*if SFAs are possible for agents at all, they would normally occur throughout our lives and more so as we mature and life becomes more complex* as we become more self-aware" (P156). In making self-forming actions as we mature, we are constantly forming, *but also reforming*, our existing characters, motives, and purposes as we go along, in ways that, while influenced by our prior characters, motives, and purposes, are not determined by our prior characters, motives, and purposes (P157). The complexity of our lives, and of our wills and motivations, that gives rise to conflicts in our wills and to self-forming actions, does not abate, but normally grows, as we develop beyond childhood (P157–P159).

Note how the *indeterminism* involved in SFAs is crucial to the arguments of these steps. For this Basic Argument to succeed, it must be supplemented by arguments to show that free and responsible actions involving indeterminism, such as libertarian views of free will require, are impossible or unintelligible. Free will skeptics who appeal to the Basic Argument must also address the Intelligibility Question about libertarian free will and show that libertarian accounts of free will involving indeterminism are inescapably subject to arguments from chance or luck. Galen Strawson himself is aware of this. In his book, in addition to presenting the Basic Argument, he offers many other arguments to show that libertarian views of free will involving indeterminism would be impossible and unintelligible—citing Nietzsche that they represent the best self-contradiction so far conceived by the human mind. I have addressed these other arguments made by him and many others in earlier chapters.

10.3. Neil Levy's Free Will Skepticism

Neil Levy's book *Hard Luck: How Luck Undermines Free Will and Moral Responsibility* (2011) is also replete with arguments, many of which are original, to show that one kind of luck or another undermines free will and basic-desert responsibility. A distinctive feature of his view is that he not only argues that luck undermines libertarian views of free will, as commonly argued, but also that various kinds of luck can also undermine compatibilist views of free will and moral responsibility. Hence free will skepticism.

Levy's central argument against libertarianism (in Chapter 3) is one we have discussed in earlier chapters. He says that "an adequate account of moral responsibility must have the resources to explain choices contrastively" (2011, pp. 43, 90). Since I have responded at length to objections of this sort concerning contrastive explanations earlier in these chapters, I'll only briefly comment on a couple of points relevant to Levy's version of the arguments.

First and foremost, it is not true, on the view developed here, that different self-forming choices might occur given exactly the same past, including the same past motives and other mental states and processes of the agents. If different self-forming choices might occur at one or another time in the course of a deliberation, *the reasoning leading up to them would be different in significant respects*. Second, while agents will have reasons for the choice made at a time rather than any other, whichever choice is made, these reasons will merely be inclining. They will not be conclusive or decisive prior reasons for making the choice to which they incline, so that effort will have to be made to overcome resistance in the agents' wills if the choice is to be made. This is a truth, I further argued, that reveals something important about free will: an undetermined free choice *cannot be completely explained by the entire past*, including past causes or reasons (P182). This is so because every undetermined self-forming choice is the initiation of a novel pathway into the future, a "value experiment," whose justification lies partly in that future and is not fully explained by the past (P183) (1996, pp. 145–146).

Levy's argument from luck concerning contrastive explanations is presented in Chapter 3 of his book. Interestingly, he gives much more attention in the book to arguments from luck against various *compatibilist* views of free will and responsibility (in Chapters 4 though 8). Most free will skeptics, Levy notes, are disappointed incompatibilists. They hold that compatibilist views of free will are not strong enough to support basic-desert responsibility, while libertarian views requiring a free will that is incompatible with determinism are impossible. Levy, by contrast, is a disappointed compatibilist. He does not believe determinism of itself rules out compatibilist free will. But he argues that compatibilist views also fail to give satisfactory accounts of basic-desert responsibility, not because of determinism, but because of *luck*. He calls this "the hard luck view."[2]

I'll not attempt to address all of Levy's complex arguments regarding compatibilist views and luck. But I will touch on some which have interesting connections to the view of this book. First, he says that when one chooses, "there are two possibilities: either one's choice is settled by one's endowment, or not" (2011, p. 90). By an agent's "endowment" he means "the traits and dispositions that make one the kind of person one is" (p. 29) and that constitute the "preexisting background of reasons (desires, attitudes, beliefs, and values) against which one is deliberating." If our choice is settled by our endowment, he argues, we face a problem of *constitutive luck* since we cannot be responsible in some ultimate way for having created aspects of our endowment. By contrast, if our choices are *not* settled by our endowment at the time they are made, they would have to be settled in part by other present features of ourselves or our environment over which we lacked control and so they would be the result of *present luck*. Levy calls this dilemma the "Luck Pincer" (p. 94). It applies, he contends, to compatibilist as well as to incompatibilist theories.

This Luck Pincer is interesting from the point of view of the arguments of this book. According to these arguments, we can be responsible for creating aspects of our endowments by way of self-forming choices. And how these self-forming choices turn out is not "settled" by our existing endowments when they are made. These existing endowments in the case of self-forming choices allow for more than one choice to be made, consistent with the "background of reasons, desires, attitudes, etc." against which we deliberate. Nor does it follow that, if our self-forming choices are not settled by our existing endowments when they are made, then their occurring one way rather than another would be mere matters of present luck. To the contrary, when SFAs occur, it is because the agents have brought them about rather than any alternative, voluntarily and intentionally, by succeeding in a teleologically guided cognitive process (an effort of will) to bring about that very choice, thereby overcoming resistance in the will to doing so. This effort may have failed, but if it had failed, later efforts may have succeeded. Or the deliberation may have ended without any decision being made. And if any effort did succeed, despite the possibility of failure, the agent would have brought about the resulting choice rather than any alternative, voluntarily and intentionally, and for the reasons inclining the agent to that choice at that time.

(P358) The indeterminism involved in such SFAs implies that any particular effort may fail to attain its goal. But such failures have their causal source in the conflicts in the agents' wills and the resistant motives involved in those conflicts which afford agents the opportunity to make either choice at a later time, having thought further about their options and their situations.

Finally, consider Levy's "Luck Pincer" from the point of view of compatibilism, at which it is specifically directed.

(P359) On the one hand, if our choices are *determined by our endowments*, Levy argues, we face a problem of *constitutive luck* since we cannot be responsible "in some ultimate way," as compatibilists would insist, for having created aspects of our endowment. On the other hand, if any of our choices were not settled by our endowments alone but were *determined by our endowments plus present events*, we could also not be responsible for them "in some ultimate way" since we could not be responsible in some ultimate way for the endowments or for the present events which together determined our action.

The assumption I would question here is that "we cannot be responsible in some ultimate way, as compatibilists would insist, for having created aspects our endowment." We can be responsible for creating aspects of our endowment by engaging in self-forming actions.[3]

10.4. Pereboom on Free Will Skepticism and Meaning in Life

Pereboom has defended free will skepticism in two very influential books (*Living without Free Will* [2001], *Free Will, Agency, and Meaning in Life* [2014]) and many articles. He calls his view "Hard Incompatibilism," distancing himself from the hard determinism of many traditional free will skeptics and emphasizing that, in the light of modern quantum physics, he remains agnostic about whether determinism is true. But like other modern skeptics he believes the kind of free will required for responsibility in a basic-desert sense cannot be had whether determinism or indeterminism is the case. And he offers influential arguments against both contemporary libertarian and compatibilist views in the attempt to show this.

Against event-causal (EC) and noncausal (NC) libertarian views, Pereboom appeals to "disappearing agent" objections. In explaining free action in event-causal or noncausal terms, he argues, EC and NC libertarians fail to give adequate accounts of the causal role of agents in free action to adequately account for basic-desert responsibility. On event-causal views, all the causation of actions is done by events, including mental events, leaving no causal role to the agents over and above the causal role of the events, including mental events. On noncausal views, an agent's choosing or acting is not spelled out in causal terms at all, neither as caused by the agent nor by reasons or motivating conditions. Reasons or motivating conditions may explain why particular choices or actions occurred, but they do not *cause* the choices or actions. Agent-causal libertarian views purport to provide the required kind of agent control. But Pereboom believes they are ruled out by our best physical theories plus other problems about the obscurity of the nature of the agent control they presuppose.

Turning to compatibilists, Pereboom argues that all compatibilist views fall prey to manipulation arguments. The most powerful and most discussed of his manipulation arguments is his own four-case argument. Case 1 of this argument describes an agent, Plum, who is manipulated by a team of neuroscientists into killing White. The scientists press a button just before Plum begins to reason about his situation, which they know will produce in him a neural state that realizes an egoistic reasoning process, which they know will deterministically result in his decision to kill White. Plum would not have killed White had the neuroscientists not intervened, since his reasoning would then not have been sufficiently egoistic to produce this decision (Pereboom 2014, pp. 76–77).

In Case 2, the neuroscientists program Plum at the beginning of his life so that his reasoning will be strongly egoistic at the time necessary to get him to decide to kill White. In Case 3, Plum is indoctrinated to be this way by his community; and in Case 4, he is this way due simply to the causal determinacy of the universe. Pereboom argues that if, as seems plausible, Plum is not accountable for killing White in Case 1, and there are no relevant metaphysical differences between Cases 1–4, then he cannot be responsible in Case 4 either. Being causally determined to do something by factors beyond one's control—the relevant feature common to all four cases—undermines accountability; and so compatibilism is false.

Manipulation arguments of various kinds have given rise to an enormous critical literature among contemporary philosophers; and this four-case argument of Pereboom's has provoked an especially large critical literature.[4] Compatibilists often counter such arguments by insisting that we must distinguish between cases where agents are intentionally manipulated by other agents and cases where they are merely caused to act as they do by impersonal, natural circumstances. In the former case, responsibility can be "transferred" to the other persons who cause the agents to act in certain ways, if those other persons are responsible agents, whereas in the latter case, responsibility cannot be transferred to natural circumstances because, as the compatibilist Dennett put it, "nature is not a person" and cannot be held responsible. In Pereboom's Case 1, therefore, responsibility for Plum's killing White can be transferred to the manipulating neuroscientists, whereas in Case 4, if the agent such as Plum satisfies all the usual compatibilist conditions for responsibility (reasons-responsive, uncoerced, etc.), since his moral responsibility cannot be transferred to any other agents, he is responsible for killing White.

Cases 2 and 3 are more complicated. Some compatibilists would say that in Case 2, if the neuroscientists intentionally program Plum from the beginning of his life to be egoistic in a manner that would lead him to kill White, then the neuroscientists, and not Plum, would be responsible, as in Case 1. But a few might say that Plum might still be responsible if he satisfies all the usual compatibilist conditions. He kills White knowingly and for reasons that he wholeheartedly acts upon at the time, is responsive to these reasons, is not coerced, and is not acting compulsively, etc. In Case 3, where Plum is indoctrinated to be the way he is by his community, some would say that responsibility would transfer to his indoctrinators, while others might say he would still be personally responsible if he satisfies all the relevant compatibilist criteria. But all compatibilists would insist that in Case 4, if Plum is merely determined to act as he does by natural causes and he satisfies all the relevant compatibilist conditions, he would nonetheless be free in a sense required for moral responsibility.

Though I am sympathetic to this four-case argument of Pereboom's and to some other manipulation arguments for the incompatibility of free will and determinism, readers who are familiar with the literature on them will have noticed that I have not used them in this book to argue for incompatibilism. This claim might be questioned, however, by noting the following:

(P360) At the end of Chapter 2, I discussed B. F. Skinner's utopian novel *Walden Two* and explained how reading it as a youth gave rise to my interest in issues about free will. This is correct as a historical note. But what I came to realize as I delved more deeply into issues about free will in later life was the following: the kind of freedom *of will* I was looking for (which was in fact missing in Walden Two) could be distinguished from mere freedom *of action* (which Walden Two had plenty of). The citizens of Walden Two could do whatever they willed to do (they had a surface freedom of action) because they were behaviorally conditioned from childhood to will to do only what they could do (they lacked a deeper freedom of the will).

(P361) This deeper freedom of will I was looking for required that agents be *ultimately responsible* (UR) to some degree, not just for acting-as-they-do-because-of-the-way-they-are, but for *being the way they are* and *having the wills* they do have. This is what Galen Strawson also called ultimate responsibility, and it is what Pereboom and other free will skeptics call basic-desert responsibility. It requires asking such questions as these: Was it ever causally possible for agents to have acted differently in the course of their lives to make themselves and their wills any different than they are? And this would not have been causally possible if determinism was true.

(P362) The question to focus on then, I came to believe, was not whether agents were manipulated to be the way they are by other agents or by natural causes. The critical question was whether it was ever causally possible for agents to have acted differently in the course of their lives to make themselves and their wills any different than they are, whether or not they were made the way they are by other agents or by natural causes or both. Whether they were made so by other agents or by natural causes, if it was never causally possible for agents to have acted differently in the course of their lives to make themselves and their wills any different than they are, they would lack ultimate responsibility for being the kinds of persons they are with the wills they had.

(P363) This, I came to see, is what troubled me about Walden Two. To the extent that the control of the behavioral conditioners was completely effective, the citizens of Walden Two would lack freedom of will, though they would retain freedom of action (being able to do whatever they were conditioned to will to do). To the extent that the behavioral conditioning in Walden Two was not completely effective, however, some agents might have some control over how their wills were formed and some of them might have ended up willing things that would disrupt the orderly life of Walden Two. The founders of Walden Two could not allow this.

(P364) But I wondered, as have many others, whether behavioral conditioning alone could ensure this. To ensure such complete control, one might have to manipulate the genes and brains of humans, like the neuroscientists of later manipulation arguments do. One would have to ensure that young and older persons in Walden Two or other such manipulated societies never had *conflicts in their wills* which the persons themselves might have resolved in ways that were *not* determined by their past conditioning or by the manipulation of others. To the extent any agents of this society could do this, they might have some freedom of will and some UR for being the way they were. This is what I thought was missing in Walden Two; and it would be missing in any world, manipulated or not, in which it was never causally possible for agents to have made themselves and their wills any different than they are.

Finally, with regard to Pereboom, in both of his books mentioned and other writings in which he defends free will skepticism, Pereboom is also much concerned, as are other free will skeptics, with what we would have to give up in thinking about our lives if we were to jettison ideas of basic-desert responsibility. The titles of the books suggest this concern: *Living without Free Will* and *Free Will, Agency, and Meaning in Life*. The main negative reactive attitudes we would have to give up, he argues, if we jettisoned ideas of basic-desert responsibility, are moral resentment, indignation, and guilt. These negative reactive attitudes, he says, presuppose "a belief that the agent deserves to be the target of... anger just because of what he has done or failed to do" (2014, p. 128).

But giving up these negative attitudes, Pereboom argues, would not rule out judgments of people's goodness or badness, or responses to people's poor judgments, so long as they had a forward-looking aim of influencing people to do better in the future. And when responding to ill will, we still have many non-basic-desert-entailing attitudes, such as disappointment, hurt feelings, shock, concern, and sadness. Indeed, Pereboom argues that making these changes could make a better world, as anger often destroys relationships and fuels conflicts (2014, p. 128). He also discusses how free will skepticism would influence views on criminal responsibility.

(P365) Retributive punishment in criminal law, Pereboom believes, is clearly a form of harm for which justifications must meet a high standard (2014, p. 158), and the standard of basic desert may be higher than we can meet, given free will skepticism. He thus advocates a *quarantine model* of criminal punishment, which is justified by forward-looking self-defense. Societies are sometimes justified in quarantining persons who have highly communicable diseases, not because they deserve blame, but simply to protect the general population. Criminal punishment, it is suggested, might be justified for similar forward-looking purposes, without assuming basic-desert responsibility. At the same time, this would lead to a greater emphasis on rehabilitation and other forward-looking aspects of our criminal justice system that would allow inmates to return to productive lives while minimizing harm to society.

10.5. Thinking It Over

I believe Pereboom and other free will skeptics may be generally right about what attitudes and practices we would have to give up, and which might be retained, if we gave up belief in the free will required for basic-desert responsibility.

(P366) But giving up the idea that anyone deserves blame or moral anger for what they have done and substituting such attitudes as disappointment, shock, concern, and sadness is quite a lot to swallow if we are not sure it is truly necessary. To be disappointed and sad in response to the behavior of cruel dictators, child abusers, ruthless seekers of profit, and many other cruel and exploitative individuals without supposing they are deserving of moral blame, any more than any other persons are, seems to undermine our views about morality as well as responsibility. To take an example (at the time I am writing), what are we to think of Vladimir Putin and other dictators of the present and past, such as Stalin, whom Putin is emulating? Not moral blame or anger, but simply disappointment and sadness? Are we to think they are all fictional JoJos who are lacking any blame at all for the kinds of persons they became?

(P367) Free will skeptics like Pereboom would undoubtedly point out, and rightly so, that they are no more sympathetic to the cruel dictators and exploiters of the world than the rest of us are. If we could stop such persons, we would be justified in putting them in quarantine. Rehabilitation might be useless for many. But in quarantine, they would no longer be able to exploit others. Meanwhile, by focusing on dictators and longtime exploiters of others, they would point out, we would be diverted from focusing on the many other persons who because of unfortunate circumstances and upbringing have committed crimes but can be rehabilitated in quarantine and return to being productive members of society. We would likewise be diverted from the cruelty and injustice of our current prison systems and practices of retributive punishment which result from beliefs that all persons have backward-looking basic desert for what they have done, no matter what their past and present circumstances may have been. Finally, free will skeptics would say that by focusing on despicable dictators and exploiters of others who provoke such emotional reactions, we would be diverted by these emotional reactions from the strong arguments against the possibility of free will of the kind required for moral responsibility in the basic-desert sense.

(P368) I appreciate all these concerns. But as a believer in basic-desert responsibility, I react to them differently than do free will skeptics. I believe such skeptics too precipitously reject the kind of free will that would support such basic-desert responsibility, namely a free will that is incompatible with determinism. They marshal all the standard objections against such a free will that we have been considering and conclude that it is unintelligible and impossible ideal. Since they also argue that compatibilist views of freedom and responsibility do not capture their notion of basic desert, free will skeptics believe we must abandon such a notion altogether.

(P369) By contrast, I think we should try to show that a free will required for basic desert (one that satisfies conditions of ultimate responsibility) is not an unintelligible and impossible ideal that cannot be made sense of. Before abandoning it, we should try to show that such a notion of free will is intelligible and something we might possibly have by answering the many objections that have been made against its possibility and intelligibility. We cannot demonstrate at present that it is empirically possible, but we can try to show that it is not ruled out by current science, so that whether or not we have it is, in Balaguer's words, an "open scientific problem." And we should not completely abandon notions of basic desert and ultimate responsibility until the scientific evidence shows definitively that we have to abandon any notion of free will that might support them.

If we do keep these notions, however, which free will skeptics tell us are archaic remnants of the past, how are we to avoid the often cruel and harsh consequences of them that are also archaic remnants of the past that free will skeptics would like us to abandon? I am thinking of the cruelty and injustice of current prison systems, the practices of retributive punishment which result from beliefs that all persons have backward-looking basic desert for what they have done, no matter what their past and present circumstances may have been, and so on.

(P370) These are important questions that I have not fully addressed in these chapters thus far. It turns out that, *if the account of free will supporting basic desert and ultimate responsibility is formulated with the aim of trying to make it empirically and scientifically possible*, as I have tried to do here and in other works, the harsher consequences of basic desert[5] and ultimate responsibility that free will skeptics decry would not follow. I have argued for this point in earlier formulations of my view, for example, in *The Significance of Free Will*, in a way that remains true of the present view. Since I cannot improve on what I said about this matter in *Significance*, I will quote further from the final section of that work, entitled "Modernity and Irony" (1996, pp. 212–15).

(P371) "Another kind of disservice that is done" by many accounts of libertarian free will is that they "may leave the impression that exercises of free will are entirely above and beyond the influences of natural causes and conditioning. This can easily lead one to think that the abused child or ghetto dweller has as much free will and ultimate responsibility . . . as one who lives in more advantaged circumstances. For if each has free will and free will is a mysterious power to rise above one's circumstances, whatever they may be, then each is responsible to the same degree, no matter what their past circumstances. The theory of this book implies no such consequence. Precisely because that theory recognizes *the embeddedness of free will in the natural order*, it recognizes that free will and ultimate responsibility are matters of degree and our possession of them can be very much influenced by circumstances. That is why, if one believes in the value of free will and ultimate responsibility, it is important to cultivate a social order in which they can flourish, rather than one like Walden Two, or some totalitarian regime, in which they cannot" (1996, p. 213).

(P372) "The fact that free will and ultimate responsibility are matters of degree is also why it is the case that if we should learn of the young rapist [discussed in an earlier chapter] that his childhood was one of horrendous abuse and mistreatment, our resentment, indignation and other negative reactive attitudes would tend to change. . . . We may not conclude he has no responsibility whatever for what he has done. But that will depend on . . . whether we think there is anything the young man *could have voluntarily done* in the past despite his unfortunate circumstances to make himself different than he was. In other words, we invoke UR" (1996, p. 213).[6]

(P373) "What is needed for a mature" view of libertarian free will and hence basic-desert responsibility "in the modern age is a recognition of the many ways in which circumstances of birth and upbringing can limit free will and [basic desert] responsibility (for this is one of the prevailing themes of modernity) without yielding to the temptation to think that we are all always helpless victims of circumstances and never have any ultimate responsibility for what we do or are. Such recognition . . . would mean rejecting the harsh political judgment that the disadvantaged of society are wholly responsible for their disadvantaged condition because they retain their free will undiminished and are therefore undeserving of government or societal support or assistance" (1996, p. 214).

(P374) "Hans Blumenberg, author of *The Legitimacy of the Modern Age* (1983), has said that the idea that we might attain complete autonomy or perfect freedom is the 'final myth' of modernity. The quest for autonomy is integral to the modern age, Blumenberg argues, but complete autonomy is an impossible ideal. If we seek an end to dependency and determination from without, he argues, we must accept an 'ineliminable contingency within' ourselves. I think this is profoundly correct. If we want to be independent sources of activity in the world, we must accept ambivalence, uncertainty, and conflict within ourselves—all of which are connected to the indeterminacy that is required for free will. The ambivalence, uncertainty and risk are in turn related to competing images of the good that must inevitably confront those who would be ultimate creators of their own ends. . . . This questing or striving for worthy ends is the goal of free will—and indeed, the goal of life itself, if we are to believe the great myths of humankind. Without this questing life would become, in the words of Herman Melville in *Moby Dick*, 'an ice palace made out of frozen sighs'" (Kane 1996, pp. 214–15).

10.6. Gregg Caruso, Creativity, and Just Deserts

Gregg Caruso is another defender of free will skepticism who has written widely and insightfully on the topic in the past two decades. His contributions include books such as *Free Will and Consciousness: A Determinism Account of the Illusion of Free Will* (2011) and *Rejecting Retributivism: Free Will, Punishment and Criminal Justice* (2021) and numerous published papers. He follows Pereboom in many of his views about, and arguments for, free will skepticism, some discussed in the previous section. In addition to luck objections against libertarians, he appeals, against compatibilists, to Pereboom's four-case argument, as well as to Levy's Luck Pincer. Caruso adds his own insights to all these topics. His 2021 book just mentioned, for example, is a full-length study and defense of the quarantine model of criminal punishment, which he calls the public-health quarantine model.[7]

I will focus here on several aspects of Caruso's work relevant to my own view that have not been covered in the previous sections. One of these topics is creativity. In an American Philosophical Association symposium on his views about this topic in which I participated, Caruso said:

One aspect of the traditional free will debate that is often overlooked is the question of *creativity*—i.e. whether free will is required for genuine creativity and whether agents justly deserve to be praised or blamed for their artistic and creative achievements. . . . The question of creativity is relevant to the topic of free will because it raises questions about human agency, ability and effort, assessment and evaluation, just deserts and reward or punishment. (pp. 593, 597, 601, 605)

As a free will skeptic, Caruso defends a notion of creativity that "relinquishes the notion that agents justly deserve to be praised or blamed for their artistic," scientific, or other creative activities. The challenge facing free will skeptics, like himself, he adds, is thus to explain how such a notion of creativity "preserves *enough* of what we care about and why life without basic desert moral responsibility would not be as destructive to creativity as many people believe."

He uses a number of examples, including that of Mozart, to show that while the kind of artistic creativity that free will skeptics could affirm would not be consistent with libertarian free will, it would be consistent with kinds of creativity compatibilists could affirm. He quotes Paul Russell in this regard: "Even if there exist deterministic causal paths leading to the emergence of Mozart's works . . . none of this would serve to show that the works concerned are not 'creative,' 'original' or 'new contributions' to the evolution of Western music." For such claims are comparative claims: "Mozart's symphonies can justifiably be called 'new' and 'original' to the extent that they introduce previously unheard themes, methods, arrangements, etc." Free will skeptics, Caruso argues, can accept all such claims about the creativity of artists and artistic works. What they cannot accept is "the notion that agents justly deserve [in the sense of basic desert] to be praised and blamed for their artistic activities."[8]

Caruso turns to the very different example of Einstein to make another point about what free will skeptics need not give up regarding claims about creativity. He notes that the year this APA symposium was taking place (2015) was "the centenary of Einstein's discovery of a new theory of gravity—general relativity." And he quotes a media commentator on that discovery (Smenk 2015): "Einstein's achievement required perseverance and enormous creativity, as he struggled over a rough and winding road for eight years to formulate the theory." Einstein is an interesting example in this regard. For he himself was an admirer of, and a hard determinist like, Spinoza. Einstein, as is well known, resisted twentieth-century developments in quantum theory that would require indeterminism and offered challenging thought experiments against them. Less well known, but with equal consistency, is that Einstein denied that he deserved credit or praise (in a basic-desert sense) for his enormous creativity.

Agreeing with this, Caruso adds, does not prevent free will skeptics from legitimately ascribing creativity to Einstein. "Since desert claims are about [responsibility in the sense of] *accountability* and ascriptions of creativity are about [responsibility in the sense of] *attributability*, there is no inconsistency in free will skeptics attributing creativity to agents." For responsibility in the sense of attributability, unlike the sense of accountability, requires only that "actions or attitudes are properly *attributable* to, or *reflective* of, an agent's" existing self. It does not require any ultimate desert for how the existing self became the creative self it is.

A second familiar notion of responsibility that free will skeptics can retain, Caruso argues, is *forward-looking answerability*: agents are responsible for their actions and attitudes in this sense if they have the capacity for "evaluative judgment in a way that opens them up to demands for justification from others." We are justified in inviting agents to evaluate critically what their actions indicate about their intentions and character and to demand apology or request reform of their future behavior. This is something we would want to do even if we believed agents were not justly deserving of being praised or blamed in basic-desert senses for their actions and attitudes, including their creative activities.

Caruso rightly adds that creativity does not only apply to the Mozarts and Einsteins of this world. Many people in everyday life are creative in various ways and degrees, some praiseworthy and some blameworthy. On the praiseworthy side, are many persons who are creative in less spectacular, yet praiseworthy, ways: the woman who is very creative at making floral designs and makes a successful business of it, or another who is a creative chef who makes a successful business of that or simply makes her family and many friends very happy on holidays. Or there are men like an uncle, whom I always admired, who could find creative ways to fix anything from household gadgets to toys. There are many men and women who do creative things in their workplaces, and parents who must be creative in one of the most important aspects of life, raising children to be competent and caring adults in a complex world. On the blameworthy side, consider investors who game the stock markets in various creative ways to cheat others and enrich themselves, or politicians who find devious ways to enrich themselves and their wealthy donors while fooling their constituents, or con men or con women who find creative ways to cheat persons of their life savings, and many others.

According to free will skeptics, Caruso suggests, we can *attribute* creativity of different sorts to each of these agents. And with the bad ones, we are also "justified in inviting them to evaluate critically what their actions indicate about their intentions and character and to demand apology or request reform of their future behavior" (forward-looking *answerability*). But none of them would be justly deserving of being praised or blamed in basic-desert senses for their creative activities, good or bad (in the sense of *accountability*).

While Caruso makes a sophisticated case for all this, I find myself with the same reactions to his arguments that were expressed earlier to Pereboom's view in P366–P369. Free will skeptics like Caruso believe we must abandon basic-desert notions of creativity as well as of morality. By contrast, as noted, I think we should try to show that a free will required for being basically deserving of praise or blame for our creative achievements is not an unintelligible and impossible ideal. Before abandoning it, we should try to show that such a notion of free will is intelligible and something we might possibly have by answering the many objections that have been made against its possibility and intelligibility (P360).[9]

Other instructive aspects of Caruso's defense of free will skepticism emerge in a more recent book coauthored with Daniel Dennett, *Just Deserts: Debating Free Will* (2021). This book is a spirited debate between the two articulate authors in which Caruso defends his free will skepticism against Dennett's well-known compatibilist views. Both reject libertarian views of free will of all kinds early in their debate as unintelligible or impossible and then move on to the disagreements between free will skeptics and compatibilists. They spend a great deal of time trying to make their disagreements altogether intelligible to each other, including disagreements about the central notion they are debating, just deserts. Thus, in their third and final debate, Caruso says the following to Dennett:

> Given the canonical understanding of "just deserts" and how it is used to justify various retributive attitudes, judgments and treatments, your use of the term lends itself to easy confusion and gives the mistaken impression that you are setting out to preserve something that you are not. . . . One may rightly wonder why it would not be better [for you] to simply eliminate the notions of *desert* and *free will*, since they come with lots of historical baggage and are likely to confuse readers into thinking you're defining a stronger thesis than you are. Why not then adopt something like the following thesis instead: Determinism . . . is compatible with agents having the kind of *autonomy* and *control* required for the kind of *forward-looking*

moral responsibility sketched earlier, where moral protest is grounded, not in desert, but in *non-desert invoking desiderata:* future protection, future reconciliation, and future moral formation. Shall I inform my fellow free will skeptics that we have a new member of the team? (Dennett and Caruso 2021, pp. 194–95, 197)

Dennett responds with a resounding no. He's not ready to sign on with team free-will-skepticism. He says,

> One more time; I am saying that people do really and truly and non-instrumentally *deserve* to be punished for their crimes because they have accepted a bargain—a promise, a contract—that stipulates that they will be treated thus. The existence of the contract and its justification is to be explained on consequentialist grounds, of course, but once it is part of a society, the desert of all participants is as real as the money in their bank accounts. There is no such thing as basic desert, just as there is no such thing as basic economic value. . . . Seeking to diagnose our failures to communicate, I have been puzzled by your frequent allusions to what is consistent with, or available to, the free will skeptic. Who might want to be a free will skeptic? Not I. These claims are guaranteed to fall flat when addressed *to me*, since only those who still think that free will (in the sense that matters) is threatened or challenged by determinism should be interested in this possibility at all. The sense of "free will" appearing in your term "free will skeptic" is one of the senses of free will that I have argued for decades *is not worth wanting*. (pp. 197–98)

This exchange makes very clear what is in dispute between free will skeptics and many compatibilists, such as Dennett.

> (P375) Caruso and Dennett agree that the kind of free will required for basic desert, and basic desert itself, are not possible and not intelligible. But Dennett as a compatibilist goes further and says that this kind of free will and basic desert is also not *worth wanting*. We can have all the free will and *desert* worth wanting, he argues, spelled out in familiar consequentialist and compatibilist terms, even if determinism should be the case. If Caruso and other free will skeptics believe that a free will requiring indeterminism is impossible and unintelligible, then why continue to believe such a free will is "worth wanting"?[10]

(P376) This is an interesting question. And it suggests another way in which those, like me, who try to make sense of a libertarian free will are not outliers in this debate between free will skeptics and compatibilists, and can contribute to it. Suppose, for example, one could give an account of free will requiring indeterminism that shows how agents can be basically deserving to varying degrees for being the kinds of persons they are with the wills they have and show that such a free will is intelligible. Then one could say why such a free will is "worth wanting" even if it might remain an open scientific question whether we have such a free will.[11]

A further response I would make to Dennett's claim that any such incompatibilist account of free will is not "worth wanting" was made earlier in Chapter 6, section 6.8 (P232–P234) in terms of evolution. As described there, and as many evolutionary theorists have argued, a higher stage of evolution is reached in humans, in which a further development of the evolutionary process allowed analogues of genetic mutations to occur in the mind and then to be subject to selection within the mental environments of agents.[12] This higher stage of evolution also allows agents to exercise a certain kind of *control* over their own behavior that was earlier called *teleological guidance control*. Agents exhibit such teleological guidance control over some of their own processes when they tend through feedback loops and error correction mechanisms to converge on a goal in the face of perturbations. Such control, as noted, is necessary for any voluntary activity and is the basis for the evolution of freedom of agency.

This kind of evolutionary development, which Dennett himself describes in his important work *Freedom Evolves* (2003), is crucial for understanding free agency and is certainly something "worth wanting." And it can be spelled out in compatibilist terms, as he argues. But there is a still further stage of the evolution of free agency, I argued, that is also worth wanting and cannot be spelled out in compatibilist terms alone, as summarized in the following:

(P234) What I now want to suggest from the point of view of the evolution of *free will* is that a still higher stage of evolution in human beings is possible and arises when their inner rational environments reach a stage of complexity that allows them to have conflicts in their wills about what to do and how to act. This further stage of evolution of their inner rational environments allows human agents to exercise not merely a compatibilist *teleological guidance control* over their own behavior—the ability to exercise control over their pursuits of certain goals or ends. It also allows them to exercise incompatibilist *plural voluntary control* over which goals or ends they choose to pursue when their wills are conflicted about which ends to pursue. This further development of the internal rational environments of human agents amounts to a further evolution from freedom *of action* to freedom *of will*.[13]

This kind of freedom of the will is also "worth wanting," I would argue, and it would ground judgments of responsibility in the basic-desert sense that free will skeptics like Caruso and compatibilists like Dennett are denying. It is desert not just for doing some of the things we do, but also for being the kinds of persons we are and having the wills we have that account for our doing those things. Such a notion of basic desert, I would argue, is not unintelligible and it remains an open question whether or not it is empirically possible.

10.7. Saul Smilansky on Free Will and Illusion

In his book *Free Will and Illusion* (2000) and subsequent writings, Saul Smilansky has introduced a novel and controversial view into current free will debates which he calls "illusionism," the claim that some degree of "illusion on free will is morally necessary." Most philosophers writing on free will, compatibilists and incompatibilists alike, reject Smilansky's illusionist view. But in doing so, they often overlook the importance of the subtle arguments that he marshals getting to this view—in particular, his rejection of what he calls the *assumption of monism* and his defense of what he calls a *fundamental dualism* on the compatibility question. These arguments, as it happens, throw important further light on debates between free will skeptics like Caruso and compatibilists like Dennett.

In a more recent article, "Free Will, Fundamental Dualism and the Centrality of Illusion" (2011), Smilansky provides an overview of his arguments. First, like free will skeptics and most compatibilists, he rejects the possibility of libertarian free will.

> I believe that robust libertarian free will is impossible. The case against such libertarian free will has already been well stated, and I have nothing substantially original to say about it. . . .[14] The libertarian project was a

worthwhile attempt: It was supposed to allow a deep moral connection between a given act and the person, yet not fall into being merely an unfolding of the arbitrarily given, whether determined or random. But it is not possible to find any way in which this can be done. (pp. 426–27)

(P377) Smilansky then argues that, once libertarian free will is rejected, "a harmful *Assumption of Monism* has seriously impaired the debate about free will" (2011, pp. 426–27). This assumption of monism is that, if libertarian free will is not possible, one must affirm either compatibilism, on the one hand, or a hard incompatibilist or free will skeptical position, on the other. It's not difficult to see that *this assumption of monism is at work in the Dennett/Caruso debate*, with Dennett affirming compatibilism and Caruso free will skepticism, the only options they believe to be plausible, since both have rejected libertarian free will as unintelligible and impossible earlier in their debate.

(P378) Smilansky argues to the contrary that rejecting this assumption of monism "allows us to stay close to the deepest intuitions of the free will issue" (2011, pp. 426–27). One need not assume, therefore, that, if libertarianism about free will is untenable, one must affirm either compatibilism or free will skepticism. He argues instead for what he calls a *fundamental dualism* which presupposes "the partial validity of both compatibilism" and free will skepticism "or, in what amounts to the same thing, from the partial inadequacy of both" (p. 431). He says: "There is a basis for working with compatibilist notions of fault and moral responsibility, based on local compatibilist-level control, even though we lack the sort of deep grounding in the 'ultimately guilty self' that libertarian free will was thought to provide. Moreover, we are morally required to work in this way. But doing so has often a 'hard determinist' moral price in terms of unfairness and injustice. We must recognize the frequent need to be compatibilists and the need to confront that price" (p. 431).

That price, as free will skeptics would emphasize, Smilansky adds, is that no persons are ultimately responsible for being the kinds of persons they are and for the actions that result from their being the kinds of persons they are. If there is no libertarian free will, then "being the sort of person one is" and having the character and motivations one has are "ultimately . . . one's luck. And one's life and everything one does, is an unfolding of this" (2011, p. 428).

Smilansky then offers an interesting response to an issue raised by Dennett in his debate with Caruso and in other works. Smilansky says

> Compatibilists may argue at this point that if libertarian free will is incoherent, then it is not "worth wanting" in the first place and we need not make such a fuss about the absence of the impossible (e.g., Dennett, 1984; S. Wolf, 1987, pp. 59–60; Frankfurt 1988, pp. 22–3). This however is a red herring. The various things that [a libertarian] free will could make possible, if it could exist, such as deep senses of desert, worth and justification, *are* worth wanting. They remain worth wanting (and regretting) even if something that would be necessary to have them cannot be coherently conceived. (2011, p. 440)

But at the same time, Smilansky insists, we cannot go all the way with free will skeptics either. "For if people are to be respected their nature as purposive beings capable and desirous of choice needs to be catered to. We have to be able to live as responsible beings in a Community of Responsibility, ... to note and give persons credit for their good actions and to take account of situations in which they lacked the abilities and opportunities to choose freely and are therefore not responsible in a compatibilist sense" (2011, pp. 430–31).

What, then, is the solution? How can we accept a measure of truth in both compatibilism and free will skepticism without fully accepting one or the other?

(P379) Smilansky's controversial answer is to appeal to illusion. Illusion, he says, is the "vital but neglected *key* to the free will problem." But he immediately adds, "I am not saying that we need to induce illusory beliefs concerning free will or live with beliefs that we fully realize are illusory. Both these positions would be highly implausible. Rather I believe that illusory beliefs are in place, and that the role they play is largely positive" (2011, p. 433). How so? People, he adds, usually are not, and "ought not to be, fully aware of the ultimate inevitability of what they have done, for this would affect the way in which they hold themselves responsible. ... We often want a person to blame himself, feel guilty, and even see that he deserves to be punished. Such a person is not likely to do all this" if he internalizes a perspective in which his "responsibility" is consistent with the thought that the actual world into which he was born and grew up was such that it was causally impossible for him to have ever done anything "except what he did do" (p. 434).

These thoughts would apply to both free will skeptics and compatibilists. For even compatibilists hold views about responsibility that are consistent with the thought that the actual world in which we were born and lived might have been such that it was causally impossible for us "to have ever done anything except what we actually did." As Smilansky rightly says, people don't usually think in terms of such an ultimate perspective. And if they did, and were to believe this about it, it would have some effect on the ways in which they hold themselves responsible. Either they would likely shake their heads and get it out of their minds as soon as possible. Or worse, like the Vladimir Putin's of the world, they would smile and get on with what they thought of as their destiny.

There is, of course, another way to go here that does not require illusion: one could try to make sense of a libertarian view of free will that is not unintelligible, that does not reduce to mere chance or luck, and is empirically possible—a free will that in Smilansky's words "could make possible, if it could exist . . . deep senses of desert, worth and justification [that] are worth wanting" (2011, p. 440).

(P380) It remains an open scientific question whether any such free will exists. But the idea is to so formulate it that its existence would be a genuine empirical possibility, and without the need for illusion or the need for a fundamental dualism requiring that we choose between compatibilism or free will skepticism. We could take on board the best of compatibilist views of free will, involving reasons responsiveness and other notions. But, while the best of compatibilist accounts would be essential to a full accounting of free and responsible agency, they would not represent all the free will and responsibility worth wanting. There would also be a deeper free will and ultimate responsibility, that free will skeptics and defenders of illusion, like Smilansky, recognize but do not believe is possible.

(P381) Smilansky is well aware of these motivations. He says that "we often want persons to blame themselves, feel guilty and even see that they sometimes deserve to be punished. Persons are not likely to do all this, if they internalize a perspective in which their responsibility is consistent with the thought that the actual world into which they were born and grew up was such that it was causally impossible for them to have ever done anything 'except what they did do'" (2011, pp. 433–44).

As a final point, I would like to suggest that there is another relevant argument against an illusionist resolution of the problems Smilansky describes. An objection of this kind is suggested by Ken Levy (2022), and here I want to take it one step further: Levy says, "While Smilansky's illusionist response to responsibility skepticism has merit, it would not work if a majority of persons were to consent, theoretically and psychologically to the belief that their usual assumptions about the moral responsibility system, in criminal as well as moral matters, were illusory."

I would take this point one step further and say that an illusionist response to responsibility skepticism would run into trouble even if a smaller number of citizens in powerful positions believed the moral responsibility system was illusory, if this minority were to have powerful motives to accept this illusionist belief: for example, would-be dictators and other seekers after power, rich people who don't want to believe the rules apply to them, robber barons, career criminals, financial actors who cheat others, and so on and on. If they are convinced that these beliefs are illusory, why should they live with beliefs that constrain their actions when they exploit others? It seems that selfish people would have every reason to latch on to illusionist beliefs to justify their ways of life. Indeed, the thought that the persons they exploit are living in illusion while they see things as they really are would be a powerful motivator for their exploitative behavior.

11

Ultimate Desert, the Dialectic of Selfhood, Kant's Three Questions, Aspiration, Eastern Views, Theism, and Predestination

11.1. A Personal Story

Why do I believe in a free will that is incompatible with determinism? It's a long story that I've been telling in this book and other writings. But if I had to describe some essentials, the story would go like this:

(P382) There are consequences of the belief that all human actions are determined that I cannot accept without further evidence of their truth. If all human actions were determined, it would always have been causally impossible for me and all other persons to have done anything differently in the course of our lives to have made ourselves any different than we in fact are, though we may have believed otherwise when we acted. I find this an unpalatable conclusion, not only with regard to my own life, but for all other humans—the good ones, who may inspire admiration and love, and the bad ones, who may have acted cruelly or harmfully to others, including at worse, evil dictators and exploiters of other persons and groups. If determinism were true, it would never have been causally possible for any of them, good or bad, to have done anything differently in the course of their lives to have made themselves any different than they are.

(P383) This would *not* mean these and other agents would have no control over their own actions. To the contrary, they might have considerable teleological guidance control over many of their actions—the powers to do what they willed to do and to guide their behavior in directions they willed to guide it. But if determinism was true, it would have been causally impossible for them to have exercised these powers in any other ways than the ways they actually exercised them. They might have considerable teleological guidance control. But they would lack plural voluntary control, the powers to will and to act in different ways at certain times, without being determined either way they will or act, to make themselves and their wills different than they actually are.

(P384) There may have been other hypothetical or possible worlds in which humans willed and acted in ways different than they do in the actual world. But they don't live in these other hypothetical worlds. They live in the actual world. And if this actual world is deterministic, it would always have been causally impossible in this actual world for them to have exercised these powers in any other ways than the ways they actually exercised them. To say that it would have been causally possible for them to do this in some other merely hypothetical worlds that did not actually exist, would be to present us with what Kant rightly called a "wretched subterfuge" and William James a "quagmire of evasion."

Because I find these consequences of the belief that all human actions are determined unpalatable in these ways, I want to believe in a free will that is incompatible with determinism, if such a free will is possible and can be made intelligible. But this desire brings us back to the deep questions that have been addressed throughout this book. Can we have such a free will? If it requires that some of our choices or actions be *un*determined, would that not reduce free will to chance or luck or mystery? Can such a free will be reconciled with modern views of humans in the natural and human sciences? Is it an intelligible ideal at all or, as Nietzsche said, the best self-contradiction conceived so far by the human mind? One may argue, as many have in the past, that such a free will would seem to underwrite deeper meanings of what many humans desire, such things as creativity and novelty; autonomy and self-creation; desert for one's achievements; moral responsibility; reactive attitudes, such as resentment and indignation; individuality and uniqueness; dignity and respect; life hopes, an open future, and others.

But compatibilists have been quick to argue that you can get most of these things in familiar forms in ordinary life and language without denying determinism and supposing anything so weird and esoteric as an undetermined free will. In ordinary affairs, we hold persons morally responsible and accountable for their actions unless some excusing or mitigating conditions are present. Were they coerced or acting under threats? Were they capable of knowing the differences between right and wrong? Were their actions intentional or inadvertent? Were they subject to hallucinations or delusions? Were they manipulated in ways they could not have reasonably resisted?

If moral responsibility can be understood in such ordinary terms without assuming the falsity of determinism, compatibilists argue, so can the other notions that libertarians claim to value, such as desert, dignity, reactive attitudes, and autonomy. Autonomy, for example, requires capacities to reflect upon and critically evaluate one's reasons or motives for action, to revise one's reasons or motives in the light of these reflections, to identify with some of them as reflective of one's "real" self, and to act upon reasons one chooses to identify with in a manner that is not coerced, compulsive, or manipulated. And none of these capacities, they claim, require the falsity of determinism. To such claims, my response is this:

> (P385) True enough. But if determinism was true, it would never have been causally possible for anyone to exercise these capacities in the course of their lives in ways that were any different from how they actually exercise them. As a consequence, it would never have been causally possible for them to have made themselves and their wills any different than they in fact are. Yet this is what I believe freedom *of will* would require over and above freedom of action. So I have set out to show here and in other writings that such a free will requiring indeterminism at certain points in our lives us coherent and intelligible by answering the many objections against it and showing that that it is both conceptually and empirically possible. This would not demonstrate that such a free will exists, but it would allow one to rationally believe in such a free will until such time as it was definitively shown to be conceptually or empirically impossible.

11.2. Kant's Three Questions and Aspiration

Beginning in several writings in 1993,[1] and later in *The Significance of Free Will* (1996), I linked these thoughts about rational belief in such philosophical matters to two further themes that comprise the title of this section, Kant's three questions and aspiration:

(P386) Near the end of his *Critique of Pure Reason*, Kant says there are three great philosophical questions humans can ask:[2]
What can I know?
How should I act or live?
What should I aspire to?
(I depart from Kant in the translation of the second two of these questions in ways, and for reasons, to be shortly explained.)

(P387) The second of these questions—"How should I act or live?"—is the ethical question. Through the centuries, philosophers have tried to answer it in terms of answers to the first question—how we should act or live in terms of what we can know. Find the facts about human nature and the cosmos, it was believed, and we will have definitive answers to ethical questions about how to live. Beginning with the above-cited works of 1993 ("The Ends of Metaphysics"), 1994 (*Through the Moral Maze*), and 1996 (*The Significance of Free Will*), I have argued that answers to the second ethical question must depend *to some degree* on answers to the first question, "What can we know?" We must learn about human nature to understand what human happiness or fulfillment requires. But that is not sufficient to fully answer the second of Kant's questions, the ethical question. To do this, we must bring in the third question as well: "What should we aspire to?"

(P388) "Aspiration" is viewed in these earlier writings of mine as a special term having to do with the search for the true and the good. Kant himself in his third question uses the term "hope" rather than "aspiration" ("What can I hope for?" *Was kann Ich hoffen?*). The two terms "hope" and "aspiration" are related, to be sure. But hope is an attitude one can have while sitting in an armchair doing nothing to obtain what is hoped for, whereas aspiration, as viewed in these works, is a form of life involving a patient spiritual or intellectual search or *quest* for the "true" and the "good" (which are the subject matters of Kant's first two questions). It is with this meaning in mind that I have altered the formulation of Kant's third question from "hope" to "aspiration." Likewise, Kant's second question is "What should I do?" (*Was soll Ich tun?*), which I have altered to "How should I act or live?"

to emphasize a connection with the broader ancient philosophical quest for a "life worth living."

(P389) By phrasing these questions in this way in earlier writings, I meant to emphasize that the move beyond the first two Kantian questions to the third question about aspiration is not a move away from rational inquiry toward "irrational" hope. To the contrary, aspiration as understood in this context does not preclude rational inquiry but requires it. What aspiration adds to rational inquiry is a recognition of the radical contingency of such inquiry, without precluding the possibility of success. The searches of scientists for the ultimate truths about the natural world or the fundamental laws of nature have the characteristics of searches in the realm of aspiration in this sense—owing to the fact that the scientists cannot know with certainty that they have attained the final truths or fundamental laws of nature *even if they have in fact attained them*. Any explanatory scheme they have may be incomplete or falsified by future discoveries or experiments.

Scientists who have such lofty goals aspire to something of great importance (the ultimate truths about nature), which for all they know is attainable, but whose attainment is difficult and not assured. There are actions they can perform (consider all available evidence, do experiments, criticize existing theories, look for more precise and comprehensive explanations) they believe will lead to the goal, not guaranteeing its attainment, but such that failing to undertake these actions would mean abandoning aspirations to attain the goal.

(P390) This illustrates how aspiration as here conceived is more than hope, though it involves hope. The point of quests in the realm of aspiration, as I argued in these earlier writings, is to highlight the difficulty, skill, character, discipline, and effort required to persist in the search for cherished goals and high ideals. "Aspiration" is an apt word for this radically contingent seeking. It signifies "an outflowing or going outward of the spirit," from the Latin *aspirare* which means "to breathe forth" (*spirare*) but also to have a fixed desire for something and seek to attain it.[3]

(P391) Questions about free will seem to be about Kant's first great question: What can we know? Indeed, questions about free will *are* about this first question. But that is not all they are about. They are also about his second question, the ethical one: How should we act and live? In short, they are about both the "true" and the "good," the two "ends" of metaphysics in Aristotle's account in his book that was placed after (*meta*) his book on physics.

(P392) The connection of free will issues to the good as well as the true comes from the connection of free will, in the sense in which it has usually been historically debated, to *moral responsibility*. Determinism poses particular problems for moral responsibility if what we are concerned with is responsibility for being the kinds of persons we are with the ill will or goodwill we may have to do the things we do. Moral responsibility of this kind seems to suggest a kind of self-formation which is not only incompatible with determinism, but (as many others believe) incompatible with indeterminism as well.

11.3. Free Will and Ultimate Moral Responsibility

(P393) It is this notion of free will, one that would support such ultimate moral responsibility, that has motivated me and I think motivates many others who believe in an incompatibilist free will. Those who may believe in such a free will, I would argue, should not claim to know with certainty that such a free will exists. They should not yet regard it as an adequate answer to Kant's first question: What can I know? There are many questions that need to be addressed concerning the existence of such a free will—to its existence and indeed to its very intelligibility and conceptual and empirical possibility.

Many of these questions have been discussed in this book, but there are undoubtedly more that need to be addressed. As we have seen in these chapters, objections to such a free will have not been made only by *compatibilists* about free will. They have also been made by *free will skeptics* who believe we must abandon notions of ultimate responsibility and ultimate desert that such a free will would support; also by *revisionists* who believe we should revise our understanding of free will and responsibility in a compatibilist direction so that these notions requiring ultimacy are abandoned; and by *illusionists* who believe we should allow as many people as possible who believe in such ultimate responsibility and desert to continue to do so since it would lead to serious disruptions of our ordinary ethical and social lives if many persons no longer believed we are ultimately responsible for being the way we are or acting as we do.

> (P394) Just as those who believe in an incompatibilist free will that would support such notions of ultimate responsibility should not claim to know with certainty that such a free will exists, they also cannot claim to know with certainly that the ultimate responsibility such a free will would support exists. In addressing these issues, I argue, they must move beyond Kant's first two metaphysical questions, about the true and the good, to his third question, about aspiration.

But they should also keep in mind what is said about aspiration in P387–P392. Aspiration in this context is not a move away from rational inquiry toward "irrational" hope. It does not preclude rational inquiry, but requires it. What aspiration adds to rational inquiry is a recognition of the radical contingency of such inquiry, without precluding the possibility of success. The searches of scientists for the ultimate truths about the natural world are exemplars of searches in the realm of aspiration in this sense. But aspiration can function in other areas of human life and inquiry far less rigorous and exacting than the empirical sciences. Yet, wherever it functions, the point of speaking of aspiration rather than mere hope is to highlight the difficulty and effort required to persist in the search for cherished goals and high ideals. "Aspiration," as I said, is an apt word for this radically contingent seeking.

> (P395) In the case of the kind of incompatibilist free will that I believe is required for ultimate responsibility, we cannot show with certainly that such a free will exists. But what we can do, *if we aspire to rationally believe in it*, is do our best to show what such a free will would have to look like if it did exist, to show how it would be related to many other important notions such as agency, choice, action, selfhood, will, control, responsibility, power, and others; and to show that it is an intelligible and possible ideal, by arguing that the most common objections that have been raised to its possibility fail to show that is an unintelligible or impossible, and by showing how it might be possible (though certainly not proven) given what is known in contemporary physics and other sciences, including the neurosciences. These are the tasks I have undertaken in this book.

11.4. Ultimate Responsibility and Ultimate Desert

(P396) Corresponding to the notion of ultimate responsibility that is related to the view of free will developed in this book is a notion of ultimate desert. It is deservingness, *not only for what you may do*, but also deservingness *for being the kind of person you are, with the will you have to do what you do*. Such considerations would make you *ultimately* deserving of praise or blame for what you do.

(P397) Such ultimate desert is closely related to, though it also adds something to, what Pereboom and other free will skeptics mean by "basic desert" when they speak of "basic desert responsibility." Pereboom says that such basic desert responsibility "is basic in the sense that the agent, to be morally responsible, would deserve blame or credit just because [the agent] performed the action, given sensitivity to its moral status, and not merely by virtue of consequentialist or contractualist considerations" (2001). The free will that is necessary for such basic desert moral responsibility, according to free will skeptics like Pereboom, is incompatible with determinism, so that compatibilist views fail to capture it.

(P398) These things can also be said of what I am here calling ultimate desert. But the way ultimate desert goes beyond consequentialist and contractualist considerations is made more explicit by its relation to ultimate responsibility. Ultimate desert, like ultimate responsibility, goes beyond consequentialist considerations because it is *backward-looking* in a deep sense: *it looks back, not only to the self and will from which a choice or action may have emerged, but also further back to the* formation *of that self and will from which the choice or action may have emerged*.

(P399) Ultimate desert is also not merely a matter of contractualist considerations. It is not *merely* the result of a tacit agreement between persons and the moral communities of which they are a part to take responsibility for their choices and actions. In the case of ultimate desert, such contractualist considerations must themselves be rooted in backward-looking considerations about the formation of the selves who are part of that moral community and take responsibility for their choices and actions with respect to it. To have ultimate desert, such persons must also be ultimately responsible to some degree for being the *kinds of selves they are with the wills they have, who take responsibility for their choices and actions with respect to the moral communities* of which they are a part.

Several other features of ultimate desert so understood are worth considering. First:

(P400) Like the ultimate responsibility to which it is related, ultimate desert is also a matter of degree. This was evident in earlier discussions of ultimate responsibility, such as the case of the young man at trial for raping a young woman in Chapter 3. Recall that the initial reactions of many of us attending the trial of this young man were filled with anger and resentment toward him, since we knew the family of the teenage girl who was his victim and who lived in our neighborhood. *He had clearly violated the norms of our moral community.* But that was not the whole story. As we listened daily to the testimony of how the young man came to have the mean character and perverse motives he did have—a sordid story of parental rejection, sexual abuse, bad role models, and other factors—some of our resentment toward the young man decreased and was directed toward other persons who abused and influenced him.

(P401) But—and here was a key point—we weren't yet ready to shift all the deservingness for blame away from the young man himself. We resisted this "transference of responsibility" and "blame" entirely to other persons and wondered whether some residual responsibility might not belong to the young man himself. Our question changed: Was his behavior *all* a matter of bad parenting, neglect and abuse, social conditioning, and like factors, or did he have any crucial role to play, despite these influences, in making himself the kind of person who could will to do such things?

Such questions bear on the young man's ultimate desert for his blameworthy behavior. Their import was spelled out further in the following piece from Chapter 3:

(P58) We know that parenting and society, genetic makeup, and upbringing have a profound influence on what we become and what we are. But were these influences entirely *determining*, or did they "leave anything over" for the young man to be ultimately responsible for? Note that the question of whether he was merely a victim of bad circumstances or had some residual responsibility for being the way he is—the question, that is, of whether he became the person he is to any degree *of his own free will*—seems to depend on whether these other factors were or were not entirely determining. It seems to depend, in other words, on whether or not it was *ever causally possible for the young man to have resisted the influences of his background and upbringing* and to have acted differently at some points in his life to make himself different than he now is. And if determinism was true, acting differently than he actually did at *any* time in his lifetime would have been causally impossible.

To the degree that it was ever causally possible for the young man to have resisted the influences of his background and upbringing and to have acted differently at some points in his life to make himself different than he now is, the young man would have some degree of ultimate desert for his blameworthy behavior; and all the ultimate desert would not "transfer" to others, such as the parents who rejected him and others who sexually abused him.

11.5. Ultimate Desert, Ultimate Responsibility, and Free Will

In *The Significance of Free Will*, I spelled out further what these features of ultimate responsibility, and, by implication, ultimate desert, have for libertarian views of free will requiring indeterminism. These features, which are worth summarizing here, continue to hold in the revised view of this book:

(P402) "A disservice is done when libertarians about free will continue to appeal to mysterious forms of agency to account for free will. Such views may leave the impression that exercises of free will are entirely above and beyond the influence of natural causes and conditioning. This can easily lead one to think that the abused child or ghetto dweller has as much free will and ultimate responsibility . . . as one who lives in more advantaged circumstances. . . . The theory of this book implies no such consequence. Precisely because this theory recognizes the *embeddedness of free will in the natural order*, it recognizes that free will and ultimate responsibility are matters of degree, and our possession of them can be very much influenced by circumstances" (1996, p. 213).

But I also cautioned in *Significance* that it is a mistake to take this embeddedness too far and reject the possibility of ultimate responsibility, and the ultimate desert related to it, altogether:

(P403) "What is needed for a mature libertarianism about free will in the modern age is a recognition of the many ways in which circumstances and upbringing can limit free will and responsibility (for this is one of the prevailing themes of modernity), without yielding to the temptation to think that we are all helpless victims of circumstances. Such recognition would provide a middle way between political extremes as well. It would mean resisting the debilitating assumption that we are all helpless victims and never have ultimate responsibility for what we do or are. But it would also mean rejecting the harsh political judgment that the disadvantaged of society are wholly responsible for their disadvantaged condition because they retain their free will undiminished and are therefore undeserving of government or societal support or assistance" (1996, p. 214).

(P404) "While a political order hospitable to libertarian free will would be a free society of the Millian sort, it would not necessarily be unrestrictedly 'libertarian' in the political sense of that term if this meant abdicating all or most government efforts of social assistance. Yet government assistance in a political order hospitable to free will would also be judged by a particular standard—namely, the extent to which it empowered recipients to be self-determining and ultimately responsible citizens rather than merely reducing them to dependence. If such self-determination and the dignity associated with it are generally what the disadvantaged want anyway, that is only further evidence of the significance of free will. Humans do not live by bread alone" (1996, p. 214).

11.6. The Dialectic of Selfhood

Why might ultimate responsibility and ultimate desert confer greater value on the other goods mentioned in relation to libertarian free will, such as creativity, autonomy, self-creation, desert, responsibility, dignity, respect, and others?

(P405) As I mentioned earlier and have argued in earlier works, such questions are baffling because we underestimate how "metaphysical" one has to become to address them. Aristotle held that metaphysics—*sophia* or "wisdom" or "first philosophy" as he called it (in his book which ancient scholars placed after his book on physics)—was the study of the ultimate sources or explanations (*archai kai aitiai*) of all things. As I argued earlier, the free will issue is metaphysical in just this sense. It is about the ultimate sources and explanations (*archai kai aitiai*) of some special things in the universe, namely, *ultimately responsible human choices and actions*. We should therefore expect debates about the significance of free will to delve deeply into the metaphysical depths—and that is what they must do.

When we take seriously the metaphysical depths of the free will issue, I have argued, we are led to what I have called the dialectic of selfhood. This dialectic of selfhood, introduced in *The Significance of Free Will* (1996, pp. 91–98), was discussed in greater detail in a later unpublished paper of mine delivered at the Metanexus Institute Conference on Science, Philosophy and Religion in Madrid Spain (July 12–17, 2008) and in a paper published in *Ideas y valores*, a Columbian journal of philosophy in a special issue entitled "Libertad, determinismo y responsabilidad moral" (December 2009). I offer an updated version of this dialectic here with reference to the further developments of the views of this book.

(P406) Stage 1: imagine a baby lying in a crib or infant seat. The baby's arms and legs shake with uncontrolled and undirected energy as she looks about the room. This shaking comes from her nervous system, and ultimately from the brain which soaks up a high percentage of the energy-producing glucose of the body. (We call children "bundles of energy" for a reason.) She doesn't know what to do with all that energy yet; her task is to gradually get more control over it.

(P407) An early stage of this process of gaining control is one many parents have observed. Objects pass in front of the infant, and she follows them with her eyes. She has no control over most of the objects and simply observes them pass by. But one passing object has a special fascination—her own hand. It is different, for it seems she can control it. One day she actually learns to hold the hand still in her visual field, make fist with it, and then open the fist again. This turns out to be fascinating. When first discovered, the act is repeated over and over, and she smiles with delight at her success. She has discovered that this passing object is something special. It is part of her; and she can control it by an act of will.

She has discovered the phenomenon of *action* and *will* simultaneously by recognizing that she can control and direct things out there in the world by attending to them and willing them to happen in her mind. No wonder she is fascinated.

(P408) Not surprisingly, this discovery is connected to the distinction the infant is learning to make between herself and world. Our full sense of *being a distinct self* is tied up with our experience of *being a distinct source of motion or activity in the world*, such that what goes on behind the screen of our mind (our will) can have effects out there in the world.

(P409) Stage 2: but doubts arise about this simple picture in a second stage of this dialectic of selfhood. For, as we develop, we find we are not separate from the world, but in it and influenced by it in many hidden ways. Behind the window to the world—where *we* are supposed to be—is the brain, which is a physical object, like the body itself, part of world and influenced by it. Perhaps we only *seem* to "move ourselves" in some ultimate way, when we are in fact moved by causes coming from the world of which we are unaware operating through our brains and bodies. Such thoughts may provoke a spiritual crisis.

(P410) One crude reaction to these thoughts is to insist that *we* are not in the natural world at all—that the self behind the window is outside the natural world altogether yet is able to influence what goes on in that world in some magical way. A more subtle reaction is to argue that, while the world influences us, we can determine just *how* the world influences us through our senses and through our processing of information. We can determine what gets in and what is screened out, what influences our thought and action, and how it influences our thought and action, and what does not.

(P411) Stage 3: alas, this solution only temporarily quells doubts about the influence of the world upon us. If we have already learned we are influenced by many things of which we are unaware, how can we be sure the very selections we make from within our inner sanctum are not determined by influences from the world in our past and present of which we are unaware and are beyond our control? What if our choices about *how* the world will influence us are *themselves* determined by the world? This thought propels us to a third stage of the dialectic of selfhood, where we encounter full-fledged threats of determinist doctrines in all their historical forms—physical, biological, psychological, social, theological, and so on.

(P412) What I am suggesting is that we view the problem of determinism and free will, not as an isolated problem, but as a stage in the dialectic of selfhood—the process of self-understanding about the relation of our self to the world. At each stage we are trying to preserve a remnant of the idea that we are in some sense ultimate sources to some degree of how the world influences us and how we react to it—against the threat that we are only ultimately products of forces coming wholly from the world.

(P413) As we come to value our selfhood, we take delight in what we are able to produce or accomplish. The baby smiles at her ability to open and close her fists. Later, like all children, she will hunger for appreciation and praise for her accomplishments, whatever they may be, from walking to painting a picture or singing a song. All parents know this inexhaustible craving in children for appreciation and acknowledgment for what they do. According to A. O. Lovejoy (1961), eighteenth-century philosophers referred to this craving as the desire for "approbation" and regarded it as a fundamental human need throughout life. This desire for approbation, I suggest, is part and parcel of a more fundamental need to affirm our selfhood as independent sources of activity in the world. It is an affirmation of selfhood that will later attach to such things as creativity, autonomy, moral responsibility, dignity, respect, and ultimate desert.

Does this mean that all persons must have desires for independent selfhood and ultimate desert or must believe that the objects of these desires are obtainable—on pain of irrationality? No, nor do I think demonstrations are possible on such matters. From my earliest writings on the subject (see, e.g., *Free Will and Values* [1985]), I have noted that

(P414) Disagreements about free will involve not only conceptual and factual disputes, but disagreements about values as well; and although these value disagreements are discussable, they cannot be conclusively settled by conceptual analyses and factual appeals alone. They are objects of aspiration, which implies that we can make sense of how *they can be objects of rational belief* even if *they cannot be known with certainty*.

11.7. The Ethical Question Revisited: Kant, Dignity, Love, Bach Crystals, and *Solaris*

(P415) Viewing free will in the context of this interpretation of Kant's third question also sheds light on his second, "ethical" question. Kant himself expressed this connection in a well-known way when he said in a version of his categorical imperative that rational beings should be treated as "ends in themselves" because they are "the ultimate creators of their own ends" (1959, p. 52). He thereby described the connection between *dignity* ("worthiness for respect from others for one's personhood") and *ultimacy* ("being an ultimate creator of one's own ends"). We are to treat others as ends in themselves and not merely as means to our own ends to the extent that they exercise capacities to be ultimate creators of their own ends.

(P416) Kant learned to appreciate such a notion of dignity from his parents. His father was a humble workingman, a harness-maker. Once in Kant's youth there was a bitter dispute between the harness-makers' guild and the saddle-makers' guild. Even as a young boy, Kant marveled at the honorableness and forbearance of his parents throughout this dispute. Though the dispute became bitter at times, his parents never spoke of, or treated, their opponents as mere adversaries or enemies, but as individuals with a right to a resolution of the conflict *that preserved their dignity as ultimate creators of their own ends*, in this controversy and in life generally. The incident had a profound effect on Kant's thinking about dignity and ethics in later life.

Another example used in my ethical writings to illustrate these points concerns Johann Sebastian Bach, who worked as an organist through much of his life. I dubbed this example the "Bach Crystals."

(P417) Suppose that during Bach's lifetime, the officials and nobles who supported his music discovered a set of amazing crystals made of an unknown substance that spontaneously produced polyphonic music like Bach's. The most knowledgeable musicians and critics could not distinguish the productions of these Bach crystals from Bach's own music. We might further imagine that the officials and aristocrats who supported Bach were a callous lot who then lost all concern for Bach the man. The crystals produced all the beautiful music they could desire, and they did not have to feed and clothe the crystals as they did Bach's large family. For these nobles Bach would have been valuable only for what he produced. If Bach lost his employment because of the miraculous crystals, he might say, "The officials and nobles seemed to care about me, but all they really cared about was what I could do for them." And this is not only how we wish to be conceived by others, as mere instruments of their satisfaction or servants who are expendable if an equivalent could be found.

One other example cited in my ethical writings (*Through the Moral Maze* [1994], *Ethics and the Quest for Wisdom* [2010a]) to illustrate further nuances to these points is from a science-fiction novel, *Solaris* (1971), by the Polish writer Stanislaw Lem. Lem writes about a planet called Solaris that is covered by an ocean with astonishing powers. Readers may be familiar with one or both of two films made from this novel. Both take a few liberties with the plot, and I will do so as well, though in a different direction. But it is Lem's original work, not the films, that inspires these reflections.

The living ocean with astonishing powers that covers the planet Solaris can conjure up what seem to be real people—people from the past of the scientists and other visitors to the planet who are studying the swirling ocean from laboratories on a space station hovering over it. The story involves one of these scientific visitors. The ocean conjures up the figure of his long-dead ex-wife. He believes she is resurrected. They renew their affair, trying to change some of the traits that pushed them apart; they make love, converse, and review the past. But a strange thought begins to dawn on the scientist. The wife-image is not a real person. It is a simulacrum reconstructed by the planet's mysterious ocean out of his unconscious mind and memories. It is a more elaborate phantom than he could conjure because the ocean has greater access to his unconscious memories than he does. But it is a phantom, nonetheless.

What interests us here is the point where this shocking revelation occurs to the scientist. Let us assume he greatly loved his ex-wife, loved her even more than the man in Lem's novel (here I depart a little from Lem for a purpose).

(P418) Let us say that, loving her as he did, the man deeply regretted the events that pushed them apart before his wife died. It is not difficult to imagine how devastating would be this realization that this phantom wife was not the real one, that the real wife had not been resurrected, as he believed, and their affair not renewed. He would grieve for his loss. But—and here is a key point—he would not *only* grieve for his own loss. He would grieve more profoundly because, loving this woman as he did, he wanted it to be the case that she was resurrected *for her sake*, not merely for his. She was an end in herself who was ultimately responsible for this renewed love and the happiness it brought to both of them. If he cared only about his own pleasures, he might find the phantom wife as good a companion as the real wife. But if he viewed his ex-wife as an end in herself, who was ultimately responsible for the love she brought to their relationship, it would be devastating to realize he was now dealing with a mere simulacrum and not the real person (cf. Levy 2023, pp. 461–62).

(P419) There are many kinds of love. But to love persons in this way, as ends in themselves, who have capacities to be ultimate creators of their own ends, *and one of whose chosen ends is to love you in this way as well*, is an especially profound kind of love. And it is particularly related to the capacities of the lovers to be ultimate creators of their own ends, including those ends that led them to enter into such a loving relationship.

For Kant, to deal with his second ethical question in this manner—to say that we should treat persons as ends in themselves since they were capable of being creators of their own ends—he argued that one would have to make sense of free will in a deep sense as a form of self-creation of one's own ends that would be incompatible with a deterministic universe. And this presented special problems for someone like Kant living in the eighteenth century in the midst of the Enlightenment and the development of modern science. For the natural sciences of his day were unforgivingly deterministic about the physical world in which we must exercise our free will.

Kant responded to this challenge in a characteristically imaginative but also controversial way. It was a way that has been thought by a majority of philosophers to the present day dealing with free will to be too outré to be taken seriously. He argued that the empirical sciences of his day gave us a correct picture of the *phenomenal world* of our common experience. But that phenomenal world was to be distinguished from what he called a *noumenal world*—a reality of how things were in themselves and not merely how they appeared to us. Our freedom of will was a manifestation of this noumenal reality which was not subject to the deterministic laws of the phenomenal world described by the empirical sciences.

The major difficulty for Kant, however, was that this noumenal world was quite mysterious as to what it involved and how an undetermined free will could function in it. It was a world beyond our ordinary phenomenal experience which escaped the determinism of that phenomenal world, but we could not say how freedom functioned in it. Kant's view thus became one of the prime examples cited by critics of a nondetermined free will—that accounts of such a free will would have to appeal to mystery.

In the phenomenal world, the subject of the empirical sciences, Kant argued, actions and other events are determined by "series of causal links":

(P420) Freedom of will, in the sense of creation of one's own ends, was impossible in the phenomenal world, he argued, due to determinism being the case there. But reason, he added, "creates the idea of spontaneity, which could start to act from itself without needing to be preceded by any other cause that in turn determines it to action according to the laws of causal connection" ([1781] 1999: A533/B361). Such a freedom Kant called "transcendental freedom" because, while it cannot exist in the phenomenal world of our experience, it can exist in the noumenal world "without its cause being determined by another previous cause" (A446/B474). The problem, however, which Kant conceded, is that "we have no cognitive access to this noumenal world, though we must for practical reasons believe it exists" (A448/B474). So we must believe in a transcendental freedom which is not subject to the deterministic laws of the phenomenal world, though we cannot know how it would function, because such a freedom constitutes the "indispensable condition of that worth which human beings ... can give themselves" (A449/B475).[4]

11.8. Treating as Ends and the Ethical Dimensions of Free Will Debates

Persons like me, who are attracted to libertarian free will, can sympathize with much that Kant says here about the ethical dimensions of free will. But they cannot and need not accept his consignment of such a free will, as he describes it, to a noumenal world which we are powerless to understand. We must first note that we do not, like Kant, live in an eighteenth-century bubble in which we must assume that the empirical sciences are unforgivingly deterministic about the natural world in which we must exercise our freedom.

Many developments in the natural sciences of the twentieth and twenty-first centuries make it possible to believe that there is indeterminism in this natural world (Kant's phenomenal world) in the behavior of elementary particles, which in many cases can percolate upward to more complex chemical and biological systems. And there is much interesting speculation, which I have discussed earlier in this work, about how this micro-indeterminism might play a role in the brains and cognitive lives of humans.

A more promising path therefore than Kant's appeal to a noumenal reality for persons in modern times who want to continue to believe in a free will that is incompatible with determinism is to try to make sense of such a free will in the context of modern natural sciences. This is the path I have pursued in this and other works. It does not require locating free will outside the causal order of nature, but rather as very much embedded in that causal order. But the causation involved in making sense of such a free will need not always be deterministic. In certain contexts of "self-formation" in which the wills of agents are torn between competing goals, the causation involved may be merely probabilistic causation. Yet whichever way it goes, if this causation succeeds in attaining its goal, the result will be a voluntary, intentional, and rational choice or action of the agent for which the agent may be ultimately responsible.

Despite differences from Kant's defense of a free will that is incompatible with determinism, the approach taken to defend such a free will in this work leads to an answer to Kant's ethical question that is also similar to Kant's, though it differs from his ethical view in significant ways. Kant argued for a version of his categorical imperative, his so-called Formula of Humanity, that rational beings should be treated as "ends in themselves" because they are "the ultimate creators of their own ends" (Kant (1785) 1998, p. 74). He thereby described the connection between "worthiness for respect from others for one's personhood" and "being an ultimate creator of one's own ends" as an undetermined free will would require (P415).

> (P421) In my ethical writings, including *Through the Moral Maze* (1994) and *Ethics and Quest for Wisdom* (2010a), I have also argued for a view that persons should be treated as "ends in themselves" and not as mere means to the ends of others. And I link these claims to a view of free will that supports ultimate responsibility and ultimate desert. But just as I depart from Kant's "noumenal" view of such a free will, I also depart in crucial respects from his Formula of Humanity, according to which rational

beings should be treated as "ends in themselves" because they are "the ultimate creators of their own ends." A key point of difference, I argue, is that one cannot ethically treat all persons as ends in themselves, *independently of what kinds of ends they themselves might create and pursue* as rational agents.

Many Kantians in moral theory, Christine Korsgaard (1998) prominently among them, have expressed similar concerns about Kant's view for similar reasons. To tell the truth to a murderer at our door who asks about the presence of his intended victim inside, as Kant suggests we should do out of respect for his rational nature, even though he is using his rational nature to choose an evil end, is grotesque, as Korsgaard rightly says. It is a kind of "idolatry of reason." She argues, as have other Kantians, that Kant's view must be modified by adding special principles for "dealing with evil" (1998, p. 282). And she suggests that, in doing this, we should appeal to a distinction, attributed to John Rawls (1971), between *ideal theory* and *non-ideal theory* in ethics.

(P422) As it happens, these features were part of the view of ethics, developed in my ethical writings (1994, 2010a) just mentioned, that were related to my views of free will. The resulting ethical view used the language of Kant's Formula of Humanity but departed from Kant's formula in important ways related to my views of free will and to these concerns about dealing with evil and it led to a distinction between ideal and non-ideal theory in ethics. This view, developed between 1990 and 2010, I have called a "Moral Sphere Theory."

(P423) According to this Moral Sphere Theory, (1) to *treat persons as ends* is to allow them to pursue their ways of life without interference to the extent that one can do so *while maintaining to the degree possible a moral sphere in which all persons can be so treated by others*, and to do this as a way of allowing persons to show by how they plan to live in relation to others that they are *ultimately deserving* of being treated as ends in this way by all others, including oneself. By contrast, (2) to *treat persons as mere means* to one's own ends is to impose one's will on them, to make them do or undergo what one wants, whatever their desires, interests, concerns, or purposes might be, in situations where one is *not* doing what one can to maintain a moral sphere to the degree possible in which all persons can be allowed to pursue their ways of life without interference (e.g., Kane 2010a, p. 48).

(P424) When "treating as ends" and "treating as mere means" are so defined, this Moral Sphere Theory allows one to make a distinction between *ideal theory* and *non-ideal theory* in ethics of a Rawlsian kind that Korsgaard and other thinkers suggest is necessary to amend Kant's Formula of Humanity. (1) *Ideal theory* would apply when the moral sphere obtains ("inside" the moral sphere, as I put it) and would require that persons allow others to pursue their ways of life without interference and hence not "break the moral sphere" which does obtain by "engaging in" what I call "moral sphere-breaking plans of action." (2) *Non-ideal theory* would apply *when the moral sphere is broken down* and would require that persons do what they can to restore the sphere when it has broken down and to depart as little as possible from the ideal of treating all persons as ends when they must depart from that ideal to some degree no matter what they do. Thus conceived, principles of ideal and non-ideal theory would follow from the general requirement to "treat all persons as ends and no one as mere means to one's own ends" *to the degree possible* in every situation (Kane 2010a, p. 49).

I discuss the application of these principles to a wide variety of ethical contexts and examples in these works on ethics that I cannot discuss here. The main takeaway for present purposes has been to show how these ethical principles are related to an account of free will according to which persons are to be treated as ends in themselves because they are creators of their own ends. This is a Kantian insight that I agree with, which he believes is linked to a notion of free will that is not compatible with determinism. But such a free will need not exist only in a noumenal world beyond our understanding, as Kant believed. I believe it is something we can make sense of that humans may have in the real world of their experience.

11.9. East and West: Hindu Vedanta and Buddhism's Eightfold Way, Karma, and Rebirth

Is a notion of free will that implies ultimate responsibility and ultimate desert merely an ideal (albeit a controversial ideal) among Western thinkers that has no place in non-Western traditions? Two of the major Eastern traditions, Hinduism and Buddhism, share doctrines of karma and reincarnation in multiple lives and they argue that to escape this endless cycle of rebirths and the suffering involved one must give up attachments to individual selfhood altogether. Because of these doctrines and others, both Hinduism and Buddhism have rich philosophical traditions that consider in depth issues of free will and moral responsibility, but often in ways quite different from how they are dealt with in Western philosophy.

Riccardo Repetti, an astute chronicler of the history of Buddhist thought on these topics of free will and moral responsibility, has said that "on free will, the history of Buddhist thought is as complex as the history of Western thought" (Repetti 2019, p. 8). This is true. But the way these topics are dealt with is often quite different in Buddhism than in the West, and the same is true of Hindu Vedanta. Nonetheless, despite the vast differences in their seminal doctrines, I believe that we can learn a great deal by considering both Hindu and Buddhist views about free will and moral responsibility and comparing them to those of this book. I begin with Hindu traditions.[5]

(P425) Hindu scriptures (shastras), including such works as the Bhagavad-Gita, Mahabharata, and others, argue that "Humans are conditioned not just by their own natures, but also by *destiny* (*prarabdha*) and *self-effort* (*purosartha*)." By "destiny," *prarabdha*, is meant the cumulative results of the actions of one's past lives manifesting themselves in one's present life. By "self-effort," *purosartha*, is meant the actions of our present lives by which we seek to overcome the harmful effects of destiny. Both thus involve self-effort in different forms, in past lives and in present lives respectively. Swami Chinmayanda says that "what one meets in life is destiny (*prarabdha*); how well one meets it is self-effort (*purosartha*)" (Swami Advayananda 2018, p. 32).

(P426) It is not possible, according to Hindu scriptures, for ordinary humans to know what destiny has in store for us because we do not remember the actions in our past embodiments. Yet such lack of memory is not a curse, they inform us, but a blessing in disguise. Instead of despairing over the past hindering our present self-effort and making us despair, we are in this present life free spirits, able to exercise our will with all confidence to overcome our destiny (*Yogavasistha* 2.6.2). Sage Varistha advises Sri Rama in *Yogavasistha* (2.5.11), "Until the evils arising from one's past self-efforts are conquered, so long one must diligently endeavor by means of self-effort." And the Mahabharata (12.155.5) adds that "just because an adequate result does not accrue to the effort put forth, one cannot conclude that all efforts are futile." The Bhagavad-Gita (16:23–24) adds, "He who, casting aside the injunctions of scripture, acts under the impulse of desire attains neither perfection nor happiness, nor the supreme goal."

A key point to note here:

(P427) None of this would make complete sense if the events of past lives *determined* everything that occurred in the present and future, including present and future self-efforts, choices, and actions. But notice also that none of it would make sense if humans were not also immersed in chains of causal conditions linking the past to the present and the present to the future. Both these features hold of my view of free will. Free will is embedded in the causal order of the universe but is not determined by that causal order. A mistake, which these Hindu scriptural views do *not* make, is *assuming that to be thoroughly immersed in the causal order of the universe means that you are determined by that causal order to do whatever you do*. If that were the case, it would be causally impossible to do what the Hindu scriptures insist we can and should do: that is, by exercising self-effort *in our present lives* to "overcome our destiny"—the cumulative causal influences of our past lives. If we were always determined by the cumulative causal influences of our past lives, we could not do this.

(P428) Of course, the ultimate goal of these Hindu views is to escape the circle of rebirth and cease to be a distinct self. This is a central conclusion of these Eastern views that follows from presupposing many births that most Westerners do not accept. But it is a mistake to assume that, in the attempt to realize this goal, persons do not have to exercise *free will of a kind that is not determined by their pasts*. They must be able to do this in order to escape the otherwise endless cycle of rebirth.

Buddhism presents somewhat different problems when compared to Western views. But in the end, similar and important lessons can be drawn from it as well about free will. The Buddha's views, as is well known, were summed up in his "Four Noble Truths." The first was (1) the truth or fact of *suffering* (*duhkha*), a pervasive feature of sentient life. The second noble truth identifies (2) two main causes of this suffering, *craving* (*trsna*) for pleasure and for continued existence, and *ignorance* (*avidya*), that is, failure to recognize that all things depend on causes and conditions with no constant underlying substances to unify them. The third noble truth is that (3) we can change from pervasive suffering to happiness or overall well-being (*nirvana*). And the fourth outlines (4) how we can make this change by following an *eightfold way*, which includes attaining *wisdom* (i) right views and (ii) right intentions; *ethical conduct* (iii) right action, (iv) right speech, and (v) right livelihood; and *meditation:* (vi) right effort, (vii) right mindfulness, and (viii) right concentration.

(P429) A constant concern that has troubled critics of Buddhist views as well as their defenders through the centuries to the present day is the following: How can one reconcile the human agency, freedom, and responsibility that seems to be required by the third and fourth noble truths—which require a change from pervasive suffering to overall well-being by following the requirements of the eightfold way—given the recognition of the second noble truth, that all things depend on causes and conditions with no underlying substances to unify them?

Related to this concern, is a constant theme in Buddhist writings, namely, the Buddha's emphasis on the importance of self-agency (*atta-kara*) and individual responsibility in his discussions of how we can overcome pervasive suffering and attain overall well-being through his eightfold way. When someone said to the Buddha that there was no such thing as self-agency (*atta-kara*), given his view, he replied by emphasizing that there is "an element of initiating (*arabha-dhatu*) in people—that is, some kind of ability to choose—which allows them to initiate and direct actions" (Swami Advayananda 2018, p. 37). Those sympathetic to Buddhism argue that this shows the Buddha put the causal locus of action origination in the individual's non-inevitable choice. But others have worried that this very notion of self-agency seems to go against the Buddhist doctrine of the insubstantiality of the self.[6]

(P430) After a thorough and careful excavation and exegesis of Buddhist texts on these matters, Asaf Federman (2010), a sympathetic supporter of Buddhist views of free will, arrived at four premises which he believes the Buddha supported: (1) The Buddha rejected the idea that we exist outside the causal nexus of events. (2) But the Buddha also rejected the idea that the will is impotent. (3) The Buddha advocated that by making the right choices, we can progress toward enlightenment. (4) But he also asserted that everything is dependently originated: that is, the choices we do make are not beyond the influences of finite causes. They do not arise uncaused or outside the causal order, for example, as some Western accounts of free will claim. All this, Federman concludes, suggests that (5) the Buddha accepted a kind of free will. But it was a *compatibilist* free will.

(P431) Riccardo Repetti (2014), who has carefully chronicled the history of Buddhist views on free will from their earliest stages after the Buddha to this century, responds to Federman's view by claiming that it is among the most plausible accounts of the Buddha's views of free will he has seen. Nonetheless, Repetti argues that while Federman's claims (1) to (4) seem to be a correct summary of the Buddha's views, claim (5)—that the Buddha accepted a compatibilist view of free will—does not necessarily follow from (1) to (4). Repetti adds, however, that if Federman's had said more cautiously that what the Buddha taught was *consistent* with a compatibilist view of free will, his case would have been much stronger.

I agree with Repetti here that, while Federman's claims (1) to (4) may correctly describe the Buddha's view, they do not imply Federman's claim (5), which is that the Buddha must therefore hold a compatibilist view of free will. But I would go even further and also question Repetti's more cautious suggestion that Federman's claims (1) to (4) might be *consistent* with a compatibilist view of free will. Let me try to explain why.

(P432) The key claim about the Buddha's view that merits more attention in this regard is Federman's claim (4)—that everything is *dependently originated*. The Buddha and his followers do indeed affirm this notion of dependent origination: no events in the created universe, including no human choices and actions, are beyond the influences of finite causes. No human choices or actions (as well as other events) arise uncaused or outside the causal order, as some Western accounts of free will have claimed. This seems to suggest the following: the Buddha's rejection of the idea that the will is impotent, and his many assertions that by making the right choices and not the wrong ones we can progress toward enlightenment, suggest he is affirming a kind of free will. But exercises of such a free will must be wholly dependent on, and immersed in, the order of causes and effects of the universe and cannot transcend that order, as many traditional

Western views of libertarian free will would claim. So the conclusion is drawn that the free will the Buddha is claiming must be a compatibilist free will, fully immersed in the causal order.

There is a certain plausibility to such a claim. But the reasoning leading to it involves the same mistake that was identified when discussing Hindu scriptural views.

(P433) It involves assuming that to be thoroughly immersed in the causal order of the universe means that we must be *determined* by that causal order to do whatever we do. This would imply, among other things, that all persons are determined by their actions in past lives to do whatever they do in this present life. And this conclusion would go against the Buddha's repeated insistence that in our present lives we can change from pervasive suffering to happiness or overall well-being by following the eightfold way, including right action, right speech, right livelihood, right effort, right mindfulness, and right concentration. We are not determined to succeed in attaining enlightenment by doing these things, but *neither are we determined to fail*. The Buddha is thus suggesting an exercise of free will that is thoroughly immersed in the causal order of the universe but is not determined by that causal order. And such a view of free will is an incompatibilist kind of free will, not a compatibilist one. Nor is it even consistent with a compatibilist free will. The causal influences on us do not determine whether we shall succeed or fail to attain the goal of enlightenment by pursuing the eightfold way in this life or any other life. It is "up to us" either way whether we succeed or fail.

(P434) To be sure, the goal of exercising such a free will in Buddhism, as in Hinduism, is to escape altogether from this causal order of many incarnations and rebirths by escaping the bonds of individual selfhood altogether. And this is a major and definitive difference in these Eastern views from many Western views. But, for the reasons given, the free will necessary to attain such a goal in both these Eastern views is an incompatibilist form of free will that must be exercised within the causal order of the universe. One might ask how one can exercise a free will that is incompatible with determinism if one is thoroughly immersed in the causal order of the universe and subject to its causes. This is a significant question that I have tried to address throughout this book.

11.10. Theism and Predestination

Those who are sympathetic to these Eastern religions will be quick to point out that the theistic religions of the West and Middle East—including Judaism, Christianity, and Islam—seem to have as much, and maybe even more, difficulty reconciling human free will with their theistic beliefs than do believers in these Eastern traditions:

> (P435) In the theological traditions of these Western and Middle Eastern religious traditions, God is assumed to be (i) *all-powerful* (omnipotent), (ii) *all-knowing* (omniscient), (iii) *all-good* (omnibenevolent), (iv) *creator* of all things and (v) *eternal*, existing beyond time. These traits pose problems for creatures who might have free will because God would have created them, knowing everything they would do for all eternity when they were created. So it might seem they would be predestined to do everything they may do for all eternity. Thinkers in these theistic traditions have wrestled with such problems of predestination through the centuries. John Milton in his classic poem *Paradise Lost* describes the angels themselves debating how some of them could have sinned of their own free wills and why they were responsible for their sins rather than God, since God had made them the way they were and had complete foreknowledge of what they would do. And while wrestling with these questions, even the angels, according to Milton, were "in Endless Mazes lost" (not a comforting thought for us humans).

Some traditions in Judaism, Christianity (e.g., Calvinism), and Islam have accepted predestinationism as an aspect of their faith. But other thinkers in these traditions have resisted it, not merely because of what it implies about human free will. They have resisted it for what it implies about the goodness of God, who would have created beings, knowing from the moment of their creation that some would do good, while others would do evil and be damned. The creatures themselves, many reasoned, would not in that case be ultimately responsible for producing the good or evil they produced. God would be. The persistent problem that worries many in these traditions is that while God on such a view would therefore continue to be all-powerful, all-knowing, and creator of all things, God would not be all good.[7]

As a final thought on these theological issues, I want to suggest, without necessarily endorsing, another way of looking at this longtime theological problem of predestination, a way that is not explicitly stated in most of the traditional and controversial solutions to it—eternalism, Molinism, etc.

(P436) Let us assume that God would possess all the perfections listed in P435, omnipotent, omniscient, all-good, etc. This would imply that creatures such as humans would not have the power to act in such ways that God would not foresee and could not control. Nor would humans have the power to act contrary to what God has foreseen for all eternity, given God's omniscience. But God, being omnipotent, which would entail *having all powers, would therefore also have the power to limit some of God's own powers. We creatures* couldn't limit God's omnipotence and omniscience, *but God could.* And God might do so insofar as God is all-good. That is, God might limit God's powers over all creaturely actions by allowing them free will and consequently limit God's powers to know from all eternity how creatures would exercise their powers of free will.

(P437) To love what you have created, as parents are supposed to love their children, involves letting go of controlling them at certain points and letting them be and become what they desire *on their own*. That is what the dialectic of selfhood is all about, becoming self-forming beings. Your children may admire and love you, as noted. But they also want to be and become themselves. If God loved creatures who were capable of self-formation, God would also treat them as a loving parent. The love of parents for children which requires at some point letting them decide for themselves who they will be, would be the model of divine love.[8]

11.11. Conclusion: Free Will as Gift and Struggle

(P438) "Free will is a gift, but it is also a struggle." I said that over twenty-five years ago when talking about Augustine's view of free will in *The Significance of Free Will*. But I didn't realize the full meaning of it back then and didn't realize its full meaning till now in writing this book more than twenty-five years later. Every exercise of effort or willpower in self-forming actions might fail to succeed. That's the *struggle*. But every exercise of effort or willpower in self-formation might also succeed. And that's the *gift*. Moreover, failure of exercises of effort or willpower in self-formation is no mere accident. It has its origin in one's own will. The struggle of free will is within oneself, within one's own will. And, most importantly, any particular failure is not the end of the story. For one might succeed later. The *struggle* means that failure is a possibility. But the *gift* is that the failure is not the end of the story so long as one is able to struggle with self-formation. The indeterminism involved in free will is not just mere chance, coming from something wholly outside us, from nature or from God. It is coming from our own will and it arises from our inner struggles, not from external sources alone, and it thereby makes possible self-formation. That is why, though free will is a struggle, it is also a gift, but one that imposes responsibilities upon us.[9]

Notes

Chapter 1

1. Rumi 1956, p. 43.
2. This refinement is explained in more detail in Chapter 5 and pieces are added to it in all later chapters.
3. Sorabji, a noted scholar of ancient philosophy and former part-time colleague of mine, claimed in his 1983 work to find such a view in Aristotle. I think there are seeds of such a view in the Aristotelian corpus, as I'll note later in this work, but many other ancient scholars have disputed Sorabji's strong claims. See, e.g., Suzanne Bobzien 1998b; Dorothea Frede 2015; Michael Frede 2011. Also see Karen M. Nielsen 2017 for an instructive overview.
4. See Kane, 2011b, 2014, 2021; Kane and Carolina Sartorio 2022, a debate.
5. See Chapter 5, sections 5.1 and 5.2.

Chapter 2

1. I believe it is John Fischer who deserves credit for bringing this image from Borges's writings into current philosophical discussions of free will.
2. An insightful modern discussion of such motivations for source incompatibilism is Tognazzini 2011. An interesting recent discussion of the issues surrounding sourcehood is David Glick and Hannah Tierney 2020.
3. A very large literature has developed in the past several decades regarding folk intuitions concerning free will and moral responsibility, on whether the intuitions of ordinary folk are compatibilist or incompatibilist about these issues. The voluminous evidence on this topic is divided, and often controversial, since ordinary folk give differing responses depending on how particular cases are described. For influential discussions of these issues see, for example, Eddy Nahmias, Stephen Morris, T. Nadelhoffer, and J. Turner 2005; Shaun Nichols and Joshua Knobe 2007; Gunnar Bjornsson 2015, 2022; G. Bjornsson and Karl Persson 2013; G. Bjornsson and D. Pereboom 2016; Adam Feltz 2017; Adam Feltz, E. Cokely, and Thomas Nadelhoffer 2009; Adam Feltz and Florian Cova 2014; William Simkulet 2014b; Oisin Deery 2015a, 2015b; Deery and Eddy Nahmias 2017; Deery, M. Bedke, and Shaun Nichols 2013; Deery, Taylor Davis, and Jasmine Carey 2014; Joshua May 2014; Hoi-Yee Chan, Max Deutsch, and Shaun Nichols 2016. Tamler Sommers (2012) relates these issues to the diversity of beliefs about free will and responsibility in different cultures. Tim

Bayne 2017 relates them to issues about free will and the phenomenology of agency. J. Neil Otte 2015 criticizes me for assuming that ordinary intuitions about free will are incompatibilist. But as I make clear in these chapters, I agree with him and others that ordinary intuitions are mixed and depend on context, some supporting compatibilism, others supporting incompatibilism. I think there is much to be learned from this literature and I have myself learned much from it. But I do not discuss it here in detail because, as just noted, I do grant that there are both compatibilist and incompatibilist features of our ordinary thinking about free will and moral responsibility that have to be taken into account. What I argue is that to see how these play out in an overall philosophical view, one needs to make distinctions concerning different kinds of freedom, different dimensions of responsibility, different notions of will, and many other distinctions (the complex tapestry of the book's title) as I will do in this chapter and the chapters to follow.

4. Peter van Inwagen (1983), who has been a leading modern defender of libertarian free will, is an example.

5. There are, of course, legitimate questions here of how actions lacking both sufficient causes and motives and hence undetermined can be free and responsible actions at all and under the control of agents. Such questions, which are part of what was called in Chapter 1 the Intelligibility Question of libertarian free will, are discussed in Chapters 4 and 5 and subsequent chapters.

6. Galen Strawson has made this case regarding free will most forcefully with his "Basic Argument" (1986, 1994, 2002). Strawson does not think UR can be satisfied and so is skeptical about libertarian free will. But he does argue, persuasively in my view, that UR is necessary, as he puts it, for a "true responsibility-grounding freedom." See Chapter 10 for more on Galen Strawson's view and other free will skeptical views.

7. Examples include Eleanor Stump 1996; Derk Pereboom 2001; Linda Zagzebski 2000; and Seth Shabo 2010, 2011.

8. Shabo (2010), who has also written insightfully on these matters, calls it "compromising" source incompatibilism. He argues for the superiority of an uncompromising source incompatibilist view over a compromising one (as do those cited in the previous note), though in the end (like some of the others mentioned in note 7) Shabo (2011) expresses doubts about incompatibilism in general. Timpe, whose 2008 is the most comprehensive study of source incompatibilism, opts, like me, for a "wide" view.

9. "Voluntarily" and "willingly" here mean acting "in accordance with one's will (character plus intentions and motives)"; "intentionally" means "knowingly" (as opposed to "inadvertently") and "on purpose" (as opposed to "accidentally"); and "rationally" means "having reasons for so acting and acting for those reasons."

10. Ken Levy (2016, 2020), argues that what is necessary for free will is not the ability to do otherwise, but rather only the weaker alternative possibility of avoiding voluntarily performing the action one ends up performing. I argue in these sections that while this criterion is necessary for free will, it is not sufficient for exercises of free will in SFAs. That requires being able to do otherwise voluntarily, intentionally, and rationally.

11. I have emphasized in many past writings that one can have a sufficient motive for an action without a sufficient cause, and vice versa (see Kane 1996, 2000a). More will be said about this in Chapters 4 and 5.
12. A particularly insightful recent work on the will from which I have learned a great deal is Richard Holton's *Willing, Wanting, Waiting* (2009). I cite it further on various occasions in subsequent chapters. Another author who has written insightfully about willpower, freedom, and responsibility is Chandra Sripada (2012, 2014, 2016, 2017). His 2017 is a useful overview of recent debates on willpower in relation to freedom and responsibility. An extraordinarily large and comprehensive study of conceptions of the will in many different traditions from ancient times to modern existentialist thinkers as well as thinkers in analytic traditions is John Davenport's 2007 book *Will as Commitment and Resolve*.

Chapter 3

1. For some crucial discussion of whether this insulation thesis can be wholly true, see, for example, Nagel 1986; Russell 2002, 2017; Fischer 2006, 2012; Fischer and Tognazzini 2011. For general discussion of the role of moral responsibility in contemporary free will debates, see DeCaro 2007; Talbert 2016; Rossi and Warfield 2017; and collections of essays edited by Clarke, McKenna, and Smith (2015) and, most recently, by Nelkin and Pereboom (*The Oxford Handbook of Moral Responsibility*, 2022). These excellent collections provide a wide range of essays on all topics concerning moral responsibility in the recent literature.
2. More precisely defined: "An event E's not occurring at a time t is *causally impossible* just in case the following is true: it is not logically possible that the past prior to t is as it is in the actual world and the laws of nature are as they are in the actual world, and E does not occur at t." If an event E's occurring at a time t is *causally determined*, then E's not occurring at t is *causally impossible* in this sense. For a technical discussion of determinism and its relation to predictability, randomness, and other notions, see Werndl 2017. Those familiar with the multitude of current debates about whether or not free will is compatible with determinism will be aware that many of these arguments have appealed to the so-called "Consequence Argument" for incompatibilism (the title given to this argument by van Inwagen, who introduced it into current debates). They will also notice that I do not appeal here to this Consequence Argument in making my case for the incompatibility of free will with determinism. I am sympathetic to the incompatibilist conclusion of the Consequence Argument, but I also believe that it introduces many complex issues that divert attention from the central arguments for the incompatibility of free will and ultimate responsibility, on the one hand, and determinism, on the other—arguments that I develop in this and subsequent chapters. For an instructive overview of arguments for and against different versions of the Consequence Argument, see Campbell 2017. For arguments favorable to the Consequence Argument, see van Inwagen 1983; Daniel Speak 2011; Michael Huemer 2000; Carl Ginet 1990; Timothy O'Connor 2000; and

Alexander Pruss 2013, among others cited in Campbell 2017. For arguments against the Consequence Argument, see Kapitan 2002, 2011; Horgan 1985; Nelkin 2011; Kadri Vihvelin 2013; and Sartorio 2016, among others cited in Campbell 2017. Finch and Warfield 1996; Warfield 1996, 2000; and Finch 2012 argue that the Consequence Argument might be salvaged against arguments, but not in ways that would make it immune from so-called mind arguments that assert an incompatibility between indeterminism and free will. Justin Capes (2019) questions the usual assumptions about what the Consequence Argument is supposed to show, as does Brian Cutter (2017). For other writings on issues relevant to the Consequence Argument from which I have learned, see Wyma 1997; Helen Beebee 2002, 2003, and 2013; Carlson 2000; Cross 1986; Holliday 2012; Horgan 1985, 2015; Huemer 2000, 2004; Jastor 2020; Kittle 2019; Lamb 1993; and Pendergraft 2010, 2012. An important earlier contributor to these debates whose writings have influenced me is Keith Lehrer (1976, 1980, 1986). More recent sophisticated defenses of a libertarian type of free will that I have learned from include Lockie 2018, which relates the consequence argument in various formulations in interesting ways to the long history in Western philosophy of "transcendental arguments" for a variety of topics, including arguments for free will. Yet another original work on free will of recent vintage that I have learned from is that Elstob 2018, which offers a new approach to a variety of issues about free will based on a notion of "independence indeterminism" and a novel naturalistic metaphysics of an open creative universe. I'm not convinced by all aspects of these works, but I have learned much from them.

3. See also Ken Levy 2005a on this point.
4. For careful studies of the notion of blame that would support these judgments see Sher 2006 and Slote 1982. For the relation of incompatibilism to blame see Michael Otsuka 1998 and Evan Tiffany 2013. For a related and instructive discussion of "ought" statements generally and their relation to abilities, see Graham 2011. For informative discussions of the relation between moral responsibility and freedom generally, see Hunt 2000 and Rossi and Warfield 2017.
5. And if one says it may matter whether agents *take* responsibility for the state of their wills when they act, indeed it may. But the question then becomes whether their doing otherwise than taking responsibility for it was now, or ever, causally possible. And if determinism is true, it was not.
6. Such transference of responsibility is very much a part of our ordinary practices of holding persons responsible; and the extent to which we are inclined to do it depends on the degree to which we believe the influences were resistible by the agents, or in Hart's terms, whether the agents had a "fair opportunity" to resist them.
7. Note that this familiar compatibilist line of argument was mentioned at the end of the previous chapter, where I said it would be considered in this chapter.
8. As noted, there was an initial resistance to transferring all of the responsibility and blame to others and a desire to continue to blame the young man, at least to some degree, for having the perverse will and being the kind of person he is.
9. Might he have been acting compulsively? Perhaps. But compatibilists must come up with further conditions for defining compulsive behavior; and they have usually done

so. One such influential condition is suggested by Harry Frankfurt's account of the unwilling addict. Frankfurt's compatibilist view is discussed later in this chapter and further in Chapter 9.
10. See Watson 1987, pp. 256–86.
11. David Shoemaker has written extensively about the relation of these three notions of responsibility—attributability, accountability, and answerability—spelling out their implications and relations to one another in enlightening detail. See his *Responsibility from the Margins* (2015a). Answerability plays a significant role in other ethical thinkers, including notably T. M. Scanlon (2008), who relates it to contractualism in ethics. James Lenman (2006) is another thinker who has related compatibilism on free will to contractualism. For further discussion of these issues see the readings cited in note 1 of this chapter, as well as readings in Nick Trakakis and Daniel Cohen 2008.
12. An instructive and insightful overview of current views on responsibility is Matthew Tallbert 2016. For other important discussions of views of responsibility, see Angela Smith 2007; Michael Zimmerman 1988; Elinor Mason 2005; Brian Warmke 2011; Tabitha Taylor 2016; and the essays in the collections on moral responsibility cited in note 1 of this chapter, Randolph Clarke, Michael McKenna, and Angela Smith 2015 and Dana Nelkin and Derk Pereboom 2022.
13. Thus, acts of free will of type 2 and most acts of type 3 involve responsibility for *expressing* the will one *has* in action, as well as responsibility for *having* the (quality of) will one *expresses* in action. I qualify here by saying "most" free acts of type 3 because the exceptions include, in addition to certain other acts in later life, the earliest SFAs of childhood when there is as yet no backlog of prior formed character that provides input into them. I discuss these first SFAs of childhood in Chapter 5. The notion of autonomy in my view involves all three kinds of acts of will and especially relates to acts of kinds 2 and 3. For insightful and contrasting views of autonomy see Nomy Arpaly 2004 and John Christman 1991.
14. The debate does not end here. Compatibilists have offered many further arguments historically in the attempt to counter these intuitions and have offered ever more sophisticated arguments in the past half century. Their arguments are discussed further in Chapter 9.
15. Some contemporary philosophers (e.g., Michael Smith 1997, 2003; Kadri Vihvelin 2004, 2013, 2017; Michael Fara 2008; Dana Nelkin 2011) have put forth so-called "dispositional" analyses of the freedom to do otherwise, which also take a conditional or hypothetical form, but are meant to be an improvement over the traditional conditional analyses of classical compatibilists. I critically examine these new dispositional compatibilisms in Chapter 9. For critical discussion of such dispositional analyses, see Randolph Clarke 2009 and Bernard Berofsky 2003, 2012.
16. For discussion of further difficulties with FSEs involving blockage, see Michael Robinson 2014. For a general critique of FSEs of all varieties, see Daniel Speak 2007. For discussion of so-called fine-grained responses to FSEs of all kinds, see Justin Capes and Philip Swenson 2017. For an interesting critical reply to Frankfurt on norm-guided formation of cares see John Davenport 2013. Ezio Di Nucci (2011) offers an original interpretation of what FSEs do and do not show about free will and responsibility.

17. The "buffered" designation comes from David Hunt (2005), who has also written insightfully on FSEs of this form. The "necessary-condition" designation comes from David Widerker and Michael McKenna 2003, p. 10. For difficulties with the tax-evasion case and subtle discussion of the difficulties of buffered cases in general, see William Simkulet 2015. For a discussion of the relation of buffered cases to blameworthiness, see Justin Capes 2016. For a useful collection of essays on blame in general, its nature, and the norms governing it, see D. J. Coates and Neal Tognazzini 2013. For a careful assessment of the relation alternative possibilities and blameworthines, see Carlos Moya 2014. For further critical discussion of Frankfurt cases of all kinds, see Justin Capes and Philip Swenson 2017 and Alfred Mele 2006, 2017a, among other works.

Chapter 4

1. Such "arguments from luck" against an incompatibilist free will have been defended in one form or another by a great variety of thinkers, including David Hume ([1740] 1978) in the eighteenth century and a great many in the twentieth century, including R. E. Hobart 1934; A. J. Ayer 1954; J. J. C. Smart 1961; Galen Strawson 1986; Bruce Waller 1988; Richard Double 1991; Ishtiyaque Haji 1998; Michael Zimmerman 2002; Michael Almeida and Mark Bernstein 2003; Mirja Pérez de Calleja 2003; Gideon Rosen 2008; Jason Turner 2009; Neil Levy 2011; Markus Schlosser 2014; Seth Shabo 2014a, 2014b, 2020; Sam Harris 2012; Daniel Wegner 2002; Benjamin Vilhauer 2010; Zac Cogley 2015; Stephen Kearns 2015;Taylor Cyr 2017, 2019; and Daniel Statman and Christopher Shields 2022; among others. For an overview of these debates from all sides, see E. J. Coffman 2015 and the collections edited by Daniel Statman (1993) and by Andrei Buckareff, Carlos Moya, and Sergi Rosell (2015). On some difficulties for arguments from luck in relation to moral responsibility, see William Simkulet 2014. For studies in experimental philosophy concerning folk intuitions on free will, responsibility, and luck, see Gunnar Bjornsson and Derk Pereboom 2016.
2. See also C. Baker and J. Gollub 1990; William Freeman 1999; Robert van Gulick 1995; R. Hilborn 2001; J. Hobbs 1991; S. Kellert 1993; A. Maye et al. 2007; William T. Newsome 2009; Chris D. Frith 2009; Peter Jedlicka 2014; Hans Briegel and Thomas Mueller 2015; Mark Pestana 2001; and numerous further references in all of these works. An interesting and insightful piece on the relation quantum physics to decision-making is John Jung Park 2016. More radical views about the role of indeterminism in the brain, which are interesting, but on which I do not rely here, include Stuart Hameroff and Roger Penrose 1996 and Henry Stapp 2007. An interesting view of a distinguished Swiss physicist who has influenced my thinking is Nicolas Gisin 2021. Adina Roskies (2014) takes issue with neuroscientist Michael Shadlen (2014) in a spirited debate concerning whether indeterminism might play a significant role in neural processing relevant to free will. See also Jenann Ismael 2016 for an informed and insightful account of the relation of physics to issues about free will. A useful collection of different views on these subjects is Uri Maoz and Walter Sinnott-Armstrong 2022. An interesting article on the implications of the cognitive

sciences for free will is Andrea Lavassa's "Why Cognitive Sciences Do Not Prove That Free Will Is an Epiphenomenon" (2019). Another important cognitive science contribution here on voluntary control and free action is John Dilworth 2008.
3. It would seem especially so if, as assumed, his reasons inclined (albeit without necessitating) that he chose to steal at that time.
4. Indeterminism would be the *proximal* cause of the *failure* of any effort to choose. Though the distal cause of failure would be the competing motives that provided resistance in the will that stirred up the indeterminism in which resistance was not overcome by the effort. Failure of effort, as noted in P72, is thus a signal to the deliberating agent that the competing motives still matter and should not be dismissed so precipitously. But, in the end, it is the success of one of the agents voluntary and intentional efforts, *despite* the indeterminism, that accounts for the choice that is made.
5. That would not necessarily absolve all such agents of all responsibility, as in the case, for example, of the assassin. But his responsibility would be for attempted murder, not actual murder, if no one else were killed. And the responsibility would be in his effort, which was voluntary and intentional, not in his failure, which was not voluntary and intentional.
6. See also Ken Levy (2020), who makes this point in a work on free will, crime, and responsibility in the law.
7. This is one reason, as we shall see in the next chapter, why I now reject the simple designation of my view as an "event-causal" view.
8. We shall see, as further pieces are added in this chapter and the next, that there are some more subtle rationality constraints that apply as well in cases of effort-making in "will-setting."
9. I have learned much in developing the views of this chapter and the next from the critical works of, and conversations with, many authors, especially with Maria Sekatskaya 2017, 2020, 2021, 2022; Mirja Pérez de Calleja 2003; Robyn Repko Waller 2014, 2015; and Alessandro (Alex) Fiorello 2020. Some other writings that have influenced me include Elizabeth Pacherie 2007; Stefan Cuypers 2006; Roman Altschuler 2010; Ilham Dilman 1999; Jan Cover and J. O'Leary Hawthorne 1996. A collection of essays critically evaluating my views of free will by some prominent figures, all of whom have influenced my work and my responses, is David Palmer 2014a. An instructive review of this volume edited by Palmer is by Jose Colen (2016). I have also benefited by correspondence with Martin Gerwin (2019) and Alessandro Fiorello (2021) on their original work and mine on the issues of this chapter and the next.

Chapter 5

1. The assumption is therefore often made that to explain an incompatibilist free will, one has to postulate a special kind of causation by an agent or substance (often designated "agent causation") that is a metaphysically primitive relation which cannot in principle be spelled out in terms of causation by states and events familiar to the sciences. Such agent-causal views are critically examined in more detail in Chapter 8.

2. In the case of SFAs, for example, it is true to say both that "the agent's making an effort to bring about the choice of A, caused or brought about the choice of A," and that "the agent caused or brought about the choice of A." Indeed the first claim which describes an event cause ("the agent's making an effort to bring about the choice of A") *entails* the second, which describes an agent cause. Such event-causal descriptions are not meant to deny that agents caused their free choices and free actions. Rather they spell out in more detail *how* and *why* the agents did so.
3. An important recent work that forcefully makes this case is John Hyman's *Action, Knowledge and Will* (2015). Hyman says in this work that events can only acquire the status of causes of actions "by participating in actions by agents and agents can only exercise causal power by dint of events" (p. 57).
4. Another author from whom I have learned much on these issues is Thomas Mueller, who emphasizes in his writings the need to appeal to both agents and events in an adequate account of the causation of action. An interesting and original further development of some of the features of this view is Thomas Mueller and Hans Briegel 2018. Ken Levy (2020, 2023) inclines as well to this sort of AC/EC view.
5. As noted earlier, the best-known modern version of this sort of regress argument against libertarian free will is made by Galen Strawson (1986, 1994), who calls it the "Basic Argument." I will be returning to this argument in Chapter 10.
6. If this were not the case, or if, for example, mental capacities never developed beyond those of a child, as happens in some cases, then ultimate responsibility (and liability for punishment and blame) would be severely limited and minimal, as with young children of similar capacities.
7. See Kane 2008.
8. This may also be true of *some* other self-forming actions at later stages of our self-formation when we reform ourselves in the face of conflicts in our wills that do not result from any prior SFAs. I'll be saying more about this in later chapters as well.
9. Kane 2008, 2009.
10. Kane 2007a, 2008. Kane 2007a is a response to insightful critical papers by Robert Allen (2007) and Katherin Rogers (2007, 2008). Rogers 2008 is an interesting study of Anselm's view of free will, and in it (and also in 2007) she identifies similarities between Anselm's view and mine. Tobias Hoffman and Cyrille Michon (2017) have written an equally interesting account of Aquinas's views on free will which shows some similarities (but also some differences) with my view as presented here. See also Scott MacDonald's informative "Aquinas's Libertarian Account of Free Will" (1998).
11. Neil Levy (2008) and Manuel Vargas (2005) have raised important objections to my view and the views of others which require that responsibility for later actions be dependent in this way on earlier actions. I have attempted to respond to Levy and to Vargas in Kane 2008 and in later chapters of this book.
12. Concerning the other end of the life cycle—as we grow older—a different kind of objection may arise. In speaking about these matters, I have frequently heard it suggested by someone or other in the audience that as people get older, they become more and more set in their ways, and so have a need to make fewer and fewer SFAs, rather than more of them. My response to this familiar observation is usually given

on a personal note. I find that the opposite is the case in my own experience, and I ask the older folks in the audience what their experience is. They usually agree that aging brings many occasions for new and different SFAs that we did not face when younger. Issues about health, retirement, illness and loss of loved ones, relations to grown children and grandchildren, and so on and on.

13. Objections of this kind are raised in slightly different ways by Mele 1998, 2006; Ginet 2014; Fischer 2007; Clarke 2003; Pereboom 2003, 2007; and Galen Strawson 2002.

14. The difference would depend on whether the motivations that give rise to the efforts had been formed by some earlier self-forming actions, such as, for example, a man's earlier resolution to go on a diet, or whether the motivations were based on desires or inclinations not so formed, such as the man's present temptation to order his favorite high-calorie dessert at a restaurant when he sees others ordering it. In either case, given the resulting conflict in his will, effort would be needed to overcome resistance in his will, if either choice is to be made. And the efforts thus initiated would be free acts of kind 1 or free acts of both kinds 1 and 2.

15. In addition, the *initiation* of such efforts or exercises of willpower will normally be *determined* by the state of the agent's will at the time they are initiated. They will be initiated when agents judge that their motives incline them toward making a particular choice to a degree that would justify making the choice at the time.

16. These efforts initiated in self-forming choice situations would, first of all, be *will-settled* acts, not *will-setting* ones like the self-forming choices the efforts might succeed in bringing about. For each particular effort would have as its goal the making of a *specific* choice (e.g., to steal from the poor box) rather than any alternative choice. Second, the *initiation* of such efforts or exercises of willpower may be *determined* by the trajectory of the agent's reasoning at the time they are initiated, in the manner described in P140. Nonetheless, if any such effort or exercise of willpower were to succeed in attaining its goal, it would *bring about* a self-forming choice or SFA which *was* both *will-setting* and *undetermined*.

17. Or, stated differently, competing cognitive processes, over each of which an agent has a kind of control similar to what Fischer and Ravizza (1998) call *guidance control*, exercised in deliberation, give rise to what they call *regulative control*, that is, the power of an agent to voluntarily bring about a certain choice and the power to voluntarily do otherwise.

18. Note where we thus arrive: different goal-directed cognitive processes (efforts or volitional streams) over each of which the agent has "one-way" or *singular* voluntary control, that is, teleological guidance control—efforts that may occur at various points in the course of a deliberation—make possible "more-than-one-way" or *plural* voluntary control. This is the case since the agent might succeed in attaining the goal of one or another of these efforts (the choice aimed at by that effort) during a given deliberation and the agents would do so voluntarily, on purpose and for reasons, whichever choice is thereby made.

19. Another objection involving agential power or control often made against event-causal views of free will like this one is that they give us no *more* power to determine what one does than compatibilists give us. (See, e.g., Pereboom 2001 and

Clarke 2003.) And (this argument continues) some further power to determine what one does than compatibilists give us is required for true libertarian freedom. This may be called *the no-more-power objection*. It is, in my view, misguided for the following reason: if agents in SFA situations can exercise plural voluntary control over undetermined alternatives, as I have argued they can, then I submit that they *do* have more power than compatibilists can give us in a determined world. For the most compatibilists can say of agents *in a determined world* who act voluntarily, intentionally, and rationally is that they may have acted otherwise voluntarily, intentionally, and rationally *if* the past or the laws of nature had been different in some way than they actually are. Compatibilists cannot say that agents have the power to have acted otherwise in these ways given the *actual* laws of nature and the past *as it actually was* at the moment of action. Not only is such a plural power more power than compatibilists can give us in a determined world, but it is the kind of power that libertarians have always demanded for free will and moral responsibility. That is, it is a power than can be voluntarily (non-coercively), intentionally (purposefully), and rationally *exercised in more than one way, in the actual world as it is*, not in some hypothetical world that might have been but never was.

20. Because of the indeterminism involved in these efforts, however, arising from the conflicts in the agents' wills, the *outputs of these* (the choices made) would not be determined by, though they would be influenced by, these causal *inputs*.
21. Cf. as well Ken Levy 2023, pp. 740–41.
22. An interesting connection with this way of viewing things is to an admirably original and influential recent work by L. A. Paul, *Transformative Experience* (2014). Paul's book focuses on life-changing choices and experiences such as becoming a parent, marrying, becoming a doctor or entering another profession, pursuing a religious vocation, etc. Paul argues that such transformative life choices pose a significant challenge to orthodox conceptions of rational choice as a matter of weighing the probabilities and subjective desirabilities of possible options and then selecting the best option. With such transformative choices you simply cannot know all that they may involve until you undertake them. As in the case of becoming a parent, they may radically transform how you think, how you feel, and how you experience. The difficulty of such choices comes from the inability to fully grasp all the possible outcomes because they are different from the life one already knows. This fits in many ways with the idea expressed in P183 that *self-forming choices* involve the initiation of novel pathways into the future, "value experiments," as I have elsewhere called them, whose justification lies partly in that future and is not fully explained by the past (1996, pp. 145–46). Not all self-forming choices involve radical changes in one's future like Paul's transformative experiences, but many do, and, interestingly, many others involve efforts to persist in dealing with novel experiences that have come about by earlier self-forming choices.
23. Shabo 2014 goes on to defend rollback arguments against libertarian views, while Franklin 2018 argues that such rollback arguments fail, as we will see in discussing Franklin's view in Chapter 7.
24. Franklin (2017, 2018) has an interesting and original argument on these issues. If all replays came out the same, he argues, this would suggest to many persons that her

decision was not free. It's an interesting argument, though, as he might acknowledge, it may not be convincing to many proponents of the rollback objections because it brings out a clash of intuitions between compatibilists and incompatibilists on the subject.
25. Cf. Ken Levy (2023) on this point.
26. This objection was pressed on me by Carolina Sartorio in an instructive published debate between the two of us on the issues, *Do We Have Free Will? A Debate* (2022), in which she defends a compatibilist view of free will and I a libertarian view. I have learned much from this debate and from other writings of Carolina despite our differences, particularly her original views about causation and free will in her book *Causation and Free Will* (2014). In our debate, I acknowledge agreement with much that she says about the role of causation in free will, arguing that much of her account of causation is relevant and important to a libertarian view like mine as well as to compatibilist views like hers.
27. I am much indebted to John Lemos for helping me think through these issues raised by Haji as well as other issues in this book. Further discussion of Lemos's view appears in Chapter 7 (7.14–7.15).
28. Haji's criticism has led me to clarify the important points made here, which is just one example of how Haji's astute criticisms of incompatibilist views of free will, in this paper and especially in his important book (2009) have informed and sharpened my own thinking about such views.
29. An insightful response to arguments regarding contrastive explanations against libertarian free will, which appeals to my account of self-forming actions, while developing this appeal in original ways, is Neil Campbell's article in *Synthese* (2020).

Chapter 6

1. As Dennett says, indeterminism occurring when a final choice is made is not something libertarians should want, since it would make the occurrence of the final choice a mere matter of chance or luck. Mele adds similarly that what libertarians typically desire, "both indeterminism and significant control at the moment of decision," is the very "desire that prompts a serious version of the worry about luck" (2006, p. 14).
2. See Ken Levy 2020, pp. 19–20.
3. Another such thinker would be neuroscientist Peter Ulric Tse (2013). Tse has produced a recent podcast on free will and neuroscience (Tse 2021) in which he further develops his original views about the neuroscience of free will in his 2013 book. He identifies how and where indeterminism may be involved in synaptic transmission in the brain and how it may influence cognitive processing. He also further develops his notion of "criterial causation" in his book, in which causes may influence and alter the criteria by which neurons will fire in future interactions. Tse's views have great promise for providing neurological support for accounts of free will like the one developed here.

4. Dennett also makes this point in chapter 4 of his *Freedom Evolves* (2003). This chapter, in an excellent book on evolution and freedom, is devoted to critically examining my view of free will, which he takes to be the most plausible naturalistic account of a libertarian free will on offer at the time. He sent me an earlier draft of the chapter to which I responded, initiating a fruitful discussion. While we agreed on certain things, he held firmly to his compatibilist convictions and his rejection of any libertarian view. Later in this chapter, I discuss some evolutionary implications of the revised view of this book, which reflect in part this fruitful exchange with Dennett.
5. See further references in Murphy, Ellis, and O'Connor 2009 and in P. Jedlicka 2014. For numerous references to all aspects of issues about free will, see Robert Doyle's comprehensive website *The Information Philosopher* in the section on free will. In this informative website Doyle summarizes in very useful ways, the views of many philosophers and scientists on free will in the past and present. In the process, he also defends his two-stage deliberative view of libertarian free will from both scientific and philosophical perspectives.

Chapter 7

1. Behind these disagreements lie more fundamental differences between Balaguer's view and my own about what is required for libertarian free will. In Chapter 2, I argued that while there are many kinds of freedom that are compatible with determinism and could exist in a determined world, there is at least one significant kind of freedom worth wanting that is not compatible with determinism. This further freedom is what was traditionally called "freedom *of will*," and it historically signified the power to be the ultimate creator and sustainer to some degree of one's own ends or purpose. Having this further freedom of will, I argued, requires sometimes being able to act otherwise than you do, that is, having alternative possibilities. But that is not enough. To see what more is required, I argued, one must revisit the long history of debates about free will, where one finds another historical condition fueling libertarian intuitions that is even more important than this alternative possibilities condition. I called this further condition "ultimate responsibility" and argued that focusing on it tells us why the traditional problem is a problem about the freedom *of the will* and not just about the freedom *of action* and why these freedoms must be distinguished if important questions about free will are to be adequately addressed. I repeat these arguments here because they provide insight into something that lies behind the disagreements between Balaguer's view and mine concerning his torn decisions and my self-forming actions. For, as it turns out, Balaguer rejects appeals to ultimate responsibility as being at all important to what should concern libertarians about free will.
2. But that doesn't mean I accept his Daring Libertarian View. For the realization that my appeal to concurrent efforts provides no significant advantage over his Daring View was further evidence that the appeal to concurrent efforts falls short of giving us an adequate libertarian account of free will. Reflecting on what lies behind this

consequence provided me further insights into the motivations behind some of the changes in my view that have been made in this book.
3. Franklin aptly quotes Michael Bratman here, who says that "the image of the agent directing and governing is, in the first instance, an image of the agent herself standing back from her attitudes, and doing the directing and governing" (2005, reprinted in 2007, pp. 195–96). Like Franklin, in my account of free will, I have absorbed and presupposed much from Bratman's groundbreaking views about reasoning, choice, rationality, and action.
4. The difference would depend on whether the motivations that give rise to the efforts had been formed by some earlier self-forming actions, such as, for example, a man's earlier resolution to go on a diet, or whether the motivations were based on desires or inclinations not so formed, such as the man's present temptation to order his favorite high-calorie dessert at a restaurant when he sees others ordering it. In either case, given the resulting conflict in his will, effort would be needed to overcome resistance in his will, if either choice is to be made. And the efforts thus initiated would be free acts of kind 1 or free acts of both kinds 1 and 2.
5. An earlier paper that anticipates some of the claims of this paper of Franklin's is Franklin 2016.
6. We can give stronger (type 1) contrastive explanations, in cases of motivational conflict such as John's, for why he chose *for the reasons he had for stealing the money rather than* for other reasons he also had for not stealing the money or vice versa (P273). We can say his reasons for stealing the money in these circumstances inclined him to a degree that would justify making an effort to make the choice to steal at this time, thereby overcoming his resistant motives for choosing not to steal. If he succeeded in overcoming these resistant motives, despite the possibility of failure due to the indeterminism stirred up by the conflict in his will, his making this choice at the time *rather than* any other would not be *unexplained*, even though it would be *undetermined*.
7. If either competing preference was formed in such manner, the formation of this preference would then be a self-forming action of the kind described in previous chapters. For the preference so formed would have resolved a conflict in the will of the agent by the agent's overcoming resistance in the will coming from the motives to form a competing preference (P207–P208). It would not then matter if the final decision terminating deliberation was determined by this prior formed preference. For the crucial indeterminism would have come earlier in the agent's successfully forming this preference rather than any other by overcoming resistance in the will to doing so (P209).
8. I have omitted the further description of the books content on this opening page because I will be returning to the pragmatic and moral justification he refers to in it when considering later the views of the free will skeptics mentioned at the end of the quotation: "In addition, the book argues that while we lack sufficient epistemic grounds supporting belief in the existence of libertarian free will, we may still be justified in believing in it for moral reasons. As such the book engages critically with the works of a growing number of philosophers who argue that we should jettison belief

in desert-grounding free will and the practices of praise and blame and reward and punishment which it supports."

9. He specifically cites Ekstrom and Clarke, who cogently make these objections, though many others have made them as well. Another powerful objection against such views is made by Thomas Nadelhoffer (2010). Other strong critical papers are by Stephen Kearns (2012 and 2015).
10. If the effort fails, and at a later time reasons incline one to make a competing choice, one would have to make a further effort at that later time to overcome resistance in one's will to making that other choice.
11. Moreover, the making of a choice in such circumstances differs consciously from making a choice where we believe the reasons favoring the choice are conclusive or decisive and there is no resistance in the will to be overcome.
12. See also Ken Levy 2001 on this possibility.
13. For a constructive and partially critical discussion of Lemos's view see Dwayne Moore 2022.
14. In addition, if the goal or telos of this teleologically guided process is to be *rationally* selected and not merely randomly or arbitrarily selected, the agent's reasoning prior to the initiation of the teleologically guided process must incline the agent to assign greater weight to this particular set of reasons rather than any other. (5) And if the outcome of this teleologically guided process is not to be determined, the reasons to be assigned greater weight by the process must not necessitate or determine the agent to assign greater weight to these reasons. (6) There would be competing motives in the will for not doing so, competing motives that would have to be overcome if this teleologically guided process is to succeed. (7) So the teleologically guided process of the agent that assigned greater weight to one set of reasons rather than another would be an exercise of *striving* will, that is, an effort or exercise of willpower or striving to attain this goal against resistance, in this case resistance in the agent's own will. (8) Assigning greater weight to certain reasons in this manner would be an integral feature of self-forming action wherever self-forming actions might occur in the practical lives of agents.
15. Lemos has further developed his view and answered objections to it in a new and recently published book (2023). This book relates libertarian free will to important topics such as criminal justice, pride, and love, in insightful ways with which I would agree. It is an important contribution to current debates.
16. Three other important defenses of a libertarian view of free will in the current literature that I have not discussed here are Carlos Moya 2006; Ken Levy 2020; and David Hodgson 2012. Moya provides excellent defenses of the claims that moral responsibility requires access to alternative possibilities as well as a kind of ultimate sourcehood that is incompatible with determinism. He discusses my earlier view at length, arguing that because the indeterminism involved in self-forming actions allows that all of the agent's dispositions, deliberations, and motivations may not fully determine whether an agent performs an action, it is unclear how the performance of the action is under the agent's rational control (2006, p. 153). These objections were made to my previous view and I have attempted to answer them in earlier chapters of

this book. He goes on to argue that the reason libertarian views of free will, including my earlier view, have failed to adequately answer luck and other common objections is because they try to locate the indeterminism in choices or decisions. He argues that they should focus instead on beliefs and other motivational states to locate the requisite indeterminism. I do not agree with this for reasons that are evident from earlier chapters of this book. While choices and decisions are not the only locations for self-forming actions in the theory developed here, they are among the most important locations and play crucial roles in our freedom as self-determination. There are many other themes in Moya's carefully argued work not addressed here, which I believe are consistent with the view of this book. It is another book I would recommend to those interested in works defending libertarian free will. Ken Levy's 2020 book and a recent paper (2023) develop a view of libertarian free will that has some similarities to that of this book. He cites my view often and relates a view like it to many issues, including issues of criminal responsibility, which is a specialty of his, as a legal theorist. Finally, David Hodgson's (2012) libertarian view is unique and would require a lengthier discussion than I can give here. But it is also worth reading.

Chapter 8

1. O'Connor has cowritten a relevant article with Jonathan Jacobs employing some of these notions (2013).
2. Among Lowe's many contributions to contemporary free will debates, perhaps the most influential and controversial is this view that all causation is substance causation. He says: "In my view, only entities in the category of substance—that is, persisting concrete objects—possess causal powers. Strictly speaking, an event cannot do anything and so cannot cause anything. For causings are a species of doings . . . and doings are themselves happenings" (2008, p. 4). Some AC theorists, O'Connor among them, have latched on to this idea in recent times as a way of supporting AC accounts of libertarian free will over EC theories (though it is not accepted by all agent-causationists. See the overview articles on agent-causal views by Meghan Griffith (2017) and O'Connor (2011). If all causation is substance causation, these agent-causationists argue, then all causation of action would be causation by a special kind of substance, an agent. Yet for reasons given here, and other reasons, I think it is highly implausible if it implies that there is no such thing as causation by events involved in free agency and free will. What Lowe might have said which is not implausible is not that events "cannot cause anything," but rather that events which do cause things to happen (such as earthquakes and planes' crashing into buildings) must be *substance-involving* events (they must involve geological plates and airplanes). This is an interesting thesis. I'm not sure it is universally true and take no definitive position on it. But it could be true. And it is true, I believe, of those event causes that are crucial for explaining actions. The event causes such as mental states and processes of the agent that are typically involved in causing actions are states and processes of an agent. But such agent-involving *event causes* are involved and crucially so in agent

causation of actions. Moreover, on the AC/EC view I defend, it is the agent qua complex system exercising guidance control over some of its own processes, who brings it about that these mental states and processes are causally involved in the manner they are causally involved. Another unusual feature of Lowe's view is that he sometimes characterizes it as less than purely agent-causal because, on it, agents do not cause their actions. In short, his view seems to be noncausalist in certain important respects. Despite these sometimes puzzling complexities, there is much to be learned from reading his work.

3. For example, in my account of self-forming actions, I suggest that three notions of *will* are involved, two of which involve appeal to *powers* of agents capable of self-formation and free will (P42–P47).

4. Griffith is intent on showing that many of the more controversial claims made by traditional agent causalists that have led to criticisms and rejection of traditional versions of the view, need not be held by agent causalists and are not held by some more recent defenders of the view, including herself. One recent defense of an agent-causal view which goes against the grain of her remarks by giving a more traditional dualistic account of agent causation is Richard Swinburne's *Mind, Brain, and Free Will* (2013b). This view is out of fashion these days, even among AC theorists of free will. But Swinburne gives it a sophisticated modern defense that is worthy of the attention especially of those inclined to AC libertarianism.

5. Another important recent defense of an agent-causal view is Helen Steward's *A Metaphysics of Freedom* (2012). This book and Steward's other carefully argued writings defend a unique naturalistic view of agent causation from which I have also learned much. She rightly, in my view, rejects Lowe's view that all causation is substance causation, arguing that what can be called causes fall into a variety of different categories, including substances and events, which accords nicely with the AC/EC defended here. One important aspect of her view that I would disagree with, however, is what she calls "Agency Incompatibilism." She says (2016, p. 162) nonhuman animals are relevant to the issues surrounding the truth or otherwise of determinism. For the thing which is most basically and interestingly in potential conflict with determinism, she argues, "is not choice, or decision, or decision based on deliberation or upon reason. The thing which is most basically in potential conflict with determinism is agency *itself*, a power which I venture to assert all animals up to a certain minimal level of complexity certainly possess. . . . I call this view Agency Incompatibilism. . . . If incompatibilism is a doctrine only about humans, then incompatibilism is bound to be vulnerable to special pleading on the part of humanity." By contrast, "if incompatibilism is a doctrine . . . about how we must think about causality and the evolution of reality over time in a world in which animals and their distinctive powers of self-direction are present, then incompatibilism immediately takes on a more hopefully naturalistic cast. Mere indeterminism in micro processes at the quantum level is not enough and would amount to mere chance if they did have some effect in the brain." She concludes that if indeterminism, and hence incompatibilism, emerge at the animal level, we do not have to explain how they emerge at the human level since they are already present at the animal level. (For criticisms of these views of Steward's,

see Helen Beebee 2014.) My responses to these claims should be evident from earlier chapters of this book. The capacity for agency is a necessary requirement for free will, to be sure. Creatures in which free will develops must be capable of agency, as she describes it. But free will is a higher evolutionary development of beings capable of agency of whatever kind who may evolve into possession of free will. They must have an inner mental life complex enough to have conflicts in their wills about what to do or how to act as agents and which can be resolved by them in a manner undetermined by their pasts. Human beings, I have argued, can develop these capacities, but the capacities need not be confined to humans. It's possible that some higher animals have them to a limited degree and also that other extraterrestrials in the universe that we may come upon may have them to a degree equal or even more advanced than our own. Thus, there need be no special pleading for humanity here. Nor do we have to assume that focusing on animal agency is needed to give incompatibilism a more naturalistic cast. The incompatibilistic view of free will developed here is something that can exist in a naturalistic worldview. Finally, insofar as we can speak of agency at the level of animal agency as she does, we are not speaking of freedom of *will* as conceived here and as it was understood in the history of debates about free will. At most we would speaking of freedom of *action* (in the sense of no constraints or impediments preventing us from doing what we want or desire to do). Freedom of will is a deeper notion than this, as I have argued throughout this book, and it is the very notion that points to a need for incompatibilism and indeterminism that have been so central for historical debates about free will. Compatibilists could say, and most would say, that the agency we find at the animal level can be explained in compatibilist terms without invoking indeterminism or incompatibilism. But these differences aside, there is much that I agree with in Steward's works and hers is another important defense of libertarian free will that is indispensable reading.

6. Another illustration of these concerns appears in an introduction to the free will problem that also defends a libertarian and ultimately an AC libertarian view, namely T. J. Mawson's *Free Will: A Guide for the Perplexed* (2011). The "perplexed" for whom his book is meant to be a guide are those persons being introduced to the problem of free will who share some initial intuitions that incline them to a libertarian view, but are perplexed by the many counterarguments in the literature against such a view. In defending an AC theory of libertarian free will, Mawson follows the playbook of modern AC libertarians summarized in this section. That is, he argues that the causal role of agents as "ultimate authors" of some of their own choices and actions cannot be reduced to causation by states or events alone, as in (EC) libertarian views, or to noncausal processes, as in NC views. Since only these three options are available to libertarians, he concludes that the only hope for those perplexed about how to make sense of a libertarian free will is thus to affirm an AC libertarian view. On Mawson's account of such a view, "for a genuinely free choice the agent himself or herself must give to the world some causal 'oomph,' as we might put it. This is the 'ultimate authorship' condition for free action" (2011, p. 144). This appeal to "causal oomph," he says, is to our experience as agents of *making* something happen rather than merely being swept up in the events surrounding us. This experiential appeal (which is made by

many AC theorists) is, I believe, genuine and must be taken into account. But doing so does not absolve one of answering many questions about *how* this causal oomph, like agent causation in AC theories generally, works and what it amounts to: What does its exercise consist in? And how does it account for ultimate authorship? Answering such questions is an important part of what the additional pieces of the AC/EC view reviewed in the next two sections are meant to do.

7. Another important work that develops these ideas of Juarrero and others on complex dynamical systems with special implications for free will issues is *Did My Neurons Make Me Do It?* by philosopher Nancey Murphy and neuroscientist Warren Brown (2007). I have been influenced in my thoughts on these subjects by this excellent volume as well as by Juarrero's book and other authors mentioned here. An important collection of readings by other influential figures who have defended notions of "downward causation" in relation to complex dynamical systems is coedited by Murphy, George F. R. Ellis and T. O'Connor and entitled *Downwards Causation and the Neurobiology of Free Will* (2009). This volume includes important essays by neuroscientists and others, including William Newsome, "Human Freedom and Emergence," George F. R. Ellis, "Top-Down Causation and the Human Brain," and Chris Frith, "Free Will and Top-Down Control in the Brain," among others. In a lengthy introduction, Murphy also discusses the important work of Robert van Gulick (1995) and Terence Deacon (2007) on these issues of emergence in complex systems such as the human brain. Two other works that have much to say about these issues of complexity in defence of a libertarian view of free will are J. Polkinghorne 2009 and Mark Pestana 2001.

8. Regarding Prigogine on "fluctuations," I gave a paper at a conference in Prigogine's honor at the University of Texas, where he taught in the spring semesters for many years. When some listeners questioned my assumption about the possibility of indeterminism in the brain that might support an incompatibilist view of free will, Prigogine rose to my defense, emphasizing the role of "fluctuations" in the brain which are crucial to its functioning and some of which, he believed might be undetermined. Several students who received master's degrees in physics at the institute named after Prigogine at Texas (Robert Bishop being one of them) subsequently came over to the philosophy department and did PhD dissertations under my direction. Bishop has since written many works, some of which I have quoted here addressing the potential relations between physics, complex systems, and libertarian free will (see, e.g., Bishop 2011 and Bishop and Atmanspacher 2011). Harald Atmanspacher has been head of the Department for Theory and Data Analysis at the Institute for Frontier Areas in Psychology in Freiburg, Germany, and founding editor of the journal *Mind and Matter*. His writings, sometimes with other scientists and philosophers, including Bishop, have also influenced my thinking about the relationship of free will to contemporary developments in the natural sciences. (See, e.g., Atmanspacher and P. beim Graben 2007.) Other figures, whose work I first encountered at a conference in the Netherlands, have influenced my thinking on these matters, include Thomas Mueller and Hans Briegel (2018), as well as others encountered at a conference in Spain in which I participated, "Is Science Compatible With Free Will?" (Antoine Suarez and

P. Adams 2013), and others at a conference in Milan, Italy, "Quantum Physics Meets the Philosophy of Mind" (Antonella Corradini and Uwe Meixner 2014). Prigogine was also sympathetic to the work of Bishop and Atmanspacher as well as to my own work on free will, which we discussed on a number of occasions.

9. And in P137–P141, P143, P154–P155.
10. AC libertarians maintain we are irreducible agents who, by acting, settle matters that aren't already settled. This implies that the neural matters underlying the exercise of our agency don't conform to deterministic laws, but it does not appear to exclude the possibility that they conform to statistical laws. Pereboom argues, in response, in his *Living without Free Will*, that, if these neural matters conform to either statistical or deterministic physical laws, the complete conformity of an irreducible agent's settling of matters with what should be expected given the applicable laws would involve coincidences too wild to be credible. Jason Runyan (2018) has effectively to my mind countered this argument by showing that the wild coincidence objection is an empirical objection lacking empirical support.

Chapter 9

1. Classical compatibilists, such as Hobbes ([1654] 1999), rejected any such notion of the will as a power to be the ultimate source of our ends or purposes and defined freedom simply as the absence of constraints or impediments preventing us from doing what we want or desire to do. Like other classical compatibilists, Hobbes tended to focus on external constraints or impediments to action, such as physical restraint, coercion, covert control, lack of ability (e.g., being paralyzed or unable to swim), lack of opportunity, political oppression, and the like.
2. A particularly insightful critique of Frankfurt's "real self" view is Lippert-Rasmussen 2003. See also Agnieszka Jaworska 2017, which is an informative survey of various "mesh theories" of libertarian free will, treating their advantages, but also some of their difficulties.
3. A related version of this reason view of Wolf's has recently been defended by Dana Nelkin (2012). Nelkin also defends an asymmetry thesis according to which praiseworthy conduct does not require the freedom to do otherwise, but blameworthy conduct does. Nelkin's work in general has contributed much to contemporary defenses of compatibilism.
4. For insightful further discussion of this "semi-compatibilist" position, see articles by Taylor Cyr (2017) and Cyr and Philip Swenson (2019).
5. Even if we could suspend them, he argues, it would be irrational to do so since the losses to human life would far outweigh any reasons we might have to suspend them. Why, he argues, should esoteric discoveries of physicists or chemists or neuroscientists about the behavior of electrons, amino acids, or nerve cells lead us to abandon these reactive attitudes toward other humans in our everyday practices?
6. For further enlightening discussion of Strawson's view and Strawsonian theories in general, see Pamela Hieronomi's insightful and comprehensive defense of a

Strawsonian view (2020); Angela Smith's (2007) discussion of holding and being responsible, which includes reflections on Strawson's views; Paul Russell's critical survey of Strawsonian theories of responsibility (2017a), and the collection of essays on Strawson's "Freedom and Resentment" edited by Michael McKenna and Paul Russell (2008).

7. Another figure who has put forth a theory of responsibility along Strawsonian lines, while adding many nuances to it, is David Shoemaker. In his important work *Responsibility from the Margins* (2015a), he distinguishes three distinct types of responsibility—attributability, answerability, and accountability—and shows how they are related to different reactive attitudes in Strawson's sense. He applies this tripartite account to various hard cases of assigning responsibility to persons who are at the "margins" of moral community, such as psychopaths. Psychopaths are not responsible in the accountability sense due to their incapacity for empathy. But they may still be responsible for some forms of rational judgment, according to Shoemaker, and to that extent may be considered responsible in the attributability and answerability senses. Angela Smith (2012) also discusses these three types of responsibility in enlightening ways and tries to develop a unified account of the three of them.

8. Other authors sympathetic to compatibilism in one form or another that I have not mentioned in this chapter, but from whose writings I have learned in writing this book include Marina Oshana (2018), Joanna Rigato (2015, 2018), Niels Miltenberg and Dawa Ometto (2019), and Patricia Greenspan (2012).

9. Vihvelin (2017, pp. 52–61) has provided an astute and informative critical survey of contemporary Dispositional Compatibilist views.

10. In a number of impressive works Scott Sehon (2005, 2016) argues that explanations of actions in terms of *reasons* and *purposes* are teleological explanations and cannot be reduced to explanations in terms of *causes*. He contends, however, that this is quite consistent with compatibilist views of free and responsible action and does not by itself require incompatibilism. This is evident in the title of his most recent book on the subject, *Free Will and Action Explanation: A Non-causal Compatibilist Account* (2016). Another original and insightful work by G. F. Schueler, *Reasons and Purposes: Human Rationality and Teleological Explanations of Action* (2003) also argues against the (Humean) idea that reasons explanations of action are causal explanations. This Humean idea overlooks two crucial points, he argues, namely that reasons explanations are teleological explanations and that they are normative explanations, since it is possible that the agent's reasons for an action are not good reasons. Schueler does not take a definite position, however, on compatibilism vs. incompatibilism. Other astute and relevant papers in this connection include Richard Feldman 2004; Andrei Buchareff 2015' Michael Esfeld 2021; and Reid Blackman 2015.

11. Lengthy and enlightening critical studies of List's view include Nadine Elzein and Tuomas Pernu 2017; Kaiserman and Kodsi 2021; and Gebharter 2020.

12. Others include C. Weigel 2013 and Kelly McCormick 2013. McCormick 2017 is an excellent overview and defense of current revisionist views. Additional influential compatibilist views I have not discussed in this chapter include Huoranzski 2011. His view has had significant influence on European philosophers on free will and includes criticisms of my former views. Hilary Bok's *Freedom and Responsibility* (1998), also

offers an original conditional and mesh account of compatibilist free will which involves improvements over traditional conditional accounts. Haji 2002 is a critical assessment of Bok's complex view.
13. Balaguer also mentions neuroscientists who make these points, including Dayan and Abbott (2001). An important work that also needs to be mentioned in this connection is Busemeyer and Bruza's *Quantum Models of Cognition and Decision* (2012). It includes an extensive bibliography of further scientific work on the relation of quantum modeling for cognitive functioning in the brain.
14. An excellent critical discussion of Vargas's revisionism that makes many of these points is Nadine Elzein 2013. Elzein is author of many articles, including this one, defending a libertarian approach to free will from which I have learned in writing this work. In another important essay, "Conflicting Reasons and Freedom of Will" (2010), she argues cogently for the critical role of conflicts in the will to libertarian conceptions of free will that is consonant with my view. Similarly, she has discussed (2018) how libertarians might respond to demands for contrastive explanations. And, as noted above (n. 12) with coauthor Tuomas Pernu (2017) she has authored a critique of Christian List's libertarian compatibilist view, which they refer to as "supervenient freedom."
15. A second and updated version of this *Four Views of Free Will* book is scheduled to be published in 2024, with updated views of each of the four contributors.
16. For the printed version of my contribution to this panel discussion, see Kane 2010b.
17. Another important recent work that throws further light on the issues discussed in this and earlier chapters but does not take an exclusively compatibilist stance is Ann Whittle's *Freedom and Responsibility in Context* (2022). She argues that an understanding of the situations in which we attribute freedom and moral responsibility to agents supports the thesis that attributions of freedom and moral responsibility are context dependent. This resulting contextualism then offers, she argues, a rapprochement of compatibilism and incompatibilism. Both positions can be said to be right, depending on the context, since there is no "right" answer to the question of whether or not determinism undermines freedom and moral responsibility. Note that there are some similarities here to the view of this book, which also holds that some libertarian free actions (namely self-forming ones) must be incompatible with determinism, while other libertarian free actions may be compatible with determinism, so long as they follow from some self-forming actions. But it doesn't follow from this view that there is no right answer to whether or not determinism undermines an incompatibilist account of freedom and responsibility. For what cannot be the case if an incompatibilist view of free will of this kind is true is that *all* free and responsible actions could be compatible with determinism. *Some* crucial choices or actions must be *incompatible* with determinism if an incompatibilist or libertarian account of free and responsible actions is to exist, even if not all libertarian free and responsible actions need be incompatible with determinism. For if some free and responsible actions must be incompatible with determinism, then if *libertarian* and hence incompaibilist free and responsible actions exist, *universal determinism must be false.* Whereas if compatibilism was true, we could have all the freedom and responsibility that was possible even if determinism was universally true.

Chapter 10

1. Views of Pereboom, G. Strawson, Levy, and Caruso are discussed in greater length in this chapter. Bruce Waller has written a number of influential works (1990, 2011, 2014) in which he is skeptical of moral responsibility and the entire "moral responsibility system," but not of free will, though he is also skeptical of incompatibilist forms of free will. Ted Honderich (1988) argues for determinism and for skepticism about free will. Tamler Sommers 2012 offers original and challenging arguments for free will skepticism based on the diversity of views about free will and responsibility in different cultures. His book is especially enlightening about the cultural diversity of views on the subject. Thomas Nadelhoffer (2011) and Benjamin Vilhauer (2015) offer novel and intriguing arguments as to why we should take free will skepticism seriously. Farah Focquaert and Elizabeth Shaw have joined with Pereboom and Caruso to found what is called the Justice Without Retribution Network, which discusses the legal and criminal implications of free will skepticism. See Farah Focquaert, Gregg Caruso, Elizabeth Shaw, and Derk Pereboom (2020).
2. Another instructive recent work on luck that does not draw Levy's free will skeptical conclusions is E. J. Coffman's *Luck: Its Nature and Significance for Human Freedom and Agency* (2015).
3. For further criticisms of Levy's view see Tognazzini 2013 and Franklin 2013b.
4. Manipulation Arguments have played an important role in free will debates. Though I do not make them central to my own arguments, there is much to learn from them. See, for example, Double 1989; Long 2004; Fischer 2012; McKenna 2008a, 2014a; Haji 2009; Todd Patrick 2011; Kearns 2012; Swinburne 2013a; Deery and Nahmias 2017; Mickelson 2017; Franklin 2018; Huoranszki 2021; Mele 2019.
5. For further discussion of this point, see Levy 2020, pp. 79–91.
6. If we accept "an incompatibilist interpretation of responsibility and the reactive attitudes" based on UR, "it would be contradictory to conclude that incompatibilist free will and ultimate responsibility cannot be matters of degree or cannot be lessened by circumstances."
7. Caruso and Pereboom have coauthored a recent book (*Moral Responsibility Revisited*, 2022) which is a comprehensive defense of the free will skepticism they both hold.
8. Russell, whose "free will pessimism" view was discussed in the previous chapter, would not follow Caruso in accepting this final conclusion.
9. For a similar response, see Ken Levy 2023, pp. 461–62.
10. Free will skeptics have an initial answer to it, which Caruso suggests in this debate by appealing to Pereboom's four-case manipulation argument, among other arguments. The answer can be best described in terms of the first two cases of Pereboom's argument. In Case 1, Plum is manipulated to kill White by neuroscientists who have control over Plum's brain. In Case 2, the neuroscientists intentionally program Plum from the beginning of his life to be egoistic in a manner that leads him to kill White. If we want to understand basic desert, as free will skeptics understand it, we must ask who is basically deserving of blame for this killing. And the answer would be the neuroscientists, who intentionally brought it about that Plum would do this in a

manner that would not allow Plum to have done otherwise. For a "hard line" reply to this four-case argument, see Sofia Jeppsson 2020.
11. Both Pereboom and Caruso, for example, allow for the possibility that agent-causal libertarian views might be conceptually coherent, but they go on to argue that such views cannot be shown to be empirically justified. They would be "worth wanting" if shown to be intelligible in this way, even if they were not empirically possible.
12. The result is a qualitative change in the evolutionary process, by which ways of living and acting within a single species are indefinitely multiplied and the importance of individuals of the species in the selection process (each with his or her own internal rational environment) is immeasurably enhanced.
13. Ways of living and acting could thereby be tested and rejected internally without requiring actual experimentation and possible harm or death to the individual.
14. Smilansky cites Galen Strawson's 1986, 1994, 2002 and notes that in Chapter 4 of his book *Free Will And Illusion*, he offers a moralized version of Galen Strawson's Basic Argument.

Chapter 11

1. "The Ends of Metaphysics" (1993), *Through the Moral Maze* (1994). An updated development of the views first introduced in these works is my *Ethics and the Quest for Wisdom* (2010a).
2. Tom Seung, an excellent philosopher and longtime friend and colleague, alerted me to these Kantian questions. Tom, who defected from North Korea to the south during the Korean War, graduated from Yale College with highest honors after the war. He went on to Yale graduate school, getting his PhD in philosophy a short time after I received my own degree there. Six years after that we were reunited in the department of philosophy at the University of Texas, where our families and children were friendly for many decades. Tom was an original thinker with a sharp critical mind, who influenced my thinking about many issues. A few years ago Tom moved with his dear wife back to his native Korea, where he passed away.
3. In the past few years, the notion of "aspiration" has been made a subject of widespread discussion inspired by an admirably original and insightful book on the subject by philosopher Agnes Callard: *Aspiration: The Agency of Becoming* (2018). To fully address the relationship between her notion of aspiration in this work and my own conception of aspiration in the earlier works beginning in the 1990s would require another book as lengthy as this one. But I will briefly discuss some of the parallels and differences in the two views here as a stimulus to further discussion. Callard says that aspiration as she understands it in her book "is a distinctive form of agency directed at the acquisition of values" (p. 4). "The aspirant sees that she does not have the values she would like to have and seeks to move herself toward a better valuational condition. She senses that there is more out there to value and she strives to see what she cannot get fully in view" (p. 5). "The work of aspiration includes, but is not limited to, the mental work of thinking, imagining

and reasoning" (p. 5). She adds that "the English word 'aspiration' is a good but not perfect label for the concept I aim to explicate, namely, *rational value acquisition*" (p. 6). Aspiration she says is a kind of work, the work of self-creation, of acquiring new values which often involves effort or struggle (p. 180). I agree with all this: it is also involved in what I refer to as "self-formation." But there are some instructive differences. By relating aspiration to Kant's three questions as I do, I include value acquisition in ways much like she does, but I also include more. Consider Kant's first two questions: "What can we know?" and "How should we act and live? They involve as I noted in these earlier works the two great topics of metaphysics—the True and the Good. And both are objects of aspiration in my view. Aspirations to the good as I see them are similar in many ways to aspiration as Callard sees it in her book. But I also emphasize the role of aspiration in connection with searches for objective truth. Consider the examples of such aspiration that I use in this book and have used in earlier works, e.g., (P389): "What aspiration adds to rational inquiry is a recognition of the radical contingency of such inquiry, without precluding the possibility of success. The searches of scientists for the ultimate truths about the natural world or the fundamental laws of nature have the characteristics of searches in the realm of aspiration in this sense—owing to the fact that the scientists cannot know with certainty that they have attained the final truths or fundamental laws of nature *even if they have in fact attained them*. Any explanatory scheme they have may be incomplete or falsified by future discoveries or experiments. Scientists who have such lofty goals aspire to something of great importance (the ultimate truths about nature), which for all they know is attainable, but whose attainment is difficult and not assured. There are actions they can perform (consider all available evidence, do experiments, criticize existing theories, look for more precise and comprehensive explanations) they believe will lead to the goal, not guaranteeing its attainment, but such that failing to undertake these actions would mean abandoning aspirations to attain the goal." The same is true of philosophical quest for the true as well as the good. And it is especially true of the metaphysical dimensions of the free will problem which have to do with ultimate responsibility and ultimate desert and which must relate these notions to what we can know about the physical world and human existence. To formulate a view that will capture these notions and be consistent with both science and philosophy will not guarantee attainment of the goal, but failing to undertake these tasks would mean abandoning aspirations to attain this goal. Yet, wherever it functions, the point of speaking of aspiration rather than mere hope is to highlight the difficulty and effort required to persist in the search for cherished goals and high ideals. "Aspiration," as I said, is an apt word for this radically contingent seeking. As stated in (P395) "we cannot show with certainly that such a free will exists. But what we can do, *if we aspire to rationally believe in it*, is do our best to show what such a free will would have to look like if it did exist; . . . and to show that it is an intelligible and possible ideal, by arguing that the most common objections that have been raised to its possibility fail to show that it is an unintelligible or impossible, and by showing how it might be possible (though certainly not proven) given what is known in contemporary physics and other sciences, including the neurosciences." By further relating it to moral responsibility of an ultimate kind, we can also say something about the implications of such a search for the Good as well as the True, the two ends of metaphysics. Callard's book tells us much about the relation of aspiration to the Good and the potential relation of aspiration to the True, since seeking the good to which we aspire is related to seeking the truth of who we are. It is an important work.

4. Instructive and insightful accounts of Kant's view of free will are Vilhauer 2010 and 2017.

5. See, e.g. Riccardo Repetti 2014, Mark Siderits 1987, "Beyond Compatibilism: A Buddhist Approach to Freedom and Determinism" and Arindam Chakrabarti's excellent survey of Indian philosophies, 2017. See also Bronwyn Finnegan's insightful 2022. I owe a special debt to Sivagami Nateson and her husband Chinna who were our neighbors in Rollingwood, Texas for many years, and provided my wife and me with many insights and readings about Indian religious and philosophical traditions.

6. Others have countered this, see e.g. Gier and Kjellberg 2004.

7. The literature on these issues in theistic traditions is vast. A selection of relevant readings includes Fischer and Todd 2015; Grant 2016; Murray 1993; and Pruss 2016. Vicens 2017 is an insightful overview of various theological positions on theological determinism and free will, including traditional positions of medieval philosophers and modern positions. She brings out difficulties in each of these views, traditional and modern, and argues that the Consequence Argument for libertarian free will poses problems for reconciling free will and theological determinism. An instructive collection of essays on theological determinism by various thinkers is Leigh Vicens and Simon Kittle 2019. Thomas Talbott (2008) argues persuasively that Christians who accept the goodness of God and the sinfulness of humans should reject theological determinism. He further argues that they should reject theological determinism, even if they also reject libertarian free will in humans. Lynne Baker Rudder (2003) offers challenging arguments as to why Christians should not be libertarians. Other works on these issues from which I have learned much include Judisch 2016; Koons 2002; and Cover and O'Leary-Hawthorne 1996. See also Zagzebski 2022 for an interesting treatment of these issues.

8. In a recent article, "Elucidating Open Theism" (2023), Joshua R. Sijuwade defends a variant of what has come to be called in recent times "open theism," the view that while God can be understood as maximally great in being, knowledge, goodness and other features, the future is nonetheless causally, epistemically and providentially open. In this article, he attempts to make sense of such an open theism and to answer many objections against it by appealing to a notion of libertarian free will in creatures of the kind developed in my works involving ultimate responsibility and self-forming actions. I agree with much that he says in this article on this complex issue. In another interesting and well-argued article, "Mormonism and Determinism," Blake T. Ostler (2023) argues that a similar openness approach would be most consistent with Mormon beliefs about God. I became sympathetic to open theism through a long-time friendship with Charles Hartshorne, who was a colleague in the Department of Philosophy at the University of Texas for many years. Hartshorne came to such a view in developing the "process philosophy" of is own teacher and mentor, Alfred North Whitehead.

9. I was surprised to find, in reading an interesting and insightful account of Hegel's views of free will by Christopher Yeomans (2017, pp. 362–63) that some of these themes in my work expressed in P436 and earlier pieces can also be found in Hegel. In making this comparison, Yeomans cites a quotation from my work (Kane 1999, p. 144): "Paradoxical as it may seem, in order to have *ultimate* control over their destinies, possessors of free will must relinquish another kind of control at pivotal points in their life histories, namely, an antecedent determining control that would guarantee how things will turn out in advance." Yeomans then adds that "Hegel deeply accepts this paradox in his analysis of human free will. On the one hand, our rational will makes possible an active mental life that is of infinite value and is worthy of fundamental respect. On the other hand, the deep necessities of character that manifest themselves in that life are always also contingent.... As with Kane, Hegel sees within each agent an internal plurality of goals that coexist ... in sometimes uneasy tension with each other. The executive function of the will involves managing that tension.... This is a tough and interminable task.... But we do sometimes succeed and such success is a real achievement. Free will would not be worthy of such respect if it were not so difficult."

References

This list of References includes, in addition to the works cited in the text and in the notes of the book, other works not cited in the text and notes, that have influenced my thinking about the issues discussed in the book and that are recommended reading for anyone interested in doing further research on the subject matter.

Acker, Shathy. 2022. "Liberal Compatibilism: A Proposal." Unpublished Manuscript.
Adams, Robert M. 1990. "Middle Land the Problem of Evil." In *The Problem of Evil*, edited by Marilyn McCord Adams and Robert M. Adams, pp. 110–25. Oxford: Oxford University Press.
Advayananda, Swami. 2018. "The Gordian Knot of Self-effort and Destiny." In *Center for Sanskrit Research and Indology*, pp.1–56. Kerala, India: Chinmaya International Foundation.
Allen, Robert. 2007. "Self-Forming Actions: The Genesis of Free Will." *Proceedings of the American Catholic Association* 81: pp. 263–78.
Almeida, M., and Mark Bernstein. 2003. "Lucky Libertarianism." *Philosophical Studies* 113: pp. 93–119.
Altschuler, Roman. 2010. "An Unconditional Will." PhD dissertation, Stony Brook University.
Altschuler, Roman. 2015. "Character, Will and Agency." In *From Personality to Virtue: Essays on the Philosophy of Character*, edited by D. Webber and R. Masala, pp. 95–109. Oxford: Oxford University Press.
Alvarez, Maria. 2009. "Actions, Thought Experiments, and the 'Principle of Alternate Possibilities.'" *Australasian Journal of Philosophy* 85 (1): pp. 61–81. https://doi.org/10.1080/00048400802215505.
Alvarez, Maria, and John Hyman. 1998. "Agents and Their Actions." *Philosophy* 73: pp. 219–45.
Amaya, Santiago. 2023."'Free Will' Is Vague." *Philosophical Issues* 33: pp. 7–21.
Anglin, W. S. 1991. *Free Will and the Christian Faith*. Oxford: Oxford University Press.
Anscombe, G. E. M. 1971. *Causality and Determinism*. Cambridge: Cambridge University Press.
Aquinas, Thomas. 1945. *Basic Writings of Saint Thomas Aquinas*. 2 vols. New York: Random House.
Aristotle. 1985. *Nicomachean Ethics*. Translated by Terence Irwin. Indianapolis: Hackett.
Arpaly, Nomy. 2003. *Unprincipled Virtue: An Inquiry into Moral Agency*. New York: Oxford University Press.
Arpaly, Nomy. 2004. "Which Autonomy?" In *Freedom and Determinism*, edited by Joseph Keim Campbell, Michael O'Rourke, and David Shier, pp. 173–88. Cambridge, MA: MIT Press.
Arvan, M. 2013. "A New Theory of Free Will." *Philosophical Forum* 44 (1): pp. 1–48.

Atmanspacher, Harald. 2006. "Quantum Approaches to Consciousness." In *The Stanford Encyclopedia of Philosophy* (Winter 2006 ed.), edited by Edward N. Zalta. https://plato.stanford.edu/archives/win2006/entries/qt-consciousness/.

Atmanspacher, Harald, and P. beim Graben. 2007. "Contextual Emergence of Mental States from Neurodynamics." *Chaos and Complexity Letters* 2: pp. 151–68.

Augustine. 1993. *On the Free Choice of the Will.* Translated by Thomas Williams. Indianapolis: Hackett Publishing.

Austin, J. L. 1961. "Ifs and Cans." In *Philosophical Papers*, edited by J. O. Urmson and G. Warnock, pp. 153–80. Oxford: Clarendon Press.

Ayer, A. J. 1954. "Freedom and Necessity." In his *Philosophical Essays*, pp. 3–20. New York: St. Martin's Press.

Ayers, Michael. 1968. *The Refutation of Determinism.* London: Methuen.

Backmann, Marius. 2013. *Humean Libertarianism.* Heusenstarm: Ontos Verlag.

Baker, G., and J. Gollub. 1990. *Chaotic Dynamics: An Introduction.* Cambridge: Cambridge University Press.

Baker, Lynne Rudder. 2003. "Why Christians Should Not Be Libertarians: An Augustinian Challenge." *Faith and Philosophy* 20 (4): pp. 460–78.

Balaguer, Mark. 2010. *Free Will as an Open Scientific Problem.* Cambridge, MA: MIT Press.

Balaguer, Mark. 2014. "Replies to McKenna, Pereboom, and Kane." *Philosophical Studies* 169: pp. 71–92.

Baumeister, Roy F. 2008. "Free Will in Scientific Psychology." *Perspectives in Psychological Science* 3: pp. 14–19.

Bayne, Tim. 2017. "Free Will and the Phenomenology of Agency." In *The Routledge Companion to Free Will*, edited by Kevin Timpe, Meghan Griffith, and Neil Levy, pp. 633–44. New York: Routledge.

Bechtel, W., ed. 2001. *Philosophy and the Neurosciences: A Reader.* Malden, MA: Blackwell.

Beebee, Helen. 2002. "Reply to Huemer on the Consequence Argument." *Philosophical Review* 111(2): pp. 235–41. https://doi.org/10.1215/00318108-111-2-235.

Beebee, Helen. 2003. "Local Miracle Compatibilism." *Noûs* 37 (2): pp. 258–77. https://doi.org/10.1111/1468-0068.00438.

Beebee, Helen. 2013. *Free Will: An Introduction.* New York: Palgrave Macmillan.

Beebee, Helen. 2014. "Radical Indeterminism and Top-Down Causation." *Res Philosophica* 91: pp. 537–45.

Beebee, Helen, and Alfred Mele. 2002. "Humean Compatibilism." *Mind* 111 (442): pp. 201–23. https://doi.org/10.1093/mind/111.442.201.

Berofsky, Bernard. 2003. "Classical Compatibilism: Not Dead Yet." In *Moral Responsibility and Alternative Possibilities: Essays on the Importance of Alternative Possibilities*, edited by David Widerker and Michael McKenna, pp. 107–26. Aldershot, UK: Ashgate.

Berofsky, Bernard. 2006. "Global Control and Freedom." *Philosophical Studies* 131 (2): pp. 419–45. https://doi.org/10.1007/s11098-004-7490-1.

Berofsky, Bernard. 2012. *Nature's Challenge to Free Will.* Oxford: Oxford University Press.

Bishop, John. 1989. *Natural Agency: An Essay on the Causal Theory of Action.* New York: Cambridge University Press.

Bishop, Robert C. 2011. "Chaos, Indeterminism, and Free Will." In *The Oxford Handbook of Free Will*, 2nd ed., edited by Robert Kane, pp. 84–100. New York: Oxford University Press.

Bishop, Robert, and Harald Atmanspacher. 2011. "The Causal Closure of Physics and Free Will." In *The Oxford Handbook of Free Will*, 2nd ed., edited by Robert Kane, pp. 101–11. New York: Oxford University Press.

Bjornsson, Gunnar. 2015. "Incompatibilism and Bypassed Agency." In *Surrounding Free Will: Philosophy, Psychology and Neuroscience*, edited by Alfred R. Mele, pp. 95–122. Oxford: Oxford University Press.

Bjornsson, Gunnar. 2022. "Experimental Philosophy and Moral Responsibility." In *The Oxford Handbook of Moral Responsibility*, edited by Dana K. Nelkin and Derk Pereboom, pp. 494–516. New York: Oxford University Press.

Bjornsson, Gunnar, and Derk Pereboom. 2016. "Traditional and Experimental Approaches to Free Will and Moral Responsibility." In edited by J. Systema and W. Buckwalter, pp. 57–75. Blackwell.

Bjornsson, Gunnar, and Karl Persson. 2013. "A Unified Empirical Account of Responsibility Judgments." *Philosophy and Phenomenological Research*.87: pp. 6.

Blackman, Reid. 2015. "Why Compatibilists Need Alternative Possibilities." *Erkenntnis* 81: pp. 529–44. https://doi.org/10.1007/s10670-015-9753-y.

Bobzien, Suzanne. 1998a. *Determinism and Freedom in Stoic Philosophy*. New York: Oxford University Press.

Bobzien, Suzanne. 1998b. "The Inadvertent Conception and Late Birth of the Free Will Problem." *Phronesis* 43: pp. 133–75.

Bok, Hilary. 1998. *Freedom and Responsibility*. Princeton, NJ: Princeton University Press.

Bramhall, John. [1655] 1999. "Bramhall's Discourse of Liberty and Necessity." In *Hobbes and Bramhall on Liberty and Necessity*, edited by Vere Chappell, pp. 1–14. Cambridge: Cambridge University Press.

Brand, Myles. 1979. "The Fundamental Question in Action Theory." *Noûs* 13: pp. 131–51.

Bratman, Michael. 2000. "Reflection, Planning, and Temporally Extended Agency." *Philosophical Review* 109: pp. 35–61.

Bratman, Michael. 2005. "Planning Agency, Autonomous Agency." In *Personal Autonomy*, edited by James Stacey Taylor, pp. 34–48. New York: Cambridge University Press.

Brembs, Bjorn. 2011. "Towards a Scientific Concept of Free Will as a Biological Trait." *Proceedings of the Royal Society B: Biological Sciences* 278: pp. 930–39. https://doi.org/10.1098/rspb.2010.2325.

Briegel, Hans J., and Thomas Mueller. 2015. "A Chance for Attributable Agency." *Minds & Machines* 25: pp. 261–79.

Brink, David, and Dana Nelkin. 2013. "Fairness and the Architecture of Responsibility." In *Oxford Studies in Agency and Responsibility*, edited by David Shoemaker, vol. 1, pp. 284–313. New York: Oxford University Press.

Broad, C. D. 1952. "Determinism, Indeterminism, and Libertarianism." In his *Ethics and the History of Philosophy: Selected Essays*, pp. 78–94. London: Routledge & Kegan Paul.

Buchareff, Andrei. 2015. "How Does Agent-Causal Power Work?" *Modern Schoolman* 25: pp. 28–43.

Buckareff, Andrei, Carlos Moya, and Sergi Rosell, eds. 2015. *Agency, Freedom and Moral Responsibility*. New York: Palgrave Macmillan.

Busemeyer, Jerome R., and Peter Bruza. 2012. *Quantum Models of Cognition and Decision*. Cambridge: Cambridge University Press.

Callard, Agnes. 2018. *Aspiration: The Agency of Becoming*. Oxford: Oxford University Press.

Campbell, C. A. 1951. "Is 'Freewill' a Pseudo-Problem?" *Mind* 60: pp. 441–65.

Campbell, Joseph Keim. 2005. "Compatibilist Alternatives." *Canadian Journal of Philosophy* 35 (3): 387–406. https://doi.org/10.1080/00455091.2005.10716595.

Campbell, Joseph Keim. 2007. "Free Will and the Necessity of the Past." *Analysis* 67 (2): pp. 105–11. https://doi.org/10.1093/analys/67.2.105.

Campbell, Joseph Keim. 2017. "The Consequence Argument." In *The Routledge Companion to Free Will*, edited by Kevin Timpe, Meghan Griffith, and Neil Levy, pp. 151–65. New York: Routledge.

Campbell, Joseph Keim, Kristin Michelson, and V. Alan White, eds. 2023. *A Companion to Free Will*. Hoboken, NJ: John Wiley and Sons.

Campbell, Joseph Keim, Michael O'Rourke, and David Shier, eds. 2004. *Freedom and Determinism*. Cambridge, MA: MIT Press.

Campbell, Neil. 2020. "Self-Formation, Contrastive Explanations and the Structure of the Will." *Synthese* 197: pp. 1225–40.

Campbell, Neil. 2023. "Quasation and the Physical Indeterminist Luck Objection: A Reply to Moore." *Philosophia* 51: pp. 1129–42.

Capes, Justin A. 2016. "Blameworthiness and Buffered Alternatives." *American Philosophical Quarterly* 53: pp. 269–80.

Capes, Justin A. 2017. "Freedom with Causation." *Erkenntnis* 82: pp. 327–38.

Capes, Justin A. 2019. "What the Consequence Argument Is an Argument For." *Thought* 8 (1): pp. 50–56. https://doi.org/10.1002/tht3.404.

Capes, Justin A. 2023. *Moral Responsibility and the Flicker of Freedom*. Oxford: Oxford University Press.

Capes, Justin A., and Philip Swenson. 2017. "Frankfurt Cases: The Fine-Grained Response Revisited." *Philosophical Studies* 174: pp. 967–81.

Carlson, Erik. 2000. "Incompatibilism and the Transfer of Power Necessity." *Noûs* 34 (2): pp. 277–90. https://doi.org/10.1111/0029-4624.00211.

Caruso, Gregg D. 2012. *Free Will and Consciousness: A Determinist Account of the Illusion of Free Will*. Lanham, MD: Lexington Books.

Caruso, Gregg D. 2016. "Free Will Skepticism and Criminal Behavior: A Public Health Quarantine Model." *Southwest Philosophy Review* 32: pp. 25–48.

Caruso, Gregg D. 2017. "Free Will Skepticism and the Question of Creativity." *Ergo* 3(23): pp. 591–607.

Caruso, Gregg D., and Derk Pereboom. 2022. *Moral Responsibility Reconsidered*. Cambridge: Cambridge University Press.

Chakrabarti, Arindam. 2017. "Free Will and Freedom in Indian Philosophies." In *The Routledge Companion to Free Will*, edited by Kevin Timpe, Meghan Griffith, and Neil Levy, pp. 389–404. New York: Routledge.

Chan, Hoi-Yee, Max Deutsch, and Shaun Nichols. 2016. "Free Will and Experimental Philosophy." In *A Companion to Experimental Philosophy*, edited by Justus Sytsma and Wesley Buchhalter, pp. 158–73. Hoboken, NJ: John Wiley and Sons.

Chisholm, Roderick M. 1964. "Human Freedom and the Self." *The Lindley Lectures*, Department of Philosophy, University of Kansas.

Chisholm, Roderick M. 1966. "Freedom and Action." In *Freedom and Determinism*, edited by Keith Lehrer, pp. 11–40. New York: Random House.

Christman, John. 1991. "Autonomy and Personal History." *Canadian Journal of Philosophy* 21 (1): pp. 1–24.

Clarke, Randolph. 1996. "Agent Causation and Event Causation in the Production of Free Action." *Philosophical Topics* 24: pp. 19–48.

Clarke, Randolph. 2003. *Libertarian Accounts of Free Will*. Oxford: Oxford University Press.

Clarke, Randolph. 2009. "Dispositions, Abilities to Act, and Free Will: The New Dispositionalism." *Mind* 118: pp. 323–51.

Clarke, Randolph. 2011. "Alternatives for Libertarians." In *The Oxford Handbook of Free Will*, 2nd ed., edited by Robert Kane, pp. 329–48. New York: Oxford University Press.

Clarke, Randolph, Justin Capes, and Philip Swenson. 2021. "Incompatibilist (Nondeterministic) Theories of Free Will." *Stanford Encyclopedia of Philosophy.* https://plato.stanford.edu/entries/incompatibilist-theories.

Clarke, Randolph., M. McKenna, and Angela Smith. 2015. *The Nature of Moral Responsibility: New Essays*. Oxford: Oxford University Press.

Clarke, Randolph, and Thomas Reed. 2015. "Free Will and Agential Powers." *Oxford Studies in Agency and Moral Responsibility* 3: pp. 6–33.

Coates, D. J., and Neal Tognazzini, eds. 2013. *Blame: Its Nature and Norms.* Oxford: Oxford University Press.

Coburn, John S. J. 2008. *Predestination and Free Will*. Milwaukee: Marquette University Press.

Coffman, E. J. 2015. *Luck: Its Nature and Significance for Human Knowledge and Agency.* Basingstoke, UK: Palgrave Macmillan.

Cogley, Zac. 2015. "Rolling Back the Luck Problem for Libertarians." *Journal of Cognition and Neuroethics* 3 (1): pp. 121–37.

Cohen, Yishai. 2017. "Fischer's Deterministic Frankfurt-Style Argument." *Erkenntnis* 82: pp. 121–40.

Colen, Jose. 2016. "Review of David Palmer (ed.) Libertarian Free Will: Contemporary Debates." *Ethical Perspectives* 23: pp. 362–66.

Compton, A. H. 1935. *The Freedom of Man*. New Haven, CT: Yale University Press.

Copp, David. 1997. "Defending the Principle of Alternative Possibilities: Blameworthiness and Moral Responsibility." *Nous* 31: pp. 441–56.

Copp, David. 2008. "Ought Implies Can and the Derivation of the Principle of Alternative Possibilities." *Analysis* 68: pp. 67–75.

Corradini, Antonella, and Uwe Meixner, eds. 2014. *Quantum Theory Meets Philosophy of Mind*. Berlin: de Gruyter.

Couenhoven, Jesse. 2007. "Augustine's Rejection of the Free-Will Defence: An Overview of the Late Augustine's Theodicy." *Religious Studies* 43 (3): pp. 279–98.

Cover, J. A., and J. O'Leary-Hawthorne. 1996. "Free Agency and Materialism." In *Faith, Freedom and Rationality*, edited by J. Jordan and D. Howard-Snyder, pp. 47–71. Lanham, MD: Rowman and Littlefield.

Craig, William. 1990. *Divine Foreknowledge and Human Freedom*. Leiden: Brill.

Cross, Charles. 1986. "'Can' and the Logic of Ability." *Philosophical Studies* 50 (1): pp. 53–64. https://doi.org/10.1007/BF00355160.

Cutter, Brian. 2017. "What Is the Consequence Argument an Argument For?" *Analysis* 77 (2): pp. 278–87. https://doi.org/10.1093/analys/anx052.

Cuypers, Stefan. 2006. "The Trouble with Externalist Compatibilist Autonomy." *Philosophical Studies* 129: pp. 171–96.

Cyr, Taylor W. 2017. "Semicompatibilism: No Ability to Do Otherwise Required." *Philosophical Explorations* 20 (3): pp. 308–21.

Cyr, Taylor W. 2019. "Moral Responsibility, Luck and Compatibilism." *Erkenntnis* 84 (1): pp. 184–214.

Cyr, Taylor W., and Philip Swenson. 2019. "Moral Responsibility without General Ability." *Philosophical Quarterly* 69 (274): pp. 22–40.

Davenport, John. 2007. *Will as Commitment and Resolve*. New York: Fordham University Press.

Davenport, John. 2013. "Norm Guided Formation of Cares without Volitional Necessity: A Reply to Frankfurt." *Philosophia* pp. 78–92.

Davidson, Donald. 1963. "Actions, Reasons, and Causes." *Journal of Philosophy* 60: pp. 685–700.

Davidson, Donald. 1973. "Freedom to Act." In *Essays on Freedom of Action*, edited by Ted Honderich, pp. 63–81. New York: Routledge and Kegan Paul.

Dayan P., and L. F. Abbott. 2001. *Theoretical Neuroscience*. Cambridge, MA: MIT Press.

Deacon, T. W. 2007. "Three Levels of Emergent Phenomena." In *Evolution and Emergence: Systems, Organisms, Persons*, edited by Nancey Murphy and William R. Stoeger, pp. 88–110. Oxford: Oxford University Press.

DeCaro, Mario. 2007. "How to Deal with the Free Will Issue: The Role of Conceptual Analysis and Empirical Science." In *Cartographies of the Mind: Philosophy and Psychology in Intersection*, edited by M. Maraffa, M. DeCaro, and F. Ferretti, pp. 255–68. Dordrecht: Springer.

Deery, Oisin. 2015a. "The Fall from Eden: Why Libertarianism Isn't Justified by Experience." *Australasian Journal of Philosophy* 93 (2): pp. 319–34. https://doi.org/10.1080/00048402.2014.968596.

Deery, Oisin. 2015b. "Why People Believe in Indeterminist Free Will." *Philosophical Studies* 172 (8): pp. 2033–54. https://doi.org/10.1007/s11098-014-0396-7.

Deery, Oisin, Matt Bedke, and Shaun Nichols. 2013. "Phenomenal Abilities: Incompatibilism and the Experience of Agency." In *Oxford Studies in Agency and Responsibility*, edited by David Shoemaker, vol. 1, pp. 126–50. New York: Oxford University Press.

Deery, Oisin, Taylor Davis, and Jasmine Carey. 2014. "The Free Will Intuitions Scale and the Question of Natural Compatibilism." *Philosophical Psychology* pp. 1–26.

Deery, Oisin, and Eddy Nahmias. 2017. "Defeating Manipulation Arguments: Interventionist Causation and Compatibilist Sourcehood." *Philosophical Studies* 174 (5): pp. 1255–76. https://doi.org/10.1007/s11098-016-0754-8.

Demetriou, Kristin. 2010. "The Soft-Line Solution to Pereboom's 4-Case Argument." *Australian Journal of Philosophy* 88: pp. 595–617.

Dennett, Daniel. 1978. "On Giving Libertarians What They Say They Want." In his *Brainstorms*, pp. 286–99. Cambridge, MA: MIT Press.

Dennett, Daniel. 1978a. *Brainstorms*. Cambridge, MA: MIT Press.

Dennett, Daniel. 1984. *Elbow Room: The Varieties of Free Will Worth Wanting*. Cambridge, MA: MIT Press.

Dennett, Daniel. 2003. *Freedom Evolves*. New York: Viking.

Dennett, Daniel, and Gregg Caruso. 2021. *Just Deserts: Debating Free Will*. Cambridge: Polity Press.

Descartes, René. 1641 [1988]. *Meditations on First Philosophy*. In *Selected Philosophical Writings*, edited and translated by John Cottingham, Robert Stoothoff, and Dugald Murdoch, pp. 73–121. Cambridge: Cambridge University Press.

Descartes, René 1644 [1988]. *Principles of Philosophy*. In *Selected Philosophical Writings*, edited by John Cottingham, Robert Stoothoff, and Dugald Murdoch, pp. 160–212. Cambridge: Cambridge University Press.

Diderot, Denis. 1746. *Pensées Philosophique*. In *The Encyclopedia of Diderot and D'Alembert*.

Dilman, Ilham. 1999. *Free Will: An Historical and Philosophical Introduction*. London: Routledge.

Dilworth, John. 2008. "Free Action as Two-Level Voluntary Control." *Philosophical Frontiers* 3:2, pp. 29–45.
Di Nucci, Ezio. 2011. "Frankfurt vs. Frankfurt: A New Anti-causalist Dawn." *Philosophical Explorations* 4 (1): pp. 117–31.
Donagan, Alan. 1985. *Human Ends and Human Actions: An Exploration in St. Thomas's Treatment*. Milwaukee: Marquette University Press.
Doris, John. 2015. *Talking to Our Selves: Reflection, Ignorance, and Agency*. Oxford: Oxford University Press.
Double, Richard. 1989. "Puppeteers, Hypnotists, and Neurosurgeons." *Philosophical Studies* 56 (2): pp. 163–73. Reprinted in Russell & Deery 2013: ch. 14. https://doi.org/10.1007/BF00355940.
Double, Richard. 1991. *The Non-reality of Free Will*. New York: Oxford University Press.
Double, Richard. 2002. "The Moral Hardness of Libertarianism." *Philo* 5: pp. 226–34.
Doyle, Robert. 2011. *Free Will: The Scandal in Philosophy*. Cambridge, MA: I-Phi Press.
Duns Scotus, John. 1986. "Questions on Aristotle's Metaphysics IX, Q.15." In *Duns Scotus on the Will and Morality*, edited by Allan B. Wolter, OFM. Washington, DC: Catholic University of America Press.
Dworkin, Ronald. 2011. *Justice for Hedgehogs*. Cambridge, MA: Harvard University Press.
Earman, John. 1986. *A Primer on Determinism*. Dordrecht: D. Reidel.
Earman, John. 2004. "Determinism: What We Have Learned and What We Still Don't Know." In *Freedom and Determinism*, edited by Joseph Keim Campbell, Michael O'Rourke, and David Shier, pp. 21–46. Cambridge, MA: MIT Press.
Edelman, G. M. 1993. *Bright Air, Brilliant Fire*. New York: Basic Books.
Edwards, Jonathan. [1754] 1957. *Freedom of Will*. Edited by Paul Ramsey. New Haven: Yale University Press.
Ekstrom, Laura. 1993. "A Coherence Theory of Autonomy." *Philosophy and Phenomenological Research* 53: pp. 599–616.
Ekstrom, Laura, ed. 2000a. *Agency and Responsibility: Essays on the Metaphysics of Freedom*. Boulder, CO: Westview Press.
Ekstrom, Laura. 2000. *Free Will: A Philosophical Study*. Boulder, CO: Westview Press.
Ekstrom, Laura. 2011. "Free Will Is Not a Mystery." In *Oxford Handbook of Free Will*, 2nd ed., edited by Robert Kane, pp. 366–80. New York: Oxford University Press.
Ekstrom, Laura. 2010. "Volition and the Will." In *A Companion to the Philosophy of Action*, edited by Constantine Sandis and Timothy O'Connor, pp. 113–29. Oxford: Blackwell.
Ekstrom, Laura. 2019. "Toward a Plausible Event-Causal Libertarian Account of Free Will." *Synthese* 196 (1): pp. 127–44.
Ellis, George F. R. 2009. "Top Down Causation and the Human Brain." In *Downwards Causation and the Neurobiology of Free Will*, edited by Nancey Murphy, G. F. R. Ellis, and Timothy O'Connor, pp. 63–82. Berlin: Springer.
Ellis, George F. R. 2016. *How Can Physics Underlie the Mind?* Berlin: Springer-Verlag.
Elstob, Michael. 2018. *Explaining Free Will*. Printed and Distributed by Amazon. ISBN 9781790603268.
Elzein, Nadine. 2010. "Conflicting Reasons and Freedom of Will." *Proceedings of the Aristotelian Society* 110: pp. 219–43.
Elzein, Nadine. 2013. "Basic Desert, Conceptual Revision and Moral Justification." *Philosophical Explorations* pp. 1–14.
Elzein, Nadine. 2017. "Frankfurt-Style Counterexamples and the Importance of Alternative Possibilities." *Acta Analytica* 32: pp. 169–91.

Elzein, Nadine. 2018. "The Demand for Contrastive Explanations." *Philosophical Studies*.
Elzein, Nadine. 2021. Undetermined Choices, Luck, and the Enhancement Problem." Erkenntnis https://doi.org/10.1007/s10670-021-00479-6.
Elzein, Nadine, and Tuomas Pernu. 2017. "Supervenient Freedom and the Free Will Deadlock." *Disputatio* 11 (45): pp. 219–43.
Esfeld, Michael. 2021. "Super-Humeanism and Free Will." *Synthese* 198 (7): pp. 6245–58. https://doi.org/ 10.1007/s11229-019-02460-x.
Fara, Michael. 2008. "Masked Abilities and Compatibilism." *Mind* 117: pp. 844–65.
Federman, Asaf. 2010. "What Kind of Free Will Did the Buddha Teach?" *Philosophy East and West* 60 (1): pp. 1–19.
Feldman, Richard. 2004. "Freedom and Contextualism." In *Freedom and Determinism*, edited by Joseph Keim Campbell, Michael O'Rourke, and David Shier, pp. 255–76. Cambridge, MA: MIT Press.
Feltz, Adam. 2017. "Folk Intuitions." In *The Routledge Companion to Free Will*, edited by Kevin Timpe, Meghan Griffith, and Neil Levy, pp. 468–76. New York: Routledge.
Feltz, Adam, E. Cokely, and T. Nadelhoffer. 2009. "Natural Compatibilism and Natural Incompatibilism: Back to the Drawing Board." *Mind and Language* 24: pp. 1–23.
Feltz, Adam, and Florian Cova. 2014. "Moral Responsibility and Free Will: A Meta-analysis." *Consciousness and Cognition* 30: pp. 234–46.
Finch, Alicia. 2012. "Against Libertarianism." *Philosophical Studies*. DOI 10; 1007/5, 11098-912-00421.
Finch, Alicia. 2013. "On Behalf of the Consequence Argument: Time, Modality, and the Nature of Free Action." *Philosophical Studies* 163 (1): pp. 151–70. https://doi.org/10.1007/s11098-011-9791-5.
Finch, Alicia, and Ted Warfield. 1998. "The *Mind* Argument and Libertarianism." *Mind* 107 (427): pp. 515–28. https://doi.org/10.1093/mind/107.427.515.
Finnegan, Bronwyn. 2022. "Karma, Moral Responsibility and Buddhist Ethics." In *Oxford Handbook of Moral Psychology*, edited by M. Vargas and John Doris, pp. 1–21. New York: Oxford University Press.
Fiorello, Alessandro (Alex) 2020. "Free Will, Values and Narrative Selfhood." *Philosophia* 44 (1): pp. 1–20.
Fischer, John Martin. 1994. *The Metaphysics of Free Will: An Essay on Control*. Oxford: Blackwell.
Fischer, John Martin. 2006. *My Way: Essays on Moral Responsibility*. New York: Oxford University Press.
Fischer, John Martin. 2007. "Compatibilism." In John Martin Fischer, Robert Kane, Derk Pereboom, and Manuel Vargas, *Four Views on Free Will*, pp. 44–84. Malden, MA: Blackwell.
Fischer, John Martin. 2012. *Deep Control: Essays on Free Will and Value*. New York: Oxford University Press.
Fischer, John M., Robert Kane, Derk Pereboom, and Manuel Vargas. 2007. *Four Views on Free Will*. Malden, MA: Blackwell.
Fischer, John Martin, and Mark Ravizza. 1998. *Responsibility and Control: A Theory of Moral Responsibility*. Cambridge: Cambridge University Press.
Fischer, John M., and Neal Tognazzini. 2011. "The Physiognomy of Responsibility." *Philosophy and Phenomenological Research* 82: pp. 381–417.
Fischer, John Martin, and Patrick Todd. 2011. "The Truth about Freedom: A Reply to Merricks." *Philosophical Review* 120 (1): pp. 97–115. https://doi.org/10.1215/00318108-2010-025.

Fischer, John Martin, and Patrick Todd, eds. 2015. *Freedom, Foreknowledge, and Fatalism*. New York: Oxford University Press.

Flanagan, Owen 2017. *Geography of Morals: Varieties of Moral Possibility*. New York: Oxford University Press.

Flint, Thomas P. 1987. "Compatibilism and the Argument from Unavoidability." *Journal of Philosophy* 74 (8): pp. 423–40.

Focquaert, Farah. 2019. "Neurobiology and Crime: A Neuro-ethical Perspective." *Journal of Criminal Justice* 65. https://doi.org/10.1016/j.jcrimjus.2018.01.001.

Focquaert, Farah, Gregg Caruso, Elizabth Shaw, and Derk Pereboom. 2020. "Justice without Retribution: Interdisciplinary Perspectives." *Neuroethics* 13: pp. 1–3.

Foley, Richard. 1979. "Compatibilism and Control over the Past." *Analysis* 39 (2): pp. 70–74. https://doi.org/10.1093/analys/39.2.7.

Foot, Philippa. 1966. "Free Will as Involving Determinism." In edited by Berofsky, pp. 95–108.

Frankfurt, Harry. 1969. "Alternate Possibilities and Moral Responsibility." *Journal of Philosophy* 66: pp. 829–39.

Frankfurt, Harry. 1971. "Freedom of the Will and the Concept of a Person." *Journal of Philosophy* 68: pp. 5–20.

Frankfurt, Harry. 1988. *The Importance of What We Care About*. Cambridge: Cambridge University Press.

Frankfurt, Harry. 2002. "Replies to J. David Velleman, Michael Bratman and Richard Moran." In *Contours of Agency: Essays on Themes from Harry Frankfurt*, edited by Sarah Buss and Lee Overton, pp. 27–31, 86–90. Cambridge, MA: MIT Press.

Franklin, Christopher Evan. 2011a. "Farewell to the Luck (and *Mind*) Argument." *Philosophical Studies* 156: pp. 199–230.

Franklin, Christopher Evan. 2011b. "Masks, Abilities, and Opportunities: Why the New Dispositionalism Cannot Succeed." *Modern Schoolman* 88: pp. 89–103.

Franklin, Christopher Evan. 2013a. "How Should Libertarians Conceive of the Location and Role of Indeterminism?" *Philosophical Explorations*: pp. 1–15. https://doi.org/10.1080/13869795.2013.723036.

Franklin, Christopher Evan. 2013b. "A Reply to Levy's *Hard Luck*." *Criminal Law and Philosophy*. http:link.springer.com/artede/co.1007/s115720139274-1.

Franklin, Christopher Evan. 2015. "Everyone Thinks That an Ability to Do Otherwise Is Necessary for Free Will and Moral Responsibility." *Philosophical Studies* 172: pp. 2091–107.

Franklin, Christopher Evan. 2016. "If Anyone Should Be an Agent-Causalist, Then Everyone Should Be an Agent-Causalist." *Mind* 125: pp. 1101–31.

Franklin, Christopher Evan. 2018. *A Minimal Libertarianism: Free Will and the Promise of Reduction*. New York: Oxford University Press.

Franklin, Christopher Evan. 2019. "The Heart of Libertarianism: Fundamentality and the Will." *Social Philosophy and Policy* 36 (1): pp. 72–92.

Frede, Dorothea. 2015. "Free Will in Aristotle." In *What Is Up To Us*, edited by P. Destree, R. Salles, and M. Zingano, pp. 39–58. Sankt Augustin: Academia Verlag.

Frede, Michael. 2011. *A Free Will: Origins of the Notion in Ancient Thought*. Berkeley: University of California Press.

Freeman, W. J. 1999. *How Brains Make Up Their Minds*. London: Weidenfeld and Nicholson.

Frith, Chris D. 2009. "Free Will and Top-Down Control in the Brain." In *Downwards Causation and the Neurobiology of Free Will*, edited by Nancey Murphy, G. F. R. Ellis, and Timothy O'Connor, pp. 199–210. Berlin: Springer.

Gawronski, B., W. Hofmann, and C. J. Wilbur. 2006. "Are Implicit Attitudes Unconscious?" *Consciousness and Cognition* 15: pp. 485–99.

Gazzaniga, M. 2011. *Who's in Charge? Free Will and the Science of the Brain*. New York: HarperCollins.

Gebharter, Alexander. 2020. "Free Will as a Higher Level Phenomena." *Thought* 9 (3): pp. 177–87.

Gerwin, Martin. 2018. *Causes, Agents, Explanations and Free Will*. Bloomington, IN: Archway Publishing.

Gier, Nicholas F., and Paul Kjellberg. 2004. "Buddhism and the Freedom of the Will: Pali and Mahayanist Responses." In *Freedom and Determinism*, edited by Joseph Keim Campbell, Michael O'Rourke, and David Shier, pp. 277–304. Cambridge, MA: MIT Press.

Ginet, Carl. 1966. "Might We Have No Choice?" In *Freedom and Determinism*, edited by Keith Lehrer, pp. 87–104. New York: Random House.

Ginet, Carl. 1990. *On Action*. Cambridge: Cambridge University Press.

Ginet, Carl. 1996. "In Defense of the Principle of Alternative Possibilities: Why I Don't Find Frankfurt's Argument Convincing." *Philosophical Perspectives* 10: pp. 403–17.

Ginet, Carl. 2014. "Can an Indeterministic Cause Leave a Choice up to the Agent?" In *Libertarian Free Will: Contemporary Debates*, edited by David Palmer, pp. 15–26. New York: Oxford University Press.

Gisin, Nicolas. 2021. "Indeterminism in Physics and Intuitionistic Mathematics." *Synthese* pp. 1–24. https://doi.org/10.1007/s11229-021-03378-z.

Glick, David, and Hannah Tierney. 2020. "Desperately Seeking Sourcehood." *Philosophical Studies* 177 (4): pp. 953–70. https://doi.org/10.1007/s11098-018-1215-3.

Glimcher, P. W. 2005. "Indeterminacy in Brain and Behavior." *Annual Review of Psychology* 56: pp. 25–56.

Goetz, Stewart C. 2005. "Frankfurt-Style Counterexamples and Begging the Question." *Midwest Studies in Philosophy* 29: pp. 83–105.

Goetz, Stewart C. 2009. *Freedom, Teleology, and Evil*. London: T&T Clark.

Grant, W. Matthews. 2016. "Divine Universal Causality and Libertarian Freedom." In *Free Will and Theism: Connections, Contingencies, and Concerns*, edited by Kevin Timpe and Daniel Speak. New York: Oxford University Press.

Grant, W. Matthews. 2019. *Free Will and God's Universal Causality: The Dual Sources Account*. London: Bloomsbury Academic.

Graham, Peter. 2011. "'Ought' and 'Ability'." *Philosophical Review* 120: pp. 337–82.

Greene, Joshua, and Jonathan D. Cohen. 2004. "For the Law, Neuroscience Changes Nothing and Everything." *Philosophical Transactions of the Royal Society of London: Series B-Biological Sciences* 359: pp. 1775–85.

Greenspan, Patricia. 2012. "Free Will and Rational Coherency." *Philosophical Issues* 22, "Action Theory," pp. 87–102.

Griffith, Meghan. 2010. "Why Agent-Caused Actions Are Not Lucky." *American Philosophical Quarterly* 47: pp. 43–56.

Griffith, Meghan. 2017. "Agent Causation." In *The Routledge Companion to Free Will*, edited by Kevin Timpe, Meghan Griffith, and Neil Levy, pp. 72–85. New York: Routledge.

Guillon, Jean-Baptiste. 2014. "Van Inwagen on Introspected Freedom." *Philosophical Studies* 168: pp. 645–63.

Hadamard, J. 1945. *An Essay on the Psychology of Invention in the Mathematical Field*. Princeton, NJ: Princeton University Press.

Haji, Ishtiyaque. 1998. *Moral Appraisability: Puzzles, Proposals, and Perplexities.* New York: Oxford University Press.
Haji, Ishtiyaque. 2002. *Deontic Morality and Control.* Cambridge: Cambridge University Press.
Haji, Ishtiyaque. 2009. *Incompatibilism's Allure: Principal Arguments for Incompatibilism.* Peterborough, Canada: Broadview Press.
Haji, Ishtiyaque. 2022. "Libertarianism and Luck." *Journal of Philosophical Theological Research* 24 (3): pp. 115–34.
Haji, Ishtiyaque, and Michael McKenna. 2004. "Dialectical Delicacies in the Debate about Freedom and Alternative Possibilities." *Journal of Philosophy* 101: pp. 299–314.
Haji, Ishtiyaque, and Justin Caouette, eds. 2013. Newcastle upon Tyne, UK: *Free Will and Moral Responsibility.* Cambridge Scholars Publishing.
Hameroff, Stuart, and Roger Penrose. 1996. "Conscious Events as Orchestrated Space-Time Selections." *Journal of Consciousness Studies* 3: pp. 36–53.
Harris, Sam. 2012. *Free Will.* New York: Free Press.
Harrison, Gerald Kingsley. "Free Will and Luck." PhD dissertation, University of Durham.
Hart, H. L. A. 1970. *Punishment and Responsibility.* Oxford: Clarendon Press.
Hartman, Robert J. (2016). "Against Luck-Free Moral Responsibility." *Philosophical Studies* 173 (10): pp. 2845–65.
Hasker, William. 2004. *Providence, Evil and the Openness of God.* Ithaca, NY: Cornell University Press.
Hasker, William. 2008. *The Triumph of God over Evil: Theodicy for a World of Suffering.* Downer's Grove, IL: InterVarsity Press.
Hasker, William. 2011. "Divine Knowledge and Human Freedom." In *The Oxford Handbook of Free Will*, 2nd ed., edited by Robert Kane. New York: Oxford University Press.
Hecht, Jonathan. 2014. "Freedom of the Will in Plato and Augustine." *British Journal for the History of Philosophy* 22: pp. 196–216.
Heisenberg, Martin. 2013. "The Origin of Freedom in Animal Behavior." In *Is Science Compatible with Free Will?*, edited by A. Suarez and P. Adams, pp. 95–103. Berlin: Springer.
Hieronymi, Pamela. 2001. "Articulating an Uncompromising Forgiveness." *Philosophy and Phenomenological Research* 62: pp. 529–55.
Hieronymi, Pamela. 2020. *Freedom, Resentment and the Metaphysics of Morals.* Princeton, NJ: Princeton University Press.
Hilborn, Robert C. 2001. *Chaos and Nonlinear Dynamics: An Introduction.* 2nd ed. Oxford: Oxford University Press.
Hitchcock, Christopher. 2012. "Contrastive Explanations." In *Contrastivism in Philosophy*, edited by M. Blaauw, pp. 11–34. London: Routledge.
Hobart, R. E. 1934. "Free Will as Involving Determination and Inconceivable without It." *Mind* 43: pp. 1–27.
Hobbes, Thomas. 1654 [1999]. *Of Liberty and Necessity.* In *Hobbes and Bramhall on Liberty and Necessity*, edited by Vere Chappell, pp. 15–42, 69–90. Cambridge: Cambridge University Press.
Hobbs, J. 1991. "Chaos and Indeterminism." *Canadian Journal of Philosophy* 21: pp. 41–64.
Hodgson, David. 2012. *Rationality + Consciousness = Free Will.* Oxford: Oxford University Press.
Hoffman, Tobias, and Cyrille Michon. 2017. "Aquinas on Free Will and Intellectual Determinism." *Philosopher's Imprint* 17 (10): pp. 1–36.

Hofmann, Frank. 2022. "Explaining Free Will by Rational Abilities." *Ethical Theory and Moral Practice* 25 (2): pp. 283–93.
Holbach, Baron. [1770] 1990. *System de la nature*. Paris: Fayard.
Holbach, Baron. [1770] 2002. "The Illusion of Free Will." Translated by H. D. Robinson. In *The Experience of Philosophy*, 5th ed., edited by Daniel Kolak and Raymond Martin, pp. 176–81. Oxford: Oxford University Press.
Holliday, Wesley H. 2012. "Freedom and the Fixity of the Past." *Philosophical Review* 121(2): pp. 179–207. https://doi.org/10.1215/00318108-1539080.
Holton, Richard. 2009. *Willing, Wanting, Waiting*. Oxford: Oxford University Press.
Honderich, Ted. 1988. *A Theory of Determinism*. Oxford: Oxford University Press.
Horgan, Terrence. 1979. "'Could', Possible Worlds, and Moral Responsibility." *Southern Journal of Philosophy* 17: pp. 345–58.
Horgan, Terrence. 1985. "Compatibilism and the Consequence Argument." *Philosophical Studies* 47 (3): pp. 339–56. https://doi.org/10.1007/BF00355208.
Horgan, Terrence. 2015. "Injecting the Phenomenology of Agency into the Free Will Debate." *Oxford Studies in Agency and Responsibility* 3: pp. 34–61.
Horst, Steven. 2011. *Laws, Mind and Free Will*. Cambridge, MA: MIT Press.
Howard-Snyder, Daniel, and Paul Moser, eds. 2002. *Divine Hiddenness: New Essays*. Cambridge: Cambridge University Press.
Huemer, Michael. 2000. "Van Inwagen's Consequence Argument." *Philosophical Review* 109 (4): pp. 525–44. https://doi.org/10.1215/00318108-109-4-525.
Huemer, Michael. 2004. "Elusive Freedom? A Reply to Helen Beebee." *Philosophical Review* 113 (3): pp. 411–16. https://doi.org/10.1215/00318108-113-3-411.
Hume, David. [1740] 1978. *A Treatise of Human Nature*. Edited by L. A. Selby-Bigge and P. H. Nidditch. 2nd ed. Oxford: Oxford University Press.
Hume, David. [1748] 1975. *Enquiries Concerning Human Understanding and Concerning the Principles of Morals*. Edited by P. H. Nidditch. 3rd ed. Oxford: Oxford University Press.
Hunt, David P. 2000. "Moral Responsibility and Unavoidable Action." *Philosophical Studies* 97 (2): pp. 195–227.
Hunt, David P. 2005. "Moral Responsibility and Buffered Alternatives." *Midwest Studies in Philosophy* 29: pp. 126–45.
Huoranszki, Ferenc. 2011. *Freedom of the Will: A Conditional Analysis*. New York: Routledge.
Huoranszki, Ferenc. 2021. "Physical Determinism, Zygote Manipulation and Responsible Agency." *Philosophia* 49 (4): pp. 1525–40. https://doi.org/10.1007/s11406-020-00307-1.
Hurley, Susan. 2000. "Is Responsibility Essentially Impossible?" *Philosophical Studies* 99: pp. 229–68.
Hyman, John. 2015. *Action, Knowledge and Will*. Oxford: Oxford University Press.
Irwin, Terence. 1992. "Who Discovered the Will?" *Philosophical Perspectives* 6: pp. 453–73.
Ismael, Jenann. 2016. *How Physics Makes Us Free*. Oxford: Oxford University Press.
Jacobs, Jonathan D., and Timothy O'Connor. 2013. "Agent Causation in a Neo-Aristotelian Metaphysics." In *Mental Causation and Ontology*, edited by Sophie C. Gibb, E. J. Lowe, and Rögnvaldur Ingthorsson, pp. 173–92. Oxford: Oxford University Press.
James, William. 1956. *The Will to Believe and Other Essays*. New York: Dover.
Jaster, Romy. 2020. *Agents' Abilities*. Berlin: de Gruyter.
Jaworska, Agnieszka. 2017. "Identificationist Views." In *The Routledge Companion to Free Will*, edited by Kevin Timpe, Meghan Griffith, and Neil Levy, pp. 15–26. New York: Routledge.

Jedlicka, Peter. 2014. "Quantum Stochasticity and (the End of) Neurodeterminism." In *Quantum Physics Meets Philosophy of Mind*, edited by Antonella Corradini and Uwe Meixner, pp. 183–97. Berlin: de Gruyter.

Jeppsson, Sofia. 2020. "The Agential Perspective: A Hard-Line Reply to the Four-Case Manipulation Argument." *Philosophical Studies* 177 (7): pp. 1935–51. https://doi.org/10.1007/s11098-019-01292-2.

Juarrero, Alicia. 1999. *Dynamics in Action: Intentional Behavior as a Complex System*. Cambridge, MA: MIT Press.

Juarrero, Alicia. 2009. "Top Down Causation and Autonomy in Complex Systems." In *Downwards Causation and the Neurobiology of Free Will*, edited by Nancey Murphy, G. F. R. Ellis, and Timothy O'Connor, pp. 83–102. Berlin: Springer.

Johnson, Alan E. 2021. *Free Will and Human Life*. Pittsburgh: Philosophia Publications.

Judisch, Neal. 2016. "Divine Conservation and Creaturely Freedom." In *Free Will and Theism: Connections, Contingencies, and Concerns*, edited by Kevin Timpe and Daniel Speak, pp. 234–58. New York: Oxford University Press.

Kaiserman, Alex, and Daniel Kodsi. 2021. Review of C. List, *Why Free Will Is Real*, 2019. *Mind* 130 (519): pp. 287–96.

Kane, Robert. 1985. *Free Will and Values*. Albany: State University of New York Press.

Kane, Robert. 1988. Review of G. Strawson's *Freedom and Belief*. *International Philosophical Quarterly* 30 (1990): pp. 260–62.

Kane, Robert. 1989. "Two Kinds of Incompatibilism." In *Agents, Causes and Events*, edited by Timothy O'Connor, pp. 115–50. Oxford: Oxford University Press.

Kane, Robert. 1994. *Through the Moral Maze: Searching for Absolute Values in a Pluralistic World*. New York: Paragon House.

Kane, Robert. 1994a. "Free Will: The Elusive Ideal." *Philosophical Studies* 75: pp. 25–60.

Kane, Robert. 1996. *The Significance of Free Will*. New York: Oxford University Press.

Kane, Robert. 1999. "Responsibility, Luck, and Chance: Reflections on Free Will and Indeterminism." *Journal of Philosophy* 96: pp. 217–40. Reprinted in Watson ed. 2003: pp. 299–321, and in Ekstrom ed. 2000: pp. 158–80.

Kane, Robert. 1999a. "On Free Will, Responsibility and Indeterminism: Responses to Clarke, Haji and Mele." *Philosophical Explorations* 2: pp. 105–21.

Kane, Robert. 2000a. "The Dual Regress of Free Will and the Role of Alternative Possibilities." *Philosophical Perspectives* 14: pp. 57–80.

Kane, Robert. 2000b. "Précis of *The Significance of Free Will*." *Philosophy and Phenomenological Research* 60: pp. 129–34.

Kane, Robert, ed. 2002. *The Oxford Handbook of Free Will*. Oxford: Oxford University Press.

Kane, Robert. 2002a. "Some Neglected Pathways in the Free Will Labyrinth." In *The Oxford Handbook of Free Will*, edited by Robert Kane, pp. 406–37. New York: Oxford University Press.

Kane, Robert. 2002b. "Free Will: New Directions for an Ancient Problem." In *Free Will*, ed. Robert Kane, pp. 222–48. Oxford: Blackwell.

Kane, Robert, ed. 2002c. *Free Will*. Oxford: Blackwell.

Kane, Robert. 2003. "Responsibility, Indeterminism, and Frankfurt-Style Cases." In *Moral Responsibilities and Alternative Possibilities: Essays on the Importance of Alternative Possibilities*, edited by David Widerker and Michael McKenna, pp. 91–106. Aldershot, UK: Ashgate.

Kane, Robert. 2005. *A Contemporary Introduction to Free Will*. Oxford: Oxford University Press.

Kane, Robert. 2007a. "Free Will: New Directions for an Ancient Problem: A Reply to Allen and Rogers." *Proceedings of the American Catholic Philosophical Association* 18: pp. 291–302.

Kane, Robert. 2007b. "Libertarianism." In John Martin Fischer, Robert Kane, Derk Pereboom, and Manuel Vargas, *Four Views on Free Will*. Malden, MA: Blackwell.

Kane, Robert. 2007c. "Responses to Fischer, Pereboom and Vargas." In John Martin Fischer, Robert Kane, Derk Pereboom, and Manuel Vargas, *Four Views on Free Will*. Malden, MA: Blackwell.

Kane, Robert. 2008. "Three Freedoms, Free Will and Self-Formation: A Reply to Neil Levy and Other Critics." In *Essays on Free Will and Moral Philosophy*, edited by Nick Trakakis and D. Cohen, pp. 142–61. Newcastle upon Tyne, UK: Cambridge Scholars Press.

Kane, Robert. 2009. "Free Will and the Dialectic of Selfhood." *Ideas y valores* 58: pp. 25–44.

Kane, Robert. 2010a. *Ethics and the Quest for Wisdom*. Cambridge: Cambridge University Press.

Kane, Robert. 2010b. "Responsibility and Free Will in Dworkin's *Justice for Hedgehogs*." *Boston University Law Review* 90 (2): pp. 611–19.

Kane, Robert, ed. 2011a. *The Oxford Handbook of Free Will*. 2nd ed. New York: Oxford University Press.

Kane, Robert. 2011b. "Rethinking Free Will: New Perspectives on an Ancient Problem." In *The Oxford Handbook of Free Will*, 2nd ed., edited by Robert Kane, pp. 381–404. New York: Oxford University Press.

Kane, Robert. 2014. "New Arguments in Debates on Libertarian Free Will: Responses to Contributors." In *Libertarian Free Will: Contemporary Debates*, edited by David Palmer, pp. 179–214. New York: Oxford University Press.

Kane, Robert. 2016. "On the Role of Indeterminism in Libertarian Free Will." *Philosophical Explorations* 19: pp. 2–16.

Kane, Robert. 2021. "Making Sense of a Free Will That Is Incompatible with Determinism: A Fourth Way Forward." *Journal of Philosophical and Theological Research* 23 (3): pp. 5–28.

Kane, Robert, and Carolina Sartorio. 2022. *Do We Have Free Will? A Debate*. New York: Routledge.

Kant, Immanuel. [1781] 1999. *Critique of Pure Reason*. Translated by Paul Guyer and Allen W. Wood. Cambridge: Cambridge University Press.

Kant, Immanuel. [1785] 1998. *Groundwork of the Metaphysics of Morals*. Translated by Mary Gregor. Cambridge: Cambridge University Press.

Kant, Immanuel. [1788] 2015. *Critique of Practical Reason*. Translated by Mary Gregor. Cambridge: Cambridge University Press.

Kapitan, Tomis. 1991. "Ability and Cognition: A Defense of Compatibilism." *Philosophical Studies* 63 (2): pp. 231–43. https://doi.org/10.1007/BF00381690.

Kapitan, Tomis. 2002. "A Master Argument for Incompatibilism?" In *The Oxford Handbook of Free Will*, edited by Robert Kane, pp. 227–57. New York: Oxford University Press.

Kapitan, Tomis. 2011. "A Compatibilist Reply to the Consequence Argument." In *The Oxford Handbook of Free Will*, 2nd ed., edited by Robert Kane, pp. 131–46. New York: Oxford University Press.

Kearns, Stephen. 2012. "Aborting the Zygote Argument." *Philosophical Studies* 160: pp. 379–89.

Kearns, Stephen. 2015. "Free Will Agnosticism." *Noûs* 47: pp. 235–52.

Kellert, S. 1993. *In the Wake of Chaos*. Chicago: University of Chicago Press.
Kelly, Erin. 2017. "Free Will and Criminal Law." In *The Routledge Companion to Free Will*, edited by Kevin Timpe, Meghan Griffith, and Neil Levy, pp. 577–89. New York: Routledge.
King, Matthew. 2013. "The Problem with Manipulation." *Ethics* 124 (1): pp. 68–83.
Kittle, Simon. 2019. "Does Everyone Think the Ability to Do Otherwise Is Necessary for Free Will and Moral Responsibility?" *Philosophia* 47 (4): pp. 1177–83.
Klein, Martha. 1990. *Determinism, Blameworthiness and Deprivation*. Oxford: Oxford University Press.
Koch, C. 2009. "Free Will, Physics, Biology and the Brain." In *Downwards Causation and the Neurobiology of Free Will*, edited by Nancey Murphy, G. F. R. Ellis, and Timothy O'Connor, pp. 31–52. Berlin: Springer.
Koons, Robert. 2002. "Dual Agency: A Thomistic Account of Providence and Human Freedom." *Philosophia Christi* 4: pp. 397–410.
Korsgaard, Christine. 1998. "The Right to Lie: Kant on Dealing with Evil." In *Ethical Theory II*, edited by J. Rachels, pp. 282–304. Oxford: Oxford University Press.
Kremer, Michael. 2004. "How Not to Argue against Incompatibilism." *Erkenntnis* 10: pp. 1–26.
Lamb, James. 1993. "Evaluative Compatibilism and the Principle of Alternative Possibilities." *Journal of Philosophy* 90: pp. 517–27.
Latham, A. J., and Tierney, H. (2022). "Defusing Existential and Universal Threats to Compatibilism: A Strawsonian Dilemma for Manipulation Arguments." *Journal of Philosophy* 119 (3): pp. 144–61.
Lavazza, Andrea. 2019. "Why Cognitive Science Does Not Prove That Free Will Is an Epiphenomenon." *Hypothesis and Theory* 10, https://doi.org/10.3389/fp-syg.2019.00036.
Layser, David. 2022. *Do We Have Free Will?* Cambridge, MA: I-Phi Press.
Lebed, Felix. 2023. "Free Will: It Unlikely Exists in the Light or It Floats in the Complexity Paradigm." *Philosophical Psychology* 19 (2): pp. 85–95.
Lehrer, Keith. 1976. "Can in Theory and Practice: A Possible Worlds Analysis." In *Action Theory*, edited by Myles Brand and Douglas Walton, pp. 242–71. Dordrecht: D. Reidel.
Lehrer, Keith. 1980. "Preferences, Conditionals, and Freedom." In *Time and Cause: Essays Presented to Richard Taylor*, edited by Peter van Inwagen, pp. 187–200. Dordrecht: D. Reidel.
Lehrer, Keith. 1986. "Cans without Ifs." *Analysis* 29: pp. 29–32.
Lemos, John. 2018. *A Pragmatic Approach to Libertarian Free Will*. New York: Routledge.
Lemos, John. 2023. *Free Will's Value: Criminal Justice, Pride and Love*. New York: Routledge.
Lem, Stanislaw. 1971. *Solaris*. New York: Berkeley Medallion Books.
Lenman, James. 2006. "Compatibilism and Contractualism: The Possibility of Moral Responsibility." *Ethics* 117: pp. 7–31.
Leibniz, G. W. [1686] 1991. *Discourse on Metaphysics and Other Essays*. Translated by Daniel Garber and Roger Ariew. 9th ed. Indianapolis: Hackett.
Levy, Ken. 2001. "The Main Problem with USC Libertarianism." *Philosophical Studies* 105: pp. 115–16.
Levy, Ken. 2005a. "Why It Is Sometimes Fair to Blame Agents for Unavoidable Actions and Omissions." *American Philosophical Quarterly* 42: pp. 93–104.
Levy, Ken. 2005b. "The Solution to the Problem of Outcome Luck: Why Harm Is Just as Punishable as the Wrongful Action That Causes It." *Law and Philosophy* 24: pp. 263–303.
Levy, Ken. 2016. "Blocking Blockage." *Philosophia* 44: pp. 573–78.

Levy, Ken. 2020. *Free Will, Responsibility and Crime: An Introduction*. New York: Routledge.
Levy, Ken. 2022. "Let's Not Do Responsibility Skepticism." *Journal of Applied Philosophy*. https://doi.org/10.1111/japp.12623.
Levy, Ken. 2023. "On Three Arguments against Metaphysical Libertarianism." *Review of Metaphysics* 76 (4): pp. 725–48.
Levy, Neil. 2008. "Restrictivism Is a Covert Compatibilism." In *Essays on Free Will and Moral Responsibility*, edited by Nick Trakakis and D. Cohen, pp. 129–41. Newcastle upon Tyne, UK: Cambridge Scholars Press.
Levy, Neil. 2011. *Hard Luck: How Luck Undermines Free Will and Moral Responsibility*. New York: Oxford University Press.
Lewis, David. 1976. "The Paradoxes of Time Travel." *American Philosophical Quarterly* 13: pp. 145–52.
Lewis, David. 1979. "Counterfactual Dependence and Time's Arrow." *Noûs* 13: pp. 455–76.
Lewis, David. 1981. "Are We Free to Break the Laws?" *Theoria* 47: pp. 113–21.
Lewis, David. 1997. "Finkish Dispositions." *Philosophical Quarterly* 47: pp. 143–58.
Libet, Benjamin. 2002. "Do We Have Free Will?" In *The Oxford Handbook of Free Will*, edited by Robert Kane, pp. 551–64. New York: Oxford University Press.
Lippert-Rasmussen, Kasper. 2003. "Identification and Responsibility." *Ethical Theory and Moral Practice* 6: pp. 349–76.
List, Christian. 2014. "Free Will, Determinism and the Possibility of Doing Otherwise." *Noûs* 48(1): pp. 156–78.
List, Christian. 2019. *Why Free Will Is Real*. Cambridge, MA: Harvard University Press.
Locke, Don. 1973. "Natural Powers and Human Abilities." *Proceedings of the Aristotelian Society* 74: pp. 171–87.
Locke, John. [1690] 1975. *An Essay Concerning the Human Understanding*. Edited by Peter H. Nidditch. Oxford: Oxford University Press.
Lockie, Robert. 2018. *Free Will and Epistemology*. London: Bloomsbury Academic.
Long, Todd R. 2004. "Moderate Reasons Responsiveness, Moral Responsibility and Manipulation." In *Freedom and Determinism*, edited by Joseph Keim Campbell, Michael O'Rourke, and David Shier, pp. 151–72. Cambridge, MA: MIT Press.
Lovejoy, A. O. 1961. *Reflections on Human Nature*. Baltimore: Johns Hopkins University Press.
Lowe, E. J. 2008. *Personal Agency: The Metaphysics of Mind and Action*. Oxford: Oxford University Press.
MacDonald, Scott. 1998. "Aquinas's Libertarian Account of Free Will." *Revue Internationale de Philosophie* 2: pp. 309–28.
Maoz, Uri, and Walter Sinnott-Armstrong, eds. 2022. *Free Will: Philosophers and Neuroscientists in Conversation*. New York: Oxford University Press.
Marchal, Kai, and Christian Helmut Wenzel. 2017. "Chinese Perspectives on Free Will." In *The Routledge Companion to Free Will*, edited by Kevin Timpe, Meghan Griffith, and Neil Levy, pp. 374–88. New York: Routledge.
Markosian, Ned. 1999. "A Compatibilist Version of the Theory of Agent Causation." *Pacific Philosophical Quarterly* 80: pp. 257–77.
Markosian, Ned. 2012. "Agent Causation as the Solution to all the Compatibilist's Problems." *Philosophical Studies* 157: pp. 383–98.
Mason, Elinor. 2005. *Moral Responsibility*. Oxford: Blackwell.
Matteson, Benjamin. 2016. "In Defense of the 4-Case Argument." *Philosophical Studies* 173 (7): pp. 1963–82.

May, Joshua. 2014. "On the Very Concept of Free Will." *Synthese* 191 (12): pp. 2849–66.
Maye, A., Chih-hao Hsieh, G. Suguhara, and B. Brembs. 2007. "Order in Spontaneous Behavior." PloS ONE 2 e443: pp. 1–14.
McCall, Storrs, and E. J. Lowe. 2005. "Indeterminist Free Will." *Philosophy and Phenomenological Research* 70 (3): pp. 683–98.
McCann, Hugh. 1998. *The Works of Agency: On Human Action, Will, and Freedom*. Ithaca, NY: Cornell University Press.
McCormick, Kelly. 2013. "Anchoring a Revisionist Account of Moral Responsibility." *Journal of Ethics and Social Philosophy* 7: pp. 1–19.
McCormick, Kelly. 2017. "Revisionism." In *The Routledge Companion to Free Will*, edited by Kevin Timpe, Meghan Griffith, and Neil Levy, pp. 109–20. New York: Routledge.
McCormick, Kelly. 2022. *The Problem of Blame: Making Sense of Moral Anger*. Cambridge: Cambridge University Press.
McGeer, Victoria. 2013. "Civilizing Blame." In *Blame: Its Nature and Norms*, edited by D. J. Coates and Neal Tognazzini, pp. 162–88. Oxford: Oxford University Press.
McGeer, Victoria. 2014. "P. F. Strawson's Consequentialism." *Oxford Studies in Agency and Responsibility* 2: pp. 64–92.
McGeer, Victoria. 2015. "Building a Better Theory of Responsibility. *Philosophical Studies* 172 (10): pp. 2635–49.
McGeer, Victoria. 2019. "Scaffolding Agency: A Proleptic Account of the Reactive Attitudes." *European Journal of Philosophy* 27 (2): pp. 301–23.
McKenna, Michael. 2003. "Robustness, Control, and the Demand for Morally Significant Alternatives." In *Moral Responsibility and Alternative Possibilities: Essays on the Importance of Alternative Possibilities*, edited by David Widerker and Michael McKenna, pp. 201–18. Burlington, VT: Ashgate Publishing.
McKenna, Michael. 2008a. "A Hard-Line Reply to Pereboom's Four-Case Manipulation Argument." *Philosophy and Phenomenological Research* 77: pp. 142–59.
McKenna, Michael. 2008b. "Ultimacy and Sweet Jane." In *Essays on Free Will and Moral Responsibility*, edited by Nick Trakakis and D. Cohen pp. 186–208.
McKenna, Michael. 2012. *Conversation & Responsibility*. New York: Oxford University Press.
McKenna, Michael. 2013. "Reasons-Responsiveness, Agents, and Mechanisms." *Oxford Studies in Agency and Responsibility* 1: pp. 151–83.
McKenna, Michael. 2014a. "Resisting the Manipulation Argument: A Hard-Liner Takes It on the Chin." *Philosophy and Phenomenological Research* 89: pp. 467–84.
McKenna, Michael. 2014b. "Compatibilist Ultimacy: Resisting the Threat of Kane's U Condition." In *Libertarian Free Will: Contemporary Debates*, edited by David Palmer, pp. 71–87. Oxford: Oxford University Press.
McKenna, Michael, and Justin Coates. 2021. "Compatibilism." In *The Stanford Encyclopedia of Philosophy*, edited by Edward Zalta, pp. 1–30. https//plato.stanford.edu/archives/sum2020/entries/compatibilism/.
McKenna, Michael, and Paul Russell, eds. 2008. *Free Will and Reactive Attitudes: Perspectives on P. F. Strawson's "Freedom and Resentment"*. London: Ashgate.
Mickelson, Kristin. 2017. "The Manipulation Argument." In *The Routledge Companion to Free Will*, edited by Kevin Timpe, Meghan Griffith, and Neil Levy, pp. 166–78. New York: Routledge.
Mele, Alfred R. 1992. *Springs of Action*. New York: Oxford University Press.
Mele, Alfred R. 1995. *Autonomous Agents*. New York: Oxford University Press.

Mele, Alfred R. 1998. "Review of Robert Kane's *The Significance of Free Will.*" *Journal of Philosophy* 95: pp. 581–84.
Mele, Alfred R. 1999. "Ultimate Responsibility and Dumb Luck." *Social Philosophy and Policy* 16: pp. 274–93.
Mele, Alfred R. 2000. "Goal-Directed Action: Teleological Explanations, Causal Theories, and Deviance." *Philosophical Perspectives* 14: pp. 279–300.
Mele, Alfred R. 2003. "Agents' Abilities." *Noûs* 37: pp. 447–70.
Mele, Alfred R. 2006. *Free Will and Luck*. Oxford: Oxford University Press.
Mele, Alfred R. 2009. *Effective Intentions: The Power of Conscious Will*. Oxford: Oxford University Press.
Mele, Alfred R. 2014. "Kane, Luck and Control: Trying to Get By without Too Much Effort." In *Libertarian Free Will: Contemporary Debates*, edited by David Palmer, pp. 37–51. New York: Oxford University Press.
Mele, Alfred R., ed. 2015. *Surrounding Free Will: Philosophy, Psychology and Neuroscience*. Oxford: Oxford University Press.
Mele, Alfred R. 2017a. *Aspects of Agency: Decisions, Abilities, Explanations, and Free Will*. New York: Oxford University Press.
Mele, Alfred R. 2017b. "Two Libertarian Theories: Or Why Event-Causal Libertarians Should Prefer My Daring Libertarian View to Robert Kane's View." *Royal Institute of Philosophy Supplement* 80: pp. 49–68.
Mele, Alfred R. 2019. *Manipulated Agents: A Window to Moral Responsibility*. Oxford: Oxford University Press.
Mele, Alfred R. 2023a. *A Companion to Free Will*. Hoboken, NJ: John Wiley and Sons.
Mele, Alfred R. 2023b. "Free Will: Looking Ahead." In *A Companion to Free Will*, edited by Joseph Keim Campbell, Kristin Michelson, and V. Alan White, pp. 477–89. Hoboken, NJ: John Wiley and Sons.
Mele, Alfred R., and David Robb. 1998. "Rescuing Frankfurt-Style Examples." *Philosophical Review* 107: pp. 97–112.
Mele, Alfred R., and David Robb. 2003. "Bbs, Magnets and Seesaws: The Metaphysics of Frankfurt-Style Cases." In *Moral Responsibility and Alternative Possibilities: Essays on the Importance of Alternative Possibilities*, edited by David Widerker and Michael McKenna, pp. 127–38. Burlington, VT: Ashgate Publishing.
Messina, J. P. 2020. "Reasonable Pluralism about Desert-Presupposing Moral Responsibility: A Conditional Defense. *Journal of Value Inquiry.* https:/doc.org?101007/5100 790-020-09746-1.
Mickelson, Kristin. 2017. "The Manipulation Argument." In *The Routledge Companion to Free Will*, edited by Kevin Timpe, Meghan Griffith, and Neil Levy, pp. 166–78. New York: Routledge.
Miller, Christian. 2017. "Situationism, Social Psychology and Free Will." In *The Routledge Companion to Free Will*, edited by Kevin Timpe, Meghan Griffith, and Neil Levy, pp. 407–22. New York: Routledge.
Miller, E., and J. Cohen. 2001. "An Integrative Theory of Pre-frontal Cortex Function." *Annual Review of Neuroscience* 24: pp. 167–202.
Miltenberg, Niels, and Dawa Ometto. 2019. "The Libertarian Predicament: A Plea for Action Theory." *Synthese* 196 (1): pp. 161–78.
Moore, Dwayne. 2017. "Mental Causation, Compatibilism and Counterfactuals." *Canadian Journal of Philosophy* 47 (1): pp. 20–42.
Moore, Dwayne. 2022. "Mental Causation and Action Theory." *Erkenntnis* 87 (1): pp. 53–73.

Moore, G. E. 1912. *Ethics*. Oxford: Clarendon Press.
Morris, Stephen. 2018. "The Implications of Rejecting Free Will: An Empirical Analysis." *Philosophical Psychology* 31 (2): pp. 299–321.
Moya, Carlos. 2006. *Moral Responsibility: The Ways of Scepticism*. New York: Routledge.
Moya, Carlos. 2011. "On the Very Idea of a Robust Alternative." *Critica* 43: pp. 3–26.
Moya, Carlos. 2014. "Doing One's Best: Alternative Possibilities and Blameworthiness." *Critica* 46: pp. 3–26.
Mudrik, Liad, Inbal Gur Arie, Yoni Amir, Yarden Shir, Pamela Hieronymi, Uri Maoz, Timothy O'Connor, Aaron Schurger, Manuel Vargas, Tillmann Vierkant, Walter Sinnott-Armstrong, and Adina Roskies. 2022. "Free Will without Consciousness?" *Trends in Cognitive Sciences* 26 (7): pp. 555–66.
Mueller, Thomas. 2022. "Let's Build an 'Anscombe Box': Assessing Anscombe's Rebuttal of the Statistical Objection of an Indeterminist-Based Free Agency." *Synthese* 200 (74): pp. 1–22.
Mueller, Thomas, and Hans Briegel. 2018. "A Stochastic Process Model of Free Agency under Indeterminism." *Dialectica* 72: pp. 219–52.
Murphy, Nancey, and Warren Brown. 2007. *Did My Neurons Make Me Do It?* Oxford: Oxford University Press.
Murphy, Nancey, G. F. R. Ellis, and Timothy O'Connor, eds. 2009. *Downwards Causation and the Neurobiology of Free Will*. Berlin: Springer.
Murray, Dylan, and Tania Lombrozo. 2017. "Effects of Manipulation on Attributions of Causation, Free Will, and Moral Responsibility. *Cognitive Science* 41 (3): pp. 447–81.
Murray, Michael. 1993. "Coercion and the Hiddenness of God." *American Philosophical Quarterly* 30: pp. 27–38.
Nadelhoffer, T. 2011. "The Threat of Shrinking Agency and Free Will Disillusionism." In *Conscious Will and Responsibility*, edited by L. Nadel and Walter Sinnott-Armstrong, pp. 171–88. Oxford: Oxford University Press.
Nagel, Thomas. 1986. *The View from Nowhere*. New York: Oxford University Press.
Nahmias, Eddy. 2014. "Is Free Will an Illusion? Confronting Challenges from the Modern Mind Sciences." In *Moral Psychology*, vol. 4, *Free Will and Moral Responsibility*, edited by Walter Sinnott-Armstrong, pp. 1–25. Cambridge, MA: MIT Press.
Nahmias, Eddy, D. J. Coates, and T. Kavaran. 2006. "Free Will, Moral Responsibility and Mechanism: Experiments on Folk Intuitions." *Philosophy and the Empirical* 31: pp. 214–42.
Nahmias, Eddy, S. Morris, T. Nadelhoffer, and J. Turner. 2005. "Surveying Freedom: Folk Intuitions about Free Will and Moral Responsibility." *Philosophical Psychology* 18: pp. 561–84.
Nahmias, Eddy, S. Morris, T. Nadelhoffer, and J. Turner. 2006. "Is Incompatibilism Intuitive?" *Philosophy and Phenomenological Research* 73: pp. 28–53.
Nelkin, Dana K. 2011. *Making Sense of Freedom and Responsibility*. New York: Oxford University Press.
Nelkin, Dana K. 2017. "Blame." In *The Routledge Companion of Free Will*, edited by Kevin Timpe, Meghan Griffith, and Neil Levy, pp. 600–611. New York: Routledge.
Nelkin, Dana K., and Derk Pereboom, eds. 2022. *The Oxford Handbook of Moral Responsibility*. Oxford: Oxford University Press.
Newsome, William. 2009. "Human Freedom and Emergence." In *Downwards Causation and the Neurobiology of Free Will*, edited by Nancey Murphy, G. F. R. Ellis, and Timothy O'Connor, pp. 53–62. Berlin: Springer.

Nichols, Shaun. 2015. *Bound: Essays on Free Will and Moral Responsibility*. New York: Oxford University Press.

Nichols, Shaun, and Joshua Knobe. 2007. "Moral Responsibility and Determinism: The Cognitive Science of Folk Intuitions." *Nous* 41: pp. 663–85.

Nielsen, Karen M. 2012. "The Will—Origin of the Notion in Aristotle's Thought." *Antiquorum Philosophia* 6: pp. 47–68.

Nielsen, Karen M. 2017. "Aristotle." In *The Routledge Companion to Free Will*, edited by Kevin Timpe, Meghan Griffith, and Neil Levy, pp. 227–35. New York: Routledge.

Nietzsche, Friedrich. 1989. *On the Genealogy of Morals*. Translated by Walter Kauffman. London: Vintage Books.

Nowell-Smith, P. H. 1948. "Free Will and Moral Responsibility." *Mind* 57: pp. 45–61.

Nozick, Robert. 1981. *Philosophical Explorations*. Cambridge, MA: Harvard University Press.

O'Connor, Timothy. 2000. *Persons and Causes: The Metaphysics of Free Will*. New York: Oxford University Press.

O'Connor, Timothy. 2009. "Agent-Causal Power." In *Dispositions and Causes*, edited by Toby Handfield, pp. 189–214. Oxford: Clarendon Press.

O'Connor, Timothy. 2011. "Agent-Causal Theories of Freedom." In *Oxford Handbook on Free Will*, 2nd ed., edited by Robert Kane, pp. 309–21. New York: Oxford University Press.

O'Connor, Timothy. 2014. "Free Will and Metaphysics." In *Libertarian Free Will: Contemporary Debates*, edited by David Palmer, pp. 27–34. New York: Oxford University Press.

O'Connor, Timothy. 2021. "Free Will in a Network of Interacting Causes." In *Neo-Aristotelian Metaphysics and the Theology of Nature*, edited by W. Simpson, R. Koons, and J. Orr. London: Routledge.

Oshana, Marina. 2002. "Responsibility: Philosophical Perspectives." In *International Encyclopedia of the Social and Behavioral Sciences*, edited by Neil J. Smelser and Paul B. Baltes, pp. 144–63. New York: Elsevier Press.

Oshana, Marina. 2018. "Self-Identity and Moral Agency." In *Autonomy and the Self*, edited by M. Kahler and N. Jelinek, pp. 32–50. Berlin: Springer.

O'Shaughnessy, Brian. 1980. *The Will*. 2 vols. Cambridge: Cambridge University Press.

Ostler, Blake T. 2023. "Mormonism and Determinism." *Dialogue: Journal of Mormon Thought*. http://scholarlypublishing collective.org/uip/dial/article-pdf/32/4/43/1246449/15226637.pdf.

Otsuka, Michael. 1998. "Incompatibilism and the Avoidability of Blame." *Ethics* 108 (4): pp. 685–701.

Otto, J. Neil. 2015. "Experimental Philosophy, Robert Kane and the Concept of Free Will." *Journal of Cognition and Neuroethics* 3 (1): pp. 281–96.

Pacherie, Elkzabeth. 2007. "The Sense of Control and the Sense of Agency." *Psychology* 13(1), pp. 1–30.

Palmer, David, ed. 2014a. *Libertarian Free Will: Contemporary Debates*. New York: Oxford University Press.

Palmer, David. 2014b. "Deterministic Frankfurt Cases." *Synthese* 191: pp. 3847–64.

Palmer, David. 2021. "Free Will and Control: A Noncausal Approach." *Synthese* 198 (10): pp. 43–62.

Paul, L. A. 2014. *Transformative Experience*. Oxford: Oxford University Press.

Pawl, Timothy, and Kevin Timpe. 2016. "Incompatibilism, Sin, and Free Will in Heaven." *Faith and Philosophy* 26: pp. 398–419.
Pendergraft, Garrett. 2010. "The Explanatory Power of Local Miracle Compatibilism." *Philosophical Studies* 156: pp. 249–66.
Pereboom, Derk. 2001. *Living without Free Will*. Cambridge: Cambridge University Press.
Pereboom, Derk. 2003. "Source Incompatibilism and Alternative Possibilities." In *Moral Responsibility and Alternative Possibilities*, edited by David Widerker and Michael McKenna, pp. 185–99. Aldershot, UK: Ashgate.
Pereboom, Derk. 2007. "Hard Incompatibilism." In John Martin Fischer, Robert Kane, Derk Pereboom, and Manuel Vargas, *Four Views on Free Will*, pp. 85–125. Malden, MA: Blackwell.
Pereboom, Derk. 2009. "Further Thoughts about a Frankfurt-Style Argument." *Philosophical Explorations* 12: pp. 109–18.
Pereboom, Derk. 2014. *Free Will, Agency, and Meaning in Life*. Oxford: Oxford University Press.
Pérez de Calleja, Mirja. 2019. "Luck and Compatibilism." In *The Routledge Handbook of the Philosophy and Psychology of Luck*, edited by Ian M. Church and Robert J. Hartman, pp. 248–65. New York: Routledge.
Perszyk, Ken. 2017. "Free Will and Providence." In *The Routledge Companion to Free Will*, edited by Kevin Timpe, Meghan Griffith, and Neil Levy, pp. 543–52. New York: Routledge.
Pestana, Mark. 2001. "Complexity Theory, Quantum Mechanics and Radically Free Self Determination." *Journal of Mind and Behavior* 22 (4): pp. 365–88.
Pink, Thomas. 2004. *Free Will: A Very Short Introduction*. Oxford: Oxford University Press.
Pink, Thomas. 2017. *Self-Determination: The Ethics of Action*. Vol. 1. Oxford: Oxford University Press.
Plato. 1997. *Complete Works*. Edited by John Cooper. Indianapolis: Hackett.
Plotinus. 1950. *The Philosophy of Plotinus*. New York: Appleton, Century, Crofts.
Poincaré, Henri. 1952. *Science and Hypothesis*. Translated by George Bruce Halsted. New York: Dover Publications.
Polkinghorne, J. 2009. *Questions of Truth*. Louisville, KY: Westminster John Knox Press.
Popper, Karl. 1972. "Of Clouds and Clocks." In his *Objective Knowledge*, pp. 206–55. Oxford: Oxford University Press.
Popper, Karl. 1982. *The Open Universe*. Totowa, NJ: Rowman and Littlefield.
Prigogine, Ilya. 1997. *The End of Chaos: Time, Chaos and the New Laws of Nature*. New York: Free Press.
Pruss, Alexander R. 2007. "Prophecy without Middle Knowledge." *Faith and Philosophy* 24: pp. 437–57.
Pruss, Alexander R. 2013. "Incompatibilism Proved." *Canadian Journal of Philosophy* 43: pp. 430–37.
Pruss, Alexander R. 2016. "Divine Creative Freedom." *Oxford Studies in the Philosophy of Religion* 7: pp. 213–38.
Ragland, Scott. 2006. "Was Descartes a Libertarian?" *Oxford Studies in Early Modern Philosophy* 3: pp. 57–90.
Rawls, John. 1971. *A Theory of Justice*. Cambridge, MA: Harvard University Press.
Reid, Thomas. [1788] 1969. *Essays on the Active Powers of the Human Mind*. Edited by Baruch Brody. Cambridge, MA: MIT Press.

Repetti, Riccardo. 2014. "Recent Buddhist Theories of Free Will." *Journal of Buddhist Ethics* 21: pp. 5–24.

Repetti, Riccardo. 2019. *Buddhism, Meditation and Free Will*. New York and London: Routledge.

Richardson, Christina. 2015. "Arguments from Kane." Unpublished paper.

Rigato, Joanna. 2015. "Reduction, Agency and Free Will." *Axiomatics* 25: pp. 107–16.

Rigato, Joanna. 2018. "Downward Causation and Supervenience." *Philosophical Explorations* 3: pp. 384–99.

Robinson, Michael. 2012. "Modified Frankfurt-Type Counterexamples and Flickers of Freedom." *Philosophical Studies* 157: pp. 177–94.

Robinson, Michael. 2014. "The Limits of Limited-Blockage Frankfurt-Style Cases." *Philosophical Studies* 169: pp. 429–46.

Rogers, Katherin A. 2004. "Augustine's Compatibilism." *Religious Studies* 40 (4): pp. 415–35.

Rogers, Katherin A. 2007. "Libertarianism in Kane and Anselm." *Proceedings of the American Catholic Philosophical Association* 81: pp. 279–90.

Rogers, Katherin A. 2008. *Anselm on Freedom*. Oxford: Oxford University Press.

Roediger, H. L., III. 1990. "Implicit Memory: Retention without Remembering." *American Psychologist* 45: pp. 1043–56.

Rolls, E. T. 2012. "Willed Action: Free Will and the Stochastic Neurodynamics of Decision Making." *Frontiers in Integrative Neuroscience* 6: pp. 202–19.

Rosen, Gideon. 2002. "The Case for Incompatibilism." *Philosophical and Phenomenological Research* 64 (3): pp. 699–716.

Rosen, Gideon. 2008. "Ignorance and Responsibility." *Journal of Philosophy* 105 (10): pp. 591–610.

Roskies, Adina. 2014. "Can Neuroscience Resolve Issues about Free Will?" In *Moral Psychology*, vol. 4, edited by Walter Sinnott-Armstrong, pp. 103–26. Cambridge, MA: MIT Press.

Rossi, Benjamin, and Ted A. Warfield. 2017. "The Relationship between Moral Responsibility and Freedom." In *The Routledge Companion to Free Will*, edited by Kevin Timpe, Meghan Griffith, and Neil Levy, pp. 612–22. New York: Routledge.

Rowe, William. 1995. "Two Concepts of Freedom." In *Agents, Causes, and Events: Essays on Indeterminism and Free Will*, edited by Timothy O'Connor, pp. 151–71. New York: Oxford University Press.

Rowe, William. 2004. *Can God Be Free?* Oxford: Oxford University Press.

Rumi, Jalalul-din. 1956. *Rumi, Poet and Mystic*. Translated and edited by R. A. Nicholson. London: Allan and Unwin.

Runyan, Jason. 2018. "Agent-Causal Libertarianism, Statistical Neural Laws and Wild Coincidences." *Synthese* 195 (10): pp. 4563–80.

Russell, Paul. 1995. *Freedom and Moral Sentiment: Hume's Way of Naturalizing Responsibility*. New York: Oxford University Press.

Russell, Paul. 2002. "Pessimists, Pollyannas, and the New Compatibilism." In *The Oxford Handbook of Free Will*, edited by Robert Kane, pp. 229–56. New York: Oxford University Press.

Russell, Paul. 2011. "Moral Sense and the Foundations of Responsibility." In *The Oxford Handbook of Free Will*, 2nd ed., edited by Robert Kane, pp. 199–220. New York: Oxford University Press.

Russell, Paul. 2017. *The Limits of Free Will*. New York: Oxford University Press.

Russell, Paul. 2017a. "Free Will and Moral Sentiments: Strawsonian Theories." In *The Routledge Companion to Free Will*, edited by Kevin Timpe, Meghan Griffith, and Neil Levy, pp. 96–108. New York: Routledge.
Russell, Paul, and Oisin Deery, eds. 2013. *The Philosophy of Free Will*. Oxford: Oxford University Press.
Ryle, Gilbert. 1949. *The Concept of Mind*. New York: Barnes and Noble.
Sapolsky, Robert M. 2023. *Determined: A Science of Life without Free Will*. London: Penguin.
Sartorio, Carolina. 2015. "The Problem of Determinism and Free Will Is Not the Problem of Determinism and Free Will." In *Surrounding Free Will: Philosophy, Psychology and Neuroscience*, edited by Alfred R. Mele, pp. 255–73. Oxford: Oxford University Press.
Sartorio, Carolina. 2016. *Causation and Free Will*. New York: Oxford University Press.
Sartorio, Carolina. 2017. "Frankfurt-Style Examples." In *The Routledge Companion to Free Will*, edited by Kevin Timpe, Meghan Griffith, and Neil Levy, pp. 179–90. New York: Routledge.
Scanlon, T. M. 2008. *Moral Dimensions: Permissibility, Meaning, and Blame*. Cambridge, MA: Harvard University Press.
Schlick, Moritz. 1939. "When Is a Man Responsible?" In *Problems of Ethics*, translated by David Rynin, pp. 83–98. Englewood Cliffs, NJ: Prentice-Hall.
Schlosser, Markus. 2008. "Agent-Causation and Agential Control." *Philosophical Explorations* 11 (1): pp. 3–21.
Schlosser, Markus. 2014. "The Luck Argument against Event-Causal Libertarianism: It Is Here to Stay." *Philosophical Studies* 167: pp. 375–85.
Schopenhauer, Arthur. [1841] 1999. *Prize Essay on the Freedom of the Will*. Cambridge: Cambridge University Press.
Schueler, G. F. 1995. *Desire: Its Role in Practical Reason and the Explanation of Action*. Cambridge, MA: MIT Press.
Schueler, G. F. 2003. *Reasons and Purposes: Human Rationality and the Teleological Explanation of Action*. New York: Oxford University Press.
Schurger, Aaron, Pengbo Hu, Joanna Pak, and Adina Roskies. 2021. "What Is the Readiness Potential?" *Trends in Cognitive Sciences* 25 (7): pp. 558–70.
Sehon, Scott R. 2005. *Teleological Realism: Mind, Agency, and Explanation*. Cambridge, MA: MIT Press.
Sehon, Scott R. 2013. "Free Will and Mystery: Looking Past the *Mind* Argument." *Philosophical Studies* 162: pp. 291–307.
Sehon, Scott R. 2016. *Free Will and Action Explanation*. Oxford: Oxford University Press.
Sekatskaya, Maria, with Natalia Popova-Nikityuk. 2017. "Robert Kane's Naturalistic Libertarianism" [in Russian]. *Filosofiya: Zhurnal Vysshey shkoly ekonomiki* 1 (4): pp. 14–45. https://doi.org/10.17323/258-8719-2017-I-4-141-189.
Sekatskaya, Maria with Alexander Gebharter and Gerhard Schurz. 2020. "Free Will, Control, and the Possibility to Do Otherwise from a Causal Modeler's Perspective." *Erkenntnis* 4: pp. 183–97. https://doi.org/10.1007/s10670-020-00281-w.
Sekatskaya, Maria. 2021. "Androids, Oracles and Free Will." *Kriterion* 35 (4): pp. 359–78. https://doi.org/10.1515/krt-2021-0010.
Sekatskaya, Maria with Gerhard Schurz. 2022. "Alternative Possibilities and the Meaning of 'Can.'" *Dialectica* 25: pp. 76–89.
Shabo, Seth. 2010. "Uncompromising Source Incompatibilism." *Philosophy and Phenomenological Research* 80 (2): pp. 349–83. https://doi.org/10.1111/j.1933-1592.2010.00328.

Shabo, Seth. 2011. "Why Free Will Remains a Mystery." *Pacific Philosophical Quarterly* 92: pp. 105–25.

Shabo, Seth. 2014a. "Assimilation and Rollbacks: Two Arguments against Libertarianism Defended." *Philosophia* 42: pp. 151–72.

Shabo, Seth. 2014b. "It Wasn't Up to Jones: Avoidable Actions and Intentional Contexts in Frankfurt-Style Examples." *Philosophical Studies* 169 (3): pp. 379–99.

Shabo, Seth. 2020. "The Two-Stage Luck Objection." *Noûs* 54 (1): pp. 3–23.

Shadlen, Michael. 2014. "Comments on Adina Roskies: Can Neuroscience Resolve Issues about Free Will?" In *Moral Psychology*, vol. 4, edited by Walter-Sinnott Armstrong, pp. 139–50. Cambridge, MA: MIT Press.

Shaw, Elizabeth. 2019. "Justice without Moral Responsibility?" *Journal of Information Ethics* 28 (1): 95–114.

Shepherd, Joshua. 2017. "Neuroscientific Threats to Free Will." In *The Routledge Companion to Free Will*, edited by Kevin Timpe, Meghan Griffith, and Neil Levy, pp. 407–22. New York: Routledge.

Sher, George. 2006. *In Praise of Blame*. New York: Oxford University Press.

Shoemaker, David. 2003. "Caring, Identification, and Agency." *Ethics* 114: pp. 88–118.

Shoemaker, David. 2011. "Attributability, Answerability and Accountability: Toward a Wider Theory of Moral Responsibility." *Ethics* 121: pp. 602–32.

Shoemaker, David, ed. 2013. *Oxford Studies in Agency and Responsibility*. Vol. 1. Oxford: Oxford University Press.

Shoemaker, David. 2015a. *Responsibility from the Margins*. Oxford: Oxford University Press.

Shoemaker, David. 2015b. "Ecumenical Attributability." In *The Nature of Moral Responsibility: New Essays*, edited by Randolph Clarke, Michael McKenna, and Angela Smith, pp. 115–40. New York: Oxford University Press.

Siderits, Mark. 1987. "Beyond Compatibilism: A Buddhist Approach to Freedom and Determinism." *American Philosophical Quarterly* 24 (2): pp. 149–59.

Sijuwade, Joshua R. 2023. "Elucidating Open Theism." *International Journal of Philosophy of Religion* 28 (2): pp. 168–82. https//doi.org/10.1007/s11153-023-09874-1.

Simkulet, William. 2012. "On Moral Enhancement." *American Journal of Bioethics Neuroscience* 3: pp. 17–18.

Simkulet, William. 2014a. "Shaky Ground: Free Will and Moral Responsibility Are Tied to the Experience of Apparent Liberty." *De Ethica* 1 (3): pp. 37–51.

Simkulet, William. 2014b. "Lucky Assassins: On Luck and Moral Responsibility." *Lyceum* 13 (1): pp. 58–93.

Simkulet, William. 2015. "On the Signpost Principle of Alternative Possibilities: Why Contemporary Frankfurt-y Cases Are Irrelevant to the Free Will Debate." *Filosofisha Notiser* 2 (3): pp. 107–20.

Simonton, Dean K. 2004. *Creativity in Science: Chance, Logic, Genius and Zeitgeist*. Cambridge: Cambridge University Press.

Singer, Ira. 2002. "Freedom and Revision." *Southwest Philosophy Review* 18 (2): pp. 25–44.

Skinner, B. F. 1948. *Walden Two*. New York: Macmillan.

Slattery, 'Trick. 2014. *Breaking the Free Will Illusion for the Betterment of Humankind*. Decatur, IL: Working Matter Publishing.

Slote, Michael. 1982. "Selective Necessity and the Free-Will Problem." *Journal of Philosophy* 79: pp. 5–20.

Smart, J. J. C. 1961. "Free-will, Praise and Blame." *Mind* 70: pp. 291–306.

Smilansky, Saul. 2000. *Free Will and Illusion*. Oxford: Oxford University Press.
Smith, Angela M. 2007. "On Being Responsible and Holding Responsible." *Journal of Ethics* 11: pp. 465–84.
Smith, Angela M. 2012. "Attributability, Answerability, and Accountability: In Defense of a Unified Account." *Ethics* 122: pp. 575–89.
Smith, Michael. 1997. "A Theory of Freedom and Responsibility." In *Ethics and Practical Reason*, edited by G. Cullity, pp. 293–319. New York: Clarendon Press.
Smith, Michael. 2003. "Rational Capacities." In *Weakness of Will and Varieties of Practical Irrationality*, edited by Sarah Stroud and Christine Tappolet, pp. 17–38. New York: Oxford University Press.
Sommers, Tamler. 2007. "The Objective Attitude." *Philosophical Quarterly* 57: pp. 321–41.
Sommers, Tamler. 2012. *Relative Justice: Cultural Diversity, Free Will and Moral Responsibility*. Princeton, NJ: Princeton University Press.
Sorabji, Richard. 1983. *Necessity, Cause and Blame: Perspectives on Aristotle's Philosophy*. Ithaca, NY: Cornell University Press.
Speak, Daniel. 2007. "The Impertinence of Frankfurt-Style Argument." *Philosophical Quarterly* 57: pp. 76–95.
Speak, Daniel. 2011. "The Consequence Argument Revisited." In *The Oxford Handbook of Free Will*, 2nd ed., edited by Robert Kane, pp. 115–30. New York: Oxford University Press.
Spinoza, Baruch. [1677] 1992. *The Ethics and Selected Letters*. Edited by Seymour Feldman. Translated by Samuel Shirley. Indianapolis: Hackett.
Sripada, Chandra. 2012. "What Makes a Manipulated Agent Unfree?" *Philosophy and Phenomenological Research* 85: pp. 563–93.
Sripada, Chandra. 2014. "How Is Willpower Possible? The Puzzle of Synchronic Self-Control and the Divided Mind." *Nous* 48: pp. 41–74.
Sripada, Chandra. 2016. "Self-Expression: A Deep Self Theory of Moral Responsibility." *Philosophical Studies* 173: pp. 1203–32.
Sripada, Chandra. 2017. "Will-Power, Freedom and Responsibility." In *The Routledge Companion to Free Will*, edited by Kevin Timpe, Meghan Griffith, and Neil Levy, pp. 444–53. New York: Routledge.
Stapp, Henry. 2007. *The Mindful Universe*. Berlin: Springer.
Statman, Daniel, ed. 1993. *Moral Luck*. Albany: State University of New York Press.
Statman, Daniel, and Christopher Shields. 2022. "Narrative Determination." *Journal of the American Philosophical Association* 48: pp. 68–84.
Steward, Helen. 2012. *A Metaphysics for Freedom*. Oxford: Oxford University Press.
Stout, Rowland. 2010. "Deviant Causal Chains." In *A Companion to the Philosophy of Action*, edited by Timothy O'Connor and Constantine Sandis, pp. 159–65. Oxford: Blackwell.
Strawson, Galen. 1986. *Freedom and Belief*. Oxford: Clarendon Press.
Strawson, Galen. 1994. "The Impossibility of Moral Responsibility." *Philosophical Studies* 75: pp. 5–24.
Strawson, Galen. 2002. "The Bounds of Freedom." In *The Oxford Handbook of Free Will*, edited by Robert Kane, pp. 44–56. New York: Oxford University Press.
Strawson, P. F. 1962. "Freedom and Resentment." *Proceedings of the British Academy* 48: pp. 187–211.

Stump, Eleanor. 1996. "Libertarian Freedom and the Principle of Alternative Possibilities." In *The Evidential Problem of Evil*, edited by D. Howard Snyder, pp. 73–88. Bloomington: Indiana University Press.

Stump, Eleanor. 2006. "Augustine on Free Will." In *The Cambridge Companion to Augustine*, edited by Eleonore Stump and Norman Kretzmann, pp. 124–47. Cambridge: Cambridge University Press.

Suarez, Antoine, and Peter Adams, eds. 2013. *Is Science Compatible with Free Will? Exploring Free Will and Consciousness in the Light of Quantum Physics and Neuroscience*. Berlin: Springer.

Swinburne, Richard. 1974. *Metaphysics*. Englewood Cliffs, NJ: Prentice-Hall.

Swinburne, Richard. 2013a. "Defending (a Modified Version of) the Zygote Argument." *Philosophical Studies* 164: pp. 189–203.

Swinburne, Richard. 2013b. *Mind, Brain, and Free Will*. Oxford: Oxford University Press.

Sytsma, Justus, and Wesley Buchalter, eds. 2016. *A Companion to Experimental Philosophy*. Hoboken, NJ: John Wiley and Sons.

Tadros, Victor. 2016. *Wrongs and Crimes*. Oxford: Oxford University Press.

Tadros, Victor. 2017. "Doing without Desert." *Criminal Law and Philosophy* 11: pp. 605–16.

Talbert, Matthew. 2016. *Moral Responsibility: An Introduction*. Malden, MA: Polity Press.

Talbott, Thomas. 2008. "Why Christians Should Not Be Determinists: Reflections on the Origins of Original Sin." *Faith and Philosophy* 25: pp. 300–17.

Tappolet, Christine. 2017. "Self-Control and Akrasia." In *The Routledge Companion to Free Will*, edited by Kevin Timpe, Meghan Griffith, and Neil Levy, pp. 565–76. New York: Routledge.

Taylor, Richard. 1966. *Action and Purpose*. Englewood Cliffs, NJ: Prentice-Hall.

Taylor, Richard. 1999. "Moral Responsibility and Alternative Possibilities: The Flicker of Freedom." *Journal of Ethics* 3: pp. 299–324.

Taylor, Tabitha. 2016. "Remixed Responsibility: Defending Compatibilist Views of Responsibility." PhD dissertation, Central European University.

Thorp, J. 1980. *Free Will: A Defense against Neurophysiological Determinism*. London: Routledge and Kegan Paul.

Tierney, Hannah. 2014. "Taking It Head-On: How to Best Handle the Modified Manipulation Argument." *Journal of Value Inquiry* 48: pp. 663–75.

Tierney, Hannah, and David Glick. 2020. "Desperately Seeking Sourcehood." *Philosophical Studies* 177 (4): pp. 953–70.

Tiffany, Evan. 2013. "Choosing Freedom: Basic Desert and the Standpoint of Blame." *Philosophical Explorations* 21: pp. 195–211.

Timpe, Kevin. 2006. "A Critique of Frankfurt-libertarianism." *Philosophia* 34: pp. 189–202.

Timpe, Kevin. 2008. *Free Will: Sourcehood and Its Alternatives*. New York: Continuum Books.

Timpe, Kevin, and Jonathan Jacobs. 2015. "Free Will and Naturalism: How to Be a Libertarian and a Naturalist Too." In *The Blackwell Companion to Naturalism*, edited by J. K. Clark, pp. 319–35. Oxford: Blackwell.

Timpe, Kevin, and Dan Speak, eds. 2016. *Free Will and Theism: Connections, Contingencies and Concerns*. Oxford: Oxford University Press.

Todd, Patrick. 2011. "A New Approach to Manipulation Arguments." *Philosophical Studies* 152(1): pp. 127–33.

Todd, Patrick. 2012. "Manipulation and Moral Standing: An Argument for Incompatibilism." *Philosophical Imprint* 12: pp. 1–18.

Todd, Patrick. 2013. "Defending (a Modified Version of the) Zygote Argument." *Philosophical Studies* 164: pp. 189–203.
Todd, Patrick. 2017. "Manipulation Arguments and the Freedom to Do Otherwise." *Philosophy and Phenomenological Research* 95 (2): pp. 395–407.
Tognazzini, Neal. 2011. "Understanding Source Incompatibilism." *Modern Schoolman* 88 (7): pp. 73–88.
Tognazzini, Neal. 2015. "Grounding the Luck Objection." *Australasian Journal of Philosophy* 93: pp. 127–38.
Tognazzini, Neal. 2017. "Free Will and Time Travel." In *The Routledge Companion to Free Will*, edited by Kevin Timpe, Meghan Griffith, and Neil Levy, pp. 680–90. New York: Routledge.
Tognazzini, Neal. 2022. "Responsibility." In *International Encyclopedia of Ethics*, edited by Hugh LaFollette, pp. 4592–602. Malden, MA: Wiley-Blackwell.
Trakakis, Nick, and Daniel Cohen, eds. 2008. *Essays on Free Will and Moral Responsibility*. Newcastle upon Tyne, UK: Cambridge Scholars Publishing.
Tse, Peter Ulric. 2013. *The Neural Basis of Free Will: Criterial Causation*. Cambridge, MA: MIT Press.
Tse, Peter Ulric. 2021. Podcast on Free Will on You Tube's Closer to Truth.
Turner, Jason. 2009. "The Incompatibility of Free Will and Naturalism." *Australian Journal of Philosophy* 84 (4): pp. 565–87.
Ulanowicz, R. 2005. "A Revolution in the Middle Kingdom." In *Micro, Meso, Macro: Addressing Complex Systems Couplings*, edited by H. Liljenstrom, U. Svedin, pp. 78–96. Hackensack, NJ: World Scientific.
Usher, Marius. 2006. "Control, Choice and the Convergence/Divergence Dynamics: A Compatibilistic Probabilistic Theory of Free Will." *Journal of Philosophy* 304: pp. 188–213.
van Gulick, Robert. 1995. "Who's in Charge Here? And Who's Doing All the Work?" In *Mental Causation*, edited by John Heil and Alfred R. Mele, pp. 67–81. Oxford: Clarendon Press.
Van Inwagen, Peter. 1983. *An Essay on Free Will*. Oxford: Oxford University Press.
Van Inwagen, Peter. 2000. "Free Will Remains a Mystery." *Philosophical Perspectives* 14: pp. 1–19.
Van Inwagen, Peter. 2008. "How to Think about the Problem of Free Will." *Journal of Ethics* 12: pp. 327–41.
Vargas, Manuel. 2004. "Libertarianism and Skepticism about Free Will: Some Arguments against Both." *Philosophical Topics* 32: pp. 403–26.
Vargas, Manuel. 2005. "The Revisionist's Guide to Responsibility." *Philosophical Studies* 125 (3): pp. 399–429.
Vargas, Manuel. 2007. "Revisionism." In *Four Views on Free Will*, edited by John Martin Fischer, Robert Kane, Derk Pereboom, and Manuel Vargas, pp. 126–64. Malden, MA: Blackwell.
Vargas, Manuel. 2013. *Building Better Beings: A Theory of Moral Responsibility*. New York: Oxford University Press.
Velleman, J. David. 1992. "What Happens When Someone Acts?" *Mind* 101: pp. 461–81.
Velleman, J. David. 2000. *The Possibility of Practical Reason*. New York: Oxford University Press.
Velleman, J. David. 2009. *How We Get Along*. Cambridge: Cambridge University Press.

Vicens, Leigh. 2016. "Objective Probabilities of Free Choice." *Res Philosophica* 93: pp. 125–35.

Vicens, Leigh. 2017. "Free Will and Theological Determinism." In *The Routledge Companion to Free Will*, edited by Kevin Timpe, Meghan Griffith, and Neil Levy, pp. 512–21. New York: Routledge.

Vicens, Leigh, and Simon Kittle. 2019. *God and Human Freedom*. Cambridge: Cambridge University Press.

Vihvelin, Kadri. 2004. "Free Will Demystified: A Dispositional Account." *Philosophical Topics* 32: pp. 427–50.

Vihvelin, Kadri. 2011. "How to Think about the Free Will/Determinism Problem." In *Carving Nature at Its Joints*, edited by J. Campbell, M. O'Rouke, and H. M. Slater, pp. 313–40. Cambridge, MA: MIT Press.

Vihvelin, Kadri. 2013. *Causes, Laws, and Free Will: Why Determinism Doesn't Matter*. New York: Oxford University Press.

Vihvelin, Kadri. 2017. "Dispositional Compatibilism." In *The Routledge Companion to Free Will*, edited by Kevin Timpe, Meghan Griffith, and Neil Levy, pp. 52–61. New York: Routledge.

Vilhauer, Benjamin. 2009. "Free Will Skepticism and Personhood as a Desert Base." *Canadian Journal of Philosophy* 39: pp. 489–511.

Vilhauer, Benjamin. 2010. "The Scope of Responsibility in Kant's Theory of Free Will." *British Journal of the History of Philosophy* 18: pp. 45–71.

Vilhauer, Benjamin. 2013. "Persons, Punishment, and Free Will Skepticism." *Philosophical Studies* 162: pp. 143–63.

Vilhauer, Benjamin. 2015. "Taking Free Will Skepticism Seriously." *Philosophical Quarterly* 62: pp. 833–52.

Vilhauer, Benjamin. 2017. "Kant." In *The Routledge Companion to Free Will*, edited by Kevin Timpe, Meghan Griffith, and Neil Levy, pp. 343–55. New York: Routledge.

Voltaire. 1977. *The Portable Voltaire*. Edited by B. R. Redman. New York: Penguin.

Von Stosch, Klaus, Saskia Wendel, Martin Bruel, and Alan Langerfeld, eds. 2019. *Streit um die Freiheit*. Munich: Ferdinand Schoningh.

Wainwright, William. 1996. "Jonathan Edwards, William Rowe, and the Necessity of Creation." In *Faith, Freedom, and Rationality*, edited by Jeff Jordan and Daniel Howard-Snyder, pp. 119–33. Lanham, MD: Rowman and Littlefield.

Wallace, R. Jay. 1994. *Responsibility and the Moral Sentiments*. Cambridge, MA: Harvard University Press.

Wallace, R. Jay. 1999. "Addiction as Defect of the Will: Some Philosophical Reflections." *Law and Philosophy* 18: pp. 621–54.

Wallace, Robert. 2019. "Responsibility and the Limits of Good and Evil." *Philosophical Studies* 10 (176): pp. 2705–27.

Wallace, Robert. 2021. "The Tension in Critical Compatibilism." *Ethical Theory and Moral Practice* 21 (1): pp. 321–32.

Waller, Bruce. 1990. *Freedom without Responsibility*. Philadelphia: Temple University Press.

Waller, Bruce. 2011. *Against Moral Responsibility*. Cambridge, MA: MIT Press.

Waller, Bruce. 2014. *The Stubborn System of Moral Responsibility*. Cambridge, MA: MIT Press.

Waller, Robyn Repko. 2014. "Revising Reasons' Reactivity: Weakly and Strongly Sufficient Reasons for Acting." *Ethical Theory and Moral Practice* 17 (3): pp. 529–43.

Waller, Robyn Repko, with Russell Waller. 2015. "Forking Worlds and Freedom: A Challenge to Libertarian Accounts of Free Will." *Philosophia* 43 (4): pp. 1199–212.
Waller, Robyn Repko. 2023. "Free Willed Self-Expression: A Compatibilist Garden of Forking Paths." *Philosophical Issues* pp. 1–15.
Walter, Henrik. 2001. *Neurophilosophy of Free Will: From Libertarian Illusions to a Concept of Natural Autonomy*. Cambridge, MA: MIT Press.
Walter, Henrik. 2004. "Neurophilosophy of Moral Responsibility: The Case for Revisionist Compatibilism." *Philosophical Topics* 32: pp. 477–532.
Warfield, Ted. 1996. "Causal Determinism and Moral Responsibility Are Incompatible." *Philosophical Topics* 24: pp. 215–26.
Warfield, Ted. 2000. "Causal Determinism and Human Freedom Are Incompatible: A New Argument for Incompatibilism." *Philosophical Perspectives* 14: pp. 167–80.
Warmke, Brandon. 2011. "Moral Responsibility Invariantism." *Philosophia* 39: pp. 179–200.
Watson, Gary. 1975. "Free Agency." *Journal of Philosophy* 72: pp. 205–20.
Watson, Gary. 1987. "Responsibility and the Limits of Evil: Variations on a Strawsonian Theme." In *Responsibility, Character and the Emotions*, edited by F. D. Shoeman, pp. 256–86. Cambridge: Cambridge University Press.
Watson, Gary. 1996. "Two Faces of Responsibility." *Philosophical Topics* 24: pp. 227–48.
Watson, Gary. 2004. *Agency and Answerability*. New York: Oxford University Press.
Watson, Gary. 2022. *Freedom and Responsibility in Context*. Oxford: Oxford University Press.
Wegner, Daniel. 2002. *The Illusion of Conscious Will*. Cambridge, MA: MIT Press.
Weigel, C. 2013. "Experimental Evidence for Free Will Revisionism." *Philosophical Explorations* 16: pp. 31–43.
Werndl, Charlotte. 2017. "Determinism." In *The Routledge Companion to Free Will*, edited by Kevin Timpe, Meghan Griffith, and Neil Levy, pp. 669–79. New York: Routledge.
Whittle, Ann. 2010. "Dispositional Abilities." *Philosopher's Imprint* 10 (12): pp. 75–90.
Widerker, David. 1995. "Libertarianism and Frankfurt's Attack on the Principle of Alternative Possibilities." *Philosophical Review* 104: pp. 247–61.
Widerker, David. 2000. "Frankfurt's Attack on Alternative Possibilities: A Further Look." *Philosophical Perspectives* 14: pp. 181–201.
Widerker, David. 2006. "Libertarianism and the Philosophical Significance of Frankfurt Scenarios." *Journal of Philosophy* 103: pp. 163–87.
Widerker, David, and Michael McKenna, eds. 2003. *Moral Responsibility and Alternative Possibilities: Essays on the Importance of Alternative Possibilities*. Burlington, VT: Ashgate.
Widerker, David, and Stewart Goetz. 2013. "Fischer against the Dilemma Defense: The Defense Prevails." *Analysis* 73: pp. 283–95.
Wiggins, David. 1973. "Towards a Reasonable Libertarianism." In *Essays on Freedom and Action*, edited by Ted Honderich, pp. 31–62. London: Routledge & Kegan Paul.
Williams, Bernard. 1986. *Ethics and the Limits of Philosophy*. London: Fontana.
Winkielman, P., and K. C. Berridge. 2004. "Unconscious Emotion." *Current Directions in Psychological Science* 13: pp. 120–23.
Wolf, Susan. 1987. "Sanity and the Metaphysics of Responsibility." In *Responsibility, Character and the Emotions: New Essays on Moral Psychology*, edited by F. D. Schoeman, pp. 167–85. Cambridge: Cambridge University Press.
Wolf, Susan. 1990. *Freedom within Reason*. New York: Oxford University Press.

Wolf, Susan. 2002. "Sanity and the Metaphysics of Responsibility." In *The Oxford Handbook of Free Will*, edited by Robert Kane, pp. 145–63. New York: Oxford University Press.

Wolf, Susan. 2005. "Freedom within Reason." In *Personal Autonomy*, edited by J. S. Taylor, pp. 258–74. New York: Cambridge University Press.

Wyma, Keith. 1997. "Moral Responsibility and the Leeway for Action." *American Philosophical Quarterly* 34: pp. 57–70.

Xin, Jin. "Hard Libertarianism and Degree: A Kanean Approach to Free Will." Unpublished paper.

Yeomans, Christopher. 2011. *Freedom and Reflection: Hegel and the Logic of Agency*. New York: Oxford University Press.

Yeomans, Christopher. 2017. "Georg Wilhelm Friedrich Hegel." In *The Routledge Companion to Free Will*, edited by Kevin Timpe, Meghan Griffith, and Neil Levy, pp. 343–55. New York: Routledge.

Zagzebski, Linda. 2000. "Does Libertarian Freedom Require Alternative Possibilities?" *Philosophical Perspectives* 14: pp. 231–48.

Zagzebski, Linda. 2022. *God, Knowledge and the Good*. Oxford: Oxford University Press.

Zimmerman, Dean. 2018. "Ever Better Situations and the Failure of Expression Principles." *Faith and Philosophy* 35 (4): pp. 408–16.

Zimmerman, Michael. 1988. *An Essay on Moral Responsibility*. Totowa, NJ: Rowman and Littlefield.

Zimmerman, Michael. 2002. "Taking Luck Seriously." *Journal of Philosophy* 99 (11): pp. 553–57.

Index

For the benefit of digital users, indexed terms that span two pages (e.g., 52–53) may, on occasion, appear on only one of those pages.

ability, 10–11, 94, 95–96
   to do otherwise, 216–18, 220–21, 229–31, 235, 237
   See also power
AC. *See* agent-causal *under* libertarianism
AC/EC. *See* agent-causal/event-causal *under* libertarianism
accident, 16, 18–20, 68–69, 82–83
accountability, 31, 40–41, 255–56, 265–66
action
   agent's mechanisms of, 219–20
   alternative possibilities and, 117, 121
   ambivalence and, 111–12, 262–63
   appropriate nonrandomness and, 139–40, 142
   arbitrariness of, 97–99
   basic, 159, 202–3
   blameworthy, 40–41, 216–18
   causal theory of, 152, 184–86, 187–91, 192–93, 196–98, 199–201
   childhood and, 87–88
   context of, 91–92
   control and, 76–79, 92–93, 107–8, 116–19, 125, 127, 133–34, 148–50, 159–60, 192–93, 201–2, 218, 220–21, 237–38, 239, 268–69, 274–75, 285–86
   decision-making and, 48, 140–43, 146–50, 155–56, 160
   desires and, 209–14
   effort and, 126–27
   endowments and, 253–54
   freedom of, 10–12, 13–15, 16–18, 20, 27–28, 41–43, 48–49, 80–81, 89–92, 108, 111–12, 133–34, 268–69, 276
   future and, 110–12
   intentional, 82–83, 101–2, 105–6, 107–8, 109–10
   motivation and, 25, 26, 103, 105, 106–8, 109–10, 119–20, 121, 128, 230, 231, 249–51
   phenomenology of, 71–72, 201–2
   practical reasoning and, 128–31, 174–75
   probability and, 140–41
   purposive, 77
   rationality and, 25, 26, 72–74, 78–79, 98, 99, 101–2, 105–6, 107–8, 109–10
   responsiveness and, 218–20
   self-forming (SFA), 12–13, 24, 26, 42, 47–49, 53, 61, 68–69, 124, 125–27, 128–29, 135, 136–38, 160–61, 180–81, 238–39, 249–51
   striving, 25–26
   sufficient cause and motive for, 21–23
   True and Good, 215–16
   undetermined, 2–3, 17–20, 21–23, 50, 64, 70, 76–77, 98, 100, 103, 108–9, 117–19, 120, 135, 139, 141–43, 146–47, 160–62, 178, 179, 191, 197, 205–6
   voluntary, 78–79, 81–82, 83, 86–88, 89–90, 92, 94, 95–96, 97, 101–2, 105–6, 107–8, 109–10, 118, 148, 185–86, 192–93, 221
   will-setting and, 21, 22–23, 40, 42, 47–49, 50–52, 53, 55–57, 61–63, 64–66, 69, 73–74, 89–92, 94, 110, 113, 119, 120–21, 124–25, 157–58, 171–73, 180–81, 185–86, 213–14, 220
   See also agency; choice; freedom
agency
   causation and, 80–83, 154
   decision-making and, 195–98
   as disposition, 229–32
   failure of, 104–8, 109

agency (*cont.*)
  free, 14–15, 82, 185–86
  intentionality and, 17–21, 97
  manipulated, 151
  natural order and, 153, 154–55
  neo-Aristotelian, 183
  non-reductive, 154, 199
  opportunity and, 94, 95–96
  possibility and, 232–35
  power and, 46–49, 53, 56–57, 92–93, 94–96, 97, 109–10, 117–18, 121–22, 148–50, 158–59, 171, 173, 174, 183, 185–86, 191, 195, 197–98
  preemption and, 52, 53–54
  preferences and, 170
  rationality and, 19, 20, 92–93
  reductionism, 152–53, 154–56, 160, 162–63, 174, 184
  responsibility and, 15, 21–22, 28, 38, 39–41, 47–48, 57, 86–88, 89–91, 111–12, 121, 125, 160–61, 188–89
  science and, 233–35, 240, 241–42
  voluntary, 8, 15, 16, 19–20, 22, 42–43, 47–49, 55–57
  See also action; choice; freedom
agent
  causality and, 5–8, 80, 83–86, 99–100, 143, 154–56, 163–65, 176–77, 182–86, 187–91, 195, 198–200, 205, 255
  disappearing, 80, 83, 85, 255
  as information-responsive complex dynamical system, 81–84, 85–86, 154–55, 159–60, 164–65, 184, 192–93, 196, 206
  mechanisms of action, 219–20
  mental states and, 82–83
  See also causation
akrasia, 127
alternative possibility (AP), 10–13, 15–16, 17, 19–20, 21–22, 46–48, 94, 95–96, 97, 117, 121, 209, 211, 214, 216–21, 222–24, 225
ambivalence, 111–12, 213–14, 262–63
Anscombe, Elizabeth, 17, 66
answerability, 41
  forward-looking, 265–66
AP. *See* alternative possibility

Aristotle, 10, 11–12, 80, 81, 183, 204, 206–7, 244–45, 278–79, 284–85
artificial intelligence, 132
aspiration, 277–79, 280, 287
attentiveness, 54–55
attributability, 40–41, 265–66
Augustine, St., 79, 98–99, 301–2
Austin, J. L., 17–19, 66–67
authorship, 139–40, 141–43
autonomy, 188–89, 262–63, 276
Ayers, Michael, 17

Bach, Johann Sebastian, 288–89
Balaguer, Mark, 136–43, 172, 194
behavior
  conditioning of, 27, 257, 258
  evolution and, 133–34, 235, 268–69
  responsibility and, 35, 37, 38, 88
behaviorism, 27
Bhagavad-Gita, 295–96
Bishop, Robert, 59–60
blameworthiness, 29–30, 31, 35, 36–39, 216–18, 221–26, 228–29, 282–83. *See also* reactive attitude; responsibility
blockage, 50–53, 55–56
Blumenberg, Hans, 262–63
Bok, Hilary, 226
Borges, Jorge Luis, 10, 116–17
brain
  indeterminism and, 17, 58, 59–60, 71, 132, 233–34
  patterns of activity in, 81–82, 192–93, 206, 240
  See also neuroscience
Brembs, Bjorn, 60, 132
Brink, 31, 218, 226
Brown, Warren, 60
Buddhism, 294–95, 296–99

capacity, 80, 93, 134
  emergent, 81, 183, 192
  love and, 290
  responsibility and, 265, 276
Capes, Justin, 203
Caruso, Gregg, 190, 191, 247, 263–68, 269, 270–71
categorical imperative, 288, 292–93
Causal Theory of Action, 152

INDEX   361

causation
  action, 152, 154
  agent (AC), 7–8, 80–86, 99–100,
    154–56, 159–60, 162–65, 167, 168,
    176–77, 182–86, 187–91, 192–95,
    196–200, 203, 206–7, 255
  control and, 201, 205–6
  deviant, 82–84, 85, 152, 155–56,
    196–97
  efficient, 183, 201, 204, 206–7
  event (EC), 80–82, 83–86, 135–36, 143–
    44, 151–52, 154–56, 159–60, 162–65,
    168, 176–77, 183–85, 187–89, 192,
    196–97, 199–200, 255
  formal and final, 183, 201, 204, 206–7
  immanent, 199
  by immaterial substances, 84
  indeterminism and, 74–76, 83–84, 103–
    4, 119–20, 193–94
  libertarianism and, 5–8
  material, 204, 206–7
  by mental states, 7, 82–84, 164–65, 184,
    185, 188–89, 192, 196–97, 199–200
  motivation and, 121, 164–67, 168, 188,
    196–97, 201, 204–5, 206
  naturalistic view of, 189–90
  noncausal (NC), 83–86, 154, 183, 199–
    207, 255
  preferences and, 168–70
  probabilistic, 74–76, 103–5, 106–7,
    197, 292
  substance, 183–84, 185, 188–89, 192
  ultimate, 244–45
  See also determinism; libertarianism
chance, 58, 66–67, 69, 70–71, 96–102,
  103, 106–7, 114–15, 117–18, 125,
  131–32, 161–62, 205, 252–54. *See also*
  indeterminism; luck
character development, 11–13, 14, 15,
  87–88, 137, 138. *See also*
  self-formation
childhood, 87–88
Chinmayananda, Swami, 295
choice
  competing, 195–98
  contrastive explanations and, 165–67
  efforts of, 144–47, 148, 149–50, 151,
    156–59, 166–67, 175–76

  responsibility and, 11–13, 14, 15
  self-forming, 48, 55–57, 64, 71–72, 73,
    74, 80–81, 87–93, 97–99, 100–1, 103,
    104–5, 106, 108–11, 148, 160–61,
    249–51, 252, 253–54
  will-setting and, 21
  See also action; decision,
    decision-making
Clarke, Randolph, 113, 114, 115–16, 163–
  64, 169–70, 186–88, 190, 196, 200,
  201–183, 203–4
Coates, Justin, 229–30
Cohen, Jonathan D., 81–82, 192–93, 206
compatibilism, 2–3, 4–5, 7–8, 9, 28,
  143, 208–9
  asymmetry thesis, 216–18
  basic deserts and, 266–68
  chance and, 252, 254
  classical, 44–46
  control and, 93, 123, 133–34, 158–59
  counterfactuals and, 218–20
  creativity and, 264
  critical, 242–46
  deliberation and, 115–16, 118
  dispositional, 229–32
  illusion and, 269–70, 272–73, 279–80
  manipulation arguments and, 255–
    58, 263
  preferences and, 170
  reasons-responsive theories, 218–20
  responsibility and, 12–13, 37, 38, 39,
    43–49, 225–29, 247, 272, 276, 279–80
  revisionist, 235–42, 279–80
  semi-compatibilism, 219–20
  symmetry thesis, 217
  ultimacy and, 227–29
  See also determinism; free will;
    libertarianism
Compatibility Question, 4–5, 9–12, 13, 29,
  41–42, 43, 57, 58, 208
complexity, 69–70, 81–82, 87, 268–69
Compton, Arthur Holly, 131
conflict, 111–12
Consequence Argument, 236
consequentialism, 243, 267, 281–82
contractualism, 243, 281–82
contrastive explanations, 108–12, 165–
  67, 252–53

control, 76–79, 92–93, 107–8, 116–19, 122–23, 125, 127, 133–34, 148–50, 159–60, 192–93, 201–2, 218, 220–21, 237–38, 239, 268–69, 274–75, 285–86
  active, 115–16, 118, 201–183
  antecedent determining, 122
  causation and, 201, 205–6
  direct, 122
  freedom and, 218, 220–21
  indeterminism and, 93–94, 95–96, 106–8, 122–23, 158–59, 239
  kinds of, 92–93
  macro vs. micro, 122
  plural voluntary, 20, 22, 92–96, 106–8, 117, 118, 122, 125, 133–34, 139, 141, 142, 158–59, 185–86, 221, 239, 268–69, 274–75
  preferences and, 170
  rational, 170
  regulative, 218, 220–21
  selfhood and, 285–86
  systemic, 82–83
  teleological guidance, 7, 81–82, 83–84, 85–86, 92–93, 97, 102, 106–7, 108, 122, 133, 134, 141, 142, 148–50, 154–55, 159–60, 162, 164–65, 173–74, 181, 185–86, 188, 192–93, 196–97, 206–7, 218, 220–21, 239, 249–50, 268–69, 274–75
  See also action; decision, decision-making
conversation, 225–26
counterfactual, 183, 218–19, 220, 230–32
creativity, 129–32, 263–66
criminal trial, 35–36, 38–39, 282

Davidson, Donald, 82–83
decision, decision-making
  agency and, 155–56, 160, 195–98
  control and, 140–43, 148–50, 159–60
  efforts of, 156–57, 164
  inclination and, 141–42
  indeterminism and, 144–45
  phenomenology of, 136–37, 142–43
  self-formation and, 141, 150, 249–51
  torn, 136–40, 141–43, 179
  will-setting and, 157–58
  See also deliberation; choice
decision theory, 110, 233, 234

deliberation, 48, 89, 94–96, 100–2, 105–6, 107–8, 109–10, 113–15, 186
  assigning weights to reasons and, 176–81
  choice and, 145–47, 148, 149–50, 198
  evaluative judgment and, 115–16, 118, 123–25, 126, 129
  evolution and, 130–34
  indeterminism and, 116–25, 129–32, 143–44, 168–70, 173, 174, 178, 180, 186, 197–98
  luck and, 205
  preferences and, 168–70, 171–75
  self and, 169
  two-stage model of, 131
  will-setting and, 171–72, 180–81
Dennett, Daniel, 12–13, 37, 114–16, 118, 130, 131, 168–69, 171, 186, 218, 226, 256, 266–69, 270–71
desert, 225–26, 266–67, 268
  basic, 247–49, 252–53, 254–55, 257, 258–61, 262–64, 266–68, 269, 281–82
  ultimate, 279–80, 281–85, 294–95
  See also responsibility
desire, 7, 20–21, 95–96, 209–15
  ambivalence and, 213–14
  contrary, 126–28
  Motivational Will and, 25, 26
determinism, 2–6, 7–8, 9
  alternative possibilities and, 225
  causal, 31–34, 83, 185, 216–17
  compatibilism and, 215–20, 221–22, 232–33
  control and, 274–75
  freedom and, 9–13, 15, 28, 29–31, 50–53, 57, 208–9, 274–76, 281, 290–92
  hard, 3, 248, 254–55, 264
  impossibility and, 224
  metaphysical, 216–17
  physical, 224, 232–35
  responsibility and, 43–57, 226–27, 247–48, 276, 281, 282–83
  revisionist views on, 235–42
  science and, 234–35, 241–42, 248, 254–55, 290–92
  selfhood and, 286–87
  of upbringing, 35–36, 37, 38–39
deus ex machina, 58–59
deviance, 82–84, 85, 152, 155–56, 196–97

Diderot, Denis, 247
dignity, 288–89
Dilemma Defense, 49
disposition, 25, 229–32. *See also* compatibilism
Doris, John, 111–12, 125
Doyle, Robert, 60, 130, 131, 132
dualism
  fundamental, 269–70, 272
  mind-body, 6, 7–8, 189–90, 199
  substance, 183
Dworkin, Ronald, 245–46
dynamical systems theory, 81–82. *See also* system

earthquakes, 183–84
EC. *See* event-causal *under* libertarianism
effort, 88–93, 95–96, 126–27
  to choose, 144–47, 148, 149–50, 151, 156–59, 166–67, 175–76
  concurrent competing, 151, 158
  context of, 161
  indeterminism and, 160, 161–62
  luck and, 161–62
  plural, 144–46, 175–76, 178–79
  regress objection, 160, 161–62
  to resolve conflicts, 128–29
  of will, 137, 138, 148, 149, 156–58, 159–62, 164, 167–68, 171–72, 174, 186, 197–98
Einstein, Albert, 264–65
Ekstrom, Laura, 114, 168–70, 171, 172, 174–75, 186
eliminative reductionism, 183
Ellis, G. F. R., 60
ends in themselves, 288, 292–94
Epicureanism, 59, 60
Escherichia coli bacterium, 133
ethics, 277, 278–79, 288, 289–93
  ideal and non-ideal theory, 293–94
evaluation, 115–16
  critical, 173–74
  judgment and, 168–69, 170–72, 265
  reflective, 169
evolution, 129–34, 268–69
  chance and, 131–33
  control and, 133–34
example
  Austin-style, 66–67, 68–69, 121
  blockage, 50–53
  buffered, 53–57
  Frankfurt-style, 46, 47–50, 151, 209–11, 212, 216, 217, 219, 220, 230–31
Existence Questions, 5
Explanatory Luck Objection, 96–99, 105–6, 109, 205

faculty, 25
fair opportunity, 31–33
Fara, Michael, 229
Federman, Asaf, 297–99
Fischer, John, 211, 216, 217–18, 219–21, 226, 242
Foot, Philippa, 17
Formula of Humanity, 292–94
Frankfurt, Harry, 12, 38, 46–48, 49, 209–17, 219, 220
Franklin, Christopher Evan, 151–53, 155–56, 157, 158–59, 160, 162–64, 165–66, 167, 168, 169–70, 184, 199
freedom
  of action, 13–15, 16–18, 20, 27–28, 41–43, 48–49, 80–81, 90–91, 108, 111–12, 133–34, 268–69, 276
  chance and, 131–32
  to do otherwise, 31–34, 40, 43–49, 50–53, 56–57, 109–10
  historical dimensions of, 212–17, 218–20, 252
  kinds of, 9–14, 17–18, 19–20, 24, 27–28, 89–92, 93, 121, 160–61, 238–39, 257–58, 268–69
  plurality conditions for, 109–10
  responsibility and, 41–57, 208–9, 211–19, 220–22, 226–27, 228–29, 231–32, 235–36, 241–43, 247–52, 254–55, 279–81, 283–84, 294–95
  of will, 10, 13–15, 19, 21, 24–26, 27–28, 41–43, 108, 111–12, 133–34, 158–59, 208–9, 268–69, 276
  See also action; agency; alternative possibility; control
free will, 1–8, 9
  alternative possibilities and, 15–16, 17, 19–20, 21–22, 94, 95–96, 97
  aspiration and, 280
  in Buddhism, 296–99
  conflict and, 135
  creativity and, 263–66

364　INDEX

free will (cont.)
　deliberation and, 116–21, 122–34
　diagnostic accounts of, 236
　dual regress of, 21–23, 121
　ethics and, 278–79, 288, 289–94
　evolution and, 113, 129–34, 268–69
　in Hinduism, 295–96
　illusion and, 269–70, 271–73
　incompatibilism and, 93
　intelligibility of, 58
　metaphysical dimensions of, 243–46, 284–85
　modern attacks on, 4–5
　motivation and, 128, 163
　pessimism, 242–43, 244, 245–46
　plurality conditions, 16, 20, 21, 22–23, 121
　prescriptive accounts of, 236
　responsibility and, 29–31, 32–41, 86–88, 89–91, 98, 99, 106, 151
　science and, 175–77, 290–92
　skepticism, 3–4, 247–49, 251–55, 258–59, 260–73, 279–80, 281
　social order and, 261–62
　as struggle and gift, 301–2
　teleological intelligibility view of, 155
　theism and, 300–1
　ultimacy condition of, 10–12, 15–16, 21–23, 58, 86–88, 89–90, 106, 209, 227–29, 279–80
　See also agency; causation; determinism; indeterminism; will
future, 2, 31–32, 69–70, 98–99, 110–11, 116–17, 131, 138, 205–6, 213–14, 232–33, 240–41, 252, 265, 275, 296. See also value experiment

garden of forking paths, 116–17
Ginet, Carl, 49, 201–3
Glimcher, Paul, 60, 132, 133
Goetz, Stuart, 201, 203–4
good, 168–69, 170, 172–73, 215–16, 226, 277–79, 280, 300–1
Griffith, Meghan, 188–90, 196, 199, 200
guilt, 78, 221, 222, 258, 271–73. See also reactive attitude

Hadamard, Jacques, 131
Haji, Ishtiyaque, 105, 106–8, 190, 191, 195, 198, 211, 218, 223–24, 225, 226

Harris, Robert, 35, 37, 212
Harris, Sam, 247
Hart, H. L. A., 31, 32
Heisenberg, Martin, 60, 132–33
Heisenberg, Werner, 132–33
hierarchical motivation theory, 209–14, 217
Hinduism, 294–95
Hitchcock, Christopher, 165
Hobbes, Thomas, 14
Honderich, Ted, 247
Hume, David, 183, 242–43
Hurley, Susan, 236

illusionism, 269–70, 271–73
inclination, 119–20, 123–24, 141–42, 166–67, 171–72, 179–81, 198
incompatibilism, 3–5, 7, 8, 9, 29–30, 34–35, 58, 59, 93
　hard, 254–55, 270
　revisionist views on, 235–42
　source, 15–16
　See also free will; libertarianism
indeterminism, 3, 5–6, 7–8, 17–20, 21–22, 58–59
　chance and, 70–71, 76–60, 96–102, 103, 106–7, 114–15, 117–18, 131–32, 251–52, 254
　control and, 76–79, 92–94, 95–96, 106, 107–8, 121–23, 158–59, 239
　decision-making and, 144–45
　deliberation and, 113–25, 129–32, 143–44, 168–70, 171–72, 173–74, 178, 180, 186, 197–98
　effort and, 161–62
　motivational conflict and, 249–50
　in nature, 59–60
　preferences and, 169–70, 171–72, 173–74
　revisionist views on, 235–42
　science and, 291–92
　will-setting and, 61–63, 64–66, 91, 171
　See also causation; responsibility
inspiration, 130
Intellect, 25
Intelligibility Question, 5, 58–59, 251–52
intelligibility, teleological, 6, 8, 80, 81, 85–86, 155
intentionality, 101–2, 105–6, 107–8, 109–10
invention, 130

irrationality objection, 175–76, 178–79
It Ain't Me Argument, 152–53, 162, 174.
    See also Franklin, Christopher Evan

Jacobs, Jonathan, 189
James, William, 44, 131, 275
Juarrero, Alicia, 81, 192
judgment, evaluative, 98–99, 115–16, 118, 123–25, 126, 129

Kant, Immanuel, 7–8, 44, 79, 243, 244, 245, 275, 276–79, 280, 288, 290–94
karma, 294–95
Koch, Christopher, 59–60
Korsgaard, Christine, 293–94

Lamb, James, 49
Layzer, David, 132
Leibniz, Gottfried Wilhelm, 62
Lem, Stanislaw, 289–90
Lemos, John, 175–79, 180–81
Levy, Ken, 273
Levy, Neil, 190, 191, 247, 252–54
Lewis, David, 202–3, 205–6
libertarianism
  agent-causal (AC), 5–8, 80, 83–86, 99–100, 143, 154–56, 163–65, 176–77, 182–86, 187–91, 195, 198–200, 205, 255
  agent-causal/event-causal (AC/EC), 7–8, 84–86, 135, 155–56, 163–65, 166, 168, 184–86, 188–93, 195–98, 200, 205–7
  centered views, 113, 135
  contrastive explanations and, 165–67
  daring, 144–45, 147–51, 155–56
  deliberative or noncentered view, 113–21, 122–32, 135–36, 143–44, 168–69, 171, 176–77, 186
  event-causal (EC), 5–8, 84–86, 135–36, 143–44, 151–52, 153, 154–56, 159–60, 162–65, 168, 176–77, 186–88, 196–97, 199–200, 205, 255
  L-freedom, 138–40
  luck and, 252, 263
  metaphysical dimensions of, 3, 6, 7–8, 84, 243–46
  modern attacks on, 4–5
  modest view of, 168

noncausal (NC), 5–8, 83–86, 143, 154, 155–56, 186, 199, 200–7, 255
  See also compatibilism; determinism; free will; incompatibilism; indeterminism
Libet, Benjamin, 151
List, Christian, 232–35
Locke, Don, 211
Locke, John, 14–15
love, 289–90
Lovejoy, A. O., 287
Lowe, E. J., 183, 189
luck
  constitutive, 253, 254
  present, 253
  See also chance; indeterminism
Luck Pincer, 253–54, 263
Luther, Martin, 12–13, 45–46, 47

Mahabharata, 295–96
manifest image, 3
manipulation argument, 236, 255, 256, 258. *See also* compatibilism
Markosian, Ned, 189–90
McCann, Hugh, 201–2, 203, 204
McGeer, Victoria, 236
McKenna, Michael, 211, 218, 225–30
Mele, Alfred, 50–52, 96, 114, 115–16, 143–46, 147–51, 168–69, 171, 186, 190–91, 195, 198, 205, 211
Melville, Herman, 262–63
mesh theory. *See* hierarchical motivation theory
metaphysics, 3, 6, 7–8, 12, 29–30, 84, 182, 183, 216–17, 243–46, 278–79, 284–85
Mill, John Stuart, 131
Miller, Earl K., 81–82, 192–93, 206
Milton, John, 300
modernity, 3–5, 14, 262–63, 284
monism, 269, 270
moral community, 221, 226, 281–82
Moral Sphere Theory, 293–94
motivation, 25, 26, 103, 105, 106–8, 109–10, 121
  causation and, 164–68, 188, 196–97, 201, 204–5, 206
  conflicts of, 128, 163, 165–68, 249–51
  dispositions and, 230, 231
  preferences and, 171–72
  resistant, 64–66, 119–20

Mozart, Wolfgang Amadeus, 264, 265
Murphy, Nancey, 60

Nadelhoffer, Thomas, 247
Nagel, Thomas, 243, 244, 245–46
NC. *See* noncausal *under* libertarianism
Nelkin, Dana, 31, 189–90, 218, 226, 229
neuroscience, 59–60, 81–82, 154, 192–94, 196, 198, 206–7, 240, 241–42
Nichols, Shaun, 34–35, 236
Nietzsche, Friedrich, 4, 209, 247, 251–52, 275
noumena, 3, 7–8, 84, 185, 243, 290–92, 294
Nozick, Robert, 6, 176–81

objection
  irrationality, 175–76, 178–79
  luck, 96–99, 105–6, 109, 205
  phenomenological, 175–76, 178–79
  regress, 160, 161–62
  rollback/replay, 99–103, 109, 168, 205
obligation, 222–24, 225, 231
O'Connor, Timothy, 182–83, 184–86, 198
ontology, 80, 185–86
opportunity, 94–96
O'Shaughnessy, Brian, 25

Palmer, David, 182, 201, 203–4, 227
Pereboom, Derek, 54–55, 169–70, 190, 191, 195, 198, 202–4, 205–6, 211, 242, 247, 249, 254–56, 257, 258–59, 260, 263, 281
phenomenology, 136–37, 138, 142–43, 175–76, 178–79
Pink, Thomas, 201, 203, 204
Plato, 1–2
Plotinus, 10
plurality conditions, 16, 20, 21, 22–23, 109–10, 121
Poincaré, Henri, 131
Polkinghorne, John, 60
Popper, Karl, 131–32
power, 4, 94–96, 97, 109–10, 117–18, 121
  causal, 191, 195, 198, 224–25
  to decide, 148–50, 158–59
  to do otherwise, 229–35
  to form preferences, 173, 174
  kinds of, 121–22, 148–49, 197–98

ontology of, 185–86
plural, 141, 142
of will-setting, 171
See also agency; control
practices, ordinary, 221–22, 224–25, 226
predestinationism, 300–1
preemption, 52, 53–54
preference, 168–70
  forming, 171–75
  moral, 172–73
  will-setting and, 171–73, 174–75
Principle of Alternative Possibilities, 12, 46–49, 52–53, 56–57, 214, 220
probability, 74–76, 103, 104–5, 106–7, 140–41
problem-solving, 113, 129–30, 132. *See also* creativity
process, 91

quantum physics, 17, 59–60, 66–67, 76, 240, 241–42, 248, 254–55, 264
quarantine, 259, 260, 263

rationality, 72–74, 98, 99, 101–2, 105–6, 107–8, 109–10
  action and, 25, 26
  aspiration and, 278, 280, 287
  control and, 170
  plural, 139
Ravizza, Mark, 211, 216, 217–18, 219, 220–21, 226
Rawls, John, 293, 294
reactive attitude, 34–35, 221–24, 225–26, 242–43, 247, 258–60, 262
real self theory, 211, 214–15. *See also* hierarchical motivation theory
realizability, multiple, 233–35
reason, 214–15
  decisive, 179–80, 181
  inclining, 179–81
  practical, 128–31, 174–75, 186
  satisficing, 110–11
regress. *See under* objection
reincarnation, 294–95
Repetti, Riccardo, 295, 298
responsibility
  accountability and, 265–66
  agency and, 38, 47–48, 57, 111–12, 121, 125, 160–61, 188–89

alternative possibilities and, 209, 211, 222–24, 225
answerability and, 265–66
attributability and, 265–66
Basic Argument of, 248–52
basic-desert sense of, 247–49, 252–53, 254–55, 257, 258–59, 260–61, 262, 263–64, 266–68, 269, 281–82
blame and, 216–18, 225–26, 228–29, 282–83
childhood and, 87–88
conversation and, 225–26
criminal, 35–36, 38–39, 258–59, 282
diagnostic accounts of, 236
dimensions of, 9, 29–36, 38–57, 89–92, 121, 160
endowments and, 253–54
fairness and, 222–25
freedom and, 151, 208–9, 211–19, 220–22, 226–27, 228–29, 231–32, 235–36, 241–43, 247–52, 254–55, 279–81, 283–84, 294–95
historical dimensions of, 212–17, 218–20, 228–29, 249–51
illusion and, 271–73
legal, 31–34, 35–36
manipulation and, 255–58
moral, 12–13, 15–16, 31–34, 44, 46, 47, 48–49, 57, 175, 203, 209, 211, 212, 213, 216, 217–18, 219, 220–22, 225, 227, 228–29, 231–32, 235–36, 237, 239–42, 243, 247–49, 252, 256, 260, 264, 266–67, 270, 273, 275–76, 279, 281, 294–95
prescriptive accounts of, 236
quarantine model of, 259, 260, 263
reactive attitudes and, 34–36, 38–39, 41, 43, 57, 221–24, 225–26, 247, 258–60, 262
self-formation and, 281–82
transference of, 35–39, 282, 283
ultimate (UR), 11–14, 15–16, 21–23, 42–43, 53, 58, 86–88, 89–90, 106, 125, 209, 227–29, 248–52, 257–58, 260–62, 279–80, 281–85, 294–95
See also agency; desert; determinism; freedom; free will; indeterminism; libertarianism
Robb, David, 50–52

rollback. *See under* objection
Rumi, Jalal ad-Din ar-, 2
Russell, Paul, 225, 242–46, 264
Ryle, Gilbert, 14

Sartorio, Carolina, 218, 226
Scanlon, T. M., 226, 245–46
Schopenhauer, Arthur, 247
science, 2–3, 5, 58, 59–60, 81–82, 133, 142–43, 176, 260–61, 272, 278, 280
  biological, 133, 175
  cognitive, 233, 234–35
  empirical, 245, 280, 290–92
  natural, 7–8, 84, 154–55, 192–93, 241–42, 275, 278, 280, 292
  philosophy of, 131–32
  See also neuroscience; quantum physics
scientific image, 3
self, selfhood, 4
  dialectic of, 285–87
  preferences and, 169, 174–75
self-control, 223
self-determination, 152–53, 162, 201, 284
self-formation, 21, 28, 42, 61–62, 69–70, 137–38, 174–75, 213–14, 250, 279, 292, 301–2
  narrative conception of, 111–12
  See also under action
self-forming action (SFA). *See under* action
Sellars, Wilfred, 3
Sen, Amartya, 245–46
SFA. *See* self-forming *under* action
Shadlen, Michael, 60, 132
Significance Question, 4–5, 9, 10–12, 13, 29, 41–42, 57
Simonton, Dean, 60
Singer, Ira, 236
Skinner, B. F., 26–28, 257, 258
Slote, Michael, 211
Smart, J. J. C., 236
Smilansky, Saul, 269–73
Smith, Adam, 242–43
Smith, Michael, 229
Sommers, Tamler, 247
Sorabji, Richard, 6
Spinoza, Baruch, 247–48, 264
Steward, Helen, 189
Stoicism, 10

368 INDEX

Strawson, Galen, 29–31, 34–35, 222, 247, 248–50, 257
Strawson, P. F., 3, 6, 7–8, 29–30, 33, 43–44, 57, 84, 221–22, 225–26, 242–43, 248–49
supervenience, 233–35
system, information-responsive complex dynamical, 7, 81–84, 85–86, 154–55, 159–60, 164–65, 183, 184, 192–93, 196, 206

theism, 300–1
Thoreau, Henry David, 27
Timpe, Kevin, 15–16, 189
True, truth, 1–2, 215–16
Tse, Peter Ulric, 60, 132
Tuomela, Raimo, 151
Twain, Mark, 111–12

ultimate responsibility (UR). *See under* responsibility
uncertainty, 61. *See also* ambivalence
undefeated authorization, 169
UR. *See* ultimate *under* responsibility
Usher, Marius, 81–82, 83, 92, 148, 154, 192–94, 206

Valerian view, 114, 136, 168. *See also* libertarianism
Valéry, Paul, 114–15, 130, 131
value experiment, 98, 131, 252
van Inwagen, Peter, 62, 99–100, 101–2, 105, 165
Vargas, Manuel, 236–42
Vihvelin, Kadri, 218, 226, 229
Vilhauer, Benjamin, 247
volition, second-order, 210–11.
 See also desire
volitional streams, 61–62
Voltaire, 247

Wallace, R. Jay, 222–26
Waller, Bruce, 247
Walter, Henrik, 236
Watson, Gary, 6, 35, 37, 40–41, 211–12
Weber, Max, 4

Wegner, Daniel, 151
Widerker, David, 49, 50
Wiggins, David, 6
will
 building, 137, 138
 conflicted, 89, 91–92, 93, 106–8, 111–12, 120, 123–25, 126, 128–29, 133–34, 135, 138, 157, 161, 163, 166–67, 171–72, 186, 195, 197, 213–14, 249–51
 desires and, 210–14
 efforts of, 88–92, 93, 95–96, 126–27, 128–29, 137, 138, 146, 148, 149, 156–57–, 159–62, 164, 167–68, 171–72, 174, 186, 197–98
 freedom of, 24–26, 27–28, 41–43, 108, 111–12, 133–34, 158–59, 208–9, 268–69, 276
 kinds of, 24–26
 Motivational, 24–25, 26, 201
 notions of, 121
 Rational, 24–25, 26, 186
 resistance in, 73–74, 94, 97, 103, 104–5, 119–20, 123–24, 126, 127, 138, 149, 157, 164, 166–67, 176, 181, 197, 198
 resolving, 123–25, 129, 135
 setting, 20–23, 40, 42, 47–49, 53, 55–57, 61–63, 64–66, 69, 73–74, 89–92, 94, 110, 113, 119, 120–21, 124–25, 157–58, 171–73, 174–75, 180–81, 185–86, 213–14, 220
 settled, 19, 20–21, 22–23, 40, 47, 49, 69, 73–74, 90–91, 95–96, 110, 121, 124–25, 156, 157–58, 180–81, 186, 213, 214, 220, 229, 253–54
 Striving, 24, 25, 26, 72, 181, 186, 197
 teleology of, 26
 weakness of, 126–27, 128, 151
 See also action; agency; free will; responsibility
Williams, Bernard, 243, 244
Wittgenstein, Ludwig, 14, 30
Wolf, Susan, 211, 214–18, 226
Wyma, Keith, 49

Yogavasistha, 295–96